EXECUTIVE GUIDE TO PC PRESENTATION GRAPHICS

Gordon McComb

BANTAM BOOKS
TORONTO • NEW YORK • LONDON • SYDNEY • AUCKLAND

EXECUTIVE GUIDE TO PC PRESENTATION GRAPHICS
A Bantam Book / February 1988

ISBN 0-553-34540-0

Published simultaneously in the United States and Canada

Bantam Books are published by Bantam Books, a division of
Bantam Doubleday Dell Publishing Group, Inc. Its trademark,
consisting of the words "Bantam Books" and the portrayal of
a rooster, is Registered in U.S. Patent and Trademark Office
and in other countries. Marca Registrada, Bantam Books,
666 Fifth Avenue, New York, New York 10103

PRINTED IN THE UNITED STATES OF AMERICA

B 0 9 8 7 6 5 4 3 2 1

Contents

Introduction

Business Presentation Graphics by Computer

Executive Guide to PC Presentation Graphics is designed to help you become a better communicator by using computer-generated business graphics in everyday work. It shows you how charts can be best applied to written and oral presentations, and how you can avoid the pitfalls common to producing business graphics on a computer.

This book tells how to make "power presentations" that sell, persuade, entertain, and most of all, communicate. With the help of this book, you'll appear more professional to your peers, allowing you to gain the respect of coworkers and clients. This is a survival manual for the increasingly competitive world of corporate business. Still, you needn't have an MBA to use it and learn how to make effective graphics. This book is also helpful to those in retail, education, church, inside sales, and other disciplines.

You'll find a wide range of topics in *Executive Guide to PC Presentation Graphics*. There is information on how to choose the right type of chart, how to make business graphics that really dazzle, and how to present graphics so that ideas are easily understood and accepted. This book also provides guidance on buying and using computer monitors, printers, plotters, film recorders, and business graphics software packages.

There is a great deal more to giving provocative business presentations than making pretty charts. Once the charts are made, they can be inserted into reports or turned into overhead transparencies for a group presentation. This book covers these details as well.

Executive Guide to PC Presentation Graphics is written for those who want to quickly and efficiently learn how to apply the various graphics tools provided by the computer and transform them into meaningful charts and graphs—graphics that communicate where words cannot.

This book is principally designed for users of the IBM PC or clone. Chapters that deal with graphics hardware and software are geared specifically to the PC family, and readers gain the benefit of the specific buyer's guidance provided.

Time is one thing that most business people don't have, and you do not need a lot of time to enjoy the benefits of this book. Each chapter details a different segment of the presentation graphics story, and you need only read those chapters that are of vital interest to you. All the chapters begin with an executive summary that condenses the information given in the chapter into one or two quick-reading paragraphs. Since this is a book on graphics, we've supplemented much of the text with examples of charts.

Here is a quick overview of what you'll find in each chapter of *Executive Guide to PC Presentation Graphics:*

Chapter 1: Graphically Yours. Learn why charts provide impact to your presentations and how they can help you achieve. This chapter also details what you need to produce charts on your PC or compatible.

Chapter 2: Choosing the Right Chart to Tell Your Story. There are five major types of graphs with many subtypes and variations. Know which one to use to effectively communicate your ideas.

Chapter 3: The Mechanics of Good Chart Design. What makes a good chart and how do you create one on your computer.

Chapter 4: Advanced Charting Techniques. Tips and techniques on turning common charts into dazzling graphics.

Chapter 5: How to Choose the Right Business Graphics Program. Everything you need to know to choose the right presentation graphics program.

Chapter 6: Graphics Adapters and Monitors. How to interface your computer to a monitor to view high-resolution graphics.

Chapter 7: On Paper with Printers and Plotters. An overview of printers and plotters for making permanent copies of your graphs. Includes the latest on laser printers and PostScript.

Chapter 8: Making Slides and Viewgraphs. Slides and viewgraphs (overheads) are used for oral presentation—here's how to make them with your computer.

Chapter 9: Graphics in Written Reports and Oral Presentations. How to effectively integrate graphics with the written word.

Chapter 10: Advanced Presentations. How to present your graphics to a live audience.

Chapter 11: Setting Up a Graphics Workstation. An overview of several popular graphics programs; how to custom-integrate the various tools of the presentation graphics trade.

Appendix A: Chart Types and Their Uses. A quick overview of the major chart types and how they are used.

Appendix B: Further Reading. Useful books, magazines, and other sources of information on computers, graphics, desktop publishing, and business presentations.

Appendix C: Sources. Where to find the software and hardware for making presentation graphics on your computer.

CHAPTER 1

Graphically Yours

EXECUTIVE SUMMARY

Presentation graphics enhance most any meeting or report. In addition, visuals make presentations go faster and smoother; the information stays with the viewer or reader longer. More information can be contained in a single chart than in several paragraphs of text. However, the misuse of graphics can be worse than not using visuals at all. Most any computer system can be used to create business graphics, but it must have these basic items: computer, monitor, display adapter, printer or plotter, and presentation graphics software.

John Baker is a vice president of a large Midwest manufacturing firm. He's traveled 500 miles, briefcase and portfolio in hand, and is about to give an important presentation to a potential client—a client that could mean a great deal in revenue for his company.

For years, John has used the same presentation, and he's been getting fairly good results. "No need to fix it if it's not broken," is John's credo, so he's never thought of updating his presentation. He doesn't need notes; he's done the presentation so many times before that he knows exactly what to say. Besides, he's come prepared with plenty of printed reports. Confidence oozes from his pores.

What John doesn't know is that, this time, he's already lost the job. His presentation, the same one he's been giving for years, has become old. It lacks dramatic impact, it lacks professionalism, and most importantly, it lacks graphic punch. At the end of the presentation John asks for the job, but is politely held off. As he walks out to his car after the meeting, John gets the feeling that he's blown it.

Where did John go wrong? Business communication—from simple memos to multimillion dollar presentations—has changed drastically in the past few years. Yet only a handful of forward thinkers have taken the steps to keep up. It's no longer enough to provide the facts and a few lines of reassuring commentary. People need to be persuaded, and some of the best persuasion comes in the form of visuals.

Instead of talking about numbers, show them. Whether the numbers are sales forecasts, industry projections, or income breakdowns, they must be analyzed to be understood. The task of comprehending the meaning behind the numbers is much easier when the numbers aren't numbers at all, but charts.

Graphics as a Communications Tool

Before personal computers came along, changing numbers into a chart meant drawing lines, bars, and pies on graph paper. For a person with less than honed artistic skills, the time spent was hardly worthwhile, the results messy and unprofessional. To make presentable charts, the businessperson was forced to hire an artist, which unduly added to the cost of giving effective presentations.

Personal computers change all this. They provide a quick and easy way to transform numbers into pictures, rows of data into easily understood concepts. If you deal with numbers, then there is every reason for you to transform at least some of them into charts, and if you have a computer, or are thinking about getting one, then there's every reason for you to create those charts on it.

Converting numbers into charts for business purposes has become so important these days that it has its own name: *presentation graphics.* Presentation graphics is different from other graphics applications for personal computers, which include computer aided design (or CAD), free-hand drawing and painting, and animation. The thrust of presentation graphics is using charts to communicate facts and ideas. The charts themselves are not the important element; it's the meaning behind the chart that is of vital interest.

Before you go off plugging numbers into your computer, take warning: Though the science of creating presentation graphics isn't a difficult one, there is a right and wrong way to go about it. Unkind words are worse than no words at all, and the same is true of presentation graphics. You may not realize that charts have their own almost subconscious language, and unless you understand the language, you may unwittingly say the wrong things to your audience.

Why Charts?

Is there truth in the old adage that "a picture is worth a thousand words"? Let's see. The average person can speak about 115 words per minute. In about 8½ minutes time, that person will have rattled off 1,000 words. A chart can contain much, or all, of the information in the same 8½-minute speech, and the chart can be completely absorbed in 30 seconds or less. Not only is a picture indeed worth a thousand words, but it is a vastly more efficient story teller.

The benefits of presentation graphics don't stop here. Consider the points that follow.

Greater Retention

Words that are spoken or read are not retained by the human brain as long as pictures. Perception studies have shown that people retain only about 10 percent of what they hear. That means in the course of the 8½-minute 1,000-word speech, about 7½ minutes are wasted—900 words forgotten. Transform some of the words into a picture, and retention jumps to 50 percent or more.

Faster Input

The brain can accept visual information about 27 times faster than oral information—sort of warp drive for business meetings, casual client get togethers, and important presentations.

Greater Productivity

A 1981 study at the University of Pennsylvania's Wharton School of Business, sponsored by meeting graphics giant 3M, revealed that good graphics help boost productivity. When graphics were added to the agenda, the average business meeting was 28 percent shorter than those without graphics.

Increased Professionalism

A later study sponsored by 3M showed that those who use business graphics in presentations were viewed as more professional.

If these benefits seem abstract, consider their results:

- *Greater retention* helps your audience (whether it be a written or oral presentation) remember what you have said long after you have said it. Your ideas are not easily forgotten.

- *Faster input* of graphics means your message comes across in a timely fashion. If you've ever had just 5 minutes to give your presentation you know how important this is.

- *Greater productivity* through graphics means that meeting time is less, which saves money. Over the course of a year, for example, the typical midmanager will spend *168 hours less* in the meeting room. This is based on spending an average of 12 hours per week in the meeting room, a conservative figure. Convert that to a typical midmanager's salary, and that's well over $3,500 saved, and that's just for one person.

- *Increased professionalism* enhances your credibility and helps you make faster progress, through your job or with your clients.

When to Use Charts

Clearly, presentation graphics are tools that help improve communication. Yet their usefulness goes way beyond this. You've learned why charts help you communicate better; here are some ways that charts can be used to dramatically increase the effectiveness of your presentations.

Use charts to:

- Show and tell facts quickly and efficiently in order to cut down on valuable presentation time
- Sell a point of view by way of visual reinforcement
- Provoke faster decisions at a company meeting
- Increase mental retention of the facts so that your ideas stay with the audience as long as possible
- Save the reader's or viewer's time, by packing dense statistics into one or more charts
- Show how numbers and other statistics relate to one another
- Compare two divergent statistics, and plot a comparison that would otherwise be difficult to mentally perceive
- Demonstrate nonvisual concepts and ideas visually
- Focus the reader's or viewer's attention on certain facts or figures
- Provide "visual relief" in an all-word report or oral presentation
- Add credence to facts and figures
- Attract attention by using the "novelty" of business graphics

Taking Your Own Test

Relying on the tests conducted by companies such as 3M is one thing; conducting your own test is another. Take a few moments to see for yourself how charts help convey information more quickly and effectively.

```
┌─────────────────────────────────────────┐
│  Chart type percentages                  │
│                                          │
│  Line Chart_____           │
│  Column Chart_____           │
│  Bar Chart_____           │
│  Pie Chart_____           │
│  Dot Chart_____           │
│  Other Chart Types  _____           │
│                                          │
└─────────────────────────────────────────┘
```

Figure 1-1.
Form for text reply.

Enlist the help of two friends. Read the paragraph that follows to one of the friends. Speak at your normal, conversation speed. Before you continue, engage in a few moments of "idle talk"— about the weather, the new medical insurance program at work, or last night's ball game. Then ask your friend to write down the figures you previously gave. Use the form that appears in Figure 1-1.

A recent survey from Frost and Sullivan, Inc., has shown that of all the commonly used business chart types, the line graph is the most often used, followed by column and bar graphs. Of these three major types, line charts account for 29 percent of graph usage; column and bar, 24 and 13 percent, respectively. The survey revealed pie graphs are used 10 percent of the time, and dot charts are used 7 percent of the time. The remaining 17 percent comprise miscellaneous chart types, such as Pert, Gantt, and organization.

Next, grab your other friend and show him or her the chart that appears in Figure 1-2. Let your friend study it for 15 seconds, then take it away. Repeat your "idle talk" once again, then ask your friend to redraw the chart, using the blank in Figure 1-3.

The results: Odds are, the friend who received the oral presentation was unable to remember most—if not all—of the six numbers mentioned in the paragraph. Wild guesses yielded equally wild and grossly incorrect results. The friend who received the visual presentation should have been able to redraw the pie chart with reasonable accuracy.

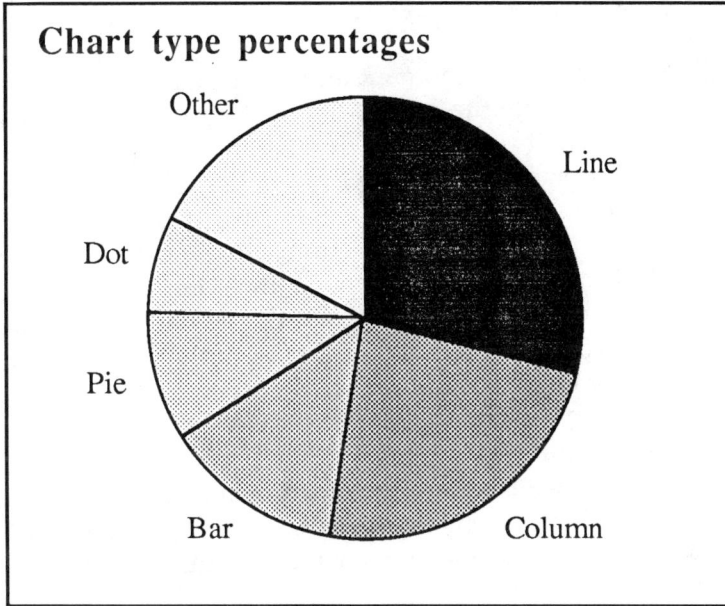

Figure 1-2.
Pie chart of data.

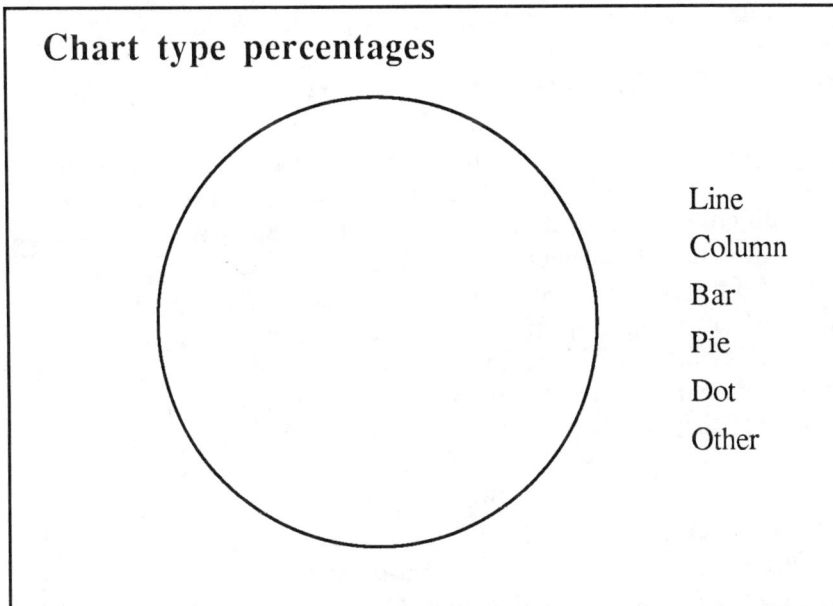

Figure 1-3.
Empty pie.

A Short History of Charting

Let's pause for a moment and see how the art of presentation graphics came into being. The history of charting is wide and varied, and it reveals why the art form has developed into a science, and why it has its own set of special rules and techniques.

For thousands of years people have used images for communicating. Humans first communicated by drawing on cave walls and the rocks that surrounded their immense and uncharted world. They "wrote" of fantastic battles with wild beasts, of conquests against unfriendly neighbors, of their gods. Only recently, well after the rise and fall of the early civilizations that made great use of "picture talk," have we created a language based on random squiggles and marks.

Unfortunately, unknown to our ancestors who created the present-day written languages, the human brain doesn't work in letters and numbers, but images and patterns. Any complex message can be written or spoken, but to interpret the message the brain must work overtime.

The return to charts for graphically communicating ideas, particularly for simplifying numbers, didn't occur until the fourteenth century. Much of the early pioneering work of transferring numbers into pictures was done by Nicole d'Oresme, Bishop of Lisieux.

A chart here and there is also in evidence in the notebooks of Leonardo da Vinci, the famous fifteenth century mathematician and philosopher. One example of a da Vinci chart plots the distance an object will fall during a particular length of time.

True chart making didn't appear until 1786, when Scotsman William Playfair published the *Commercial and Political Atlas*. This definitive work included over 40 charts, most of them line graphs, showing import and export trade between the major countries of the world. As in our modern charts, Playfair's brand graphed years on the horizontal axis and amounts on the vertical axis. Because statistical charts were so new, Playfair wisely included the raw numbers in a separate table, and each chart was fully annotated. In later editions of the *Atlas*, Playfair included bar charts and pie charts.

Others contributed greatly to the basic groundwork layed out by Playfair. One was Jacques Quetelet (1796–1874), who pioneered new methods for generating and reporting statistics. In the early 1920s Otto Neurath, director of the Vienna Museum of Social and Economic Studies, began converting statistics into artistic graphics.

By the time Neurath began developing his charts, however, others had begun to abuse the state of the art. To help prevent the further loss of credibility, interested parties from around the globe joined together and formed the Joint Committee on Standards for Graphic Presentation in 1915. Most of these standards are still in use today; they are the ones we will discuss throughout the course of this book.

Types of Graphics Programs

So far, we've talked about charting facts and figures, and yet there are other forms of computer graphics programs. Some of these are used in the course of preparing charts, and so it's helpful to know about them. One popular form is computer painting or drawing, where the computer acts as an electronic easel. You draw with light, splashing a little color here, some texture there.

Also rising in popularity is computing designing and drafting, sometimes called computer aided design (CAD). CAD programs take the place of rudimentary drafting tools—like the T-square, triangle, and ruler—and let you compose complex schematics, floor plans, and charts with the aid of a computer.

The Difference Between Good and Bad Graphs

It's easy enough to make bad charts by hand, and even easier to generate awful graphs with a computer. Remember the maxim: *Just because a computer made the graph doesn't mean it's good.*

The ease with which a computer lets you plot a set of numbers leads you blindly into trying different graph types until you get one that "looks right." That's not the way to do it. As explained in the following chapter, each type of graph is used for a specific kind of comparison. For example, you wouldn't ordinarily use a pie graph to compare sales revenue for the past 4 years—that's a job of a column chart. By using the wrong kind of chart, you mislead and confuse your audience.

In addition, graphics programs are limited in their features and flexibility. Enhancements such as different colors or patterns may not be possible, given your computer hardware and limitations of the software. The software may even promote poor chart design. Although this problem is no longer as prevalent today as it used to be, there are older software packages still in use that produce poor charts.

Some Examples of Good and Bad Charts

Figures 1-4 to 1-6 are three computer-generated charts that— while they look professionally produced—do not communicate anything of real value. Let's take a close look at each one and discover what's wrong with it, and how to make it right.

Accuracy of Manufacturing Methods

Joe Simpleton, the lead staff engineer for Hi-Pitch Nut and Bolt Company, wants management to invest $50,000 on a new laser measuring system. He's completed a graph, shown in Figure 1-4, that supports his claim of improved accuracy for the manufacture of a new product line. The graph shows three lines: one for the experimental laser system already in place, and two for the mechanical and manual measurement systems in wide use in the company.

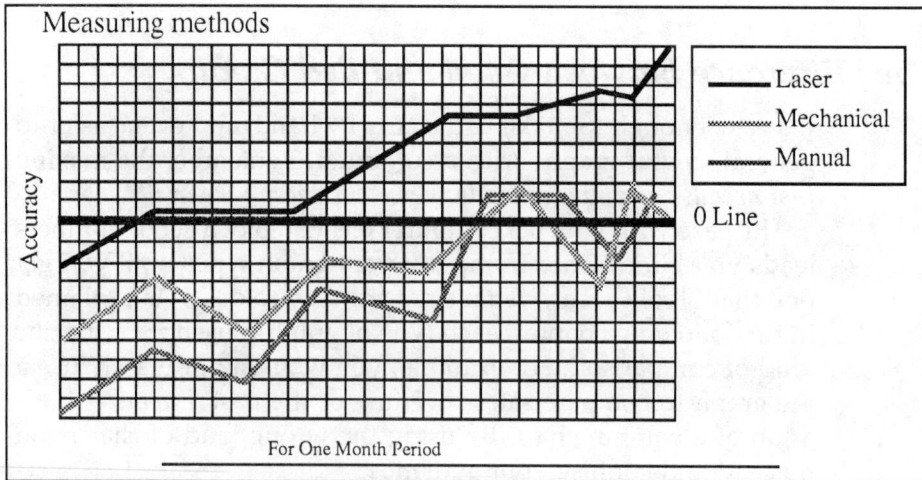

Figure 1-4.
Accuracy of manufacturing methods, bad.

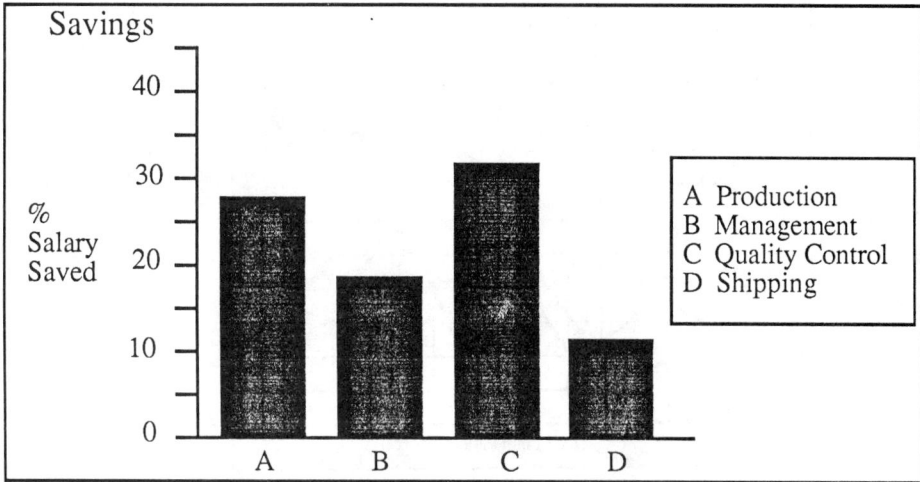

Figure 1-5.
Savings, bad.

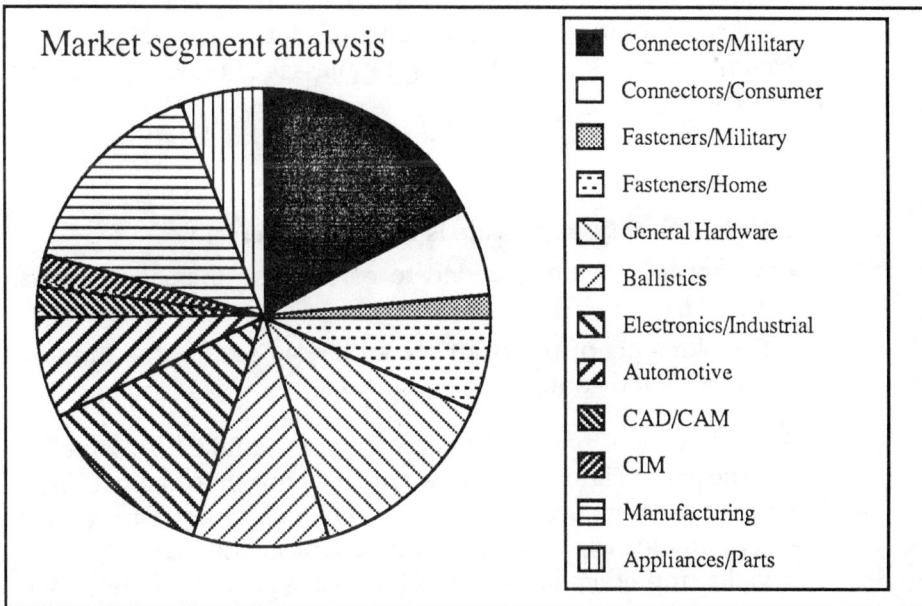

Figure 1-6.
Market segments, bad.

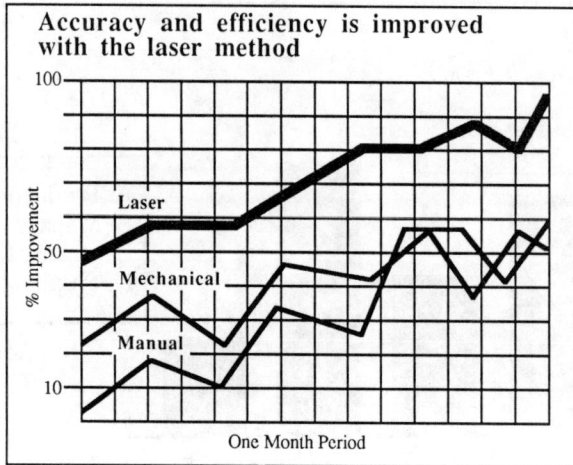

Figure 1-7.
Good accuracy chart—1.

Joe's graph doesn't lie—it shows that the laser system is indeed a great improvement. But the chart says nothing, and so the management at Hi-Pitch nixes Joe's idea. The chart just doesn't communicate, it doesn't sell. In fact, the chart raises more questions than answers. What is the message? How is accuracy measured?

The chart in Figure 1-7 shows how the chart may be improved.

- The vertical (Y axis) scale is marked in percent.
- A descriptive title is added to convey the message behind the chart.
- The elements of the chart are enhanced so that the line for "laser" stands out.

Another way to present the accuracy of manufacturing methods is shown in Figure 1-8. Here, the lines for "mechanical" and "manual" systems are graphed in their own chart. During his presentation, Joe explains that the mechanical and manual methods yield unpredictable results, but the accuracy of the laser method improves at a more or less steady rate the more it is used. Given this new improved chart, Joe just might get the go ahead for his costly laser system.

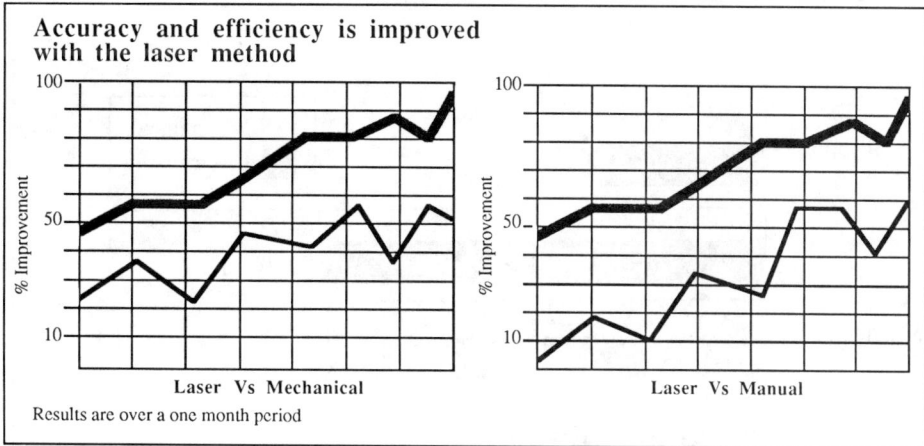

Figure 1-8.
Good accuracy chart—2.

Salary Savings

Elizabeth Brock, Joe's assistant, came up with the column graph in Figure 1-5. It's supposed to show how salaries can be cut using the laser measurement system. Elizabeth's chart fails on several counts, not the least of which is a lack of a substantial comparison. The graph compares salaries for four departments in the company, but doesn't show clearly how the old and new salaries compare with one another.

The improved chart in Figure 1-9 clearly shows the salary savings of using the laser system over using the older mechanical system.

- The four departments are graphed as "items" on a horizontal bar chart, so they no longer appear to be competing against one another.
- The lengths of the overlapping bars actively show the difference between salaries when using the laser and mechanical systems.
- The chart is given a descriptive title.
- The savings realized in each department is provided beside each pair of bars.

Figure 1-10 illustrates a similar way of proving salary savings if the laser measurement system is employed. The emphasis of

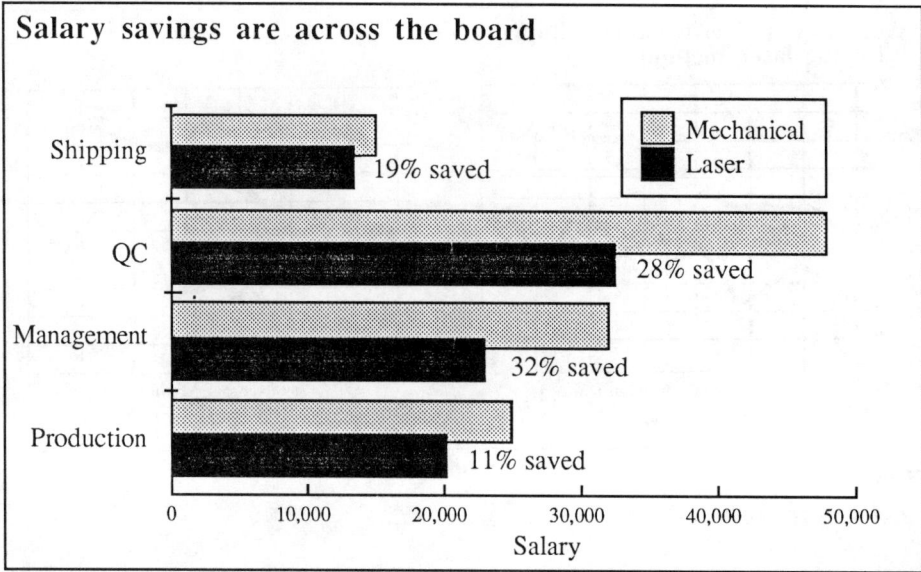

Figure 1-9.
Good salary chart—1.

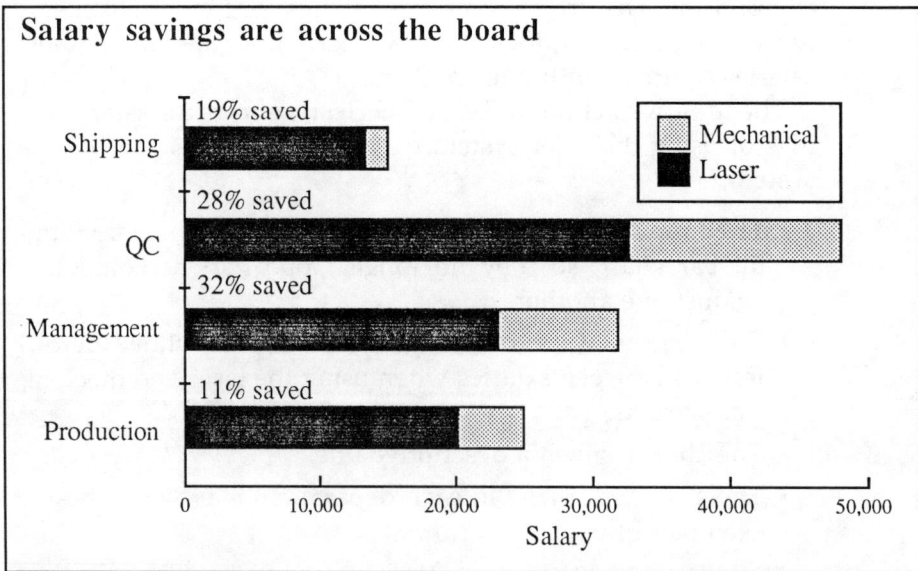

Figure 1-10.
Good salary chart—2.

the chart is stated as the title: "Your money goes farther with the laser system." Instead of overlapping bars, the bars are "stacked," dramatically emphasizing the potential savings.

Market Segments

Herb Yankovic, in the sales department, has his pitch for the laser measurement system, too. He says that the new technology will help the company enter into markets dominated by competitors. His own estimates, illustrated in Figure 1-6, show a pepperoni pizza-like pie graph that supposedly is a market analysis. Not only is the pie chart ugly and disorienting, it says absolutely nothing.

The new graph in Figure 1-11 is much better for a number of reasons:

- New markets are ranked in the order of estimated market share, and the dollar amount that can be expected by competing in that market.

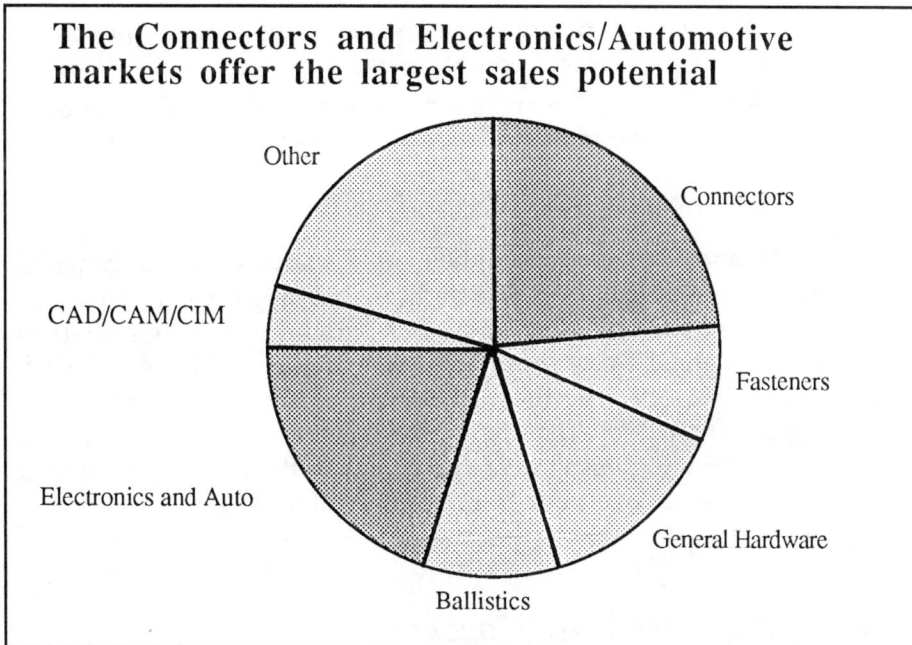

The Connectors and Electronics/Automotive markets offer the largest sales potential

Other · Connectors · CAD/CAM/CIM · Fasteners · Electronics and Auto · General Hardware · Ballistics

Figure 1-11.
Good market chart—1.

Half of the targeted markets offer greater than $1 million a year in sales potential

Percent of Total Market Share

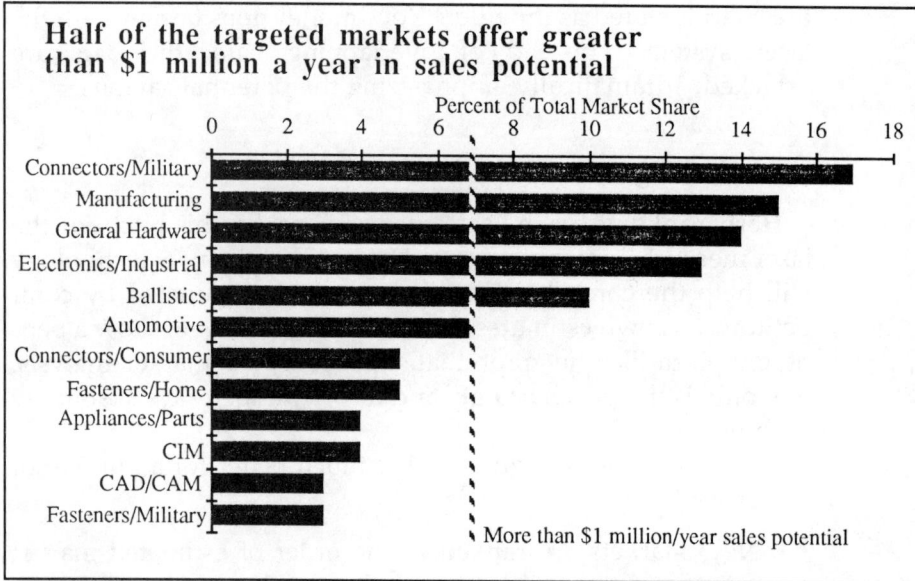

More than $1 million/year sales potential

Figure 1-12.
Good market chart—2.

- By using the horizontal bar graph instead of the pie chart, the chart is simplified but no items are removed.
- A "sales angle" is included in the chart—markets that offer $1 million or more in revenue for the company. A dotted line shows those markets that are below and above the $1 million-a-year mark.

Yet another approach to the market analysis chart is shown in Figure 1-12. Here, Herb has decided that only the major markets need be addressed, and so he has pared down the pie chart to seven items. Two of these items, connectors and job shop manufacturing, offer the most lucrative prospects, so he has highlighted them. Note that the message behind the chart is given in the title. Herb doesn't even have to be in the meeting to present this chart, yet everyone in the room will understand it and gain by it.

The Computer Ties It All Together

These topics are covered in more depth in coming chapters, but it's worthwhile to mention them here. You need five basic ingredients to make presentation graphics:

- Computer
- Monitor
- Display adapter
- Printer or plotter
- Graphics software

At the heart of the system is the computer itself. The type of computer doesn't really matter, nor do vast amounts of random access memory (RAM). You can get by with a bare bones PC or one compatible with a minimum amount of memory. Depending on the graphics software, a PC with 128K or more of RAM is sufficient for making business charts.

The computer alone isn't enough. You need a way to view the graphics. That requires a monitor and display adapter. You can use either a color or monochrome monitor. In the IBM PC, XT, and AT (as well as clones), the display adapter is a separate circuit board installed in one of the expansion slots. In the IBM PS/2 computers, the display adapter is built into the machine, although another one can be added.

Unless you plan on only viewing the charts yourself, you'll need some type of printer or pen plotter to get the graphs from the computer onto paper. There are numerous types to choose from—all have their advantages and disadvantages. Some print in black only; others print in vibrant color. Depending on the type of printer or plotter you get, you may be able to print directly on both plain paper or clear acetate film, the latter for creating fast and easy overhead transparencies.

To create the charts in the first place, you'll need a presentation graphics program. In all programs, you enter a series of numbers and tell the computer what type of chart to create. Some presentation graphs are enhanced or embellished using freehand painting or drawing programs. You use the computer and paint/draw program to change the appearance of the graph, such as add boxes, lines, or special text.

The Extras

If your use of computer graphics gravitates to the esoteric, or if you're really serious about graphics and want a full-blown system, then there are several other hardware items you may want to consider. First and foremost is an alternate input device—a mouse, touch tablet, or light pen. These input devices give you more control over the graphics you create, especially if you're going to be using a paint/draw program.

You may not want to hand draw each picture you create with your computer. To your rescue are video digitizers and image scanners. Video digitizers use a standard TV camera to capture an image and transfer the information into your computer. It's the same technology used to make computer printout novelty T-shirts and "wanted" posters. Image scanners are stand-alone units that quickly transform a full page of text or graphics into computer-readable data.

The quality of the picture you see on the screen depends on the digitizer/scanner and the design of your computer. The pictures you receive can be edited (usually with a painting program), printed out, or included with a graph. For example, you could use an image scanner to capture a drawing of a car. After editing the car with a painting program, you combine it with a chart that shows the increase in car leasing over car buying.

Printers and plotters do a fine job of providing paper output of the pictures you make with your computer, but for a really professional job, you may need a film recorder. These produce a 35-mm slide of the graphic as viewed through a special monitor. The film recorder uses a color wheel to generate different hues, so the slides come out vibrant and sharp.

A telephone modem lets you share data with colleagues, clients, and computer-slide service bureaus. You can create a chart and almost instantly transfer it over the phone lines to the corporate office. A computer-slide service bureau accepts slide data over the phone, then mails you back the finished graphic.

The Final Ingredient

There's one element that's missing from the graphics setup outlined above. It's called experimentation, your willingness to try new ideas. The software and hardware mentioned can be purchased from your local computer dealer, but experimentation comes only from you. Summon up a little willingness to experiment, stir it in with your computer and graphics program, and mix it well. The magical concoction you discover will be your personal stamp toward better communication.

Choosing the Right Chart to Tell Your Story

E X E C U T I V E   S U M M A R Y

The process of picking the right chart involves three steps: Identify the message; determine the comparison; select the chart. Identifying the message behind the chart helps focus the chart and makes its meaning clearer to the audience.

There are five types of comparisons: parts, which compare the components of a total; item, the ranking of components; time, the changes over a specific time period; frequency, the number of items that fit into predetermined categories; and correlation, which compares the relationship between two sets of values.

The five charts match the five types of comparisons. The charts are: pie, column, bar, line, and dot. Pie charts are used for parts comparisons, column charts for time and frequency comparisons, bar charts for item and correlation comparisons, line charts for time and frequency comparisons, and dot charts for correlation comparisons.

On the outside, numbers look much the same. A stack of figures showing a rise in interest rates may look the same as a stack showing a fall in grain production. But on the inside, the numbers may tell a different story. It is this story—and how you want to tell it—that dictates the type of chart you should use to effectively plot the numbers.

Picking the right kind of chart makes a lot of difference if your message is to come through to your audience. Even if the charts you make are for your own use, you'll want to choose the right kind so you can more easily and accurately analyze the numbers.

A Process of Elimination

There are five major types of business graphs, with lots of variations of each. Picking the right one out of all the possible choices can seem a monumental task. Fortunately, the job is made easier by a process of elimination.

For every chart you want to make, follow these three steps:

Step 1: Identify the message.
Step 2: Determine the comparison.
Step 3: Select the chart.

Don't forget step 1—identifying the message. It's the key to creating successful business graphics. You'd be surprised how many charts are made each day that don't have a meaningful message.

Why is it so critical to have a message? With a message in mind, it's far easier to pick a suitable chart for your numbers. More importantly, your audience is more likely to perceive the purpose of the chart and to readily accept the information contained within it. Without a firm message in mind, you run the risk of your audience misinterpreting the chart, which can lead to disastrous results.

Remember this point: *The message is the reason behind your presentation.* You wouldn't call a meeting and then sit around the table and talk about nothing. Likewise, you wouldn't make a chart that has nothing to say.

Identify the Message

Suppose you want to create a chart showing the performance of three divisions in a company. There are several ways you could

Company sales			
	A	B	C	Total
1983	325	119	84	528
1984	330	156	81	567
1985	319	171	87	577
1986	328	181	93	602
Total	1302	627	345	

Figure 2-1.
Data for message chart.

reveal the facts, depending on the message you want to convey. Figure 2-1 shows the data that each of the next three charts will use.

Now let's make some charts. In Figure 2-2, the message says that the total overall performance for the company is going up. The chart includes each department and the contribution it makes to the revenue of the company.

Figure 2-3 looks like a completely different chart, though it's made from the same data in the example above. The difference is that the message has changed—from showing increasing revenue to comparing the three departments with one another, ranking them in order of performance.

Another message produced the graph in Figure 2-4. It shows that department B has slowly improved its performance during the past several months, while the other two have remained fairly static.

Stressing the Message

Even though you may have a good idea of the message in your chart, your audience may not be so quick to catch on. Consider

Sales are steadily rising

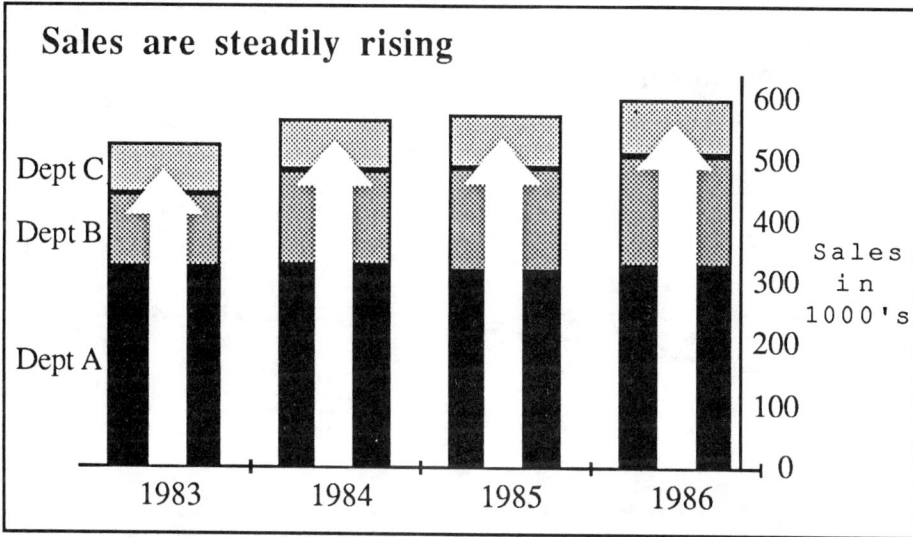

Figure 2-2.
Total performance.

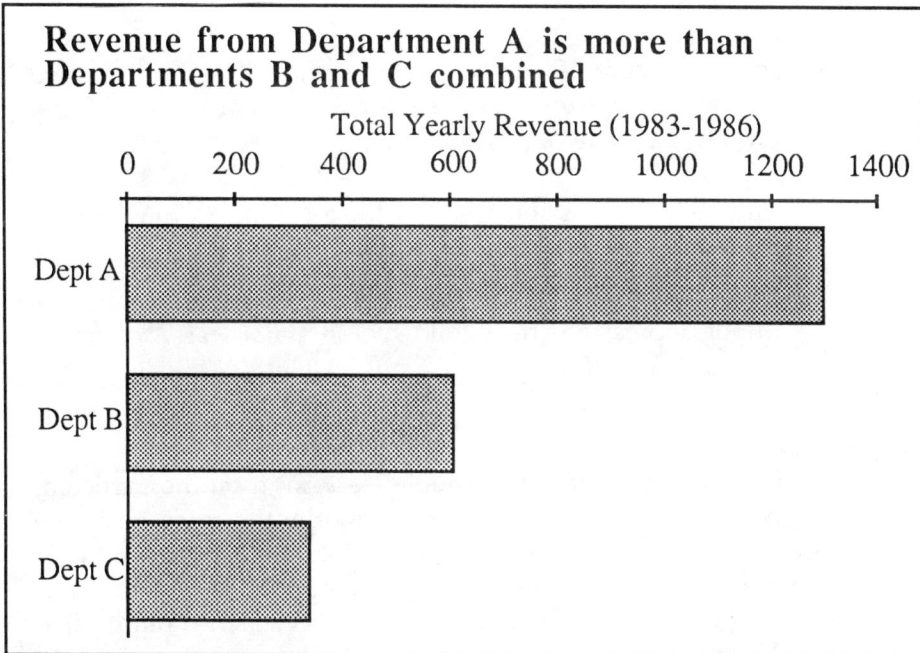

Revenue from Department A is more than Departments B and C combined

Total Yearly Revenue (1983-1986)

Figure 2-3.
Department ranking.

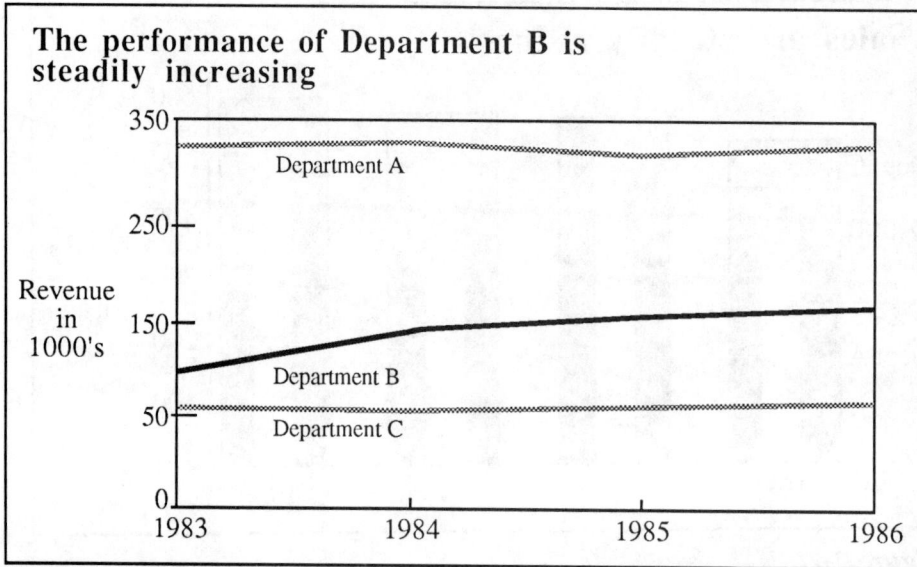

The performance of Department B is steadily increasing

Figure 2-4.
Department B getting better.

the chart in Figure 2-5. Even though it may have been created with a firm message in mind, it's not really clear in its final form. Right off, a couple of possible messages come to mind:

- The 1929 Depression was the lowest point in our nation's economic history.
- Wars have stimulated the economy.
- Minor depressions have followed all major wars.
- The economy is now more stable and prosperous than ever before.

The best way to help your audience zero in on the particular message you're trying to convey is to write the message as the title of the chart. Replace the nondescriptive title in the example above with one of the four message examples, and you give new meaning to the chart. Now the message is clear and unmistakable. If the message is too long for a title (more than 8 or 10 words), it is acceptable to pare it down into a manageable chunk. However, don't reduce the message so much that it is cryptic and impossible to understand.

title too long if 8 to 10 words

Economy trendline

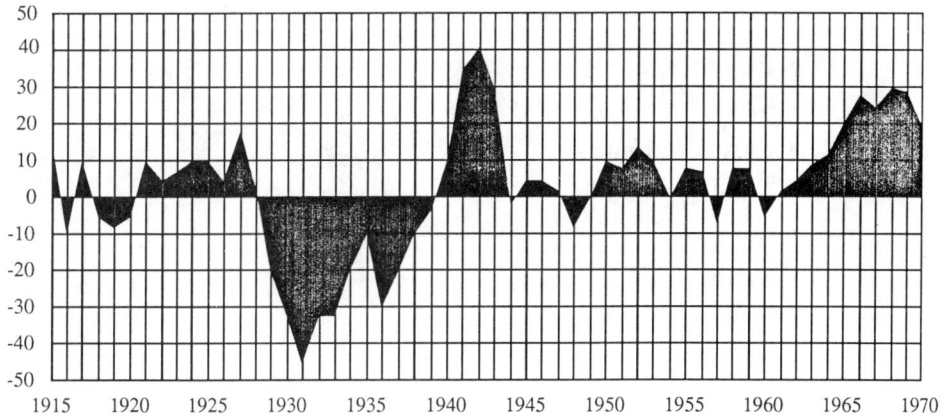

Source: Ameri Trust Company

Figure 2-5.
100-year economy trend line.

Determine the Comparison

Your proposed message will *lead you to a comparison* of one type or another. There are five types of comparisons: parts, item, time, frequency, and correlation.

- *Parts.* The percentage of components that make up the total
- *Item.* The ranking of items
- *Time.* Change over time
- *Frequency.* The number of items that fit into predetermined categories
- *Correlation.* The relationship between two sets of numbers

Following is a rundown of each of the five types of comparisons.

Parts

The *parts comparison* shows the size of individual components (or parts) and how they contribute to the total picture. As an example, assume five components make up a finished product. The cost of manufacturing that product is a known value, say, $5. Each component or part contributes some percentage to the total cost—some more, some less.

To find out if your proposed chart compares parts as they relate to the total, look for these key words in the message:

- Percentage
- Share
- Contribution
- Total
- Sum
- Ratio
- Proportion

Item

An *item comparison* depicts how things rank. The comparison may show that the items in the chart are less than, more than, or equal to one another. You'll know you're looking at an item comparison if you encounter these key words (or their synonyms) in the message:

- More than
- Less than
- Equal to
- Ranks
- Higher
- Lower

Time

The *time comparison* shows how something changes over time—how a person gets tall as she grows up, for example. That time can be in hours, days, weeks, months, years, or whatever. You can tell you're dealing with a time comparison if words such as the following are in your message.

- Change
- Increase
- Decrease
- Grow
- Decline
- Rise

- Fall
- Now/then
- Fluctuate

Frequency

A *frequency comparison* shows how many items fall into a set of predetermined categories. One good example of a frequency comparison is showing how many students in a class got A's, how many got B's, and so forth. Look for the key words:

- Frequency
- Distribution
- Range
- Fall into
- How many
- How often

Correlation

The *correlation comparison* pits two sets of numbers together, to see if there is a relationship between them. For example, there would likely be a comparison between car sales and the selling price of the car. The lower the price, the more people are likely to buy it. Key words to consider are:

- Related to
- Changes
- Increases/decreases with
- Varies

Locating Key Words

Don't worry if your message doesn't include one of the key words mentioned above. Write down the message (so you can study it), and consider alternative words for it. Consult a thesaurus and dictionary if you need help.

Here's an example. Earlier in this chapter it was suggested that you title your charts with a message. One of the messages was "Wars have stimulated the economy" (sad but often true). The word "stimulated" also means to grow or increase. Both "grow" and "increase" are key words for a time comparison. This provides you with the necessary clue—that you are comparing time. You can now choose the proper chart.

Select the Chart

The hard part is over. Now that you know the message behind the chart, and what you're comparing, you have *automatically arrived at the correct type of chart to use*. Although there are many varieties of business graphics, 95 percent of the charts you will use will fall into one of the following five major types shown in Figure 2-6: pie, column, bar, line, and dot.

Selecting the recommended chart is even easier if you refer to the table in Figure 2-7, which was adapted from the excellent tutorial on business graphics, *Say It with Charts* (Gene Zelazny, Dow Jones-Irwin, Homewood, Il., 1985). The five types of comparisons are listed on the top, the main chart types along the side.

Keep in mind that the table represents the recommended choice; it is not meant to be an absolute authority. Presentation graphics is an art, never an exact science, and you are urged to experiment. But the table provides a clearer view of what types of charts best fit the various kinds of comparisons. Exceptions will be noted along the way.

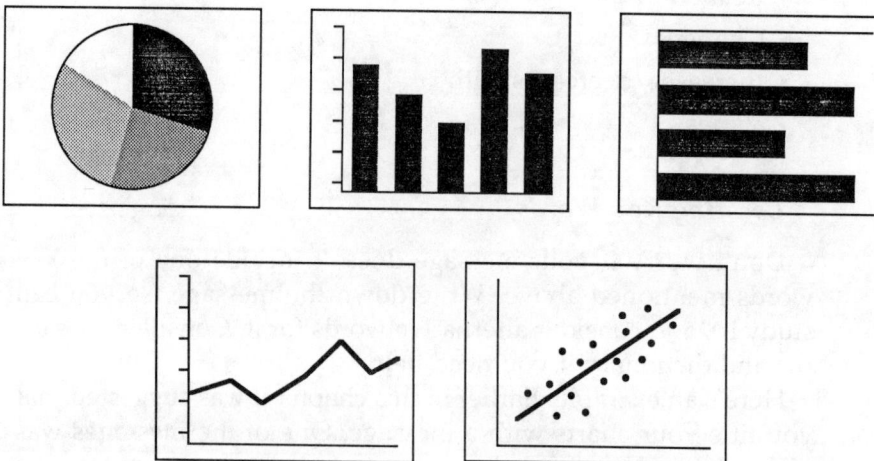

Figure 2-6.
Chart types, plain examples.

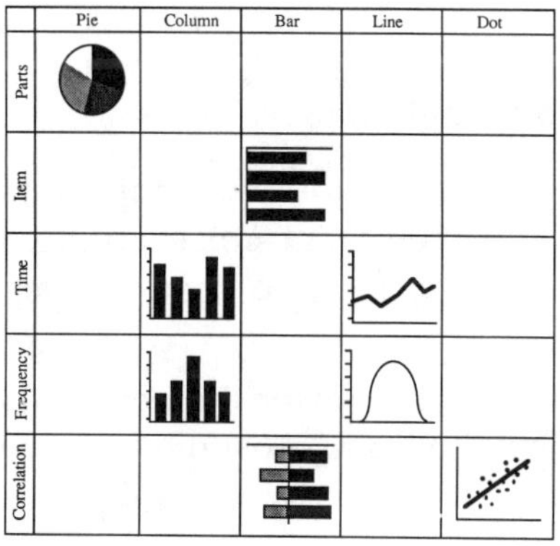

Figure 2-7.
Chart matrix.

Pie Chart

Pie charts are popular because they're easy to make and easier for an audience to comprehend. They're used almost exclusively in parts comparisons. The pie—a finite circle—is divided into portions, or slices. *Each slice represents an individual component,* a percentage or share of the total. That's perfect for a parts comparison. As you can see in Figure 2-8, the larger the part, the bigger the percentage, and so the thicker the slice.

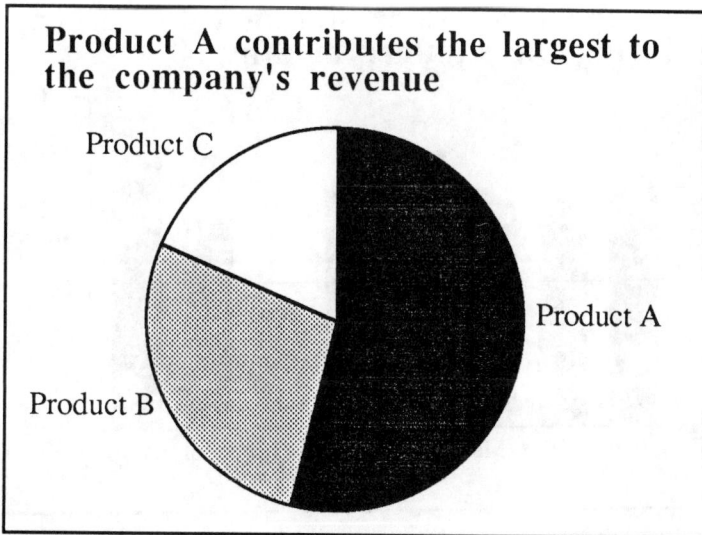

Figure 2-8.
Pie chart.

Pie Chart Limitations

Pie charts suffer from some limitations.

- By their nature, pie charts cannot show the parts of more than one total at a time. You can't, for example, show the totals of office expenditures for two separate years in the same chart.

- Pie charts should be limited to fewer than eight slices. With more slices, it's difficult to compare how the parts relate. Combine some of the smaller parts (use the ubiquitous "other" label).

Column Chart

Column charts are best used to show the change of a single item over time. *Each period of time has its own column.* As you can see in Figure 2-9, the taller the column, the greater the value of the item. Because of their design, column charts *emphasize levels of magnitude.* Differences from one time period to another are easy to spot.

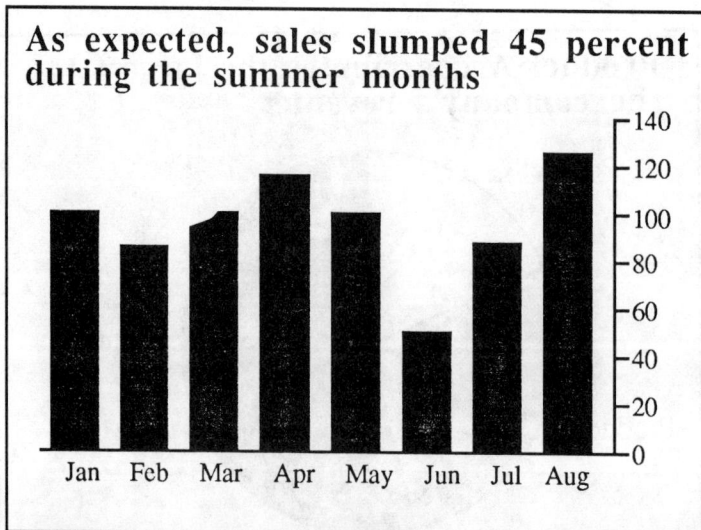

As expected, sales slumped 45 percent during the summer months

Figure 2-9.
Basic column chart—one series.

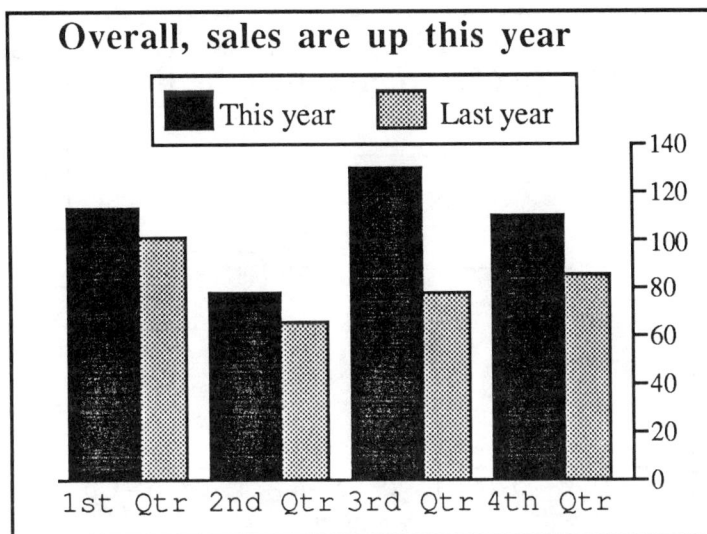

Figure 2-10.
Multiple series column chart.

Charting Several Sets of Data

It's possible to compare an item during several sets of time in one column chart. Each set is called a *series*. Let's say, for example, that you are plotting the quarterly sales of a company. The columns for the four quarters in the current year are shown in black. The columns for the quarters of last year are shown in gray. You can use patterns, stripes, or colors to differentiate each series. See Figure 2-10 for an example.

Some caveats:

- You should limit yourself to stuffing no more than four series in one column chart.

- Avoid plotting no more than six or eight numbers for each series. Lots of columns make the chart difficult to understand.

Column Charts for Frequency Distribution

An exception to the "few columns" rule above is when creating a *frequency distribution chart*, or *histogram*. In such a chart, the columns represent *ranges*, not periods in time. The height of each

Those aged 15-29 comprise the largest percentage of population in the US

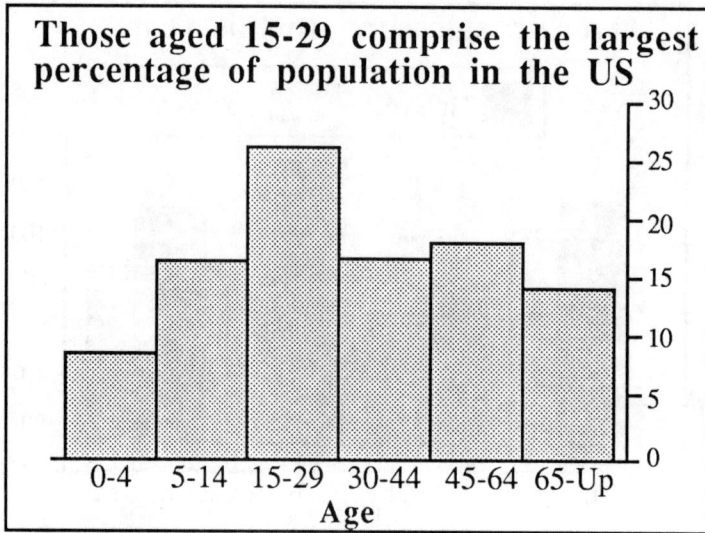

Figure 2-11.
Frequency distribution column chart.

column is dependent on the number of values that fall into each range. A good example of a columnar frequency distribution chart, as illustrated in Figure 2-11, is one that shows the population of the United States broken down into age groups (each of the age groups is one range).

Stacked Column

Stacked column charts (also called *subdivided column charts*) can be used in place of several pie charts. The two (or more) columns are both the same height. Each stack represents 100 percent, so this type of chart is sometimes referred to as a *100 percent stacked column chart*. Instead of slices, as in a pie chart, you have columns stacked on top of one another. As shown in Figure 2-12, lines can be drawn to connect the columns of the stacks (done either with the graphics program or by hand), which helps the viewer visualize the difference between them.

Other Column Chart Varieties

As you've seen, a stacked column chart shows the items that make up the total. The total, however, needn't represent 100 percent. As an example, the chart could show the sales of two

Company C has been the market leader for the past three decades

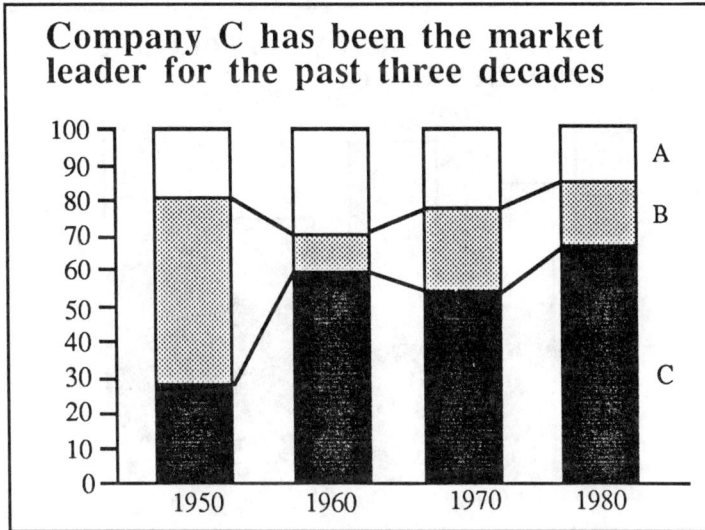

Figure 2-12.
Stacked column chart.

salespeople during four quarters of the year. The total could be real dollar amount, as depicted in Figure 2-13, or a percentage.

A *deviation column chart*, shown in Figure 2-14, ranks items with both *positive and negative values*. The items with positive values (the winners) are on top of the dividing line; the items with negative values (the losers) are on the bottom.

Most column charts start at zero and go up (or down, as in a deviation column chart). The *range column chart* shows the point spread between high and low amounts. Take a look at Figure 2-15. The bottom of each column is the low point for that data set; the top of each column is the high point.

A type of range column chart uses thin lines instead of broader columns. This type of graph, usually referred to as a *high-low chart*, is familiar to you if you follow the stock market. Additional tick marks are sometimes added to note other information within the range—specifically, the closing price of the stock—as shown in Figure 2-16.

Bar Chart

Bar charts may look like column charts turned sideways, but there's more to them than that. Bar charts are predominately

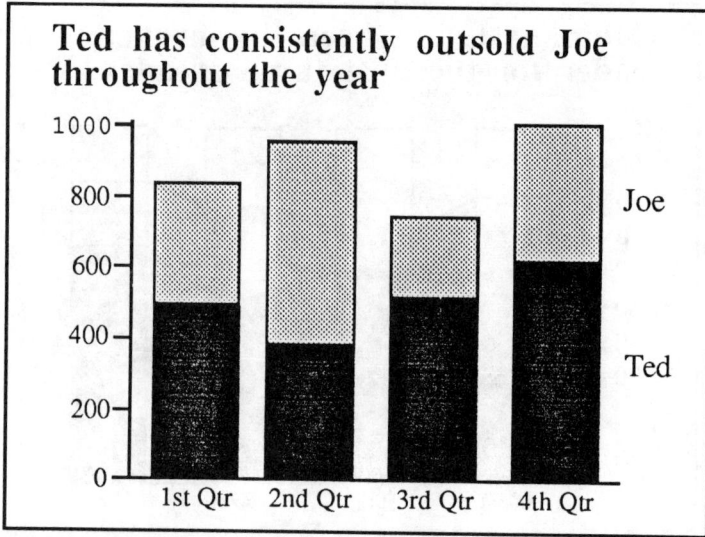

Figure 2-13.
Real dollar amount stacked column.

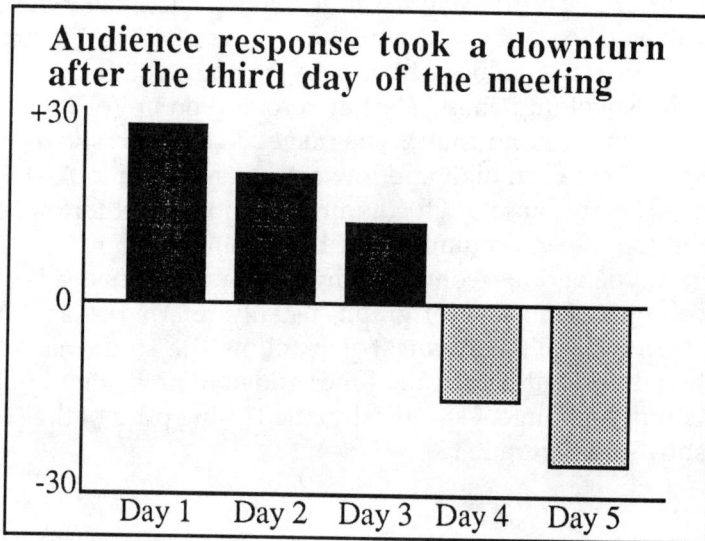

Figure 2-14.
Deviation column chart.

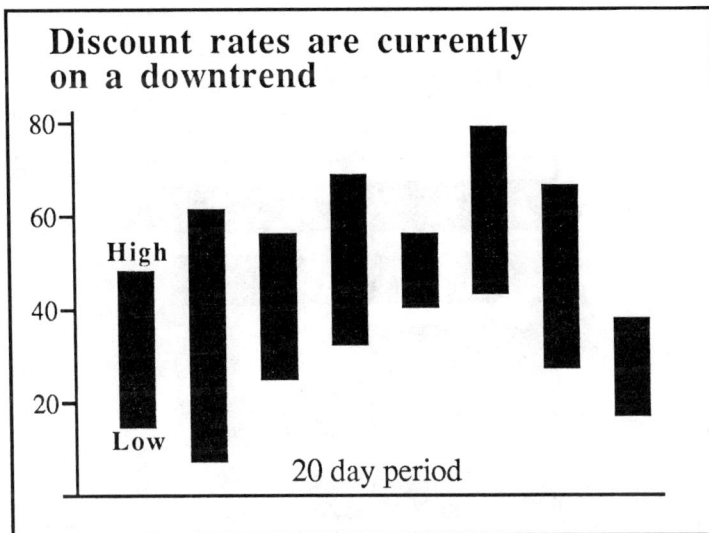

Figure 2-15.
Range column chart.

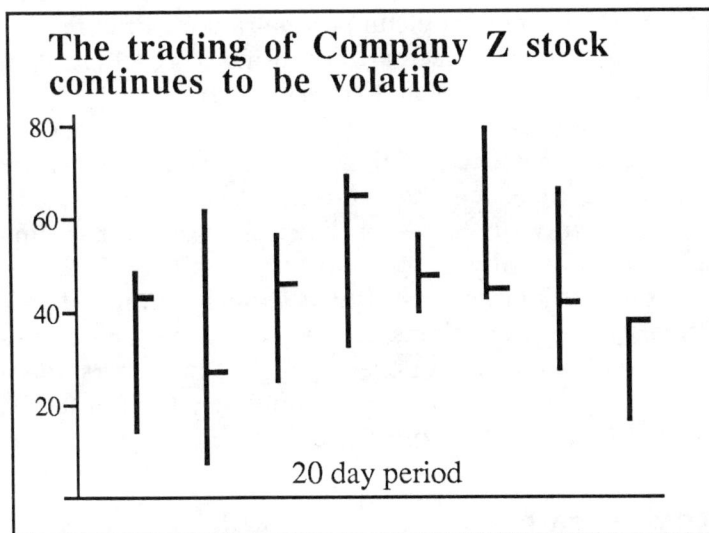

Figure 2-16.
Stock hi-low chart.

Group C ranked the lowest in our recent surveys

	0	30	60	90

Group A

Group B

Group C

Group D

Group E

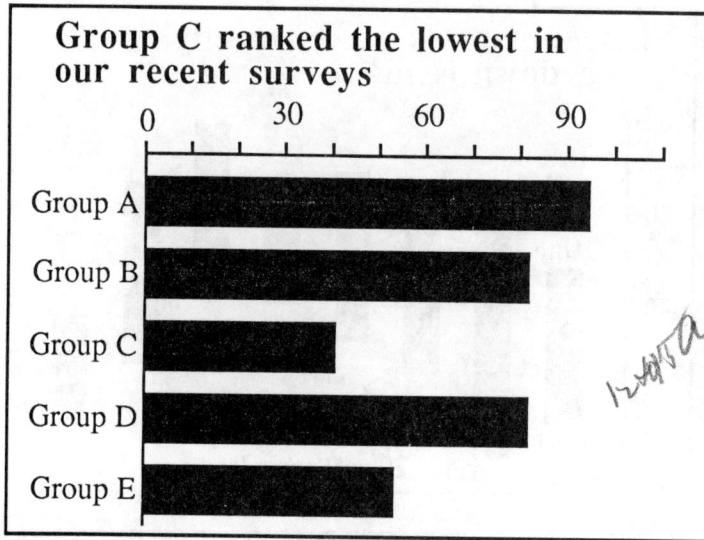

Figure 2-17.
Basic bar chart.

used to display *rank of several similar items.* The bars are stacked lengthwise, almost like lumber. As you can see in Figure 2-17, the eye can easily compare the different lengths of the bars and make a quick mental picture of the ranking of items. Magnitude isn't the important factor when using a bar chart; it's how the lengths of the bars relate to one another.

The real beauty of the bar chart is that it provides extra space on the side for labels. Column charts require labels under each bar to be close together or written vertically. In a bar chart, there's plenty of space—on both sides of the bars, in fact—to place even lengthy labels.

Unlike column charts, which should be limited to no more than six or eight columns, it's perfectly acceptable to create a bar chart with a couple of dozen bars. The more bars, the taller the chart. In practice, though, you should try to limit the bars to no more than 12 or 15. Comparisons are more easily made.

The Paired Bar Chart

The main use of bar charts may be to show the raw ranking of items, but they have additional applications. One in particular, the *paired bar chart,* can be used to show a relationship between

As the ad rates go up, the number of ads go down

Ad Rates   0   Ad Pages

[handwritten annotations: "6-8 at most", "all bars are same size ea = 100%"]

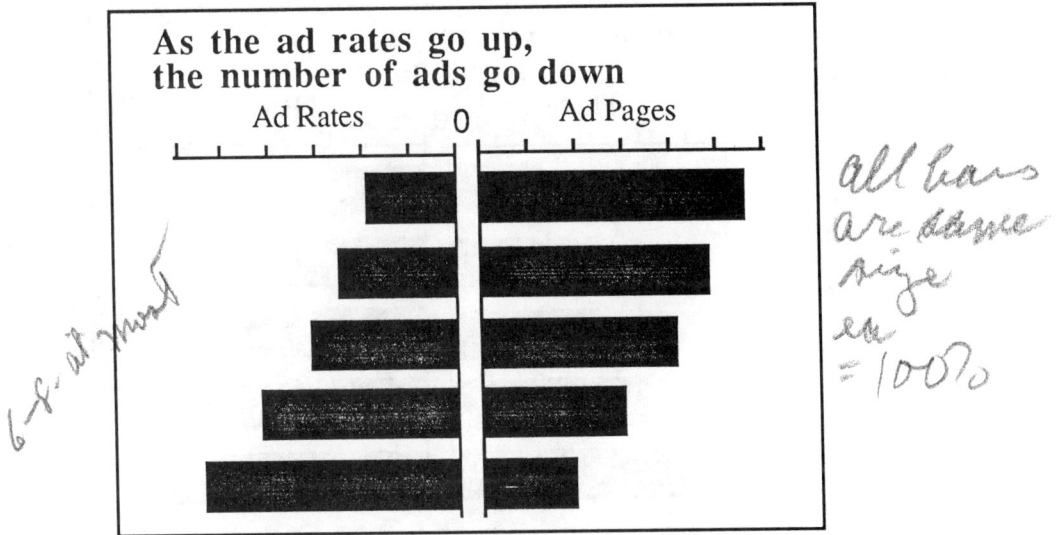

Figure 2-18.
Positive paired bar. *[handwritten: "neg correlation ?"]*

paired items. In this way, the bar chart is being used for a *correlation comparison.*

Imagine a chart divided equally down the middle. On the left side are bars for one series of items, ranked from smallest to largest. These bars show the average ad rates charged by several national magazines. On the other side are another set of bars, these showing the number of full-page ads in each of the magazines.

If there's a *negative correlation* between the cost of ads and the number of ads (higher cost, less ads), as there is in Figure 2-18, the bars on either side will be an upside-down image of one another. If there's a *positive correlation* (higher cost, higher ads), as in Figure 2-19, the bars will be a mirror image of one another. Finally, if there is *no correlation*, the bars on the right will have varying lengths of no particular pattern.

Other Bar Chart Varieties

A *sliding bar chart* shows the different mix of two items. The two items comprise a total, and the bars are of equal length. The centerline of the chart shows the 50 percent mark. Depending on the percentage mix of the two items, as illustrated in Figure 2-20, the bar will slide one way or another.

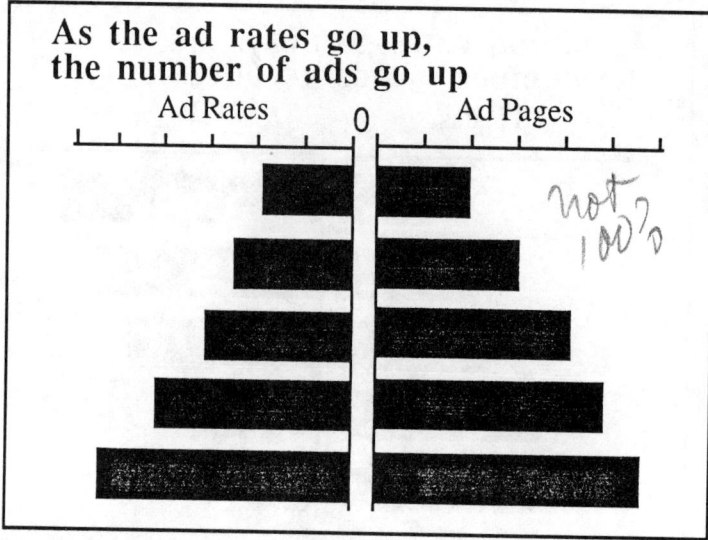

**As the ad rates go up,
the number of ads go up**

Figure 2-19.
Negative paired bar.

A *stacked bar chart* (or *subdivided bar chart*) shows the items that make up the total. The total need not represent 100 percent, but it can. For example, the chart could show the contributions to revenue from two profit centers for a variety of products. The total could be real dollar amount, as in Figure 2-21, or a per-

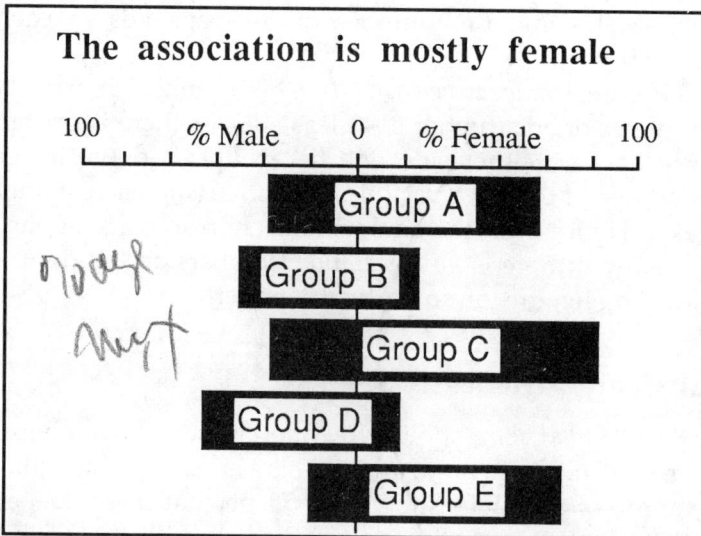

The association is mostly female

Figure 2-20.
Sliding bar chart.

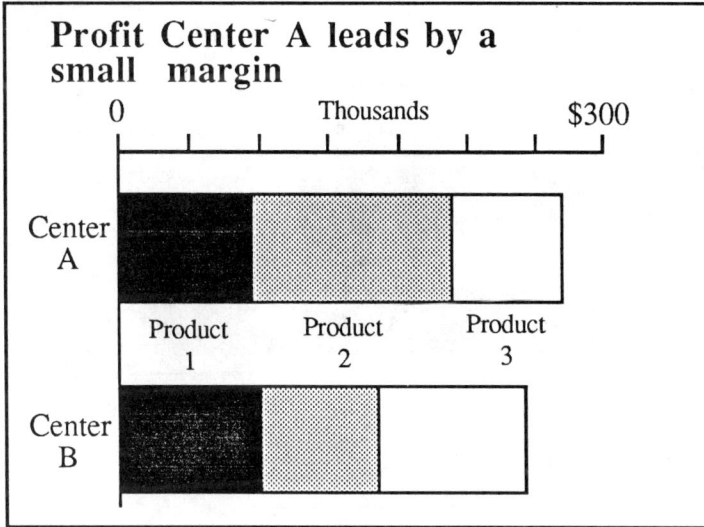

Figure 2-21.
Real dollar amount stacked bar.

centage (see Figure 2-22). An alternative to stacking is to create a *grouped bar chart,* shown in Figure 2-23. Each group compares different aspects about the same item—revenue from profit centers A and B side by side.

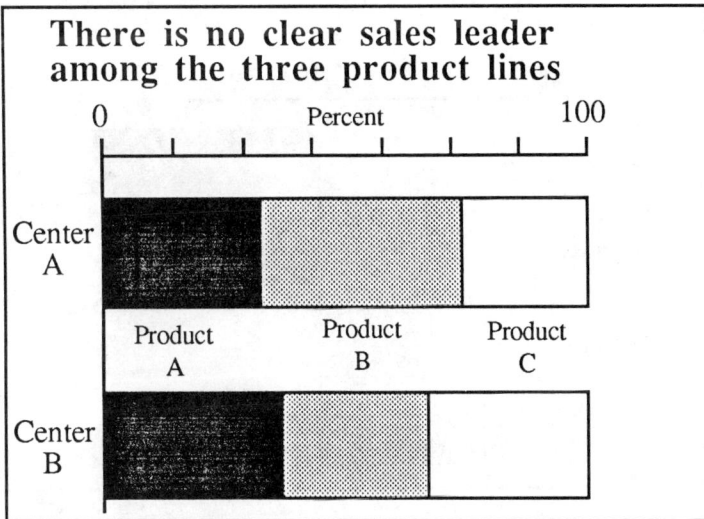

Figure 2-22.
100 percent stacked bar.

Product B is the only line to reach the $125,000 mark

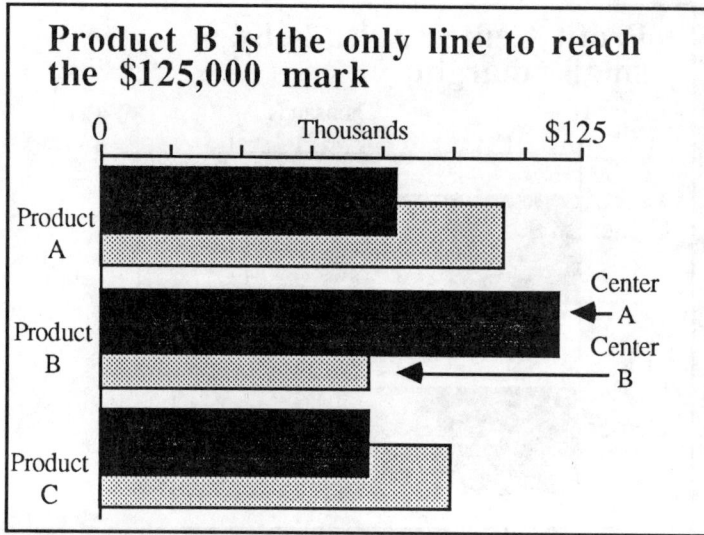

Figure 2-23.
Grouped bar chart.

A *deviation bar chart*, like the one in Figure 2-24, ranks items with both positive and negative values. The items with positive values (the winners) are on the left of the dividing line; the items with negative values (the losers) are on the right.

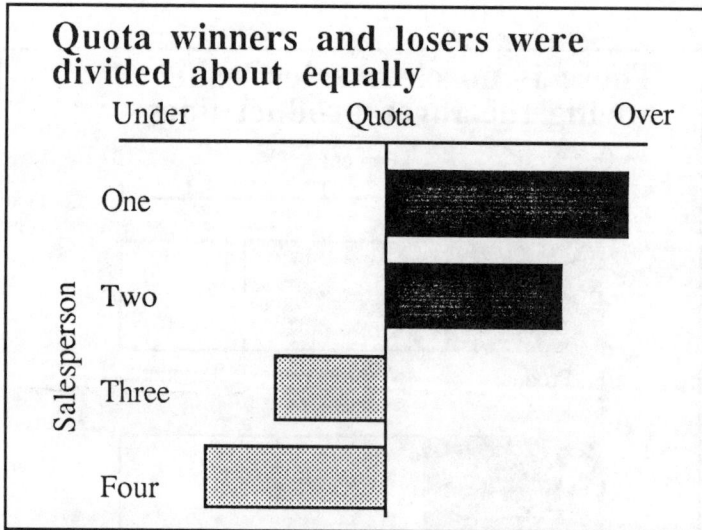

Quota winners and losers were divided about equally

Figure 2-24.
Deviation bar chart.

As expected, sales slumped 45 percent during the summer months

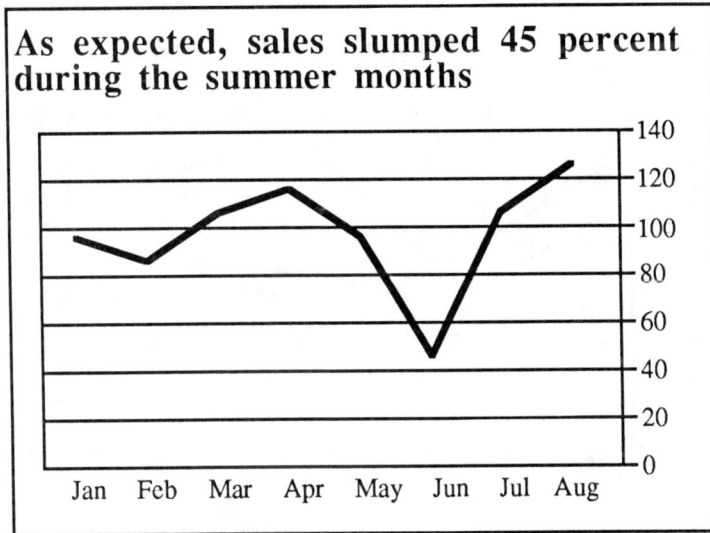

Figure 2-25.
Basic line chart.

Line Chart

Column and *line charts* are used for much of the same thing, namely, plotting the course of an item through time. Because the line of a line chart is unbroken, the effect of change—either up or down—is dramatically emphasized. Sometimes, this is exactly what you want; other times it isn't. The moral: Be extra careful when making a line chart. Be sure the dramatic impact of the line won't distract your audience from your idea. See Figure 2-25 for an example of a basic line chart.

Multiple Line Charts

Like column charts, line graphs can plot one item over several different series of time periods. This is the *multiple line chart.* One line could be for this year's expenditures, for instance; another line could be a projection for next year. Different colors, symbols, or textures are used to denote each series of data. A legend, usually placed off the side of the chart or within it, as in Figure 2-26, explains the meaning of each line.

Unlike column charts, line charts can also plot more than one item. One line could be the revenue of store A for 1 year.

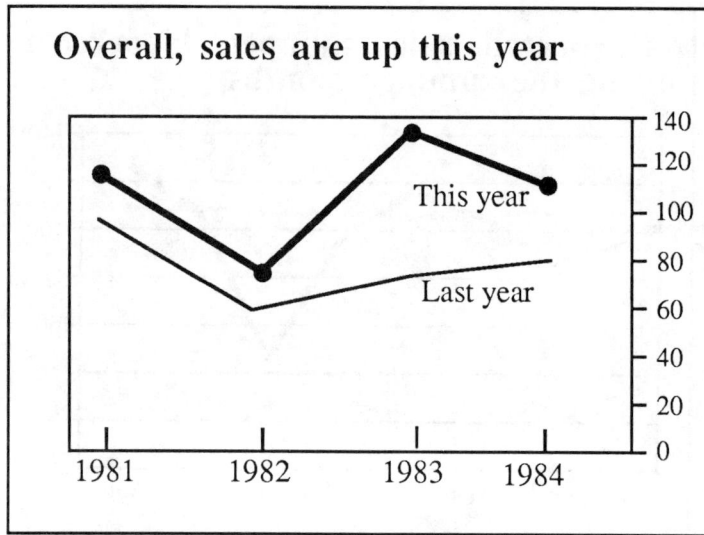

Figure 2-26.
Multiseries line chart.

Another line could be the revenue of store B for a year, and so forth. You should exercise caution and avoid plotting more than four or five lines in one chart or you may end up with a *spaghetti graph*, like the one in Figure 2-27.

Line Charts for Frequency Distribution

Line charts can also be used for *frequency distribution comparison*. Instead of graphing some type of value (usually money) against time, a line frequency distribution, or *histograph*, plots the number of items that fall into specific ages. Consider Figure 2-28, which compares diameters of a harvest of tomatoes. The line chart can be used over the column chart for a frequency distribution comparison when you want to emphasize the change, or some specific pattern.

Area Charts

A special kind of line graph is the *area chart*, also called a surface, layer, or band chart. In an area chart, the portions under the lines are filled in with a pattern or color. More than that, however, the

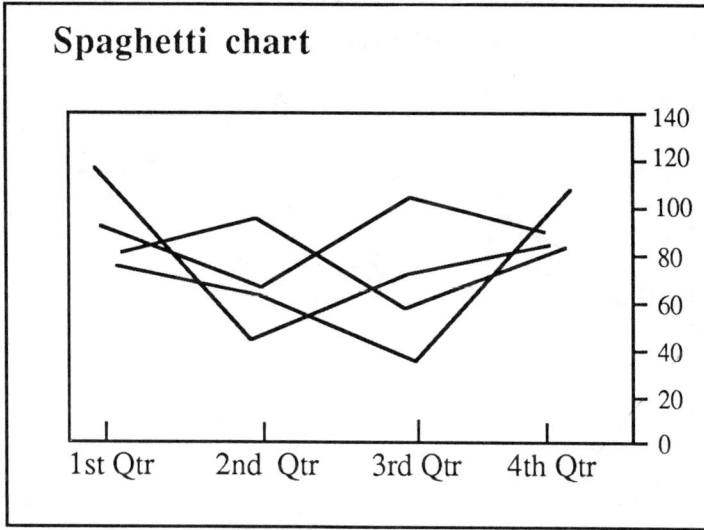

Figure 2-27.
Spaghetti graph.

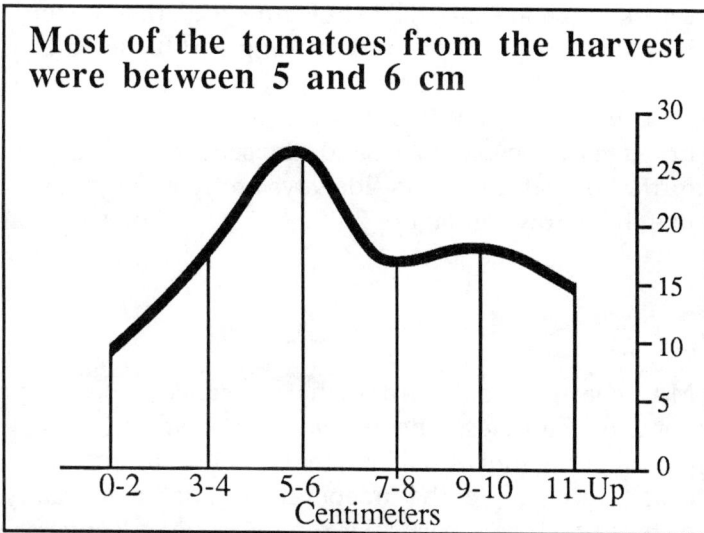

Figure 2-28.
Line chart as frequency distribution.

Another spaghetti chart

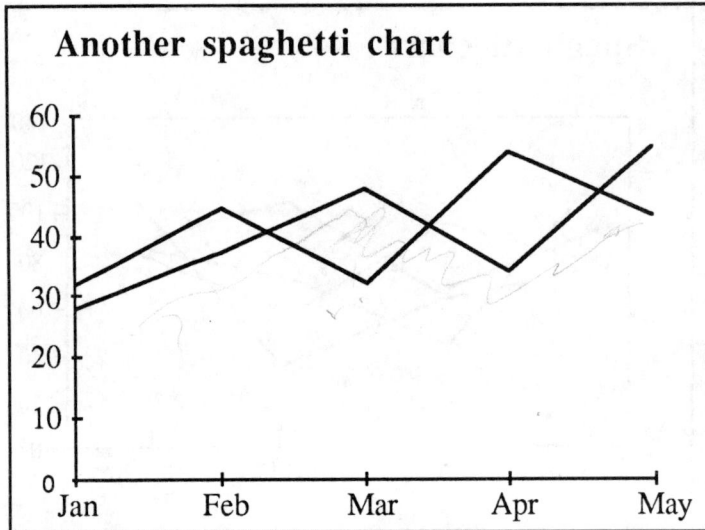

Figure 2-29.
Line chart of data.

"areas" stack on top of one another—the charts shows a *cumulative total of all the series you're plotting.*

Suppose you are graphing two series of numbers, series A and series B. In a line chart, like in Figure 2-29, the line for each series may cross over other lines, making it difficult to comprehend. But in an area chart, area B is physically stacked on top of area A. You can think of this stacking as pouring grains of sand. The first layer is one color of sand, the second another color, and so forth. Look at the layers sideways and you might get something like that shown in Figure 2-30.

Dot Chart

Most charts are made from what are called dependent and independent variables. The *independent variable* is usually a time period or the individual item that is being compared. In a column chart, for example, the independent variable is usually a period of time, such as a particular month or year. Conversely, *dependent variables* are the values for each specified item or time period. One month, the dependent variable could be 10. The next month, it could be 7, and so forth.

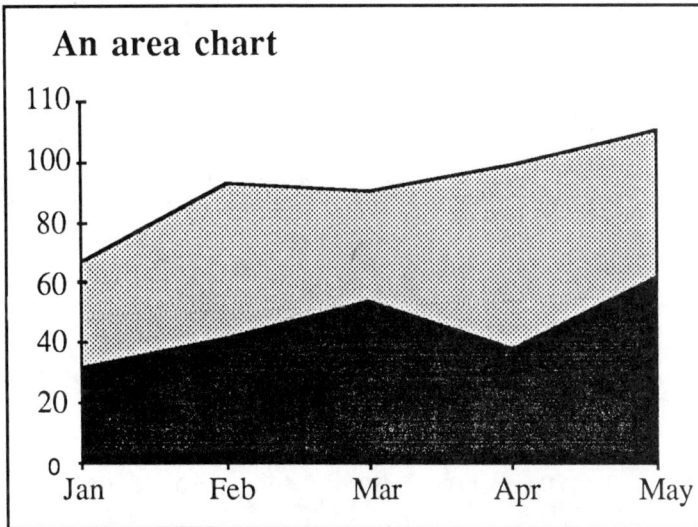

An area chart

Figure 2-30.
Area chart of data.

In a *dot chart* (also called an *X-Y chart*), there are *two sets of dependent variables*. Dots are placed on the intersection of the two variables on the chart grid. Figure 2-31 illustrates a typical dot chart.

Dot charts are specifically designed for correlation comparisons. The dots will line up in some orderly fashion if there is some logical commonality between the two series of numbers. When the two series of numbers don't have anything in common, the dots appear in the chart in a seemingly random, scattered fashion (see Figure 2-32 for an example). That's why dot charts are sometimes called *scatter charts*.

Adding Trend Lines

Often, the visual correlation of the two dependent variables is hard to grasp, because the dots don't appear to follow a strict pattern. Still, a pattern may exist, and it's important to show it. There are several statistical formulas that can be applied to the numbers to reveal a pattern, like the *trend line* in Figure 2-33. That pattern is then drawn as a line going from one corner of the chart to another. For more on statistical analysis, see Chapter 4, Advanced Charting Techniques.

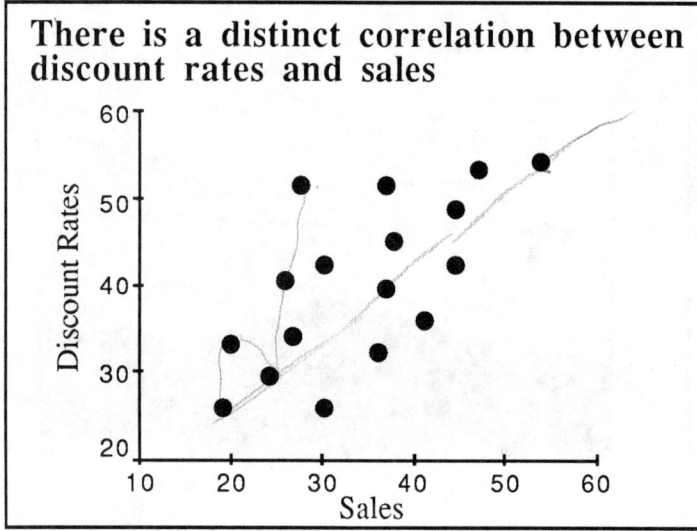

Figure 2-31.
Basic dot chart.

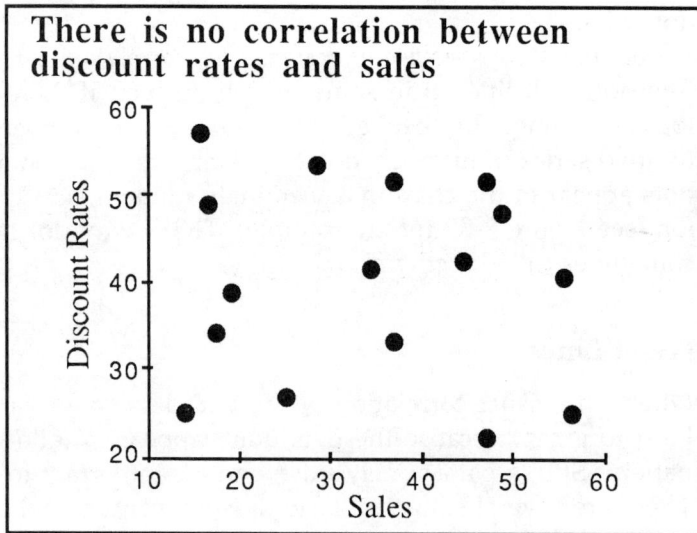

Figure 2-32.
Comparison/no comparison examples.

Radio interference increases as sunspot activity increases

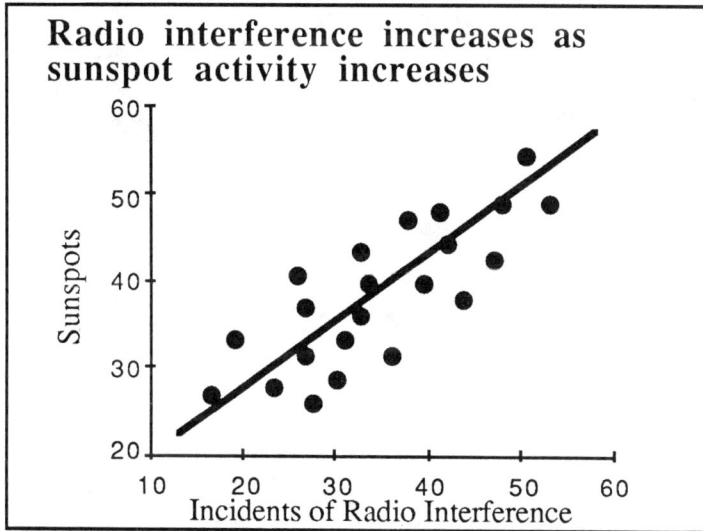

Figure 2-33.
Dot chart with regression line.

Reinforcing the Expected Trend

Dot charts are often used to answer a question, such as, "Is there a relationship between the age of our salespeople and their commissions?" The dot pattern quickly answers the question. The chart may show you that your expected answer is wrong: The older members of your sales force may not necessarily earn higher commissions. The *expected trend* may be important in your analysis, and it can be helpful to draw a line or arrow, showing the pattern as you expect it.

Identifying the Dots

One problem inherent in dot charts is identifying the data points. Identification of the individual dots is often unnecessary, however—you're just interested in showing a trend. If you need to include identification of the data points, furnish the information in table form in addition to the chart.

When the dots are few, you can use symbols instead of dots for each data point, as in Figure 2-34. Include the meaning of each symbol in a legend. When you must identify the dots, and

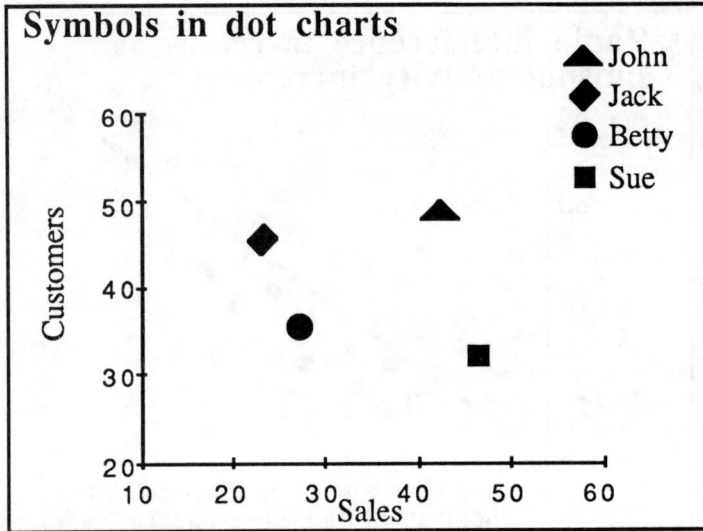

Figure 2-34.
Symbols in dot chart.

there are more than a half dozen of them, it's better to abandon the dot chart and use a sliding bar chart instead. *more than 6*

Other Chart Types

The five charts described above are primary to the discussion of presentation graphics, but there are other varieties. Let's review some of the most important ones.

Text

The five major types of business graphs are good when converting numerical data to picture form. But what happens when the data you're trying to convey aren't numbers? Use a *text chart*. A text chart, as shown in Figure 2-35, includes a few choice words that you want to stress to your audience. By highlighting your main thoughts on a subject, your audience can more easily zero in on your idea. Text charts are also ideal when interspersed between pictorial graphs. They break up the pattern of graph after graph, which helps prevent monotony.

It's important to remember that text charts work best when

1987 Objectives

- Improve customer relations

- Develop general merger guidelines

- Start employee bonus compensation package

- Tighten Quality Control

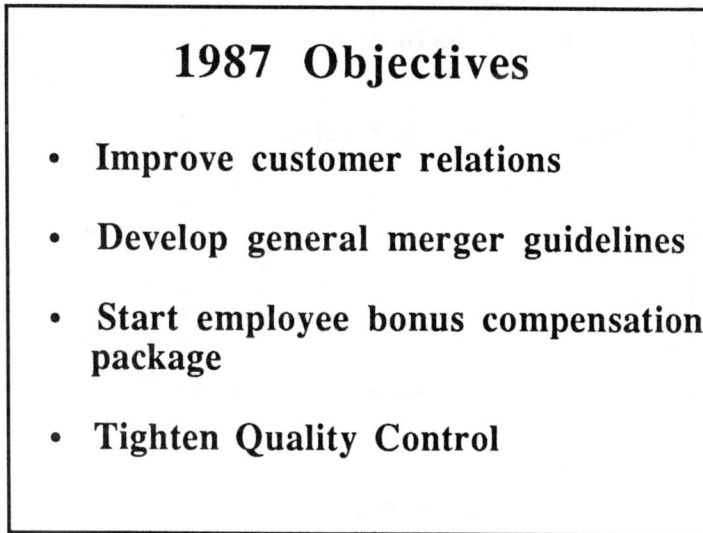

Figure 2-35.
Text chart.

they are composed of few words. As a general rule, limit text charts to no more than six lines with six words each. Whether you include the chart in a report or an oral presentation, the text should be large and crisp, to draw your audience's attention.

Using Builds in Text Charts

A *build* is when you present a series of charts one after the other and add something new to each chart. Text charts are particularly well-suited to builds—you can add one line of text to each new graph. The previous lines can be dimmed or shaded, as illustrated in Figure 2-36; this accentuates the new topic.

Bubble

The *bubble chart* is a unique variation of the dot chart. In a typical dot chart, you place a dot at the exact intersection of two whole-number variables. But when the values are ranges, not specific values, you should use a bubble chart instead. As you can see in Figure 2-37, the size and shape of each bubble is dependent on the range. If the range is uneven for one of the variables (greater for variable A than variable B), the bubble may be more oval

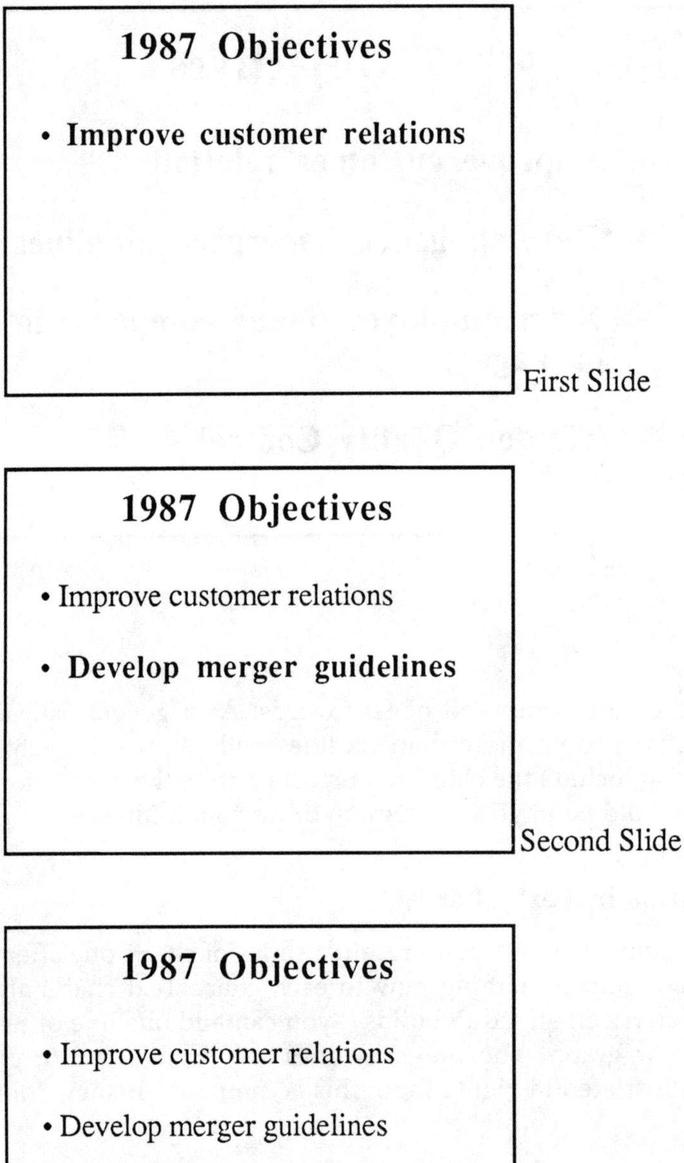

1987 Objectives

• **Improve customer relations**

First Slide

1987 Objectives

• Improve customer relations

• **Develop merger guidelines**

Second Slide

1987 Objectives

• Improve customer relations

• Develop merger guidelines

• **Tighten Quality Control**

Third Slide

Figure 2-36.
Text build.

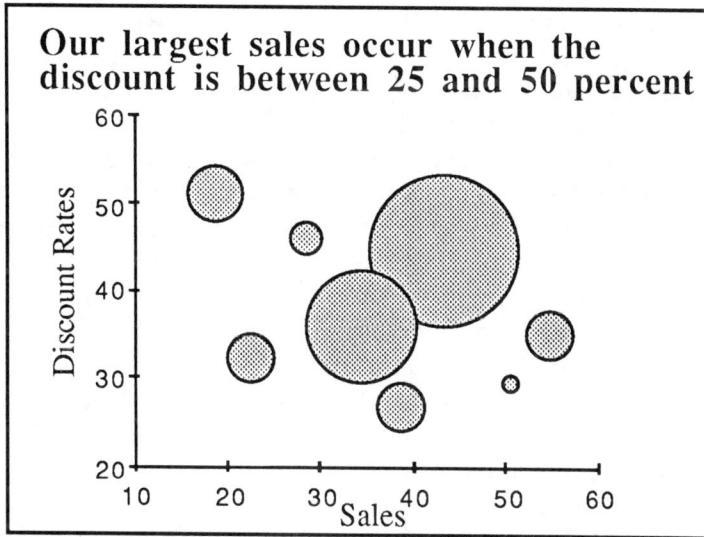

Figure 2-37.
Bubble chart.

shaped. Bubble charts are often used to show the ratios, such as the ratio of price to performance, of a particular line of product.

Gantt

Henry L. Gantt was a consulting engineer who lived during the turn of the twentieth century. His claim to fame is that he developed a unique way of managing people. He believed people were human beings, not machines, and that proper management of workers entailed considering more than just the amount of raw labor that could be done in an 8- or 10-hour shift. During World War I, Gantt developed a system of visually showing the flow of work from one task to another—a *time line* that took into account all the people and variables involved in getting something done.

Though Gantt's ideas took a while to catch on, the *Gantt chart* is now a staple of modern business management. By their nature, Gantt charts require constant updating, so a computer is an ideal tool for creating them. You can use Gantt charts as part of your presentations. You might show that a job is going on schedule as planned, or that you need more time, people, or money to get a job done.

The main element of a Gantt chart, shown in Figure 2-38, is a listing of all the tasks required to complete a job. Along with the tasks is information on the person responsible for doing the work. On the other side of the chart is the time line itself. Bars are drawn by each task, showing the start and finish dates. Tasks that can be done concurrently may share the same dates. Tasks that must follow one another start when the other one is completed.

A typical Gantt chart looks a lot like a stair step, easily revealing which tasks are dependent on the other. Gantt charts can be made from the due date and work backwards, or from some other date. If the job is a big one, it can easily be broken down into phases. *Milestones* are added to the chart, which are important due dates that can be used to determine if a job is going as scheduled.

Gantt charts are not the only visual projection management tools available. A *pert chart* shows tasks as "things-to-do" boxes, with connecting lines between tasks. Pert charts are good, but better suited for showing the work flow from one task to another, rather than the time line of particular job.

Organization

An *organization chart* shows the hierarchy of people or things. Each person or item is enclosed in a box; lines connect the boxes to one another, according to which ones are dependent on the others.

For example, take a look at the organization chart in Figure 2-39 of that most secret organization, the Central Intelligence Agency. The head of the CIA is the director. Reporting to the director is the deputy director, and so that person's box is placed under the director's. Below that are six offices and four major sectional components, each headed by a subordinate deputy director.

As you can see, the organization chart for the main offices and personnel of the CIA are probably not that much different from the ones in your company. The point is that organization charts are ideal for reducing the machinations of a company or process by placing the components in a visual step-by-step outline form. Things seem much less complicated, and that's exactly the purpose of charting.

Gantt chart for Michelson report

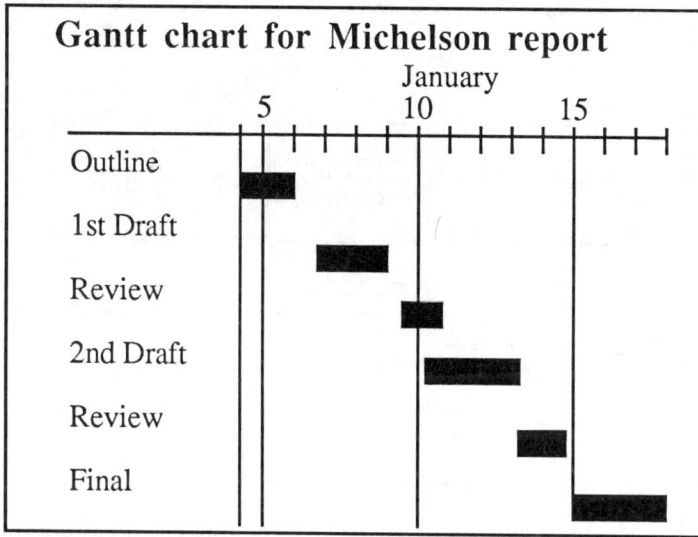

Figure 2-38.
Gantt chart.

Central Intelligence Agency

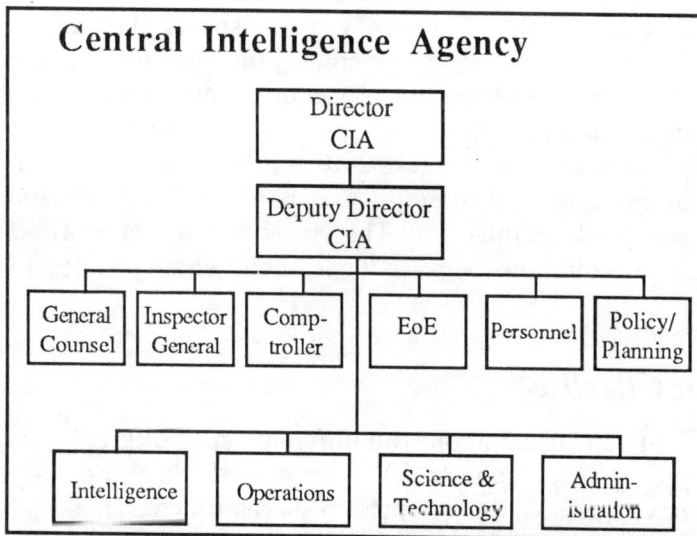

Figure 2-39.
CIA organization chart.

Manufacturing Process of XYZ Radio

```
┌───────────┐     ┌───────────┐     ┌───────────┐
│ Inventory │ ──► │  Quality  │ ──► │ Assembly  │
│           │     │  Control  │     │           │
└───────────┘     └───────────┘     └───────────┘

        ┌───────────┐     ┌───────────┐
        │   Wave    │ ──► │ Packing/  │
        │  Solder   │     │ Shipping  │
        └───────────┘     └───────────┘
```

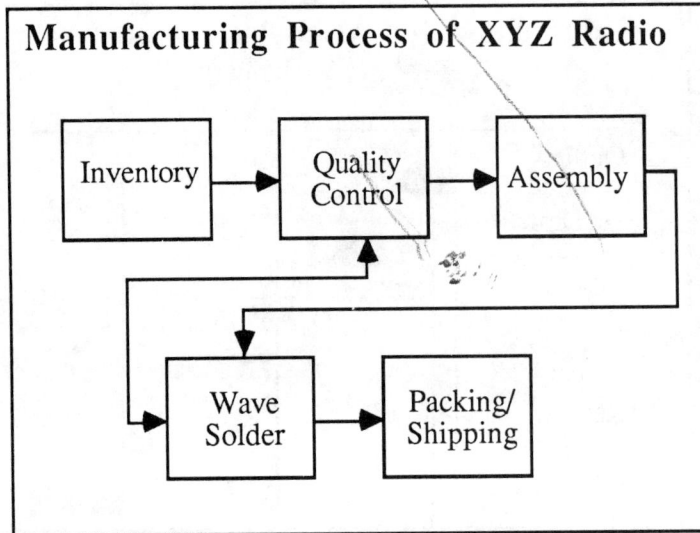

Figure 2-40.
Flow diagram.

Flow Diagram

A cross between an organization chart and pert chart is the *flow diagram*. A flow diagram visually shows the flow of people, machinery, inventory, or some other variable at critical times throughout a process or procedure. One good example is tracking a particular part of subsystem throughout the manufacturing process, such as in Figure 2-40, for the purpose of making its trek in the factory more productive. Bottlenecks and redundant stops are clearly pointed out. The visualization of a process is helpful in presentations because it can show where problems exist.

More on Charting

You've learned about the different types of graphs and how to pick the right one to tell your side of the story. As you might have guessed, there's more to successful chart making than this. In Chapters 3 and 4, you'll learn more about how to make sure the charts you create have the maximum possible impact. You'll also learn how to avoid the common pitfalls in chart design, and what you can do to turn a ho-hum chart into a real zinger.

The Mechanics of Good Chart Design

E X E C U T I V E   S U M M A R Y

One of the most important (and often overlooked) aspects of good business graphics is that charts should be as simple as possible.

Patterns and color can be used to emphasize, differentiate, or identify specific graphic elements. Darker patterns and colors tend to dominate, so use them for emphasis. The style of text in your charts should be plain and simple, making the graph easier to read.

The grid behind a chart can be horizontal, vertical, or both horizontal and vertical. Many charts don't require a grid at all, if knowing the actual values isn't important. With few exceptions, the scale in all charts should start at zero.

Incompatible data can make a chart's accurate comparisons impossible. Solutions? Break up the largest element(s), plot the values as percentages, or use an indexed or logarithmic scale. If data is missing from a chart, its absence should be clearly noted.

Throughout the years, chart making has matured into a scientific artform. There is more to making a pie chart than drawing a circle and bisecting it with lines. There are design factors to consider as well. Where should the slice that represents the important piece of data be placed? What color or pattern should it have? How many slices can a pie chart have before it's cut up into too many pieces?

Poor chart design—either accidental or deliberate—can destroy the functionality and credibility of any graph. As you discovered in Chapter 1, a carelessly constructed chart can be worse than no chart at all.

Let's take a look at the mechanics of good chart design and find out how you can avoid the pitfalls that can ruin an otherwise promising graph. This chapter starts with an overview of the design criteria common to all business graphics, followed by five sections that quickly identify the important elements of each major type of chart: pie, column, bar, line, and dot.

Chart Design Basics

There are a number of design elements that are basic to every chart you create. These elements can be broken down into nine categories: simplicity, unity, pattern, color, text, chart mechanicals, scale, proportion, and perspective.

Anatomy of a Chart

All charts, except pies, have a horizontal and vertical axis. The horizontal axis is often referred to as "X" and the vertical axis is referred to as "Y." In most line, area, and column charts, the horizontal, or X, axis plots time; the vertical, or Y, axis plots value. The X and Y axes on bar charts are rotated so that the vertical axis plots items and the horizontal axis plots value. In dot charts, both X and Y axes plot values.

The parts of the typical chart are shown in Figure S3-1.

- *Title.* The descriptive title of the chart.
- *Subtitle.* A secondary title.

- *Legend.* Text that identifies the data series (or categories) plotted in the chart.
- *Labels.* Text that identifies the purpose or meaning of a plotted element or value.
- *Key* (or annotation). Explanatory text, usually for references.
- *Axis line.* Defines the X or Y axis.
- *Scale.* Shows the graduations of the values plotted in the chart.
- *Grid line.* Major (and sometimes minor) graduations of the scale.
- *Tick marks.* Partial major or minor grid lines.
- *Element.* Identifies the item of comparison and marks its value. Can be a line, bar, column, dot, pie slice, etc.
- *Border.* An aesthetic frame that encloses the chart.

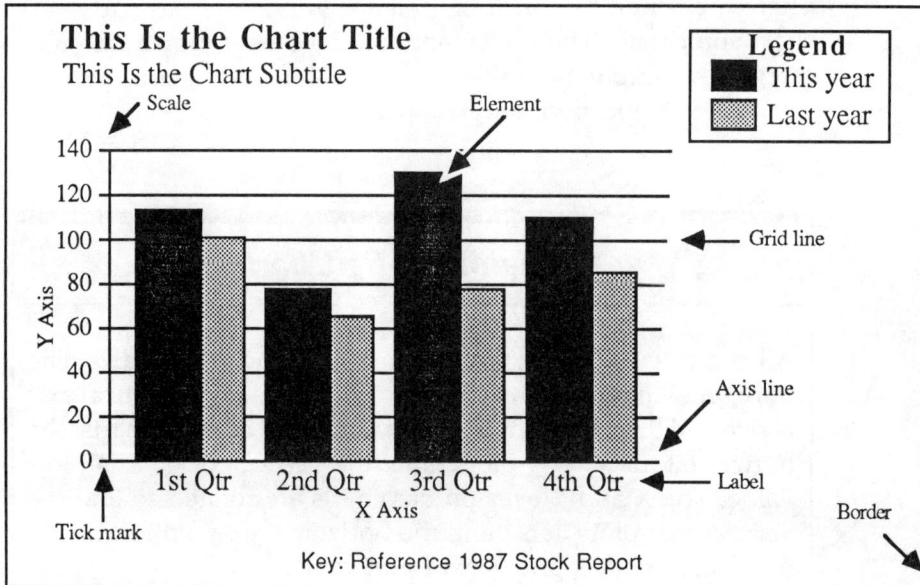

Figure S3-1.
Chart anatomy, with callouts.

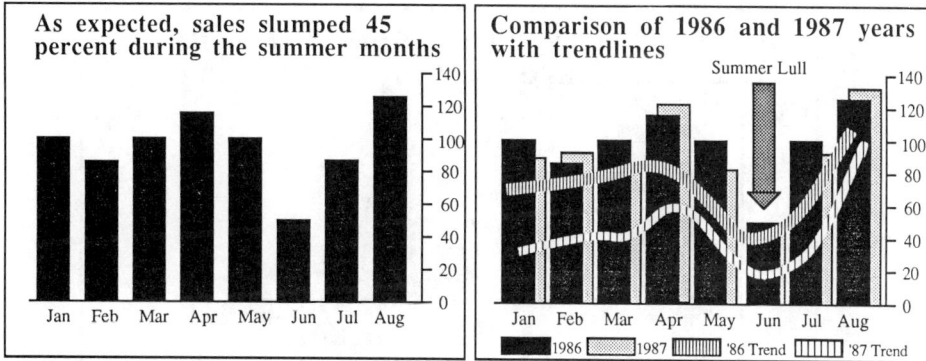

Figure 3-1.
Simple/complex chart.

Simplicity

The best chart is a simple chart. One of the most common flaws in chart making is trying to cram too much information in at once, as in the chart in Figure 3-1. A chart that tries to say too much often ends up not saying anything at all. The message isn't clear, and the chart is too difficult to read.

Each chart should have a *single focus,* the message. And that message should be a rudimentary, well-defined concept. If you can't state your message in a short sentence, then the concept is probably too general. It's far better to break the concept down into its component parts and make separate charts of each.

Unity

A chart is a picture, and it is meant to tell a story in a very short amount of time. To help convey that story, the chart should have a *uniform appearance.* Incongruous elements are distracting, and they hinder the speed at which the message in the chart can be digested.

Unity is as important as simplicity, because it helps focus the audience's attention on the specific message you're trying to make. A good example of unity is using the same typeface for text throughout the chart, as illustrated in Figure 3-2. Use one type of text for the title, and a totally different one for the labels, and the disparate appearance can be distracting.

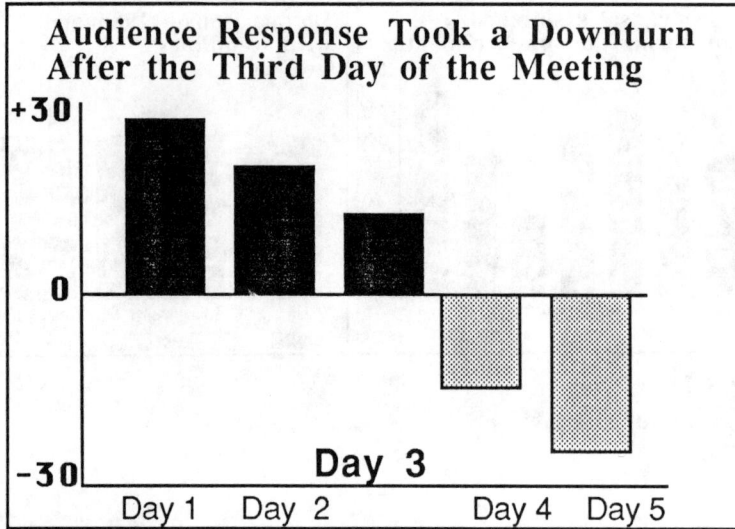

Figure 3-2.
Unified/different text style.

Unity is also important when you're presenting a series of charts. Each chart can have its own personality, and its looks can vary somewhat from the rest of the crowd. You get the best results when all the visuals have a common design, a thread to link them together.

Patterns

Empty bars, columns, and pie slices can look bare and undramatic. *Fill the elements with a pattern* to make them stand out (you can omit the outline of the element when filling with a pattern). For the greatest impact, the most important element in the chart should have the darkest pattern (black or dark gray). As illustrated in Figure 3-3, less important elements can be lighter, even white. You can use patterns for more than emphasis. Patterns can also be used to differentiate or identify certain elements.

Bear in mind that you needn't fill each element with a different pattern. Let's take a look at a simple pie chart. If your intent is to show the proportion of brand A sales over brands C, D, E, and F, fill the brand A slice with black and leave the others white

As expected, sales slumped 45 percent during the summer months

Figure showing a column chart with months Jan through Aug on the x-axis and values 0 to 140 on the y-axis.

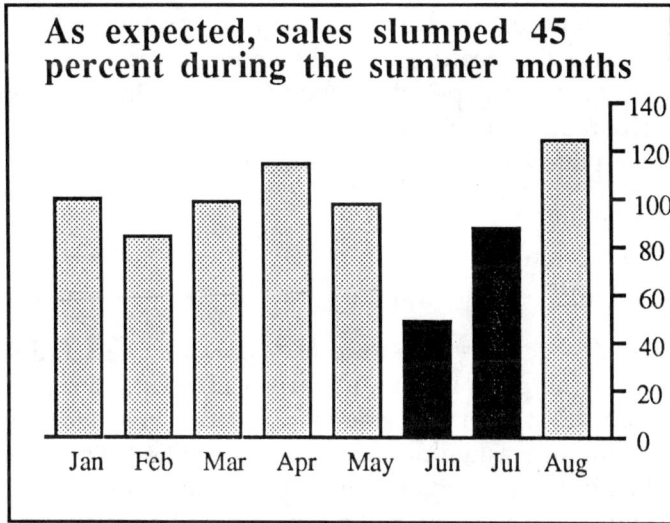

Figure 3-3.
Light/dark patterns.

or a light gray. The more contrast between the patterns, the greater the darkest element will stand out from the others.

Different patterns are often used to separate data series within a bar or column chart, such as last year's sales from this year's. Make sure the patterns don't clash.

Patterns are also used in line graphs. Like bar and column charts, the lines have different patterns so the viewer can differentiate between them. Use solid black for the line you want to emphasize. Striped and dotted patterns can be used for less important data. Again, make sure that the patterns you choose don't clash, especially if the lines cross one another. If you have a choice, experiment with different patterns until you get an arrangement that looks pleasing to you.

Patterns can be used either in place of or in addition to color.

Color

Tests have shown that only the human eye can see the full spectrum of visible light colors. Other animals may be able to see at night, or discern objects farther away, but we have been given the ability to perceive millions of colors. Why waste that gift? If your computer, software, and printer or plotter can produce color, use this feature to make more forceful charts. Surveys have shown that people respond to color images much more readily than monochrome images.

Like patterns, you can use color to:

- Emphasize
- Differentiate
- Identify

The *dark primary hues tend to dominate* a chart and should be used for the parts in a graph you want to stand out. The chart elements that are inconsequential to your message can be filled with a light, washed out color, or left unfilled. You can omit the outline of the plotted element when filling with a color.

If you want to point to the comparison between elements, use *contrasting colors*. Figure 3-4 shows a color wheel of the three primary and three secondary colors. For example, one set of columns in a column chart could be green, the other red. Red is perceived as a darker, more dominant color, so use it for the data series you want to emphasize.

Red is also believed to have an "active" psychological effect— it's a "buy me" color. Green is believed to connote serenity, inaction, or passiveness. The psychology of colors is a fascinating, if not subjective study. But it's beyond the scope of this book.

Limit Colors

A colorful chart is one thing, but don't overdo it by using more than four or five different colors, unless your computer can generate subtle hues of the same color. You can use as many variations on a basic color as you want. Too much of a good thing can be overkill, and can make your charts look like circus billboards.

Instead of using different colors, *combine coloration with patterns*—a blue and a striped blue, for example. You can also use this technique if your business graphics program or printer/plotter can't produce more than a handful of basic colors.

Text

Even though a chart may be worth a thousand words (or more), almost all charts have text of one kind or another for the title, legend, labels, and annotations.

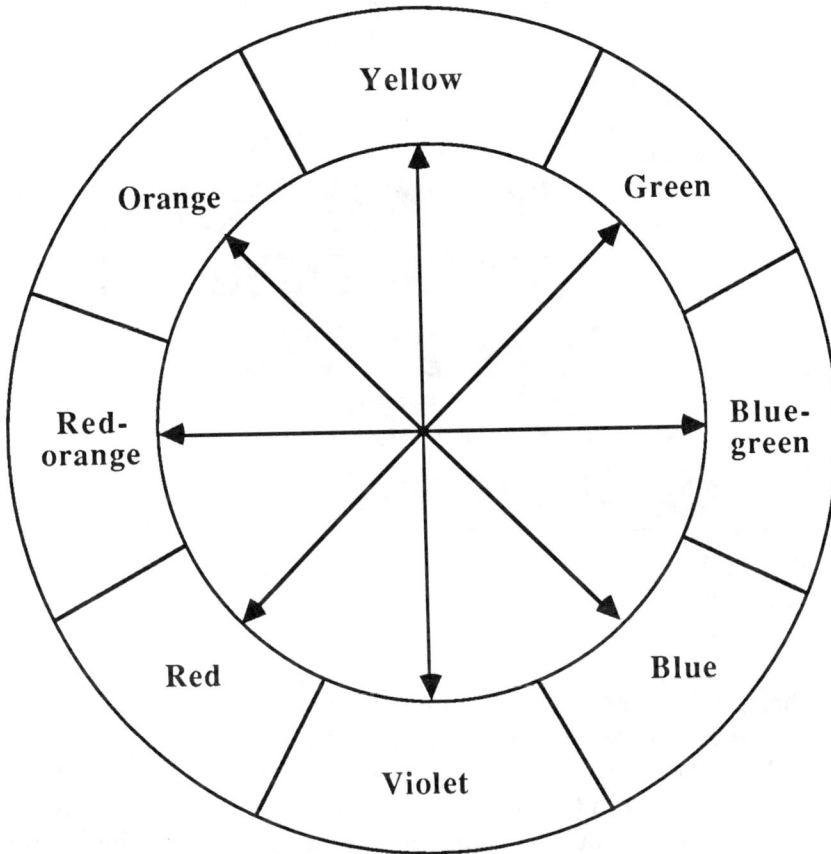

Figure 3-4.
Color wheel.

Text Size and Placement

The *title* almost always goes on top of the chart, and is large and bold, to attract attention. The text style should be plain and simple, like the example in Figure 3-5. The title doesn't have to be centered on the page, but often is. The title is the one major element that can be easily moved to any spot on the chart. If the chart looks unbalanced because there's too much on one side or the other, move the title to rebalance it.

Subtitles should be added only when the chart requires it. The best subtitles further establish the message of the chart. The subtitle can also indicate the *unit of measure* or the *source of the chart*. If the source of the chart isn't vital to the understanding of the

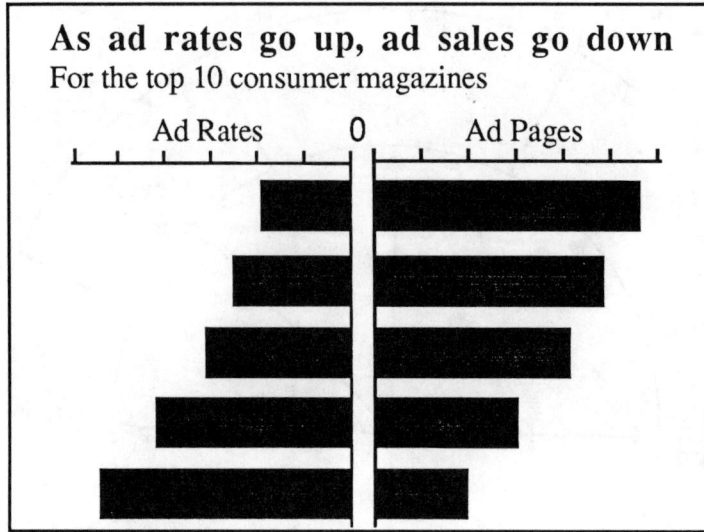

Figure 3-5.
Title/subtitle placement.

chart, it should be placed in small print at the bottom, under the horizontal (X) axis scale. This is an annotation.

Axis label text is smaller and less bold than title text, and is placed as close to the two axes as possible. Label text should be written horizontally whenever possible. When there's not enough space, it's acceptable to rotate the entire label 90 degrees so it reads bottom to top, as shown in Figure 3-6. It's *never* acceptable to write labels where the letters are stacked on top of one another (even though a number of business graphics programs let you do it).

Consistency is important with labels. If you write a label on the outside of one bar in a bar chart, all the labels should be on the outside. Likewise, if you are labeling directly in the bars, each bar should be filled with text, as shown in Figure 3-7. If a label won't fit because the bar is too short, *all* the labels should go on the outside. Direct labels on line charts should be placed as close to the start of the line as possible.

Labels may not always fit. Writing the years from 1960 to 1980 on a column chart may make all the years run together. The alternatives? Choose different major divisions (2- or 5-year periods, for example), or abbreviate the labels. Start with 1960, then go to '61, '62, '63, and so forth, as illustrated in Figure 3-8.

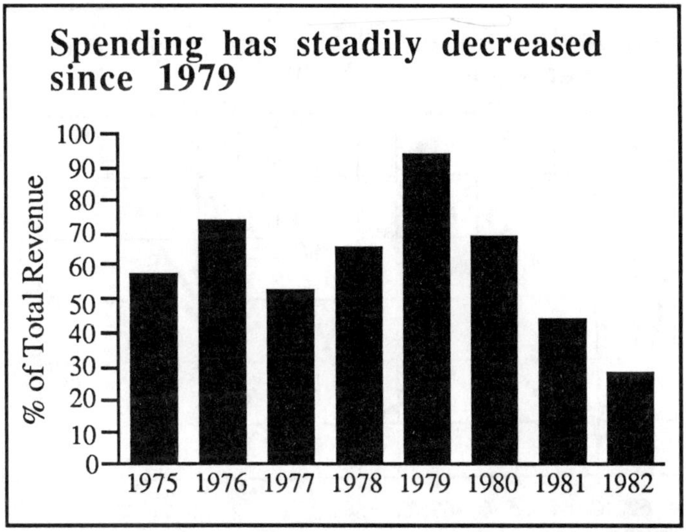

Spending has steadily decreased since 1979

% of Total Revenue

100
90
80
70
60
50
40
30
20
10
0

1975 1976 1977 1978 1979 1980 1981 1982

Figure 3-6.
Rotated label text.

For one reason or another, some labels can't be abbreviated. At other times, abbreviating the labels may confuse the audience. If the chart will be presented in written form (where it can be studied for a longer period of time), consider using a *footnote* or *key* to explain the meaning of the abbreviations. As a last resort, you can stagger the labels so they fit better.

Legends and *annotations* are usually placed to the right or bottom of the chart (legends to the right; annotations on the bottom,

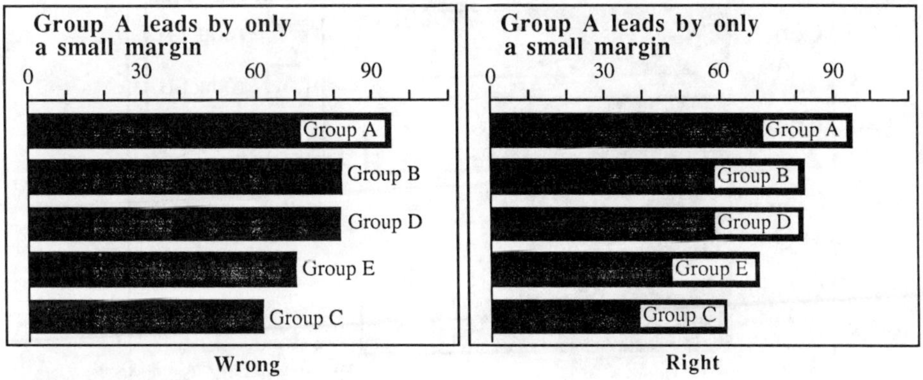

Group A leads by only
a small margin

0   30   60   90

Group A
Group B
Group D
Group E
Group C

Wrong

Group A leads by only
a small margin

0   30   60   90

Group A
Group B
Group D
Group E
Group C

Right

Figure 3-7.
Inside/outside bar label.

The company's smallest change in profit was during the early and late 1960's

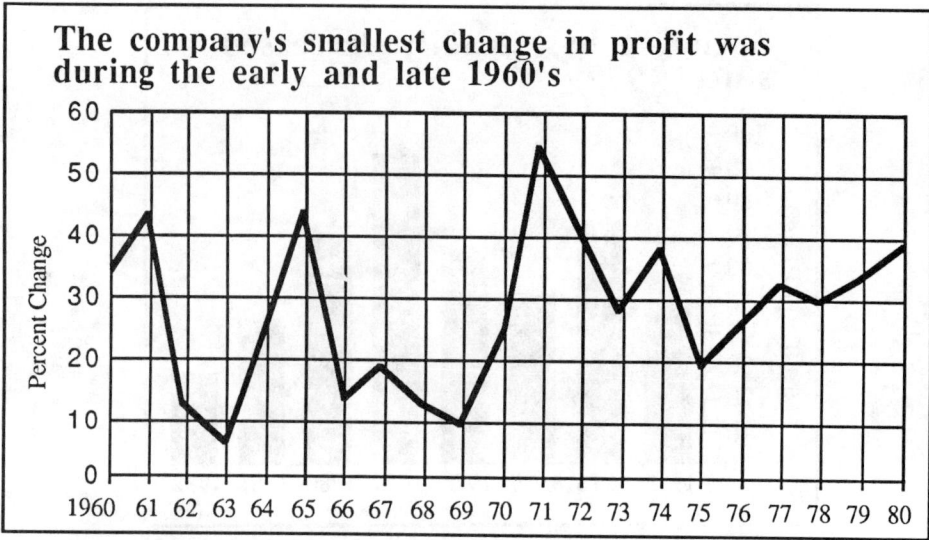

Figure 3-8.
Overlapped labels/abbreviated labels.

as in Figure 3-9). A legend (also called a key) can be placed under the title of the chart and function as a kind of subtitle, as shown in Figure 3-10. Both legends and annotations can be written in small text, but it shouldn't be so small that no one can read it—especially if the chart is to be projected.

Profit Center C had the lowest revenue

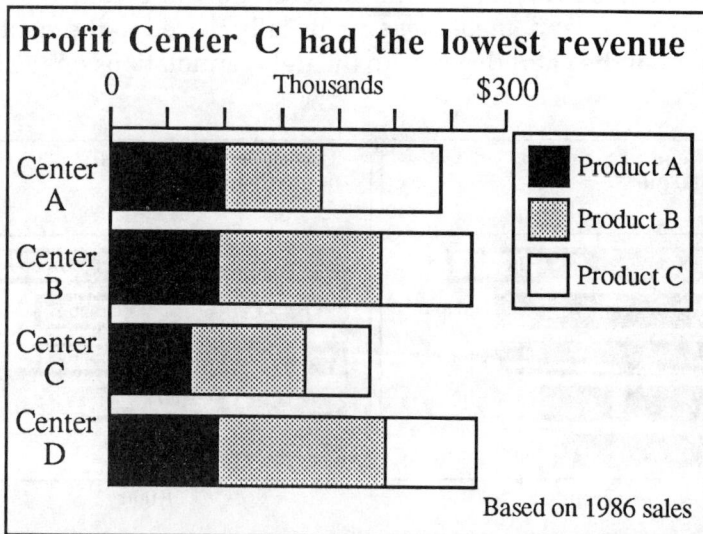

Figure 3-9.
Regular annotation/legend.

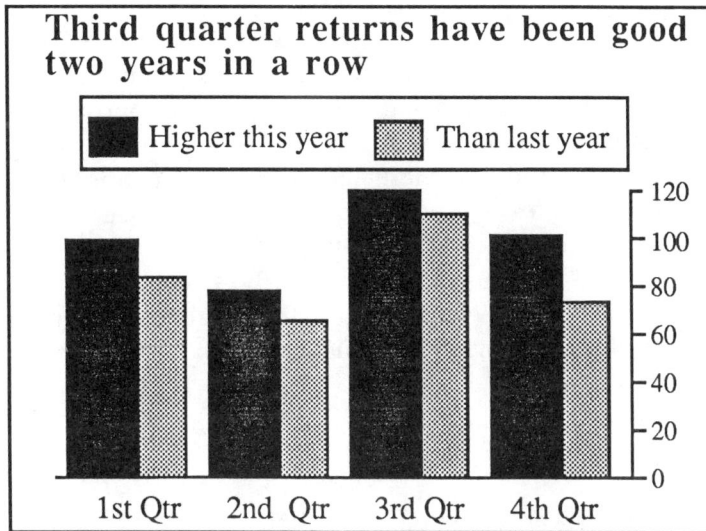

Third quarter returns have been good two years in a row

Legend: ■ Higher this year   ▨ Than last year

(bar chart with quarters: 1st Qtr, 2nd Qtr, 3rd Qtr, 4th Qtr; y-axis 0, 20, 40, 60, 80, 100, 120)

Figure 3-10.
Legend as subtitle.

Text Style

Use a plain, undecorative text style (or font) whenever possible. Fancy, curlicue text, like Old English, is hard to read and distracts the audience's attention. If you want to highlight text, use boldface or italics. If you feel you must use a decorative font—to enhance the chart message, for example—choose one that can be read quickly and doesn't diminish the visual appeal of the rest of the chart. For more details on fonts and styles, consult any good book on desktop publishing mechanics. Several books on the subject are noted in Appendix B, Further Reading.

Mechanicals

The grid behind a chart acts as a kind of picture frame. It draws your eye to the important parts of the chart. The grid also serves as a calibrator, to help you better visualize the relationships and values represented in the chart. Many presentation graphics programs allow you to change the characteristics of the grid along with other chart mechanicals, such as the weights of lines and the position of tick marks. Follow these suggestions if you have the flexibility to custom design your charts.

Grid

Column, bar, line, and dot charts are often made with a grid background. The spacing of the grid corresponds with the major divisions in the X and/or Y scales—10's, 50's, 100's, etc.

Most dot and line charts use both X and Y (horizontal and vertical) grid lines, so the eye can more easily see the relationship between the variables being plotted. Column charts are typically graduated with horizontal lines only, which mark off the values in the Y axis. Bar charts are just the reverse: The lines are drawn vertically for marking off just the X axis. See Figure 3-11 for examples of grid designs.

Whole vs. Partial Grid

The grid can be whole or partial:

- *Whole grid.* A grid line is placed at each major division in the X or Y axis.
- *Partial grid.* A grid line is placed at every two or three major divisions in the X or Y axis.

As illustrated in Figure 3-12, the fullness of a chart determines which type of grid to use. If the chart is densely packed, with several series of data, reduce the number of grid lines. Simple charts, or those that require an accurate reading of the data, should use a whole grid.

Linear or Log Grid

Most grids are evenly spaced, because the data is plotted *linearly*. The progression from one number to the next is an even

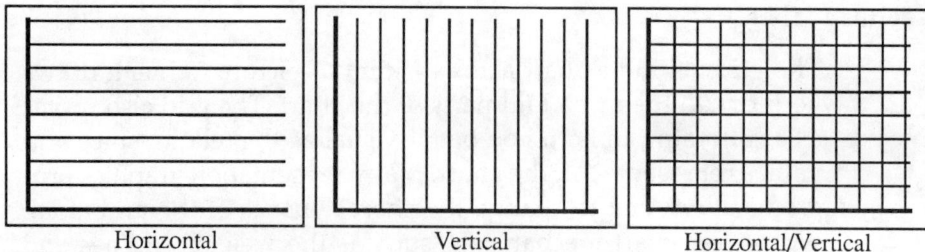

Horizontal   Vertical   Horizontal/Vertical

Figure 3-11.
Different types of grids.

Income has steadily declined since 1975

Economic downturns have been followed by sharp increases

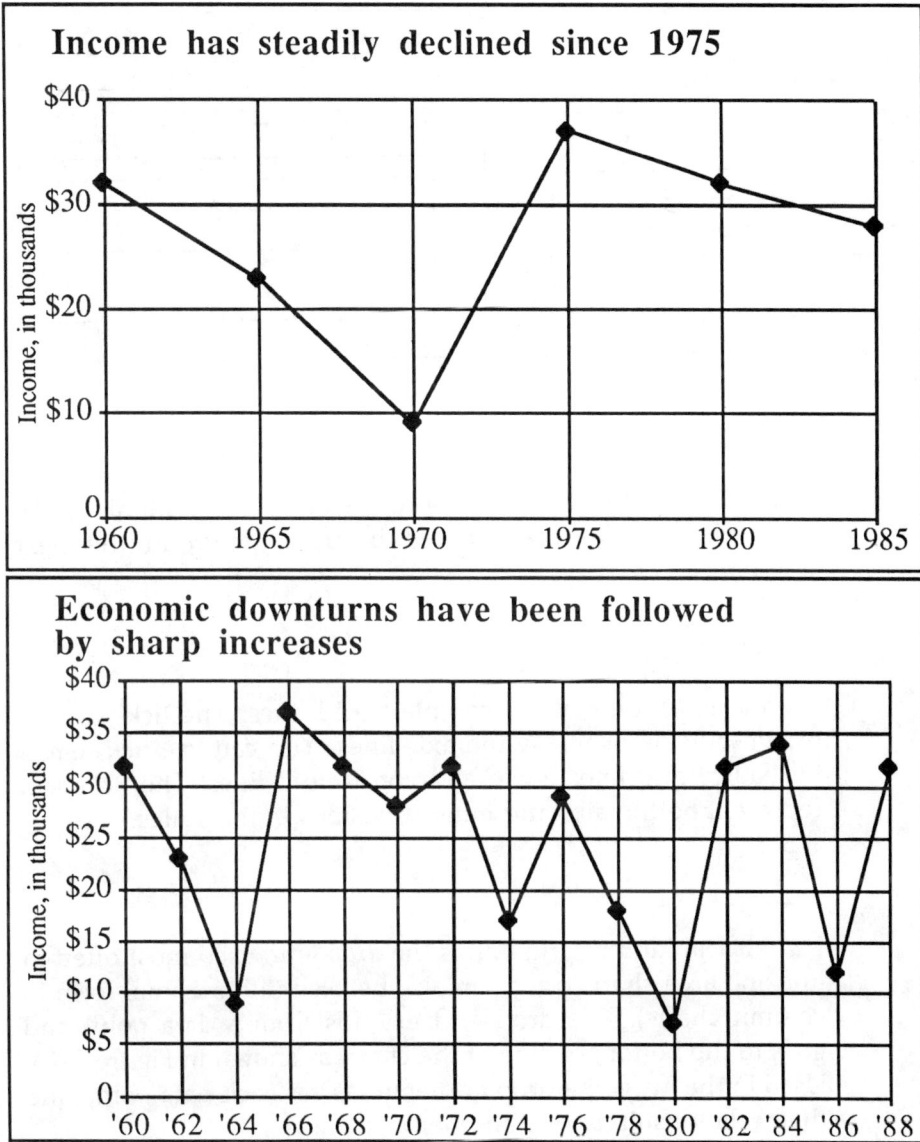

Figure 3-12.
Whole/partial grids.

unit. A *logarithmic* grid, on the other hand, shows the *percentage rate of change* (or *ratios of change*). With a logarithmic (or log) grid, an increase from 1 to 2 is 100 percent. So is an increase from 2 to 4, and 4 to 8. Charts created on a logarithmic scale show the *rate of change*, not the actual change in absolute values. Refer to

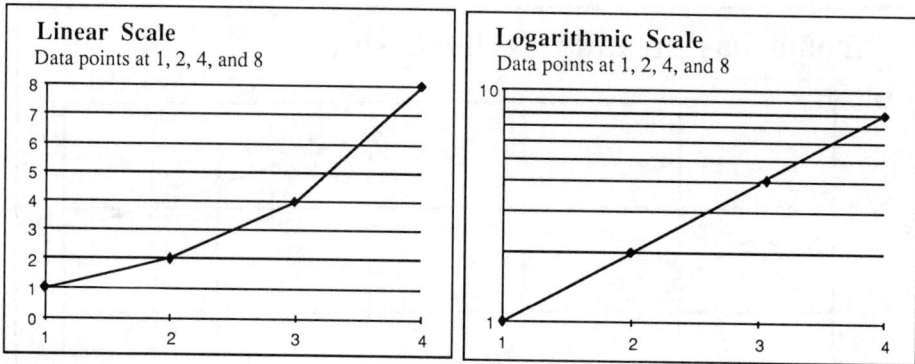

Figure 3-13.
Linear/log grids.

Figure 3-13 for examples of both linear and logarithmic grids. Logarithmic scales are covered in more depth in the next chapter.

Tick Marks

Tick marks are really incomplete grid lines. The ticks can be drawn outside or inside the axis lines. You can use tick marks instead of grid lines, or in addition to grid lines. The ticks can represent both major and minor divisions in the scales.

Drop Grid

A special kind of grid line is the *drop grid,* used most often in line and area charts (they can also be used in horizontal form in column charts). The drop grid extends from a data point and goes to the bottom or side of the chart, as shown in Figure 3-14. Used in this way, the drop grid emphasizes each data point, and their relationship to one another.

Line Weights

Much has been written about the weights of lines used in charting. Should line A be thicker than line B, or the other way around? Only a few presentation graphics programs let you alter the line weights, so you probably don't have to worry about it. Nor should you need to. If the program was designed properly, you'll never need to bother with line weights, because there's

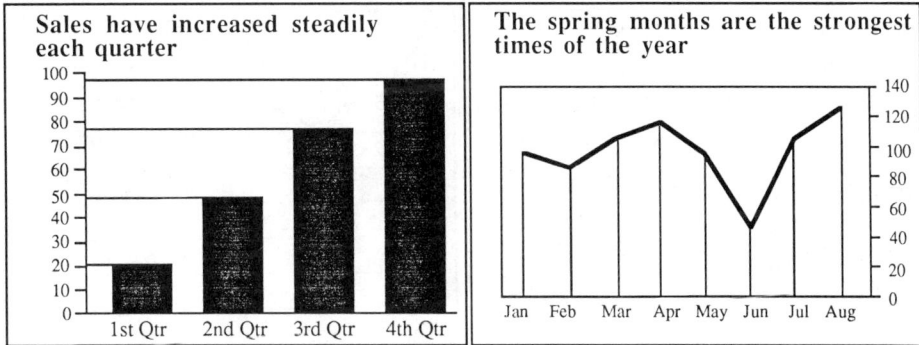

Sales have increased steadily each quarter

(1st Qtr, 2nd Qtr, 3rd Qtr, 4th Qtr bar chart; scale 0–100)

The spring months are the strongest times of the year

(Jan Feb Mar Apr May Jun Jul Aug line chart; scale 0–140)

Figure 3-14.
Horizontal/vertical drop grids.

seldom reason to deviate from the norm. Here's the order of line weights you should use in your charts. It goes from thick to thin as shown in Figure 3-15.

- Graph line (line chart, high-low chart, etc.).
- Axis line.
- Arrow line.
- Grid line.
- Tick mark line (grid lines and tick marks can really be the same thickness).

Scale

Since charts are used to compare numbers, a *scale* is used to indicate the value of those numbers. When that scale is distorted, the

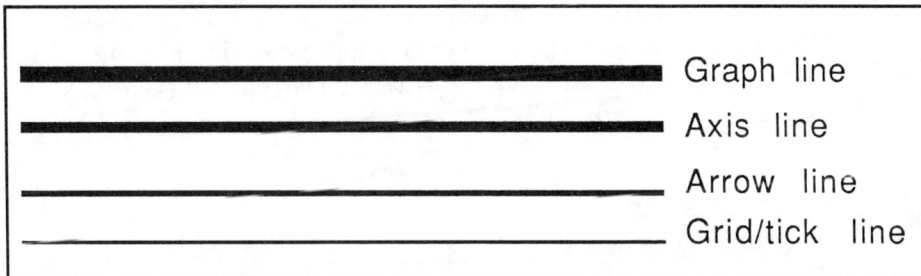

Graph line
Axis line
Arrow line
Grid/tick line

Figure 3-15.
Visual comparison of line weights.

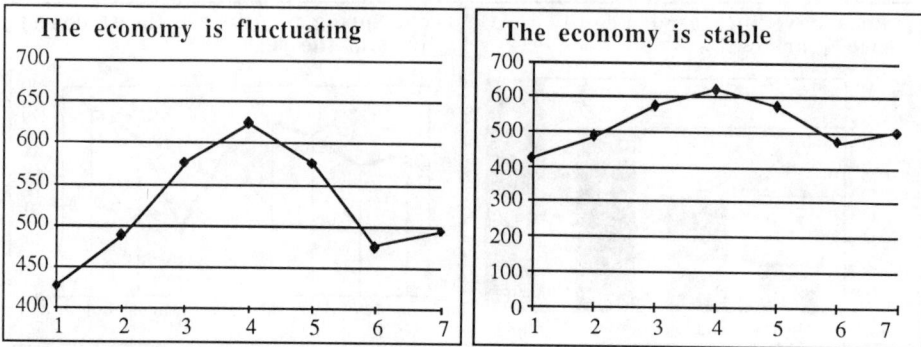

Figure 3-16.
Zero/no-zero bottom scale.

numbers become distorted. With very few exceptions, you should always start the scale of a chart at zero. You can occasionally bend these rules, when creating indexed or log charts, for example, as you'll see in the next chapter.

What happens when you don't start the chart at zero? Take a look at Figure 3-16. The chart on the left begins at 400 and extends to 700. Notice the *volatility* of the line. The excessive movement is caused by starting the Y axis scale at a point other than zero. The Y axis in the chart on the right starts at zero and accurately represents the values compared in the chart.

A similar rule applies for the uppermost limit of the chart. You should stop the scale at an even increment just above the largest value in the chart. If the largest value is 325, for instance, and the scale is divided in increments of 50, the top scale should be 350. The chart will be improperly compressed if the upper scale limit is too high, as you can see in Figure 3-17.

Manipulating the scale of a chart is probably the most common tactic people use to purposefully mislead their audience. This and other ways of false charting are described in the satirical study, *How to Lie with Statistics*, by Darrel Huff (W. W. Norton Co., New York, 1954).

Breaking the Scale

Sometimes the amount scale cannot remain intact for your chart to meaningfully represent the numbers you are comparing. For example, suppose you are comparing the performance of two companies in a multiple line chart. The values of the two series

Things aren't changing

Things are changing

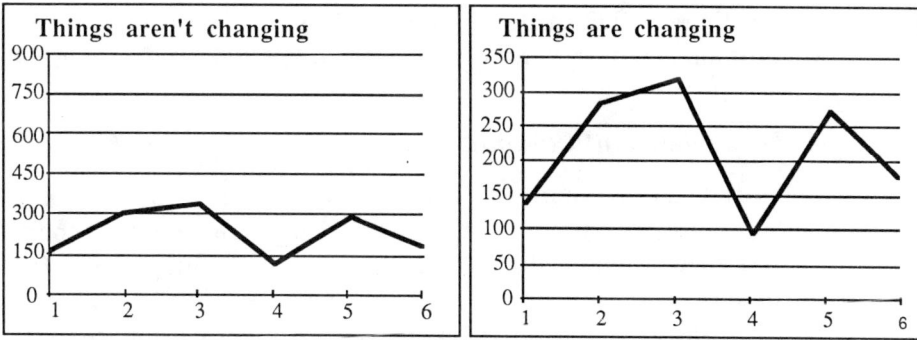

Figure 3-17.
High/normal top scale.

are drastically different, so the resultant chart looks awkward. The lines are so far away that it's nearly impossible to use them for comparison.

By splitting the scale, as illustrated in Figure 3-18, you can pull the lines closer together. You can use a similar approach when many of the columns in a column chart are grossly oversized compared with the others.

You'll most often break the scale on the vertical axis. The scale can also be broken on the horizontal axis. You'd use this technique, for instance, if you wanted to compare two disparate peri-

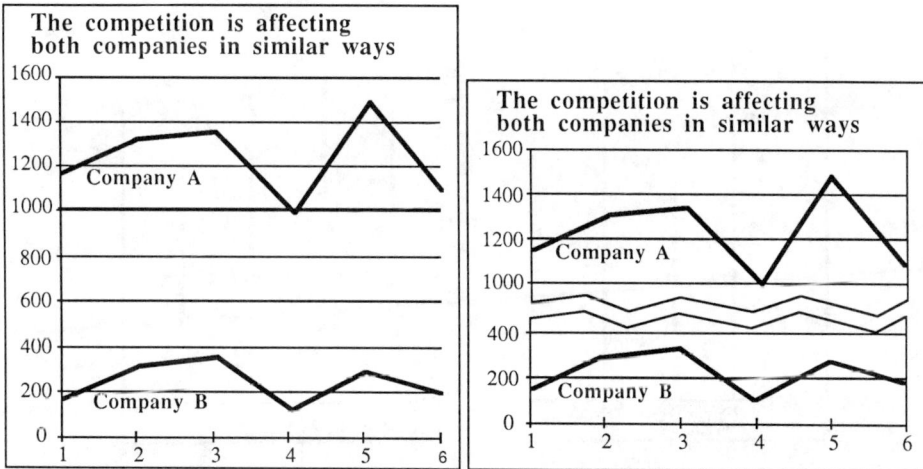

The competition is affecting both companies in similar ways

Company A

Company B

The competition is affecting both companies in similar ways

Company A

Company B

Figure 3-18.
Normal/split scales.

ods of time—1923 through 1940, and 1978 through 1985. The horizontal axis in bar and dot charts can be similarly broken.

Range Bars and Columns

By their nature, some values, like stock market quotes, don't start at zero. As illustrated in Figure 3-19, a range column chart can be used to show the highest and lowest selling prices of a particular stock (called, in this instance, a high-low chart). Depending on how well the stock is doing, the lowest point may never reach zero.

In this case, it's perfectly acceptable to start the chart at a number other than zero. The emphasis is the high-low spread, not the actual value of the stock (although that *is* an important consideration to an investor, but it needn't be graphed in the example chart). It's wise to provide the scale, either on the vertical axis or by each column.

Like column charts, the bars in a bar chart can "float" as well. But the comparison isn't the same. Range bar charts always use the zero centerline.

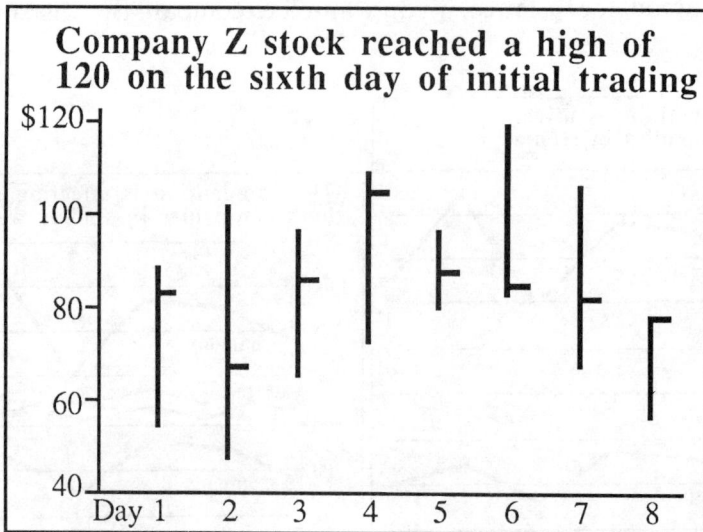

Figure 3-19.
High-low range chart.

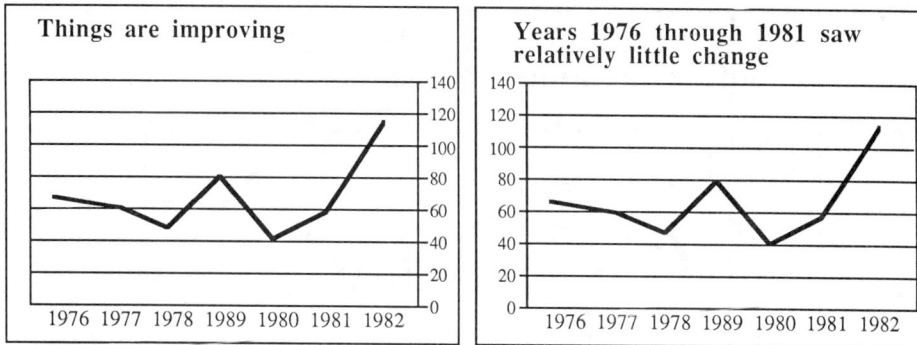

Figure 3-20.
Scale on left/right.

Scale Placement

Should the scale in a column chart go on the left or right side? It all depends. Convention says to put the scale on the left side of the chart. But if the values get larger on the right side, or the movement or values are more important on that side, put the scale there. Refer to Figure 3-20 for an example. The same suggestion goes for line charts.

Bar charts measure quantity from left to right, instead of up and down as in column or line charts. The scale in a bar chart should be placed on the top (or occasionally, the bottom).

Multiple Amount Scales

Some line and column charts require two different vertical (Y) axis scales. Take a look at the line chart in Figure 3-21. It is based on the same information in Figure 3-20. Only this time, two different scales are used. The left scale is graduated from 0 to 500. The "company B" line is plotted according to this scale. The right scale, on the other hand, is graduated from 0 to 1,800. The "company A" line is plotted according to this scale. The upper limits of the two scales were chosen so that the lines would be as close to each other as possible.

The biggest problem with multiple amount scales is that it's hard to know which lines or columns belong to which scale. The lines, columns, and scales must be clearly marked. If you're working in color, you can use different colors for the lines/col-

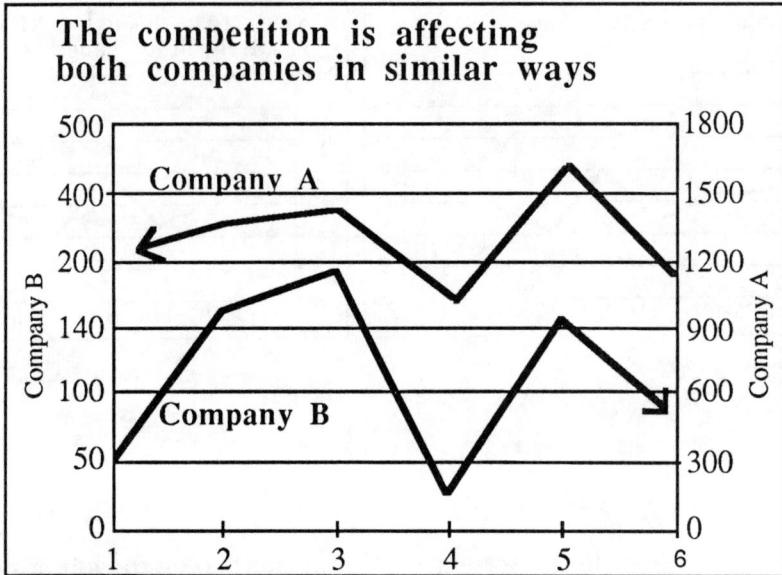

Figure 3-21.
Multiple scale line chart.

umns and scale. For instance, one line and scale can be red, the other blue.

Scale or Actual Values?

The X and Y axes or your charts needn't be scaled, especially if you're only interested in showing the comparison between values and not the actual values. Most viewers, however, prefer to know the quantity expressed in the chart. If you don't want scaled axes, identify the values by writing them alongside the columns, bars, or lines.

Proportion

Akin to scale is proportion. Line, dot, and column charts are often drawn so that they are semirectangular in shape. The exact aspect ratio isn't important, but the horizontal axis is usually about 1.25 times longer than the Y axis. Pie and bar charts don't follow this convention. Pie charts are square and the proportion of bar charts is dependent on the number of items plotted.

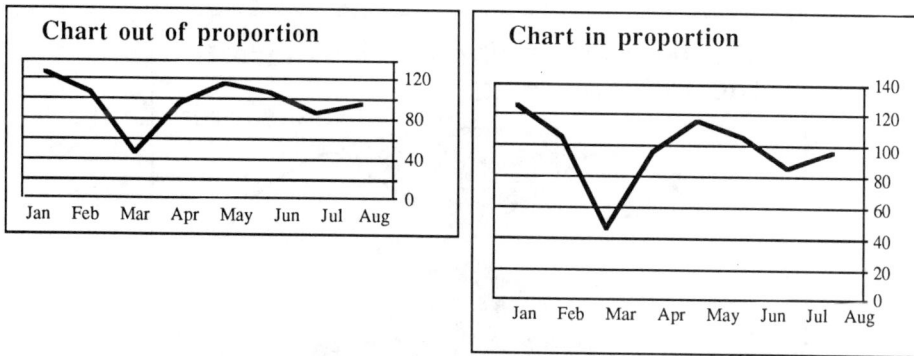

Figure 3-22.
Chart in/out of proportion.

Charts that violate the small and often overlooked rule of proportion not only look awkward, but can be misleading. Consider the graphs in Figure 3-22. The X axis of the chart on the left is inordinately stretched out. This has the effect of compressing the chart—just like not starting the scale at zero. You get the reverse effect when the chart is squeezed sideways, as if in a vise.

The graphic elements within a chart should also be in proportion to one another. After all, proportion is what allows you to use charts for making comparisons. When you fiddle with the natural proportion of a chart, the value of the graph is greatly diminished.

One way to falsely add emphasis to a particular column in a column chart, for instance, is by making it thicker than the others. This tactic upsets the unity of the chart. Use contrasting colors or patterns to emphasize a particular element in a chart.

Perspective

Computers make it easy to make striking 3-D charts. Some presentation graphics programs let you control the amount of perspective used in creating the 3-D effect. Too much perspective can grossly distort the chart. Excessive perspective reduces or eliminates the value of the chart, and can make it misleading. A pie chart with an extremely low perspective, like that in Figure 3-23, provides no real clue to the true sizes of the slices.

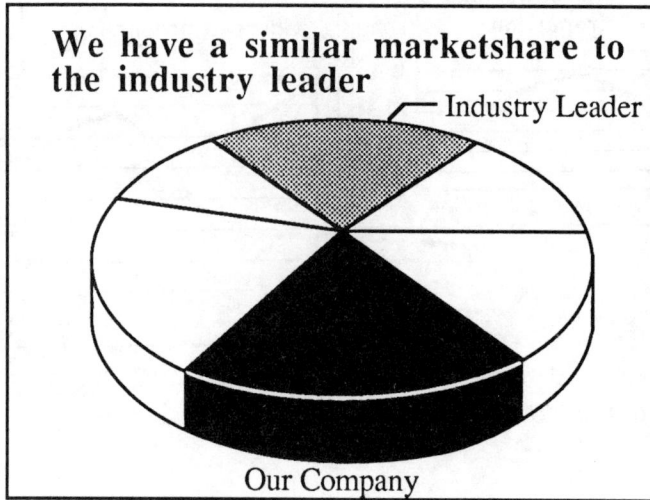

Figure 3-23.
Highly 3-D pie chart.

The Critical Eye

One of the best ways to learn professional presentation graphics techniques is to see how others do it. National magazines and major newspapers are good sources of chart examples. *Time, Business Week, U.S. World and News, USA Today,* and several other publications rely heavily on graphics, and their treatment of charts can provide you with many useful, creative ideas.

When you see a chart you like, clip it out and save it for future reference. Keep a file folder of your chart clippings and refer to the contents when you are preparing your own graphics.

Specifics—Pie Chart

Purpose: Pie charts show the proportion of parts to the whole.

Maximum number of data points per series: Six to eight.

Maximum number of data series: One. Use additional pies to present more than one series.

Grid: Not applicable.

Labels: Inside slices if all labels will fit. Otherwise outside slices. Size of slice (in percent) can be placed inside if all the labels are on the outside.

Variations

- Flat, two-dimensional.
- Coin-shaped, three-dimensional.

General Notes

- The most important slice should start at the 12 o'clock position. Position the remaining slices in descending (largest-to-smallest) or ascending (smallest-to-largest) order.
- If these is no single important slice, order all the slices in descending or ascending numerical order.
- Pie charts suffer from three problems: lack of accuracy, difficulty in comparison of small or closely related items, and difficulty in labeling. If these problems can't be overcome, choose a stacked column chart instead.
- When necessary, use arrows or lines to connect labels with pie slices.
- Important slices can be pulled away from the rest of the slice to add emphasis. This is called an *exploded* pie chart.

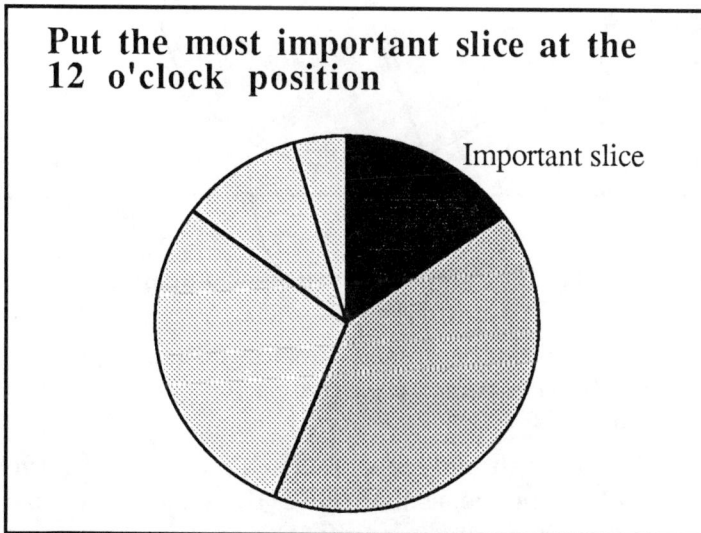

Put the most important slice at the 12 o'clock position

Important slice

(a)

Figure 3-24 (Continued).

If there are no important slices, put them in largest-to-smallest order

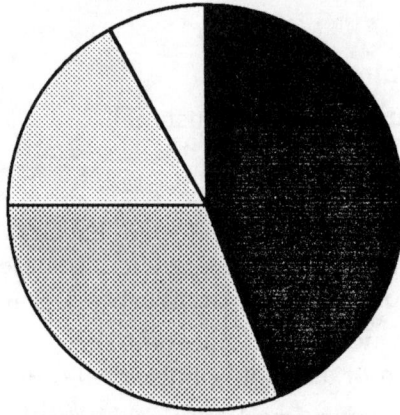

(b)

Pull out the important slice

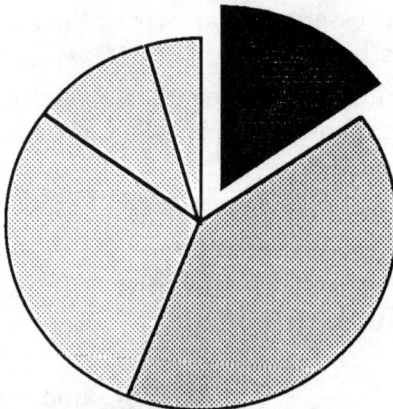

(c)

- Avoid pulling out all the slices. Comparisons are harder to make.
- Pie slices can be broken down into subgroups by the use of additional (smaller) pies, or by a 100 percent stacked column chart.
- The labels should repeat for each pie in a chart. Avoid labeling just one pie, as that causes the viewer's eye to dart back and forth to get all the information.
- See examples in Figures 3-24(a)–(e).

Break out a single slice into a stacked bar chart

100%

(d)

Duplicate labels when creating multiple pie charts

Fourth   First   Fourth

Third   Third   *(e)*

Second

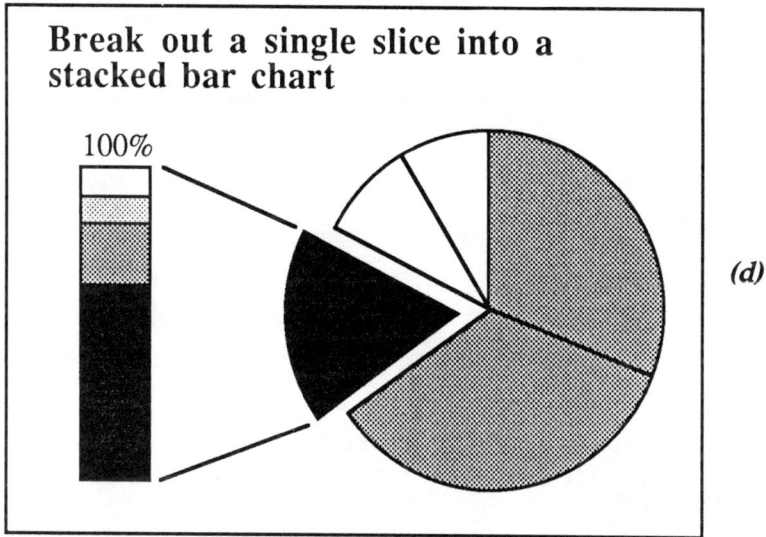

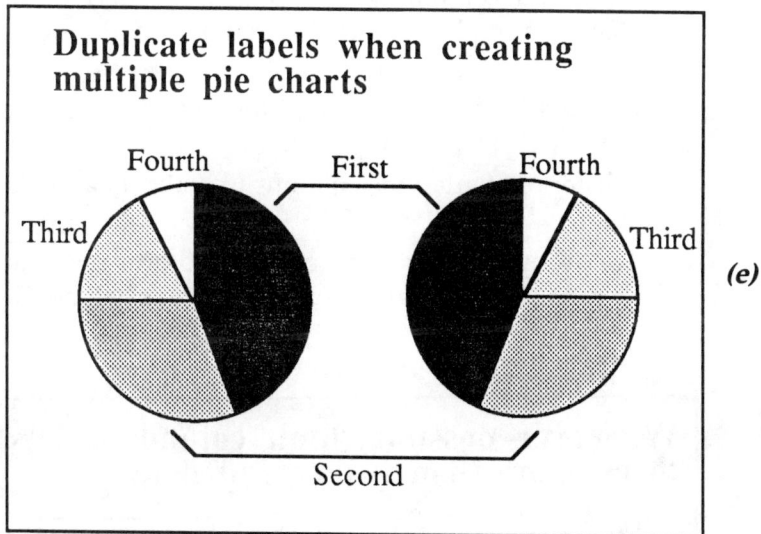

Figure 3-24.
Pie chart gallery.

Specifics—Column Chart

Purpose: Column charts compare one item through different, equal points in time.

Maximum number of data points per series: Twelve.

Maximum number of data series: One to four (more series can be placed on the graph if fewer data points are graphed).

Grid: Horizontal or (much less often) combination horizontal/ vertical.

Labels: Labels for X axis along bottom; labels for Y axis on right or left side (depending on whether data is increasing or decreasing).

Variations

- Grouped columns
- Stacked columns (absolute value or 100 percent)
- Deviated columns (above and below zero line)
- Range columns for high-low spread
- Stepped column (most often used for frequency distribution)

General Notes

- Avoid thin columns. Break up the graph into several smaller charts when plotting many data points and series.
- Column charts should be limited to plotting no more than two series of data, although they can accommodate up to four.
- Cluster or overlap the columns to make it easier to read the chart.
- The front columns in an overlapped grouped chart should be consistently shorter than the columns behind. Remember

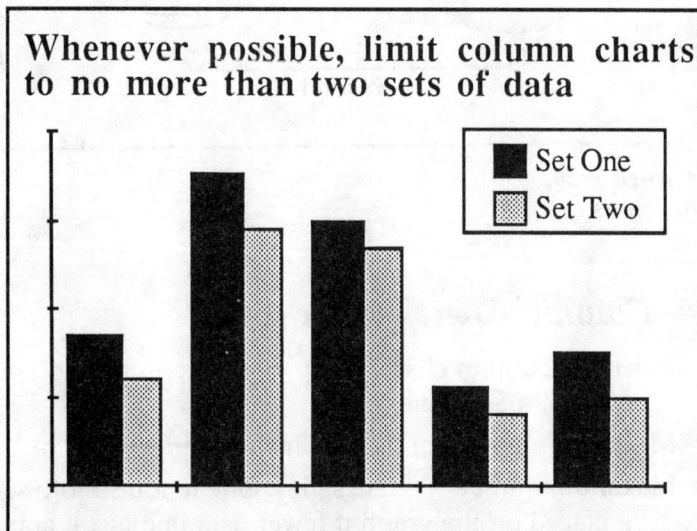

Whenever possible, limit column charts to no more than two sets of data

■ Set One
▨ Set Two

(a)

Cluster the columns when you want to emphasize the difference in height

Emphasized   De-emphasized
Difference in Height

(b)

Keep the spaces between columns smaller than the columns themselves

Yes   Column Spacing   No

(c)

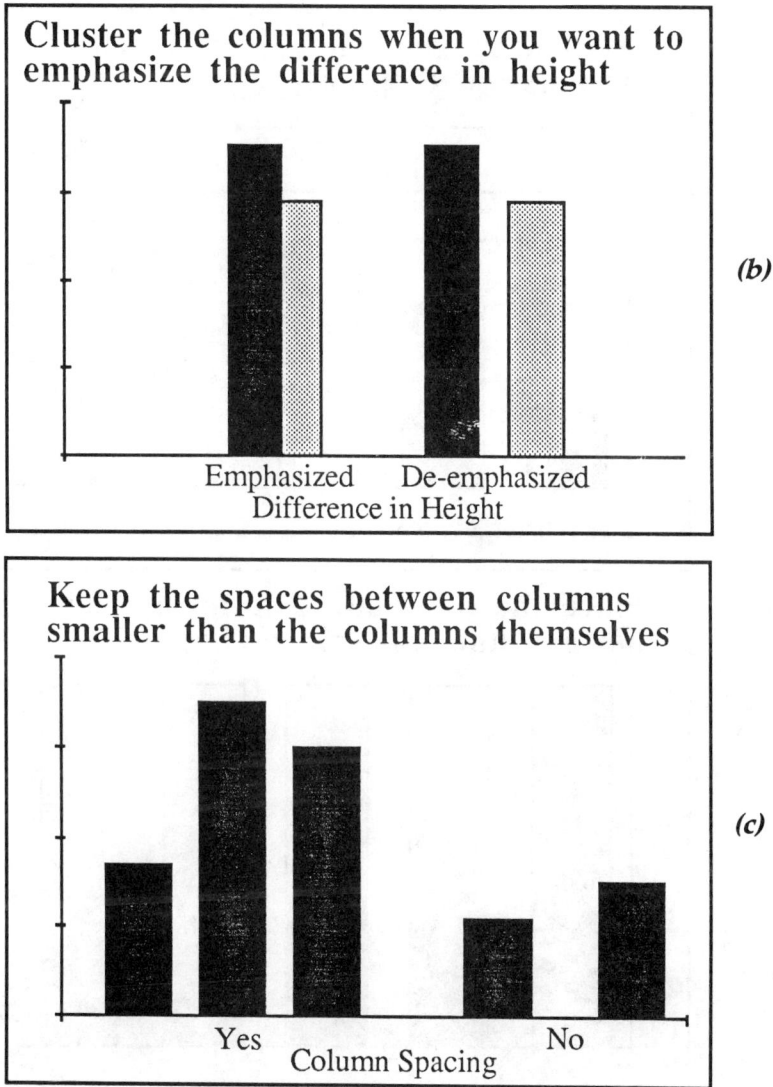

Figure 3-25 (Continued).

that overlapping stresses the difference between the lengths of the columns.

- The space between the columns should be no wider than the width of the columns themselves, preferably smaller.

- Column charts designed primarily to point out a comparison don't require a grid. A grid should be added when it's important to show the actual values represented by the columns.

Use a drop grid and direct labelling for maxium emphasis

(d)

Place the dominate column on the bottom, and make it darkest

(e)

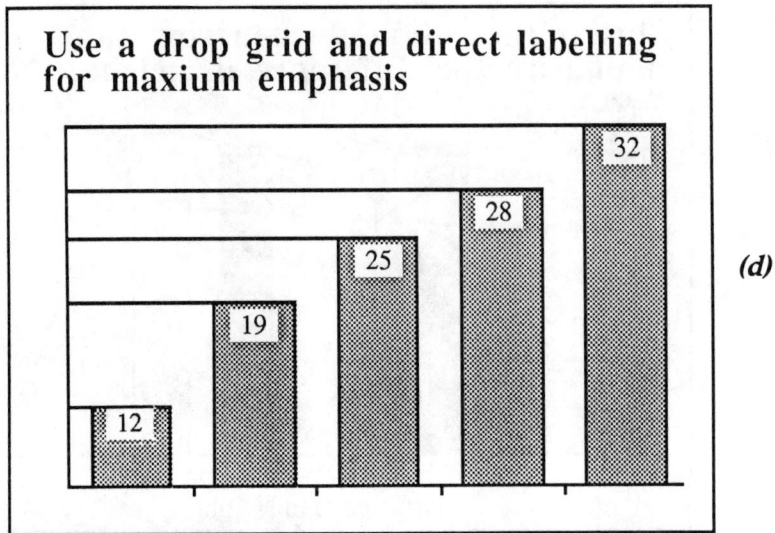

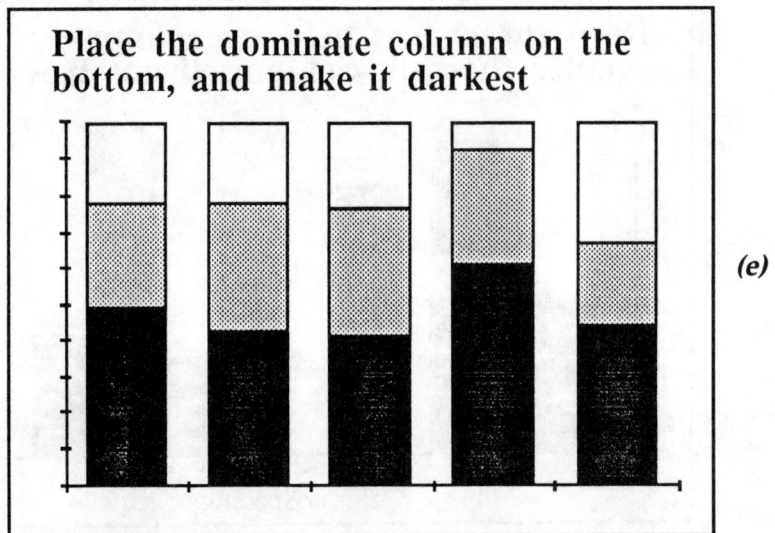

Figure 3-25.
Column chart gallery.

- A drop grid can be used to emphasize the data, or to show the absolute values of the columns. Absolute values can also be presented by labeling inside the columns.
- When creating a stacked (or subdivided) column chart, place the dominant or most important element on the bottom. Use different colors or patterns to help distinguish each of the segments.

- Join the tops of segments in a grouped column chart to emphasize the trend or relationship between similar items.
- When plotting a histogram, choose the proper number of ranges to adequately reveal the frequency distribution. Too few or too many ranges hide the pattern. All the ranges should be of equal size, and all ranges should be clearly labeled.
- See examples in Figure 3-25(a)–(e).

Specifics—Bar Chart

Purpose: Bar charts compare similar items at one point in time.

Maximum number of data points per series: Twelve to twenty (but the fewer the better).

Maximum number of data series: One to four (more series can be placed on the graph if fewer data points are graphed).

Grid: Vertical or combination vertical/horizontal.

Labels: X axis label on top; Y axis labels on left side, right side, or inside of bars. Labels can also be placed in the middle of the bars in a paired bar chart.

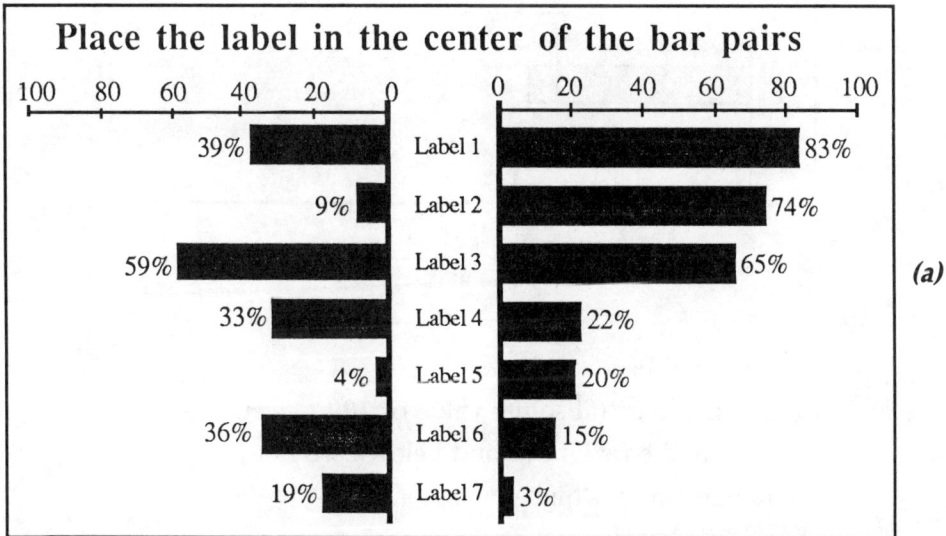

Place the label in the center of the bar pairs

	100 80 60 40 20 0		0 20 40 60 80 100	
39%		Label 1		83%
9%		Label 2		74%
59%		Label 3		65%
33%		Label 4		22%
4%		Label 5		20%
36%		Label 6		15%
19%		Label 7		3%

(a)

Figure 3-26 (Continued).

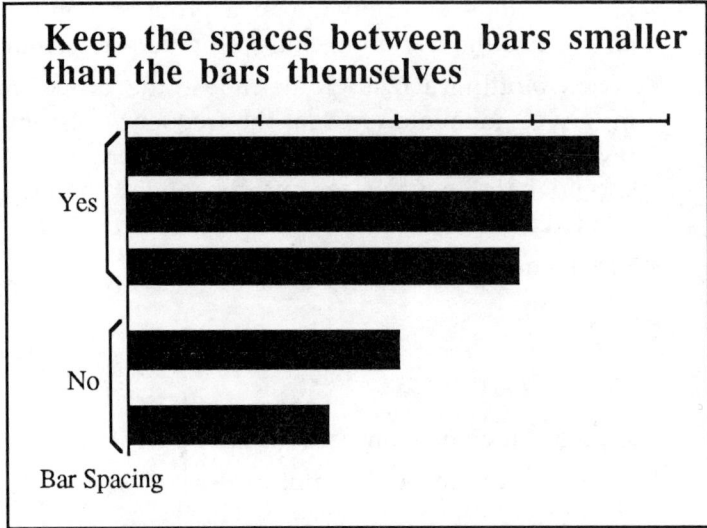

Keep the spaces between bars smaller than the bars themselves

(b)

Yes

No

Bar Spacing

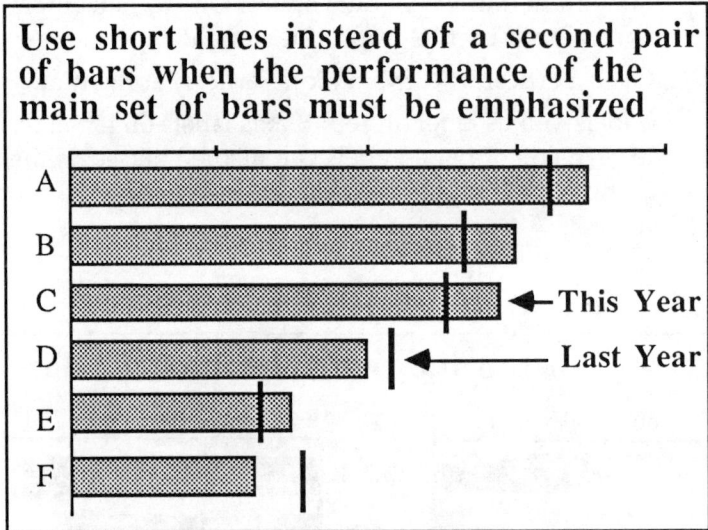

Use short lines instead of a second pair of bars when the performance of the main set of bars must be emphasized

(c)

A
B
C ← This Year
D ← Last Year
E
F

Variations

- Grouped bars
- Stacked bars (absolute value or 100 percent)
- Deviated bars (above and below zero line)
- Range bars for high-low spread
- Sliding bars
- Paired bars

Place the dominate bar closest to the Y axis, and make it darkest

(d)

Use the most logical ordering sequence, but make it consistent and easy to understand

(e)

Alphabetical Order, etc.   Descending Order

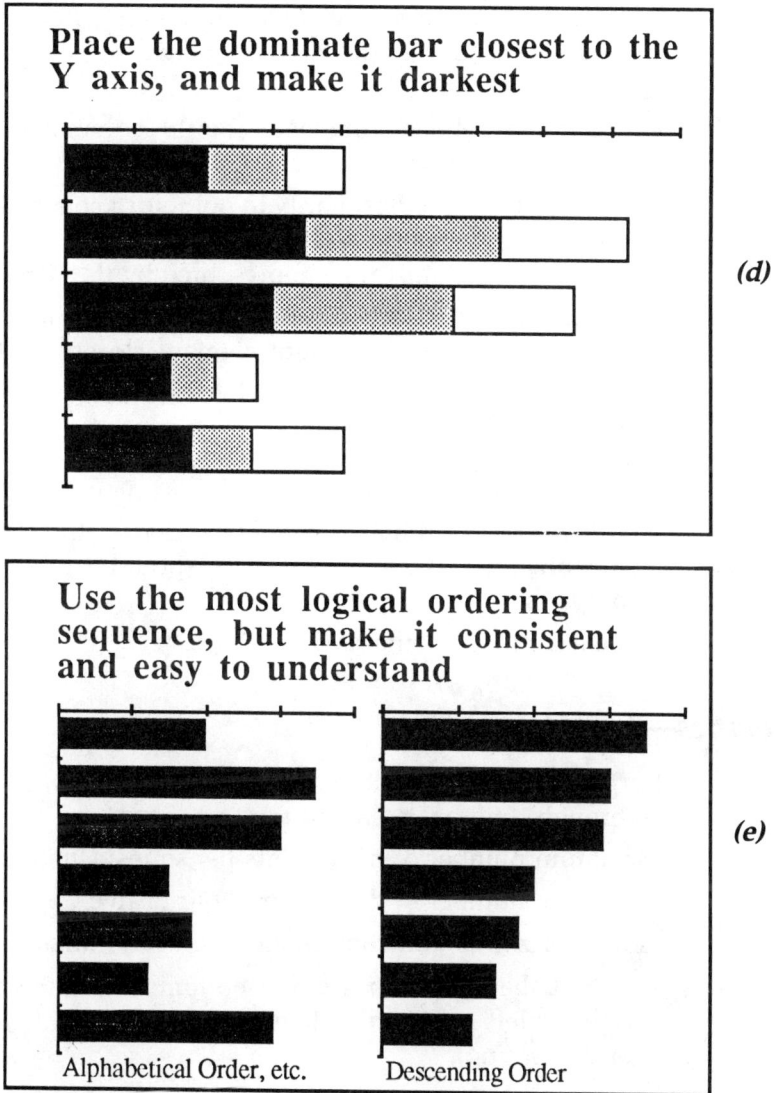

Figure 3-26.
Bar chart gallery.

General Notes

- Avoid thin bars. Break up the graph into several smaller charts when plotting many data points and series.
- Bar charts should be used to plot just one set of data, although they can accommodate up to four. Cluster or over-lap the bars to make it easier to read the chart.
- The front bars in an overlapped grouped chart should be

consistently shorter than the bars behind. Remember that overlapping stresses the disparity between the lengths of the columns.

- The space between the bars should be smaller than the width of the bars.
- Bar charts designed primarily to point up a comparison don't require a grid. A grid should be added when it's important to show the actual values represented by the bars.
- When creating a stacked (or subdivided) bar chart, place the dominant or most important element closest to the Y-axis scale. Use different colors or patterns to help distinguish each of the segments.
- You can arrange the bars in just about any sequence—by size (smallest to largest, or vice versa), time (forward or backward), by alphabet, etc. The order should be instantly recognizable, however, and should reinforce the comparison.
- See examples in Figures 3-26(a)–(e).

Specifics—Line Chart

Purpose: Line charts show fluctuations of one or more items through different points in time.

Maximum number of data points per series: Unlimited.

Maximum number of data series: Four or five.

Grid: Horizontal and combination vertical/horizontal.

Labels: Labels for X axis along bottom; labels for Y axis on right or left side (depending on whether data is increasing or decreasing).

Variations

- Single line
- Multiple line
- Band (area chart)
- Histograph (frequency distribution)

General Notes

- Lines in a multiple-line chart should have different weights, patterns, color, or symbols. The lines should be keyed directly on the chart or in a legend.

Use different line weights or patterns to distinguish between data sets

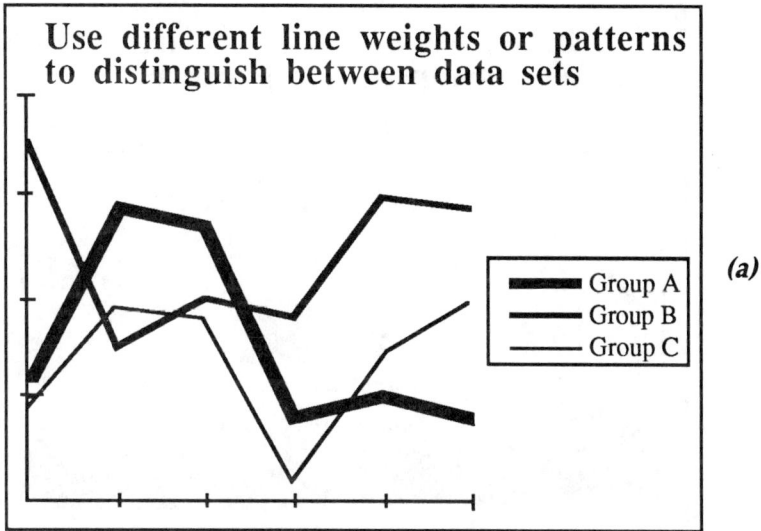

(a)

Line charts, superimposed over another type of chart, can be used to show trends, growth rates, etc.

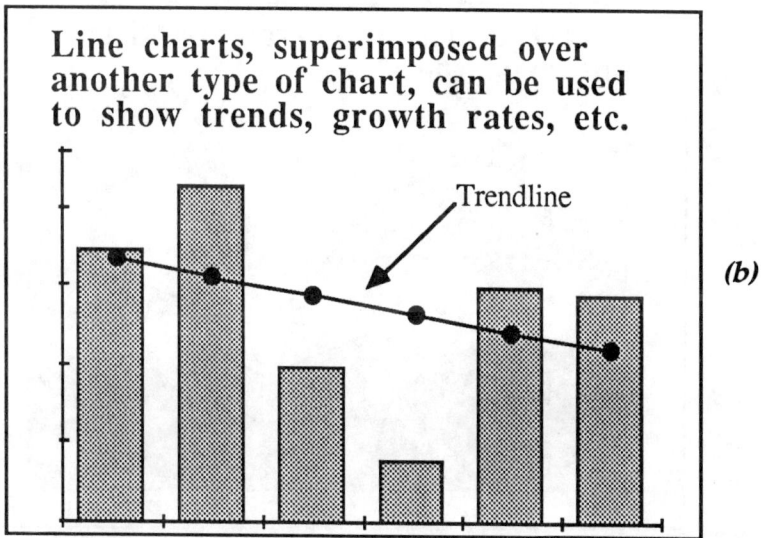

(b)

Figure 3-27 (Continued).

- Grouped multiple line charts should not have more than four or five trend lines, especially if the lines cross each other. If the chart is difficult to decipher, break it into multiple charts.
- A line chart can be combined with another chart for trend analysis.
- The plotted line should always be thicker than the grid and axis lines, but not excessively thick.

The bands of an area chart are actually stacked on top of one another

Normal View   Exploded View

(c)

Place the most important band on the bottom of the stack

(d)

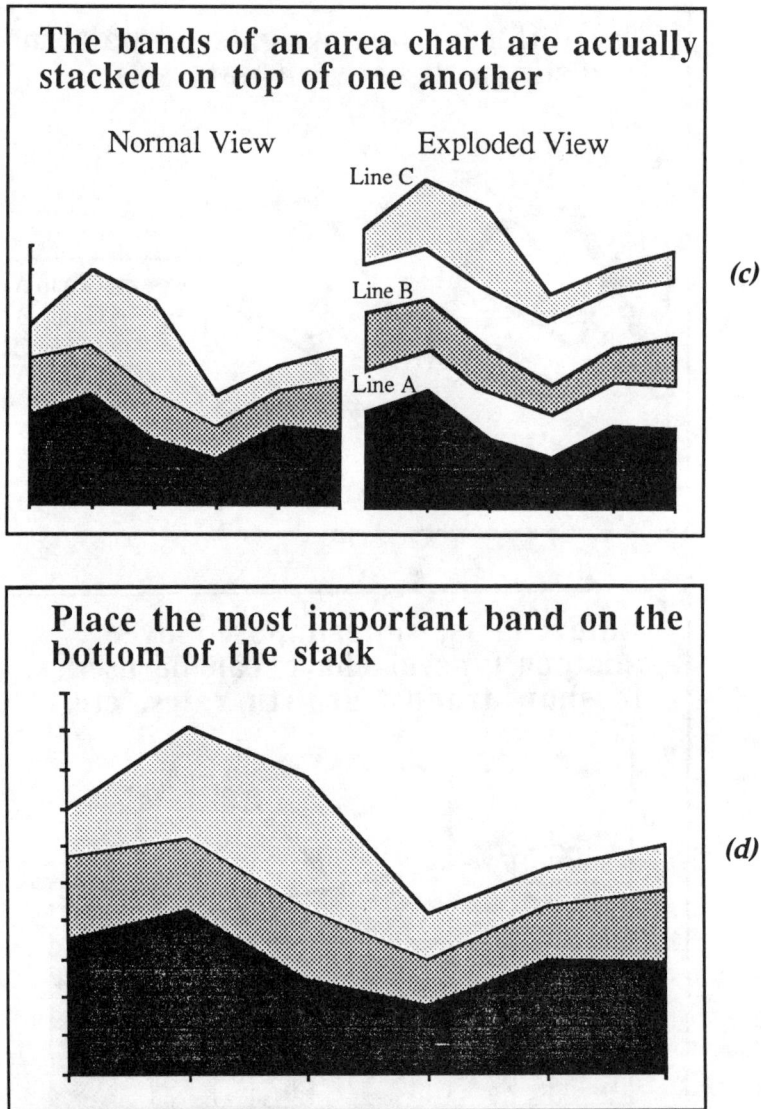

Figure 3-27.
Line chart gallery.

- When plotting a histograph, choose the proper number of ranges to adequately reveal the frequency distribution. Too few or too many ranges hide the pattern. All the ranges should be of equal size, and all ranges should be clearly labeled.

- Area charts are *not* line charts with coloring added below the lines. Area charts show cumulative effect—area B is physically stacked on top of area C; area D is stacked on top of area C, etc.

- The bottom band of an area chart should be the most dominant or important element. When there is no dominant element, place the least fluctuating band on the bottom. Why? The excessive fluctuations on the bottom band may incorrectly influence the appearance of the rest of the bands.
- See examples in Figures 3-27(a)–(d).

Specifics—Dot Chart

Purpose: Dot charts show the correlation between two sets of values.

Maximum number of data points per series: Unlimited.

Maximum number of data series: Three or four (if dot groups are confined in the chart or are identified by symbols).

Grid: Horizontal and vertical.

Labels: X-axis and Y-axis labels; dots may be individually labeled (or use symbols which are keyed in a legend).

Variations

- Grouped dot chart
- Bubble chart

General Notes

- An actual trend line can be drawn through the dots to point up the correlation.
- An expected trend line can be drawn through the dots, whether or not there is a correlation between the numbers.
- The individual clusters in a grouped (multiple series) dot chart should each have a trend line.
- Each cluster in a grouped dot chart should have a unique dot style (black dots, hollow dots, diamonds, etc.).
- See examples in Figures 3-28(a)–(d).

What to Do with Incompatible Data

It'll happen sooner or later, it always does. You enter a set of numbers into the computer, and the graph comes out looking

The regression line can show the actual correlation...

(a)

...or it can show the expected correlation.

(b)

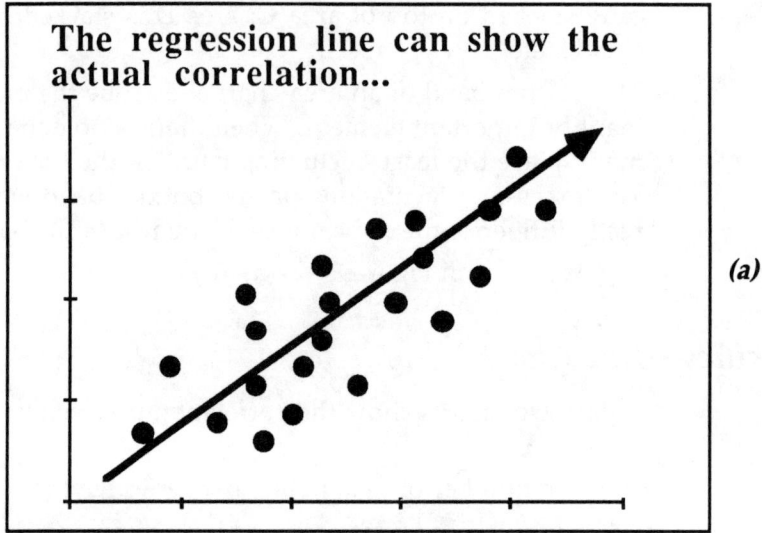

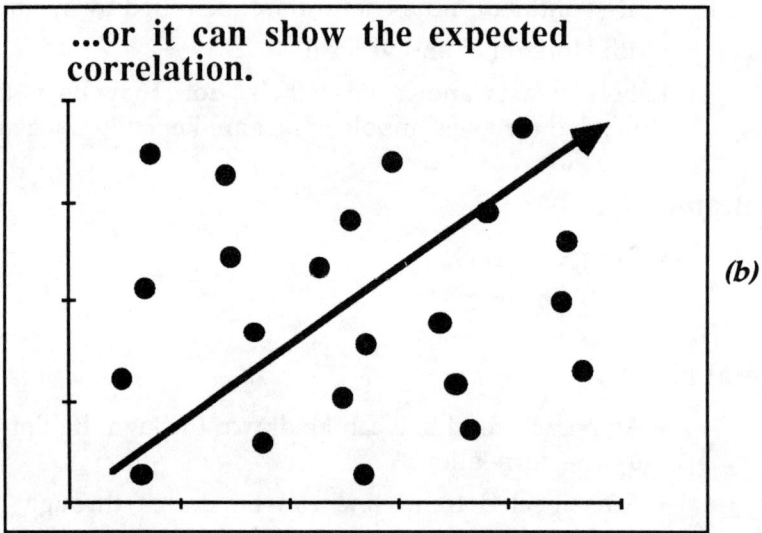

Figure 3-28 (Continued).

ridiculously lopsided, as in Figure 3-29. The cause? Incompatible data. The computer scales the chart according to the largest value. If the other values are considerably less, you'll end up with one tall bar, and several miniature ones. There are several alternatives, discussed below.

Dot clusters should be keyed with a different symbols, and can have separate regression lines

(c)

• Group A
○ Group B

Direct labels can be used if the chart has relatively few data points

(d)

● Bit
● CPU
● Printer
● Disk Drive
● Plotter
● Nybble
● Keyboard
● Monitor
● Byte
● Software
● Hardware   ● I/O Port

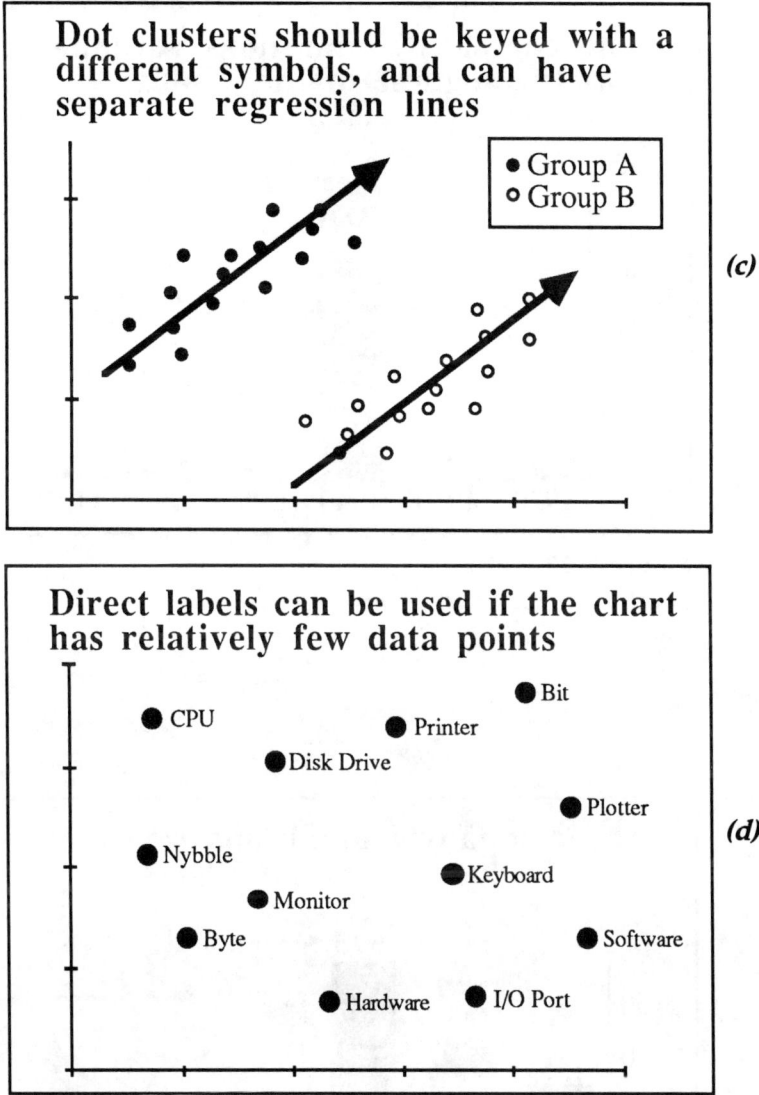

Figure 3-28.
Dot chart gallery.

Reduce Data Value

The best, and often easiest, way to avoid a lopsided chart is to replot the chart with a lower value for the tall column. Regraph the numbers and the other columns will be a normal height.

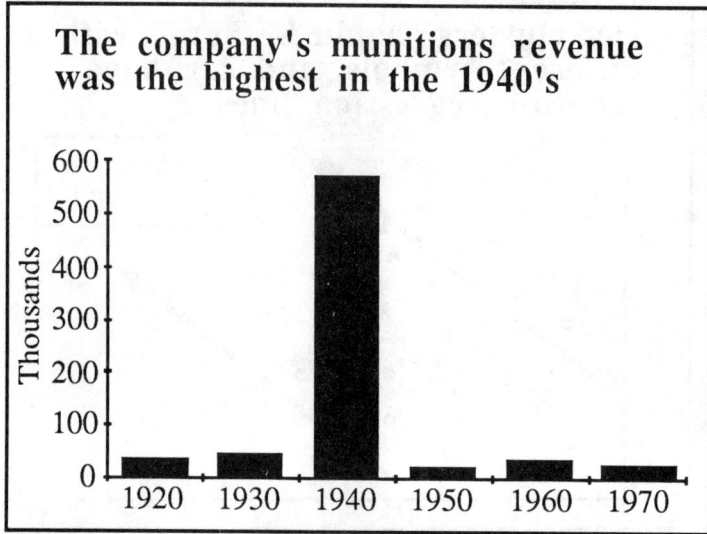

Figure 3-29.
Chart with incompatible data.

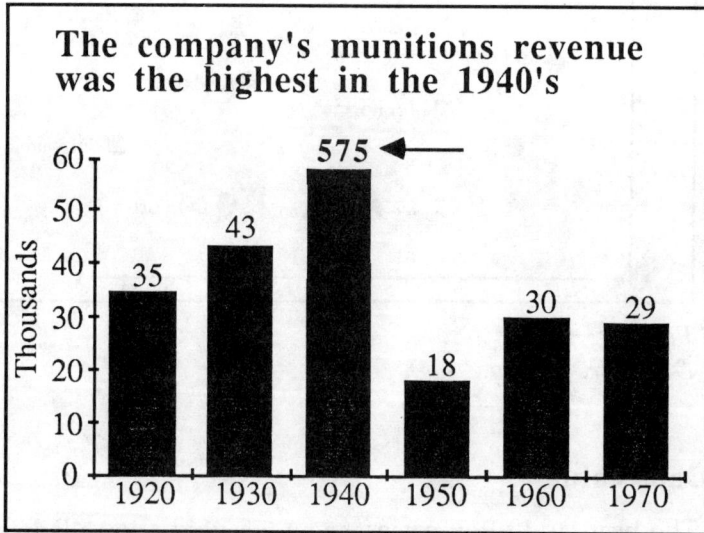

Figure 3-30.
Direct labeling.

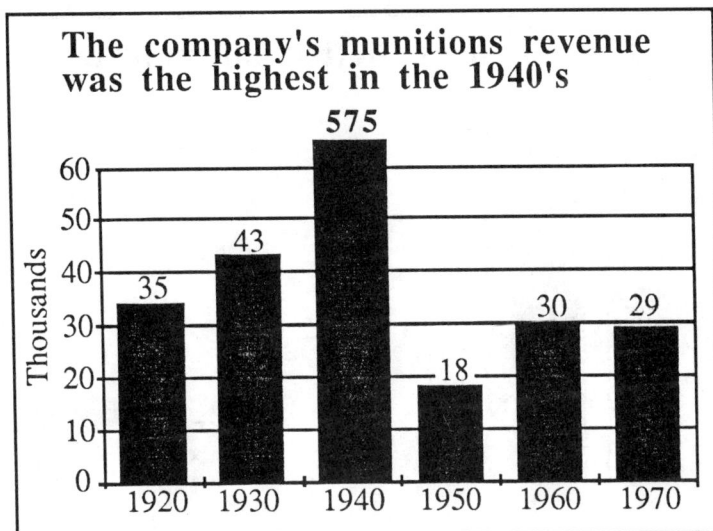

Figure 3-31.
Bar popping through top.

The tall column no longer represents the original value, so you'll have to tell your audience that the column has been chopped down to size. Use your presentation graphics program to write the actual value directly over the column, as illustrated in Figure 3-30. Should the program you're using not allow this flexibility, use a freehand painting program to manually enhance the chart, as explained more fully in Chapter 4.

Out of Scale

If you're using a painting program, you can try another technique. As shown in Figure 3-31, you can extend the bar beyond the top of the chart, as if it's popping through the top. Or cut the bar in the middle, showing a break in the scale. In both cases, you should write the actual value immediately above the chart.

Converting to Percentage

Another approach is to not plot the actual values of the numbers. Instead, plot the numbers as percentages. Your graphics program

The numbers plotted normally...

(a)

The same numbers as percentages (note that there's no apparent size difference)

(b)

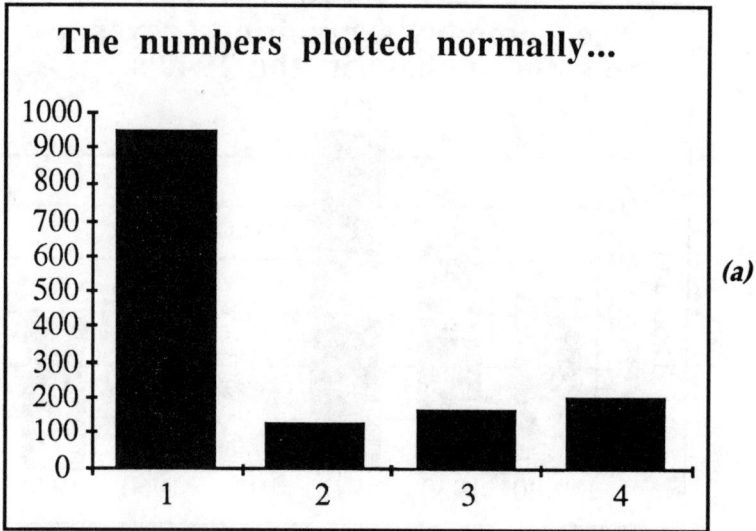

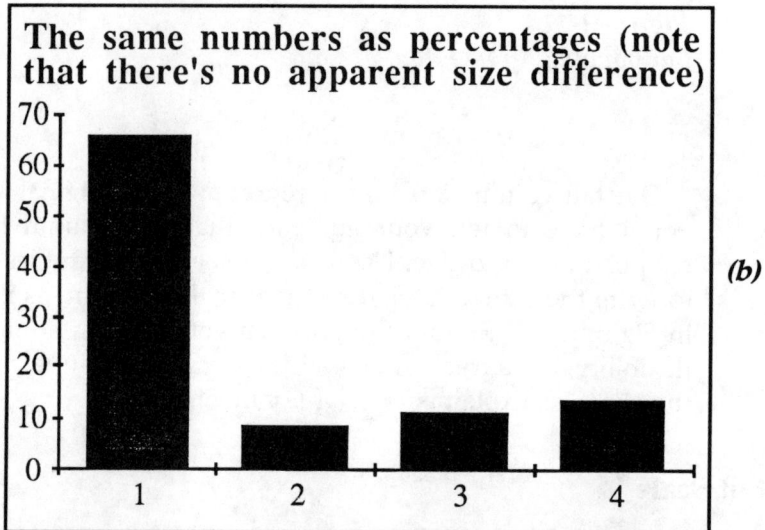

should be able to automatically convert the numbers to percentages for you.

If the program can't do the arithmetic for you, it's easy enough to do yourself. First, add all the numbers together. The sum will represent 100 percent. Then divide each value in the chart into the sum. Here is an example:

Numbers to chart: 950, 126, 164, 201
Sum of numbers: 1,441
950 is 66 percent of total (1,441).

But when plotted as a pie graph, the various percentages are easy to see

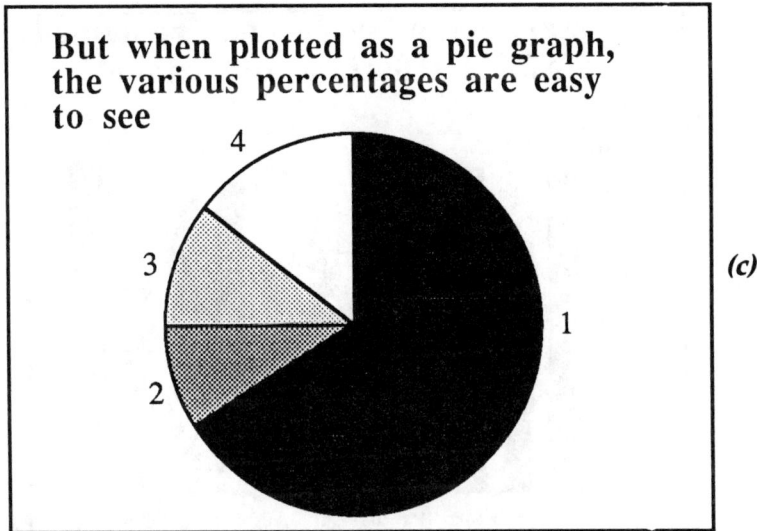

(c)

Figure 3-32.
Column/pie chart of above numbers.

126 is 8.7 percent of total.
164 is 11.3 percent of total.
201 is 13.9 percent of total.

Add up all the percents, and you get 100 (actually 99.9, because of rounding error).

Plotting these numbers on the column chart used before still doesn't provide a very striking chart, and in fact, it shouldn't. *Since you've converted the numbers to percentages, use a pie or 100 percent stacked column chart.* See Figure 3-32 for a before and after look.

Other Methods

You can also use an indexed or logarithmic scale to deal with incompatible numbers. Depending on the original values, this may produce a usable chart. The techniques of using indexed or logarithmic scales are more fully detailed in Chapter 4.

Bear in mind that using a new scale, or plotting the numbers as percentages, may drastically alter the look of the chart. This may not be what you want. Analyze the chart in its new form before you commit to it. Remember that your audience may not understand the chart as readily.

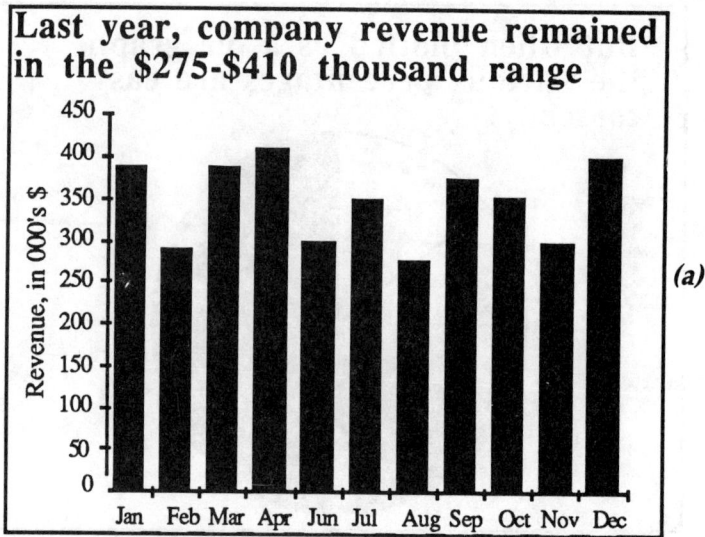

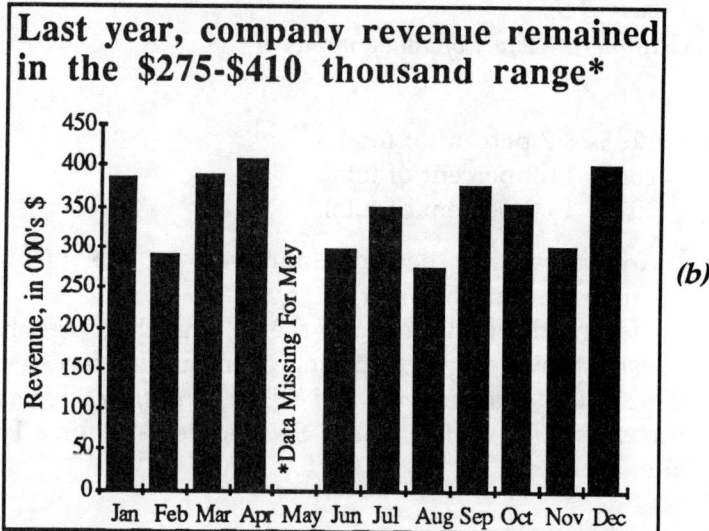

Figure 3-33.
Chart with missing month.

What to Do with Missing Data

It's easy to spot missing data when you're looking at a table. There's a blank where there should be a number. But missing data can be harder to spot when the numbers are in chart form. You can easily jump from April to June, and few people will notice. You may have simply forgotten May, or the data may not have been available. Or the numbers for May were so disappointing that you decided to leave them out!

Column charts are most often used to plot numbers against equal intervals of time. Notice the word "equal." If you start the chart at 1980 and proceed to 1986, a year at a time, there should be a column for every year in between. When the data for a particular time period is missing, enter the value as zero, as depicted in Figure 3-33. Note on the chart the information for that time period is missing.

If the information you have for that month is an estimate or approximation, fill that column with a distinctive pattern, to set it off from the rest. Note on the chart that the data is approximate. You can use the same technique when *projecting* into the future.

Dot and sliding bar charts suffer the effects the most from incomplete data. Both charts rely on examining the correlation between two sets of numbers. If a value from one set of numbers is missing, the corresponding value in the other set is useless. If several numbers from both sets are missing, you should steer away from making a chart. It will have little meaning.

When Not to Make a Chart

So far in this book presentation graphics has been praised as the eighth wonder of the world. But are there times when it's best *not* to make a chart? You can bet on it. If your aim is to impress somebody, but you don't have impressive figures to work with, don't rub salt in the wound by showing off the poor numbers in a chart. Resorting to graphics trickery—manipulating the scale, perspective, or proportion—rarely pays off. The more sophisticated the audience, the more likely they are to catch you trying to fool them. Even if only one chart in a presentation is misleading, your audience will assume they've been duped all along. It's a risk you can't afford to take.

Your concept may also be too abstract to be effectively converted into a chart. Though the numbers may be there, you may have nothing to compare. And since the purpose of a chart is to show some type of numerical comparison, a graph that compares nothing is meaningless.

Concepts that are too simplistic, specific, or familiar are also

not good candidates for charting. An example of an overly simplistic chart is a column diagram showing absolutely no growth.
The chart adds nothing to the perception of the data being
presented.

Specific data, particularly if it will be used by someone, may
be best left in tabular form. Charts force approximation of the
numbers. For example, you probably wouldn't want to provide
your accountant with a line chart that shows your aged accounts
receivables. Your accountant needs the actual numbers to work
with.

Data that's familiar to your audience needn't be charted,
because your viewers already know the numbers. If it's widely
held among your group that it's doing 20 percent less business
than other departments within the company, a chart pointing
out this fact is hardly necessary.

Advanced Charting Techniques

E X E C U T I V E   S U M M A R Y

There are a variety of tricks you can use to enhance your graphs, as well as display more quantitative or useful information about the numbers you are charting. Enhancing your charts may require the use of a utility program, such as a software package primarily designed for freehand drawing. Most drawing and graphics enhancement programs work with printers only. Almost all business graphics packages work with both printers and plotters.

Color and pattern should be used as the first step to enhancing charts. Three-dimensional perspective and drop shadows add depth and visual appeal to otherwise static charts. Feel free to use different types, styles, and sizes of fonts in your charts, but be consistent with your choice.

Combo charts combine two (or more) graphs on the same printout or screen. The graphs can be side by side or overlapped. Pictographs use symbols instead of columns and bars.

Many business charts plot statistical data, typically mean, mode, and median. Also popular is the standard deviation, the most commonly applied and useful analysis of numerical variability. A moving trend averages only a select range of numbers presented in a chart. Linear scales show the amount of change; logarithmic scales show the rate of change. An index scale compares values with an arbitrary standard or quota.

There's nothing wrong with a plain, old-fashioned pie chart: nothing fancy, just a circle with colored or patterned slices inside. It gets the job done, and it's easy to make. Indeed, plain charts have their purpose for routine presentations. But true *power presentations* require more dazzle.

You will have plenty of opportunity to create charts that sparkle with extra pizzazz. You may want to turn that plain, old-fashioned pie chart into a three-dimensional coin. Or you may want to replace the columns in a column chart with unique symbols that help convey the message or subject of the graph.

A number of presentation graphics programs have all the tools you need to make stunning, art department quality charts. Use these features whenever you can. The extra effort you make in adding life to your charts will go a long way to impressing your message upon your audience.

Even if your graphics software lacks the capabilities to make sophisticated looking charts, you can still enjoy the benefits of enhanced graphics by using an enhancement program. These enhancement programs literally add dimension to the otherwise dry and lifeless charts created by analytical business graphics programs.

Take a look at the advanced features that the higher-end presentation graphics and enhancement programs provide, and note how you can use these features to make better charts. You'll also learn how to use pictures with your charts, how to juggle complex statistics, and how to design graphics with unusual index and logarithmic scales.

Adding Visual Appeal

Visual appeal can be added to charts in a number of ways. You'd be surprised how much difference it can make to add color to a black and white chart, or to use a different size text for the title than for the rest of the chart. Here is a quick rundown of the major techniques you can use to add more appeal to all your charts. But first, a quick note about the features of your graphics software.

Do You Need an Enhancement Program?

As you are probably aware, all presentation graphics programs are not created equally. Depending on the complexity, some of the enhancement techniques discussed in this chapter can be applied directly with your charting program. But other techniques may require the use of an enhancement utility program.

Most enhancement programs are drawing or painting packages that let you "capture" the image displayed by your presentation graphics program. You can then edit the image using the various tools provided by the enhancement program. After the image is modified, you may not be able to view it in your presentation graphics program, but it can be shown on the computer's video monitor, or printed out with a printer (and sometimes a plotter).

In many cases, the enhancement program needn't be directly compatible with your business graphics software. There is no link, other than the computer's display memory, between the charting program and the enhancement program.

One exception is when you're working with high-resolution graphics. Many enhancement programs currently out accept pictures displayed in high-resolution form—either the enhanced graphics adapter (EGA) resolution of 640 by 350 picture ele-

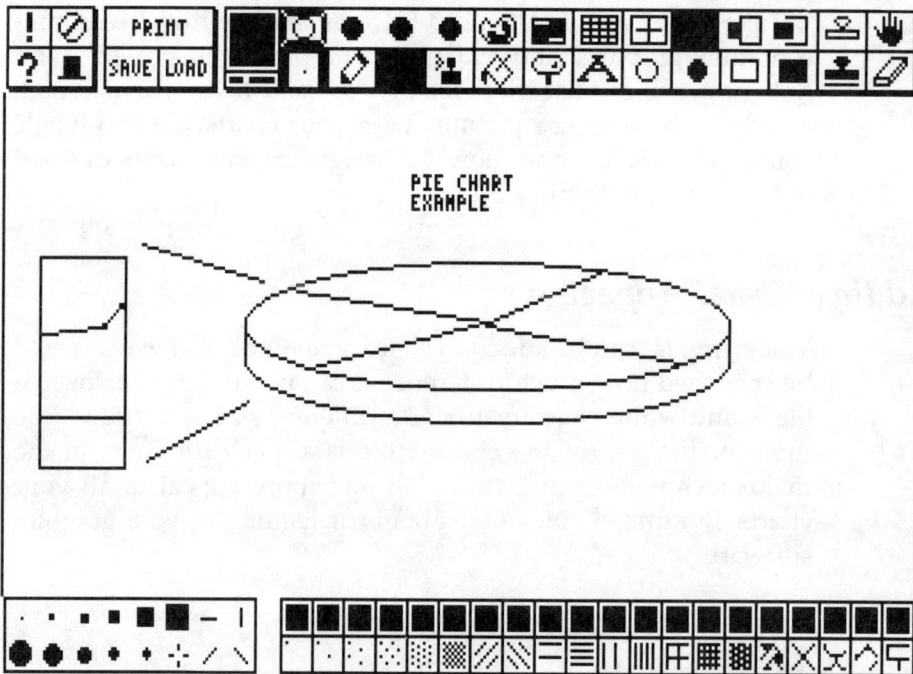

Figure 4-1.
Using a painting program.

ments (pixels) or the video graphics array (VGA) resolution of 640 by 400 pixels. But some software is limited to working with the older color graphics adapter (CGA) standard of 320 by 200 pixels. If your presentation graphics program is capable of high-resolution graphics, be sure that the enhancement software is compatible with it. See Chapter 6 for more details on screen resolution.

A number of enhancement packages are freehand painting programs, like the one in Figure 4-1. The editing procedure varies from one drawing program to the next, but it usually involves redrawing or manipulating the individual dots that make up the image. You can also use the program to draw original artwork.

Other enhancement packages are drawing programs. These work with discrete shapes—like boxes, lines, and circles—rather than dots. You can manipulate the elements created by the presentation graphics program by using the drawing tools, as illustrated in Figure 4-2. Note that software compatibility is much more important when using a drawing program as opposed to a

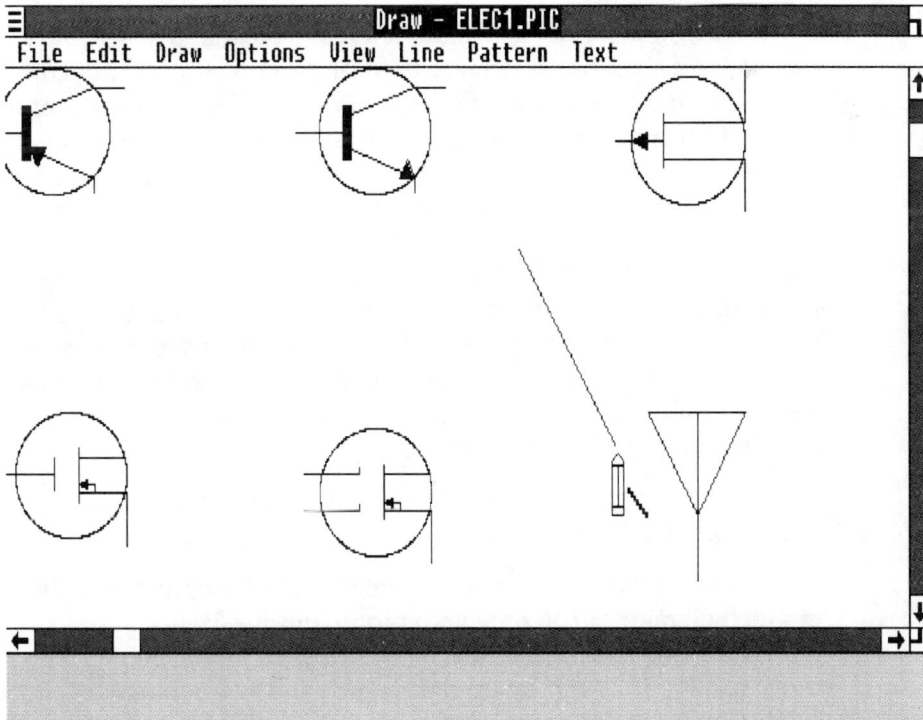

Figure 4-2.
Using a drawing program.

painting program. The drawing program must understand the format of the elements created by the presentation graphics software.

Read Chapter 5 for more details on the difference between painting and drawing programs, and how they are used with presentation graphics packages.

A Limitation with Enhancement Programs

The majority of presentation graphics programs create images— on screen and on paper—out of lines. To the graphics program, a bar chart appears as a series of lines arranged on the screen in a specific order. To you, the lines combine to make bars, a horizontal and vertical grid, X and Y axes, and so forth.

Because the charting program has generated the image from lines, it can reproduce the picture on a plotter, which works by duplicating the lines drawn on the screen. These images are called vector graphics, because they are created by starting a line at a certain vector (x-y position) on the screen or plotter, and ending at another.

All freehand painting programs create bit-mapped graphics. Bit-mapped graphics are created out of individual dots, not connecting lines. These dots are the pinpoints of light on the computer monitor, or the splotches of dots laid down on paper by a printer.

Plotters aren't made to draw bit-mapped images, which is why you can't normally use one to print a graph embellished by a painting program. You should consider this limitation before using an enhancement program of any type. If the painting program you get claims to work with plotters, make sure it is compatible with yours, and that the results are acceptable. Note that most drawing programs create vector graphics, so they are directly compatible with plotters.

Added Colors and Patterns

Color and pattern can be used in charts to help highlight or distinguish elements. You may use color to emphasize a certain column in a column chart, or an important slice in a pie chart. Patterns and textures can be used for much the same thing.

Unfortunately, the monitors used with the IBM PC and clones are not capable of reproducing a wide palette of colors. When used with CGA card (as discussed in Chapter 6), the monitor can display no more than four colors at once out of a total palette of 16 hues. The EGA, MCGA, and VGA adapters provide additional colors, depending on the software and monitor. See Chapter 6 for more information on available color palettes using the various display adapters.

No program can display more colors than the graphics adapter and monitor can show, but the software may let you select different colors for printing or plotting. This is an important feature.

Bit-Maps and Objects

There are two forms of computer graphics: bit-maps and objects. The difference is shown in Figure S4-1. Images created with *bit-maps* are made from dots, like a painting made by a pointillist. Bit-map images can be edited by adding or removing the dots. Images created with *objects* consist of primary shapes, including lines, boxes, circles, and polygons. The orientation and layering of the objects determine the look of the graphic. Object-oriented images can be edited by removing or adding shapes, or by redefining the existing shapes.

Bit-maps are easily reproduced by a graphics printer because the printer reproduces the images with dots. Object-oriented graphics can also be reproduced on a printer, but the graphics software first converts the shapes into dots before sending the data to the printer.

Pen plotters work by reproducing the outlines of the objects created with the graphics programs. The program sends the coordinates of the objects directly to the plotter, with no conversion necessary. You can't ordinarily use a plotter to reproduce a bit-map graphic, although some software allows this. To plot the image, the pen plotter places dots over the page. This technique yields acceptable results, depending on the graphic, but it quickly wears out the point of the pen.

Bit-map images are often referred to as raster or raster-scan graphics. Similarly, object-oriented images are often referred to as vector graphics.

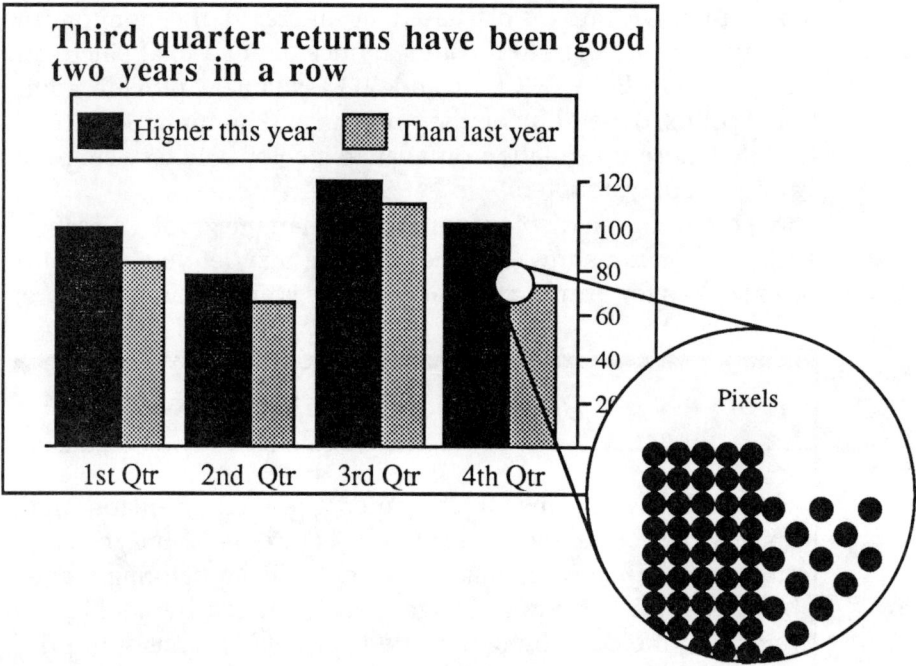

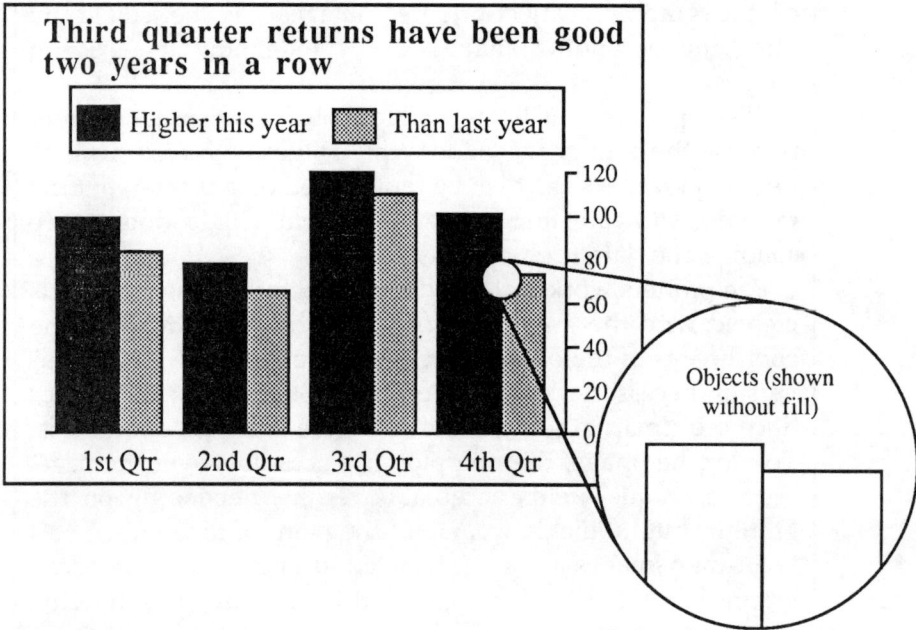

Figure S4-1.
Bit-map vs. objects.

Screen Pixel   Area filled with color

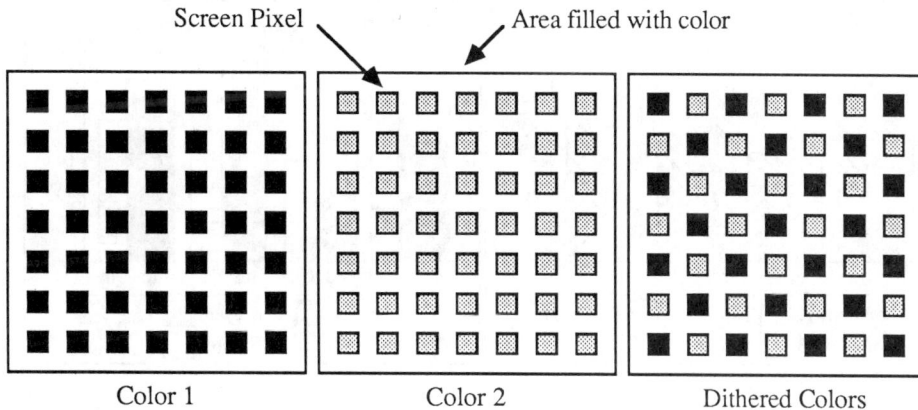

Color 1   Color 2   Dithered Colors

Figure 4-3.
Dithering illustration.

The software may also let you use a technique called dithering, illustrated in Figure 4-3. Dithering is mixing two or more colors in a small space to make an additional color. The process works for the video display as well as with most color printers. Dithered colors, however, aren't as sharp and clear as solid colors.

You'll want the ability to assign colors to specific parts of the chart. Let's say you're doing a column chart. You may want the title and subtitle in one color, the columns in another color, and the remaining elements of the chart in a third color.

Many graphics programs offer only a certain set of standard patterns for use as filling inside pie slices, columns, and bars. The patterns are usually stripes, which can be easily duplicated by a plotter (grays created out of different dot patterns are much more difficult for a plotter to reproduce). Carefully select the patterns used in your chart, so that they all go together. It's bad form, for example, to mix downward-sloping stripes with upward-sloping stripes in the same column chart, as you can see in Figure 4-4. Instead, fill one set of columns with black, the other with stripes.

Unless you find a pattern that looks good both displayed and printed (or plotted), stay away from unusual designs. Some graphics programs, both the charting and enhancement varieties, let you design your own patterns. Keep the design simple, especially if you'll be using several patterns in the same chart.

When using a painting program to add or change colors and patterns, design the original chart with empty elements—that is,

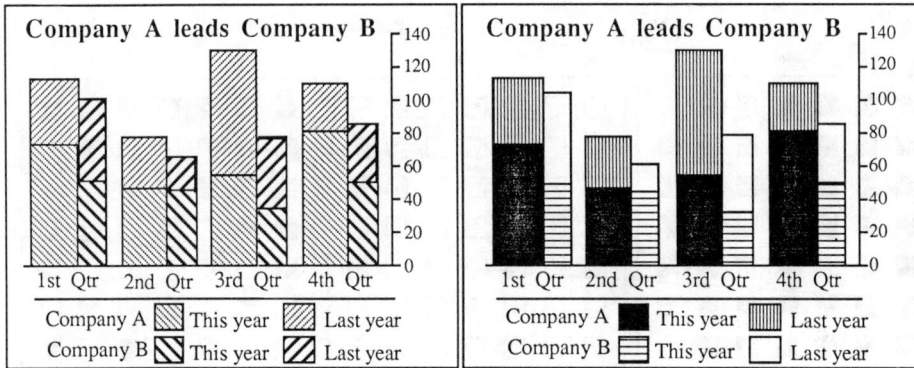

Figure 4-4.
Bad/good mix of patterns.

leave the pie slices, bars, and columns unfilled. That way, you can easily use the enhancement program's automatic fill feature to add color or pattern to the insides of the elements.

3-D Charts

Charts in three dimensions have more presence than those in flat two dimensions. Place a 2-D and 3-D chart side by side, and the 3-D version will immediately draw your attention. The better business graphics programs let you create 3-D pie, bar, and column charts. An example is shown in Figure 4-5. Some even let you make 3-D line and area charts.

If your charting software lacks a 3-D feature, you'll have to manually create the 3-D effect using a drawing program.

1. First, make a copy of the original elements using the program's cut and paste feature.

2. Slide the copy off to one side of the original (sliding it right or left gives you a side-to-side perspective; sliding it up or down gives you an up-and-down perspective). See Figure 4-6.

3. Connect lines to the front and back elements.

You can vary the depth of the image by positioning the copied elements farther away from the original. The connecting lines are longer and the perspective is lengthened. You may have to selectively erase certain parts of the background image to make the 3-D effect look right. A "zooming" feature, where you can

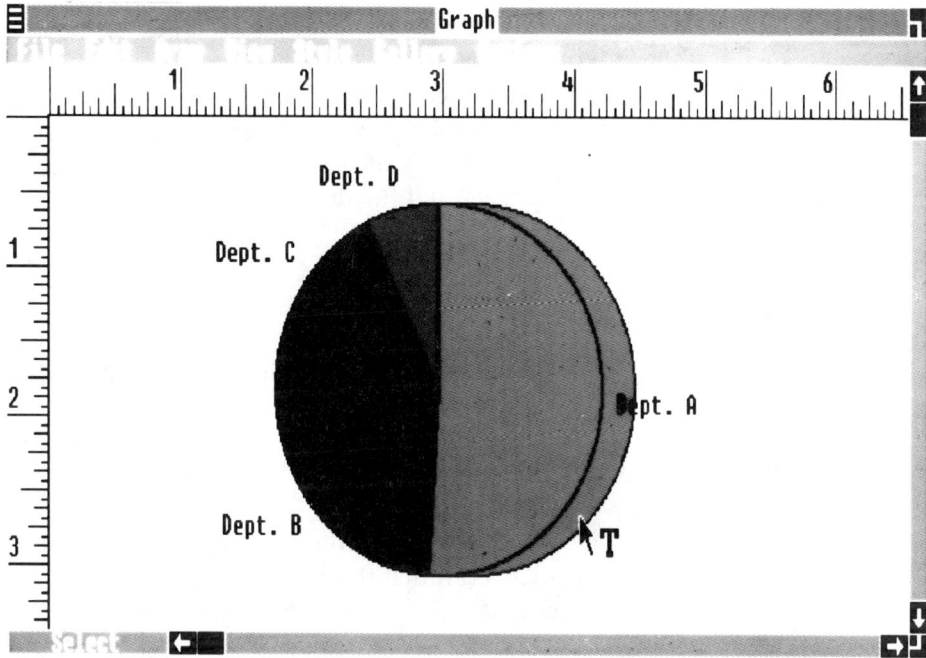

Figure 4-5.
3-D from graphics program.

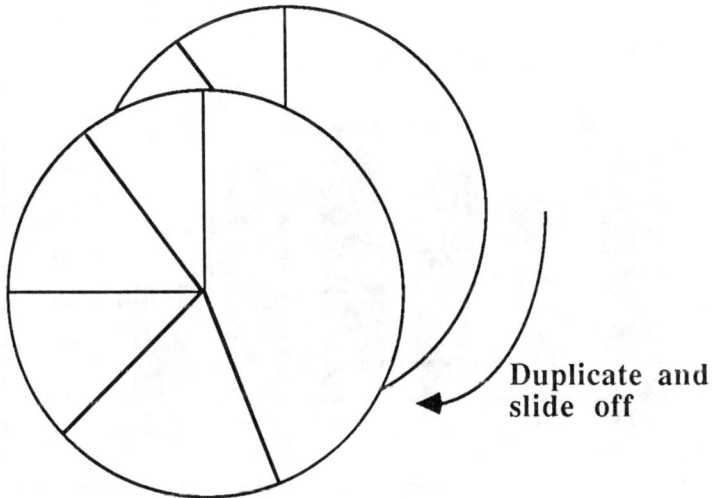

Duplicate and
slide off

Figure 4-6.
Handmade 3-D chart.

work with individual pixels, is handy for this because of the exacting work involved.

Care should be taken when creating 3-D images, no matter how you make them. Too much perspective can distort the original image. Or worse, too much of the 3-D effect can disorient your audience, making it more difficult to comprehend the chart.

Drop Shadows

One way to add depth to a chart without resorting to the full 3-D effect is to add drop shadows. The shadows, which are all a light color or pattern, are placed behind the elements of the graph and create the illusion of depth. The greater the distance between the original elements and shadows, the greater the implied depth.

When not automatically created by the charting program, drop shadows can be constructed much the same as the 3-D perspective. Figure 4-7 shows a sample chart with drop shadows.

1. Make a copy of the chart, but instead of positioning the copy over the original chart, copy it temporarily into the computer's cut-and-paste buffer.

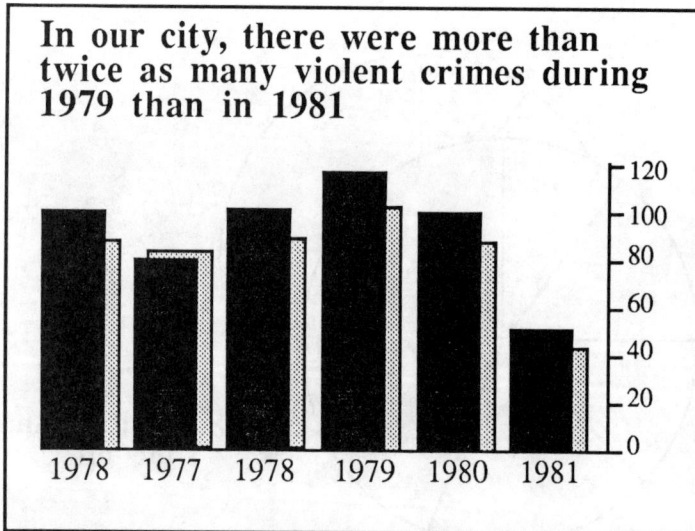

Figure 4-7.
Chart with drop shadows.

2. "Dim" the original chart elements with a new color or pattern.

3. Erase selected portions of the chart, such as the title, grid, and axes, as necessary.

4. Call up the original of the chart from the computer's memory, and place it over the shadow. Position the chart to one side of the shadow.

Special Fonts

A number of charting and drawing programs let you choose the font type, size, and style for any text in your chart. You can make your charts more lively by altering the font, and by using fonts in various styles and sizes, as shown in Figure 4-8.

Fonts for these programs are often contained in special computer-readable files. You can add or delete font files to your work disks as needed. Some programs even let you create your own fonts, or edit existing ones to better suit your needs.

The fonts are available in a variety of sizes and styles, as

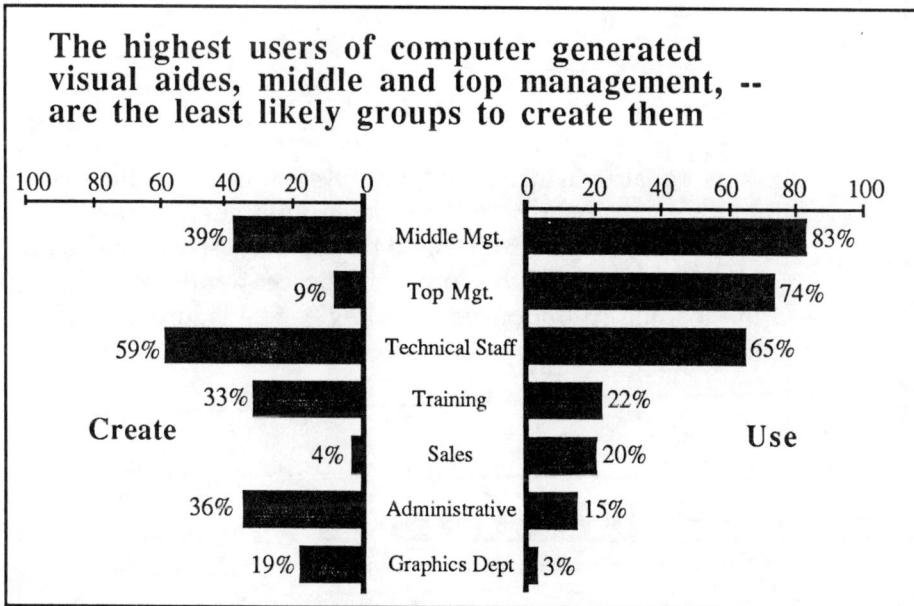

The highest users of computer generated visual aides, middle and top management, -- are the least likely groups to create them

Create		Use
39%	Middle Mgt.	83%
9%	Top Mgt.	74%
59%	Technical Staff	65%
33%	Training	22%
4%	Sales	20%
36%	Administrative	15%
19%	Graphics Dept	3%

Figure 4-8.
Chart enhanced with fonts.

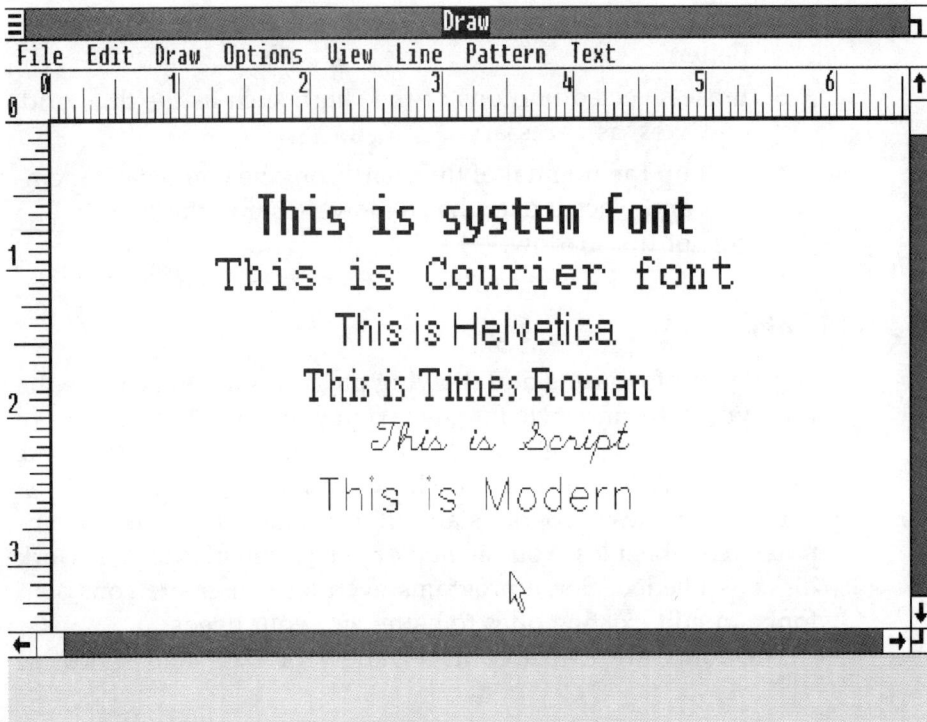

Figure 4-9.
Font gallery.

shown in Figure 4-9. Sizes are usually expressed in points, with 72 points equal to 1 inch. The point system can be a little confusing (it's a carryover from the typography trade), because a 72 point font is not 1 inch from top to bottom. The size includes the "invisible" portions of the font—the descent and ascent lines, and the leading (pronounced "ledding"). See Figure 4-10 for a graphic rendition of a typical font.

Figure 4-10.
Font anatomy.

Font styles include boldface and italics. Some programs can synthesize boldface and italics from one font. Others need a separate font file for each style.

Font Suggestions

Here are some suggestions when working with fonts.

- Stick with one or two fonts per chart. Mixing a lot of styles can be distracting to your audience.
- When you want variety, vary the font size. For example, you can make the title one size, say, 36 points. The subtitle can be smaller, say, 18 points, the other text in the chart, including the labels, X and Y scales, and legend, can be 12 or 14 points.
- As with fonts, it's best to stick with a few sizes, and keep the sizing consistent. That is, labels for the Y axis should be the same size as those for the X axis.
- Reserve boldface, italics, and other style variations for special occasions. Use italics when including the source of the information on the chart, for example. Italic fonts don't show up well on most computer displays or printers (except laser printers).

Plotter Fonts

Most all plotters have but one font built inside them. Under software control, you can vary the size of this font in a few steps, from the equivalent of about 8 point to about 48 point. Plotters may not be compatible with the special screen fonts available with most presentation graphics programs. You'll be limited to the built-in font and sizes.

Some presentation graphics programs print special fonts with plotters by generating a font bit-map file. Text is drawn on the plotter as a series of dots, as it is with a dot matrix printer. The results are mixed, depending on the font, size, and style. Try a few samples before making all your charts this way.

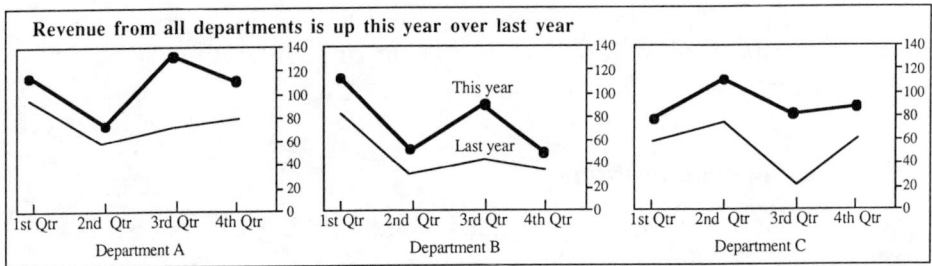

Figure 4-11.
Several charts side by side.

Combo Charts

Combo charts are those that either combine two or more graphs in one display or printout, or those that stack two graphs over one another. *Multiple charts* in one printout can be handy when splitting up data to make it easier to compare, like that in Figure 4-11.

Some presentation graphics programs let you combine two or more charts on the same page. If your program lacks this capability, you may duplicate it with a drawing or painting program. Use the program to capture the individual graphs created by the

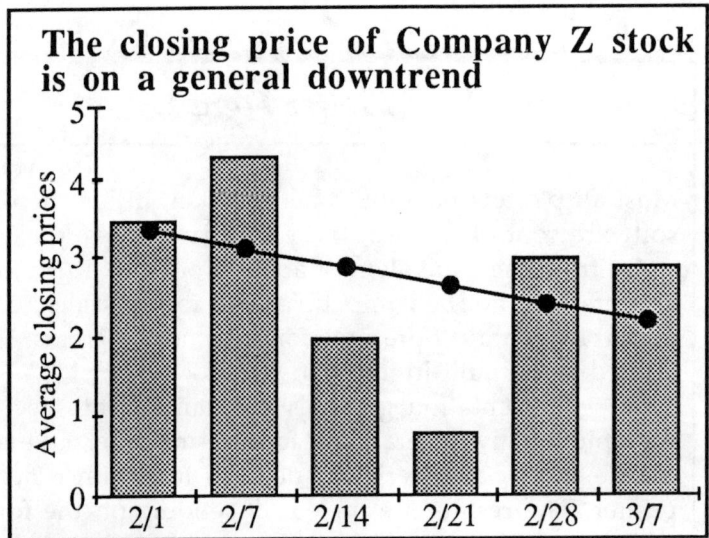

Figure 4-12.
Trend line over column chart.

charting program. Then use the enhancement program's cut-and-paste feature to place them all in one document.

Overlaying one chart over another to make a *composite graph* is a more involved matter and requires some serious thought. The most common composite graphs are those that superimpose a trend line over a column, line, or dot chart (see Figure 4-12). Many business graphics programs can do this automatically, but others can't. If yours doesn't, you'll have to combine the two manually with a drawing or painting program.

Another common composite graph is the *exploded pie chart*. In such a chart, one of the pie slices is further broken down into its component parts, as illustrated in Figure 4-13. The chart within a chart can be another, smaller pie, or a stacked column. You can manipulate the exploded piece so that it's partially covering the main pie, or positioned slightly off to one side.

Composite charts aren't difficult to create with a drawing or painting program, but care must be taken so that the graphs you sandwich together are properly aligned. The top chart *must* be created using the same scale as the bottom chart.

1. Start by capturing the top chart with the enhancement program and saving it to disk.

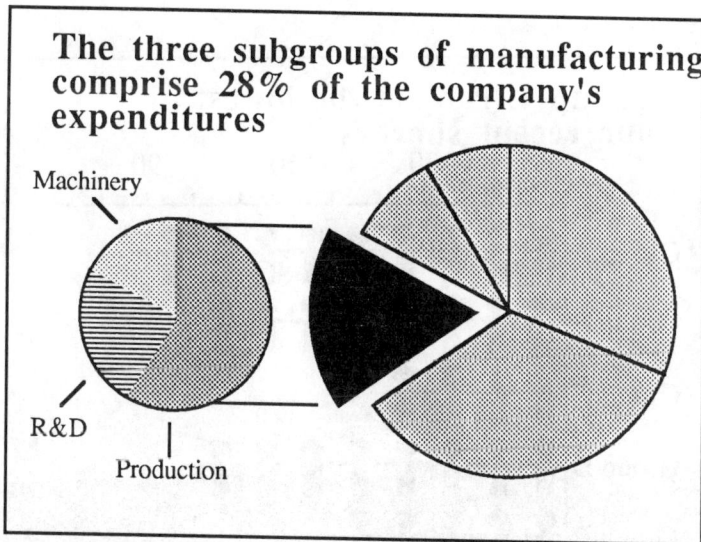

Figure 4-13.
Exploded pie chart.

2. Capture the second chart. You'll probably want to delete the grid, scale, and other elements, since they are already in place in the bottom graph. When erasing the parts you don't want, leave a small dot at the intersection of the X and Y axes.

3. Copy the remaining piece(s) of the chart into the computer's cut-and-paste buffer.

4. Call up the saved bottom chart. Paste in the top chart. Use the dot you kept in the top chart to align the two graphs precisely.

Pictographs

A *pictograph* is a chart that uses symbols instead of whole bars and columns. A typical pictograph is shown in Figure 4-14. The bars have been replaced with symbols that represent the subject matter of the chart. The more symbols, the longer the bar. A pictograph can be made out of one symbol, stretched to the length of the bar or column. Instead of plain, black columns, the column chart in Figure 4-15 is composed of missiles.

Multiple-symbol pictographs are made by placing individual copies of the symbol over the line or bar. Parts of the original

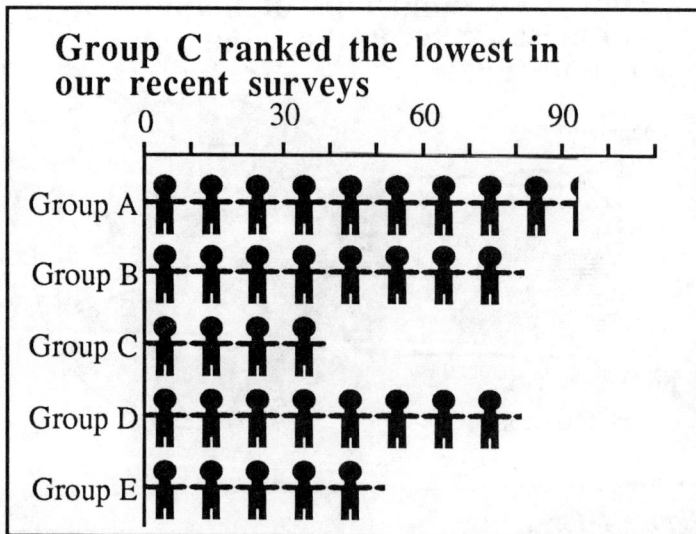

Figure 4-14.
Multisymbol pictograph.

Nuclear deployment is on the rise

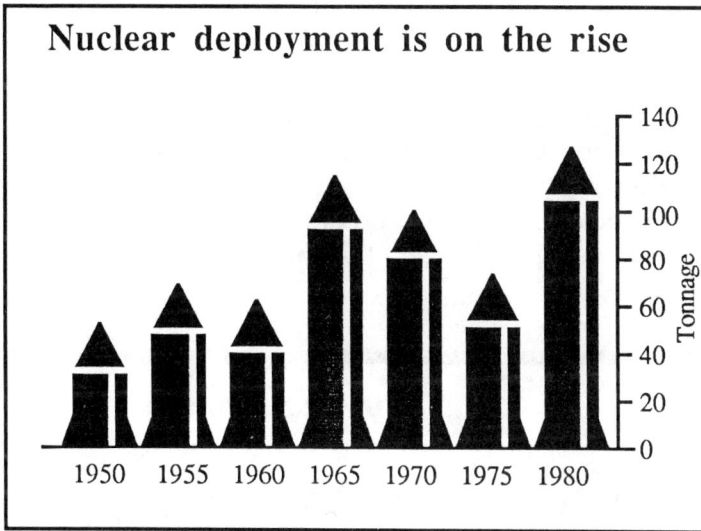

Figure 4-15.
Stretched symbol pictograph.

bars or columns are deleted in the process, or else erased prior to pasting in the symbols. Crop symbols that won't fit the length of the bars or columns as needed. Each symbol can represent any quantity—whether it be 1 pig or 1 billion bushels. That quantity must be specified in a key.

One interesting use of multiple-symbol pictographs is using different symbols for different series of data. In a column chart, for example, one symbol can represent one series of data, another symbol a second series, and so forth. You'll want to limit the variety of symbols you use, and you'll want to keep the symbols the same general size and proportion. Otherwise, it may be difficult to make comparisons.

Single-symbol pictographs are made by taking one symbol and stretching it out to fit the length of the original bar or column. This requires the painting or drawing program to have a stretch feature. Alternatively, you can redraw the symbol for each bar or column in the chart.

Sources for Pictograph Artwork

You can create your own pictograph symbols with a drawing or painting program. Symbols are also available on "picture library" disks. These disks contain dozens of images that are compatible with the graphics program you are using. They are transferred from the library files to the graphics program using a cut-and-paste feature.

A third method of creating pictograph symbols is to digitize them using a video digitizer or page scanner. These hardware devices connect to the computer and capture graphic images from books, magazines, and other sources. You can then edit the graphic using the tools in the painting program.

Using a Scanner

Desktop scanners let you capture the image of text or graphics from a page and convert the data into computer-readable codes. Once in the computer, you can paste the image into a desktop publishing document, edit the image with a painting program, or send the image through the telephone lines to a fellow worker.

Scanners are available from a number of companies, and although the features and capabilities of the different makes and models of scanners are different, their basic operation is the same.

Scanner Basics

Scanners work by sensing the light and dark patches on a page and converting those patches to digital data. The scanner has a built-in light source and paper feeding mechanism. Because scanners see each page as a collection of dots, they have a maximum resolution. Most scanners made these days have an upper resolution of 300 dots per inch, the same as the typical laser printer. At 300 dots per inch on an 8½ by 11 inch page, there are about 8 million dots.

System Requirements

Most scanners are designed for use with the IBM PC (or clone) or the Apple Macintosh. Make sure you get the model for your computer; interface cables, software, and other peripherals are different depending on the make of the machine.

When working with an IBM PC or clone, the computer should be outfitted with at least 512K of memory, preferably 640K. The more memory you have, the easier it is to use the scanner and all its features. The reason? Scanner images take up a lot of RAM. A full 8½ by 11 inch image can consume up to 1 megabyte of memory (assuming 300 dot per inch scanned resolution, the current standard). Most scanner software can accommodate originals that take up more memory space, but it often entails breaking up the page into many smaller documents or storing excess data in temporary disk files.

You can reduce the memory requirements by scanning only the important parts of the page (the scanner software does this) or by reducing the resolution of the scanner.

The computer should be outfitted with a hard disk drive, to save the large image files created by the scanner. The size of the hard disk drive is not important, as long as there is enough room for your scanned images and all other documents and files.

Setting Up the Scanner

Some scanners connect to the computer via a serial or parallel port. However, many scanner models require you to install a special interface cord in your computer. The length of the cord can be critical, so resist the temptation to place the scanner 20 feet away from the computer and attach it with an extension cable. Use only the recommended cable with the scanner and place the unit close enough to the computer so that the cable doesn't bind or cinch.

Vibrations can cause poor images, so place the scanner on a sturdy surface. Avoid the top of your computer or monitor, laser printer, or a card table. Most scanners require easy access to the top, back, and front of the machine—for proper paper feed—so make sure there is plenty of room for proper operation. Rearrange your computer and printer on your desk, if necessary, to make room for the scanner.

Scanning the Original

After installing the scanner, start the operating software. Many scanners use special scanning software; others use a free-form painting program. Most scanner software lets you adjust the contrast, brightness, and other variables before you make the scan. Once the settings are to your liking, you insert the original into the scanner, and make the scan. The scan takes from 5 to 20 seconds, depending on the scanner model and the settings.

Careful adjustment of the settings is critical to making a good scan. If you have experience with black and white darkroom photography, you know that there is a critical balance between exposure time, the contrast of the negative, and the time the paper sits in the developer (indeed, there are even more variables to contend with). Variations in any of these upset the entire process.

In scanning, there is a direct relation between contrast and brightness, and changing the setting on one alters the effect of the other. Experiment to find the best settings. Each original will have slightly different requirements. You will find that line art, black and white originals, and color originals all require slightly different settings, so don't expect to find one universal setting for all your originals. After you obtain satisfactory results, make a record of your settings and use them as starting points for future scans.

Most scanners are the *sheet-fed* variety, which means that the original is fed through the scanner, and by the internal optics, by a set of rubber rollers. You put the original in the top or front, and it exits the scanner through the back or bottom. More advanced *flat-bed* scanners operate like plain paper copiers. You place the original on a glass stage and the scanner optics take a "picture" of the stationary page. Flat-bed scanners can accept originals of just about any size or thickness. They can also be used to scan material from books.

Obviously, you cannot feed anything but single sheets through a sheet-fed scanner (make copies of book materials). The sheets must not be very thin or thick, and the paper finish must not be too slick. Thin or slick paper will slip when passing between the rollers. You get better results by mounting the original on a piece of bond paper, or enclosing it in a "carrier."

Carriers are available at some photocopy stores (they are usually intended for infrared or thermal copiers), or you can make your own. On one end, attach a piece of clear acetate (the kind for overhead projection is a good choice) to a sheet of regular bond paper. Before you scan a document, slip the original between the acetate and paper, and feed it through the scanner. The scanner optics read the image through the clear sheet. If the original is on heavy paper, you should make a photocopy of it before passing it through the scanner. Photocopies can also be made of originals that are on thin or slick paper.

Most scanners cannot accept paper sizes smaller than about 3 by 5 inches. If you are scanning a small document, mount it on a larger sheet, slip it into the acetate/paper carrier, or make a photocopy of it. Originals that are too large to fit through the scanner must be reduced on a photocopy machine that is capable of reduction. Note that although most scanners can accept paper up to 8½ by 11 (or 14) inches, the actual scanned image area is smaller. On the typical scanner, the maximum image size is approximately 8 by 10½ inches. You must accommodate for this when scanning large originals.

Making photocopies of originals is fine for some applications, but it can diminish the quality of some kinds of artwork. If you can, change the print density when making photocopies; adjust for best results. You may need to make the copies darker or lighter, depending on the original. For example, if you are after a high contrast scan, darken the copy.

If photocopying still doesn't do the trick, consider making a photographic duplicate of the original. Most local print shops can make a photo positive (or negative) of any original in just about any size. Feel free to specify a reduction or enlargement if the original is too large or too small to scan properly.

Scanning high-contrast line art is easier than scanning images with varying levels of gray. All scanners approximate the level of gray by a process called *graining* that inserts a certain number of dots for any given matrix in the image. Your eye blends the dots together and you see gray. Depending on the mode of the software and scanner, the matrix may consist of 4, 9, or 16 dots. Filling the matrix with dots, as shown in Figure S4-2, yields different levels of gray.

Using Scanned Images

Once the original has been scanned you have two choices: Save the image directly on the disk or use the scanner software to manipulate the picture. Not all scanner software lets you alter the image, but most do. You can flip the image horizontally or vertically, change black portions to white, or vice versa, even merge parts of several scans into one picture.

If your scanner software doesn't have a great deal of editing features, you can use a painting program to make alterations. Many of the better paint programs allow you to manipulate the images at the full resolution of 300 dots per inch. You can zoom in close and edit the image pixel by pixel.

Transferring Scanned Images

You'll often want to import a scanned image into another application. That application might be a picture-based database management program, a desktop publishing program, or a word processor. When working Windows-based programs, most scanned pictures can be cut and pasted using the integral Clipboard feature. Make a copy of the original scan and paste it into the application.

When working with the PC without Windows or some other operating environment, you usually must import a copy of the image that's been previously saved onto disk. That requires the software you use to scan and edit the picture to save the image in a file format that can be read by your other applications. Most scanner and painting software save pictures in a variety of file formats, included TIFF, used by a number of desktop publishing programs.

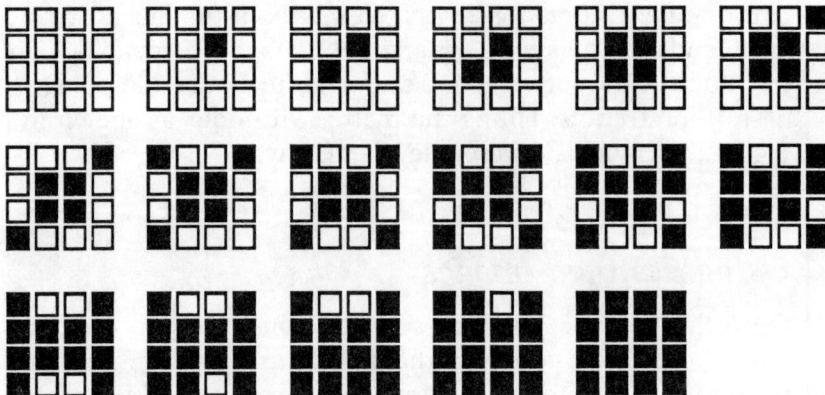

Figure S4-2.
Graining technique.

As expected, new car sales slumped 45 percent during the summer months

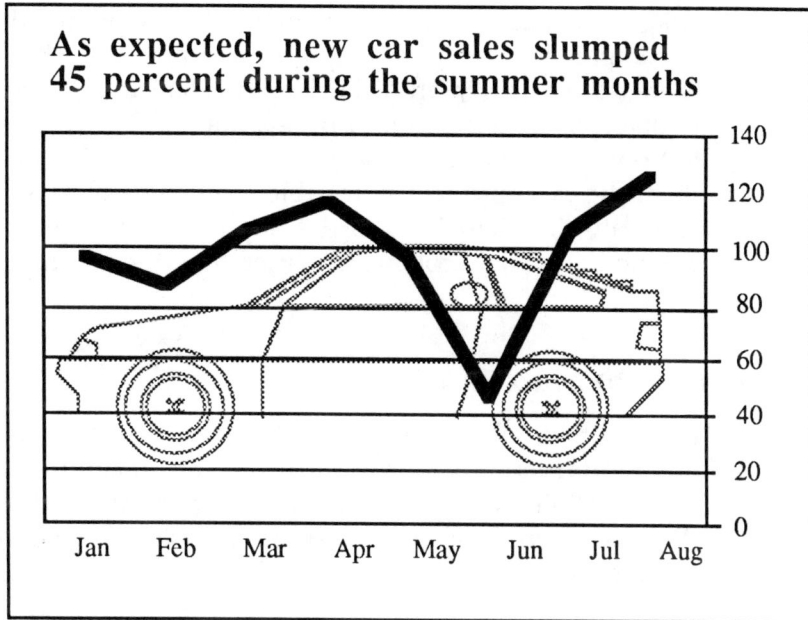

Figure 4-16.
Underlay chart.

Image Underlays

A favorite graphic trick that many classy newspapers and magazines use is to superimpose a chart over a computer-generated picture. This is the *image underlay*. Some business graphics programs allow this flexibility, but not all do. If your program doesn't permit underlays, marry the chart and graphic with the help of a painting or drawing program. You could, for instance, lay a line chart over a picture of a car, as in Figure 4-16.

Sources for Artwork

As with pictograph art, the image you use for the underlay can come from many sources. If you have a talent for art, you can draw it yourself using the painting tools available to you in the drawing program. Using a mouse, graphics tablet, or some other alternate input device comes in handy when drawing free-form art.

Disks filled with ready-made pictures, called clip art, are also available. You can grab just the illustration you want, edit it to suit your needs, and use it in your charts. Just be sure the clip art is compatible with your graphics program. See Chapter 5 for more details on clip art disks. Finally, you can digitize a picture or object using a digitizer or page scanner.

No matter where you get your pictures, you'll want to make them dimmer and less noticeable than the rest of your chart. After all, the chart itself is the important part, not the image behind it. Use light colors and patterns for the graphic underlay.

Working with Statistics

By definition, all numbers are statistics. But the kind of statistics of importance here are the kind that say something about the numbers that are being graphed. If charts *show* you the relationships between numbers, statistical analysis *tells* you about the relationships.

You may have occasion to perform some sort of statistical analysis on the numbers you're charting. A number of presentation graphics programs have statistical functions built in, so you don't have to do the math yourself. You're lucky. Statistics is a science unto itself.

If you are really interested in learning more about statistics, visit the library and check out a few introductory books on the subject. There are hundreds to choose from; a few are listed in Appendix B. In the meantime, here is a short course on statistics as it relates to business graphics.

The Three M's

There are three basic statistical measurements: mean, mode, and median. Each takes a group of numbers and analyzes something different from them.

- *Mean.* Another word for "average." That is, the mean is the average of a group of numbers. Example: The mean of the numbers 2, 5, 7, and 9 is 5.75. Means are calculated by taking the sum of the values and dividing it by the number of values.
- *Mode.* The typical value of a group of numbers. By typical, we mean the most frequently occurring value. If there are few or no numbers that repeat, the mode is the peak of the frequency curve. In the numbers 2, 3, 4, 3, 5, 3, the value 3

is the mode, because it occurs the most. There can be more than one mode in a set of numbers (the frequency curve is then said to bimodal or multimodal). Modes are found by counting the number of occurrences of each value and plotting them on a graph.

- *Median.* The median is the center value where 50 percent of the other numbers are higher and 50 percent are lower. Consider the numbers 21, 24, 34, 53, 56, 71, and 87. There are seven numbers. The number 53 is smack dab in the middle (50th percentile), which means that there are three numbers that are smaller and three numbers that are larger.

Using Statistics

How might you use the three M's in everyday chart making? Averaging comes in handy when you want to find a balancing point, for the purpose of starting at some specific base to make an objective observation or decision. Let's say that you're averaging the age of students attending a university. You have several ages from 17 through 26. The average age is the number of students divided by the number of total years in the span (10 years). A visual representation of the mean of the student ages is depicted in Figure 4-17.

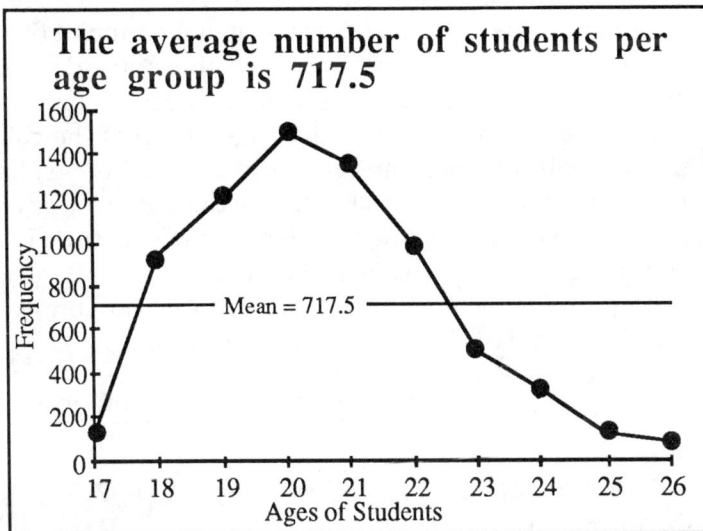

Figure 4-17.
Mean age.

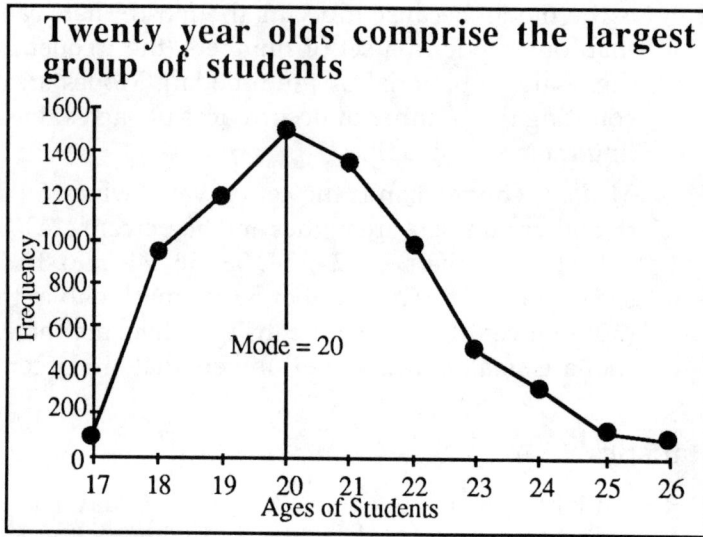

Figure 4-18.
Modal age.

The modal age group is helpful when you want to find out if students are a specific age. By graphing the ages, as shown in Figure 4-18, you find that there is a higher frequency of students 20 years old than at any other age group.

The median is perhaps the most useful of the three statistical observations, because it shows the actual midpoint of a given set of values. Unusual deviations from the norm do not have as great an influence on the result as the mean and mode.

Figure 4-19 shows the median age group of the college. Half the students are the same age or older than this age; half are the same age or younger. Finding the median of the ages entails taking the age of every student, stringing the data from low to high, and picking the one that's in the middle.

If you have an even number of values, and you want to find the exact median, use the following formula:

$$\text{Median} = \frac{\text{first} + \text{second middle numbers}}{2}$$

Therefore, out of the numbers 2, 3, 4, 6, 6, 7, 7, 9, 9, and 10, the formula would be:

$$\text{Median} = \frac{6 + 7}{2} \text{ or } \frac{13}{2} \quad \text{which equals 6.5}$$

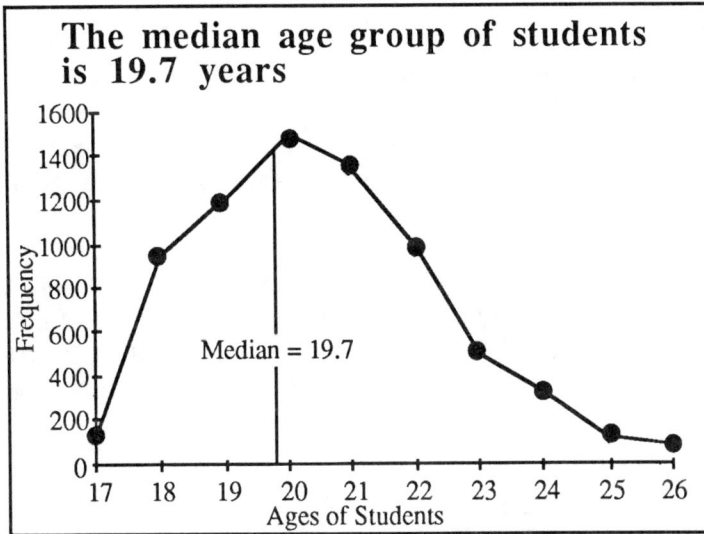

Figure 4-19.
Median ages.

Skew

For any set of numbers, you can find the mode, median, and mean. Rarely are all three symmetrically distributed along the curve. Often, the mode will be larger than the mean, or vice versa. When the mean is greater than the median and mode, the distribution curve is said to have a *positive skew*. When the mean has a lower value than the median and mode, the distribution curve is said to have a *negative skew*. The skew, one way or the other, can be helpful when showing the relationships between the mean, mode, and median. See Figure 4-20.

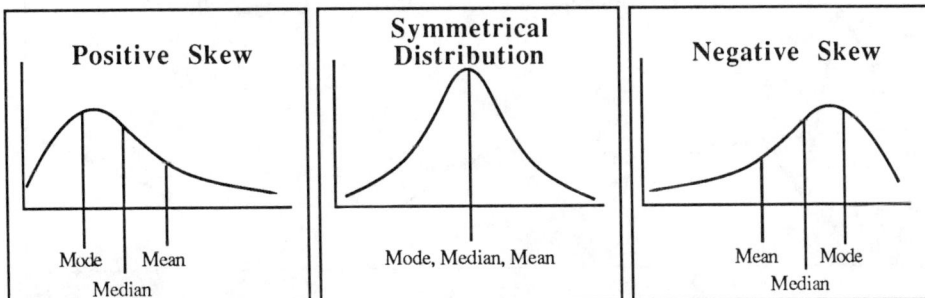

Figure 4-20.
Examples of skews.

Variability

Someone great probably once said, "Numbers invariably vary invariably." It may sound like gibberish, but there's a lot of truth in the statement. Given a set of numbers, for just about anything, you'll most likely find that those numbers don't follow any set rhyme or reason.

The numbers may not obviously be the same, but that doesn't mean that they don't have something in common. It can be extremely helpful to find just how much a group of numbers differ from one another. Two common statistical expressions of variability—mean deviation and standard deviation—come in. A quick rundown:

- *Mean deviation.* The extent to which each value differs from the average.

- *Standard deviation.* The square root of the variance, or more specifically, the square root of the mean of the squared deviation scores about the mean. Although computing standard deviation requires some heavier math (which a number of the better business graphics programs do for you), it is a more useful and accurate measure of variability than mean deviation.

Trends

Is your stock going up a little or a lot? Is it going up at all? Like its name implies, a *trend line* smooths the volatile action of the typical stock and reveals an overall trend. The most common kind of trend line is the *moving average,* shown in Figure 4-21. In a moving average, only the numbers that have occurred up to

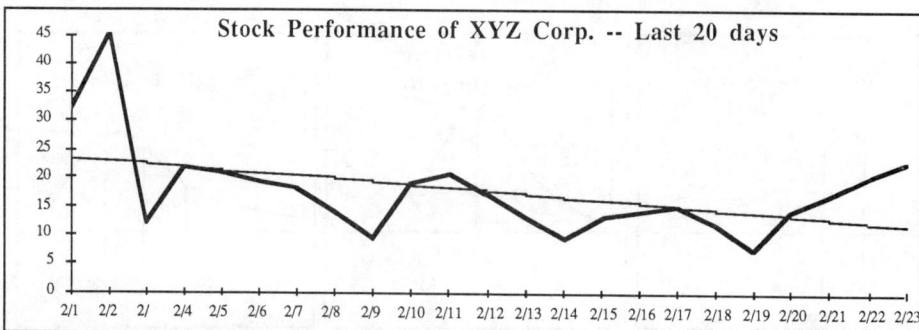

Figure 4-21.
Moving average.

a certain point are averaged. As the trend line continues, the oldest points along the way are dropped as new ones are picked up.

Moving averages are based on some specific range of periods. In the stock market, that range is usually 30 trading days (a "30-day period moving average").

Regression Analysis

Regression analysis has a fancy name but a simple concept: predicting the value of one variable based on observations made of another variable. For example, police know, from past experience, that the number of drunk drivers will be higher during major holidays than during other times of the year. They also know that the more drinks someone has had, the more likely that person will be in a serious automobile accident.

You can make a graph of the number of drinks someone has had in one evening in correlation to the number of automobile accidents for that evening. From that information, you can plot the exact correlation between the two, and predict, with a reasonable amount of accuracy, the number of accidents that might occur given an even greater number of drinks consumed in one evening.

For example, the number of drinks are plotted in one axis, the number of accidents in another, as shown in Figure 4-22. A cor-

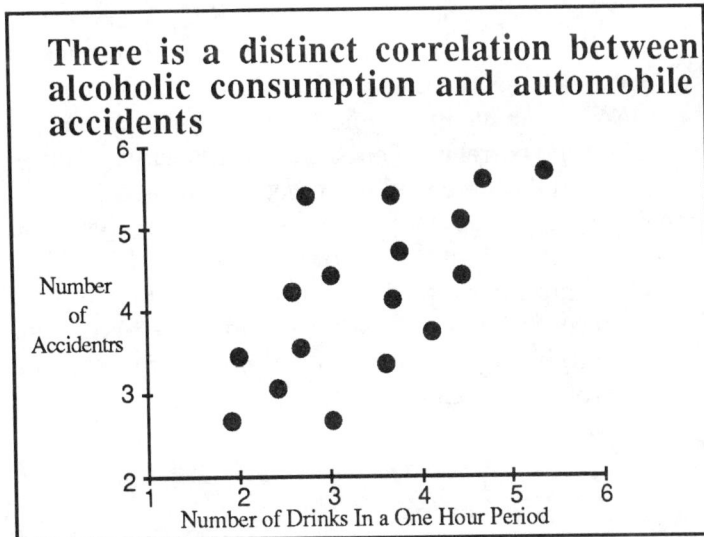

Figure 4-22.
Drunk driving chart.

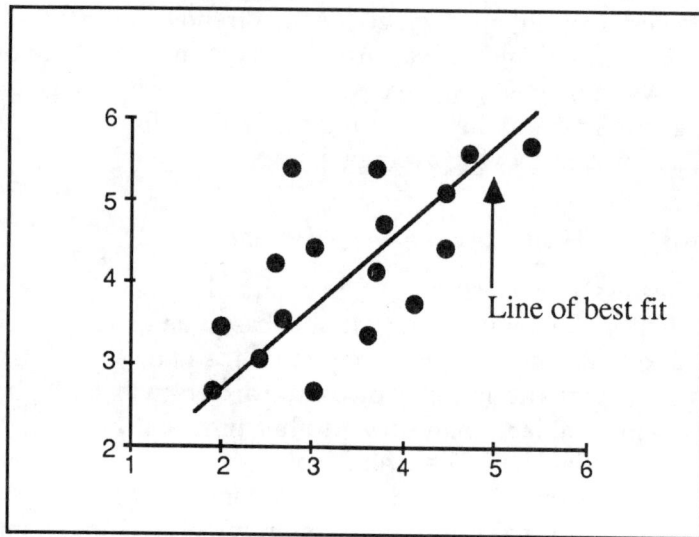

Figure 4-23.
Line of best fit.

relation coefficient (represented by ''r'' by statisticians) describes the relationship between the two axes.

By applying some math, a *regression line* showing the best relation between the X and Y values can be plotted on the chart. This line, shown in Figure 4-23, is the *line of least squares*, also called the *line of best fit*.

A correlation coefficient approaching 1 or −1 creates an obvious regression line, and the more that the values in the X and Y axis have in common. The closer the correlation is to zero, the less they have in common.

When the correlation coefficient is a positive number, the two sets of variables are said to be *positively correlated*. As one variable gets bigger, so does the other, and the regression line slopes up from left to right, as illustrated in Figure 4-24. The drinking/driving graph has a positive correlation, for example. If the correlation coefficient is a negative number, the two sets of variables are said to be *negatively correlated*, and the regression line slopes down from left to right (see Figure 4-25).

Inside Logarithmic Scales

Most charts use a linear or arithmetic scale. The X or Y numerical axis is numbered consecutively from zero on up to the largest

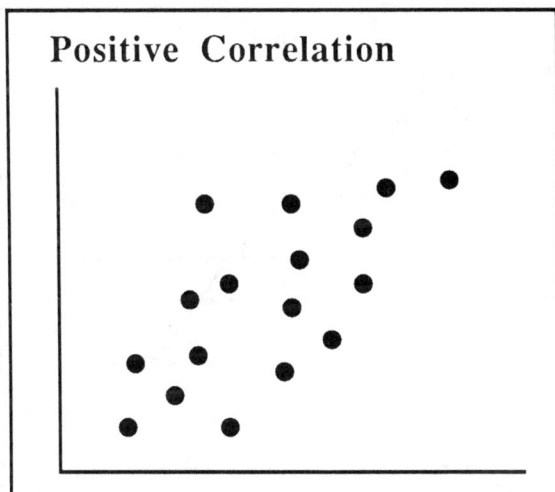

Figure 4-24.
Positive correlation.

value in the chart. The distance between each numbering increment is equal. Linear charts show the *amount of change* from one
value to the next.

Another kind of scale occasionally used in presentation graphics is the logarithmic (log) scale. Log charts show the *rate of
change* from one value to the next. In a log scale, the distance

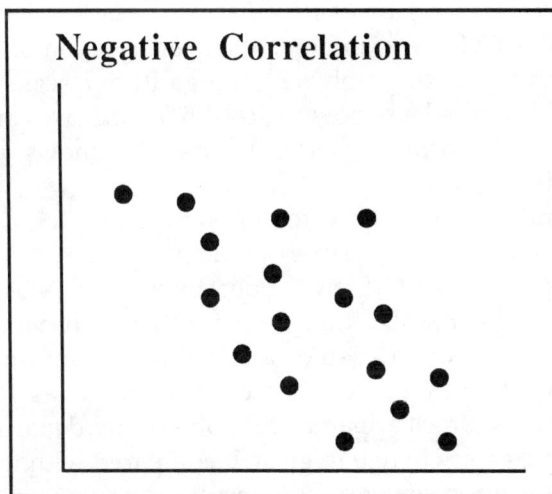

Figure 4-25.
Negative correlation.

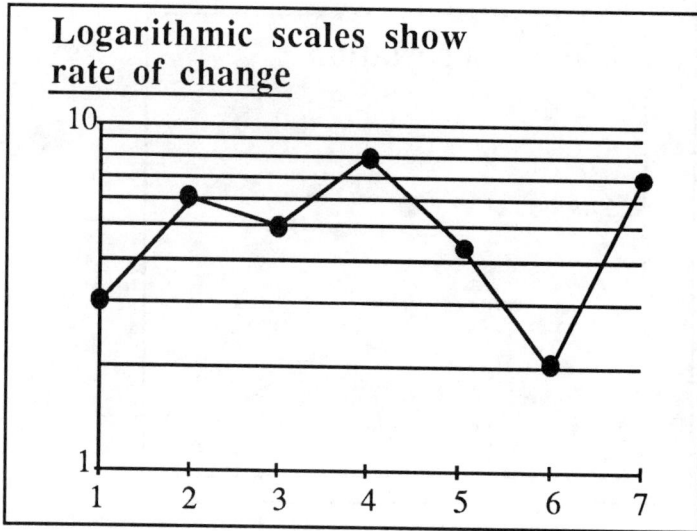

Figure 4-26.
Basic log chart.

between the numbering increments are not the same. The X or Y numerical axis starts from 1 and goes to 10, or some multiple of 10 (100, 1,000, and so forth). As the scale goes up, the distance between each numbering increment decreases by a factor of 2.

Here's an example. As illustrated in Figure 4-26, the distance between 1 and 2 is the same as the distance between 2 and 4, which is the same as the distance between 4 and 8. Log charts *represent increases compared with other values in the chart,* rather than the values of the numbers based on a common starting point—usually zero. A graph with a logarithmic scale in the X or Y axis only is called a *semilog chart.* When both axes are scaled as a logarithm, it's a *log-log chart.* Figure 4-27 shows examples of both kinds.

Showing rate of change is often important, and log charts are perfectly suited for the job. For example, you may want to compare the performance of two departments in a company. Graphed on a linear scale, it may appear that both departments are growing at about the same rate (although one does more business than the other). Graphed on a log scale, as shown in Figure 4-28, it becomes apparent that one of the departments is experiencing greater change in growth compared with the other.

A word of caution. Beware of logarithmic scales. Few people know how to read them. Log charts tend to present the data in

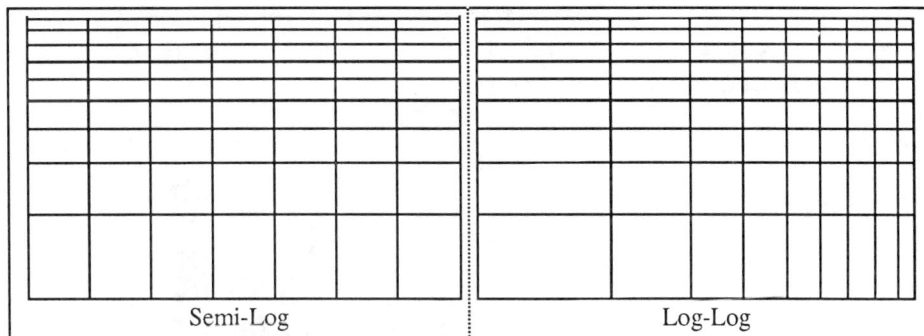

Figure 4-27.
Semilog and log-log examples.

a way that's not immediately recognizable. Though the oddly spaced grid in a log chart may be a dead giveaway, most people won't recognize its significance. They'll assume the data is presented on a natural linear scale, and accept it as such. Save log charts for more sophisticated audiences.

The Index Scale

Another unique way of charting data is to use an *index scale*. An index scale is very much like the old and reliable linear scale, but with a twist: The scale is based not on zero but on some number that represents 100.

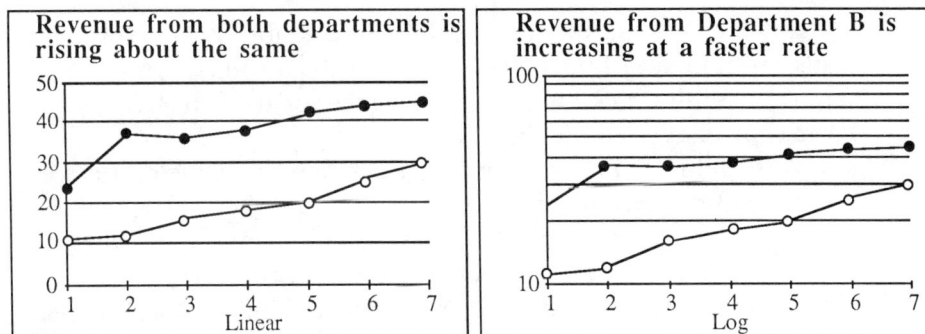

Figure 4-28.
Linear/log scales of same company chart.

Except for 1977, the cost of living has increased at a steady pace

1975=100

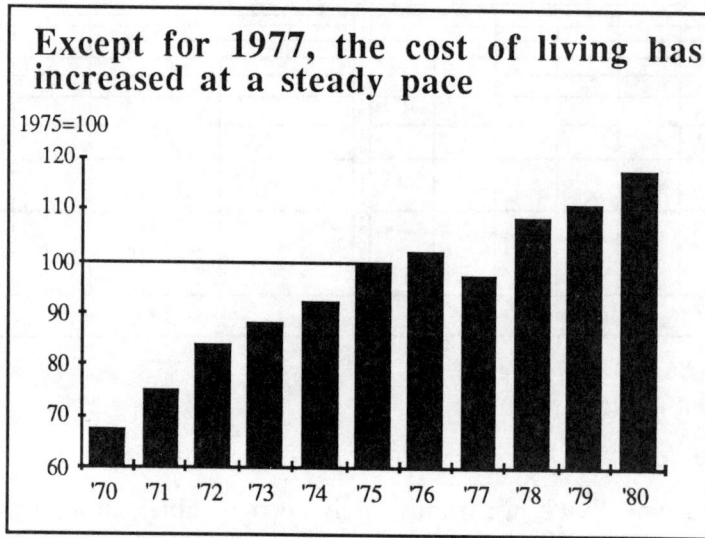

Figure 4-29.
Cost of living index chart.

The cost-of-living chart is a good example of a graph based on an index scale. In such a chart, the price of housing, food, rent, and all that is compared with the cost in years past. Because of inflation, and other monetary fluctuations, it's necessary to fix the value of the dollar at some arbitrary level.

For instance, the value of the dollar in 1975 may be considered 100, as it is in Figure 4-29. If the cost of living goes down (fat chance) in subsequent years, the line in the index charts goes below the 100 mark. If it goes up, the line goes above the 100 mark.

Index charts are helpful because they enable you to compare similar statistics. But they can also lead you into trouble. You must carefully pick an appropriate base, or the effectiveness of the chart may well be diminished.

You could, for instance, pick a year when the value of the dollar was unreasonably high. Your chart would then show that the cost of living has actually gone down, compared with this inflated year. If your aim was just the reverse—you wanted to prove that the cost of living is ridiculously high—choose a base year when the dollar value was low, as shown in Figure 4-30. No matter what base you choose, you must identify it somewhere on the chart.

The cost of living has increased dramatically since 1970

1971 = 100

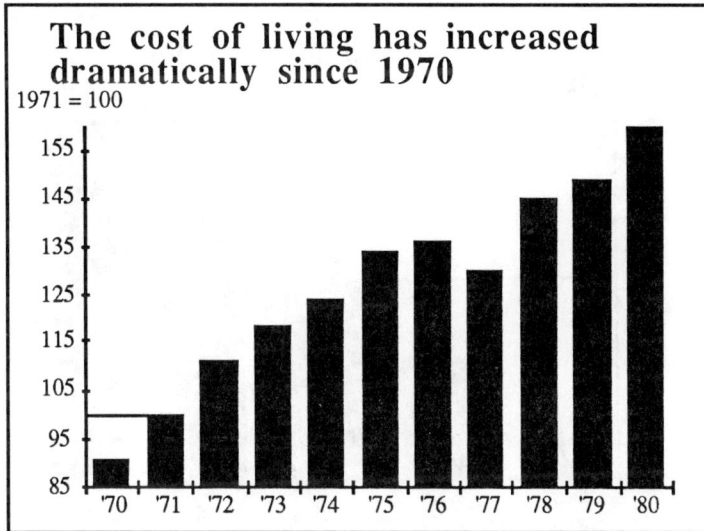

Figure 4-30.
Too high/low base year.

Some programs will index a set of numbers around a common base, but many will not. You'll have to do the math yourself, which fortunately, is easy.

1. Locate a value in your chart that you want to be 100.
2. Divide that number into 100. The result will be a "constant" that you'll use for the other numbers.
3. Take each number in the chart and multiply it by the constant.

Suppose your chart consists of the values 10, 12, 14, 16, and 18. You choose 14 to be the base index of 100. Dividing 14 into 100 gives you the constant of 7.14. Therefore:

- 10 is equal to 71.4.
- 12 is equal to 85.7.
- 16 is equal to 114.2.
- 18 is equal to 128.5.

When charting these numbers, as shown in Figure 4-31, it is necessary to override the program's auto-scaling feature. You'll want to choose a bottom scale limit just below the smallest index value, and the top scale limit just above the largest index value.

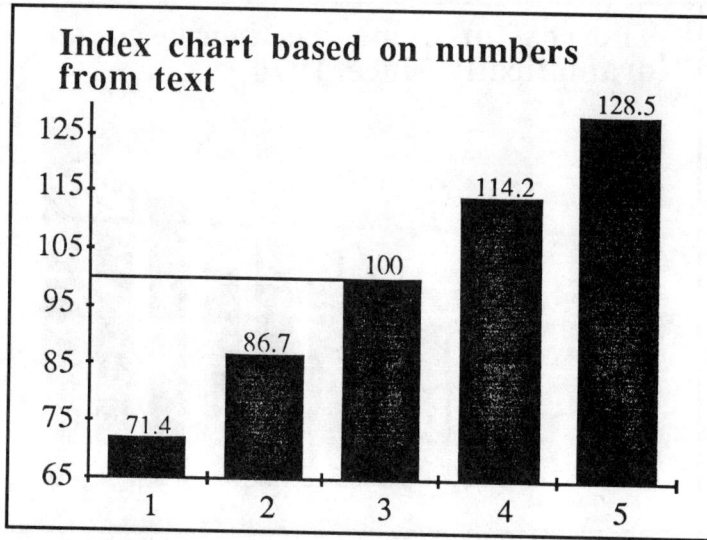

Figure 4-31.
Index of sample numbers.

If you can, make the 100 mark a heavy line, to highlight it for your audience.

Choosing a Program

Know what is expected of a good presentation graphics program—read about how to choose one in the next chapter. Apart from the different charts that the program can reproduce, and the special charting features such as 3-D and special fonts, you'll want to choose a presentation graphics program based on your computer hardware, charting requirements, and ability to share data with other programs.

How to Choose the Right Business Graphics Program

EXECUTIVE SUMMARY

There are three general types of computer graphics programs: painting, drawing, and presentation graphics. Of the presentation graphics group, analytical business graphics are designed for your own personal use, to help you better see the relationship between numbers. True presentation business graphics are designed for sharing your ideas with others. Presentation graphics offer more flexibility and look more professional.

A key to choosing the right presentation graphics program is to analyze the audience (who will view the graphs), the type of charts you want to create, how long you have to prepare the graphics, and the level of expertise of the person(s) using the program.

Data interchange formats, such as DIF, SYLK, and WKS, let you use information you've created with one program and use it in another, without the need of reentering the numbers.

There are two ways to interact with business graphics programs: by choosing a command from a menu or by typing the command explicitly from the keyboard. Menu-driven programs are easier to learn and use, but command-driven software lets you work faster. Adequate answers to your questions are a must. The better the instruction manual, the easier it is to learn and use the program. On-line help and call-in customer support can also be helpful in answering questions.

When talk turns to computers, most of us speak of them as wonderful tools to help us write reports, calculate sales, maintain household budgets, that sort of thing. But draw pretty pictures? A pad of paper and a box of Crayons are just as good, right?

With the right presentation graphics program, you can type a long series of numbers into the computer, and out will come a colorful graph, a picture that's easy for just about anyone to look at and comprehend. That graph might be a pie chart, or perhaps a bar chart. It's up to you.

Presentation graphics is big business. Everybody, it seems, wants to make pictures with their PC, and there's been no shortage of software to help achieve this goal. Having a number of worthwhile presentation graphics programs to choose from allows you to pick the package that has the features you want.

But the glut of graphics software also means that choosing the right one is much harder. This chapter takes a close look at the "three F's" to buying the right business graphics program: features, flexibility, and functionality.

Types of Graphics Software

There are three general categories of computer graphics software: painting, drawing, and presentation graphics. Although presentation graphics packages are the main thrust of this book, the other program types are important because they can be used to enhance or modify charts. Let's briefly overview the differences in the individual programs.

Painting

Painting programs let you create pictures from scratch. The world of painting programs is a big one, with software costing from next to nothing to several thousand dollars. Painting programs include those that let you doodle and draw, as well as those that let you create complex electronic portraits, such as the kind you see on movies and television news broadcasts.

Many of the least expensive painting programs provide little

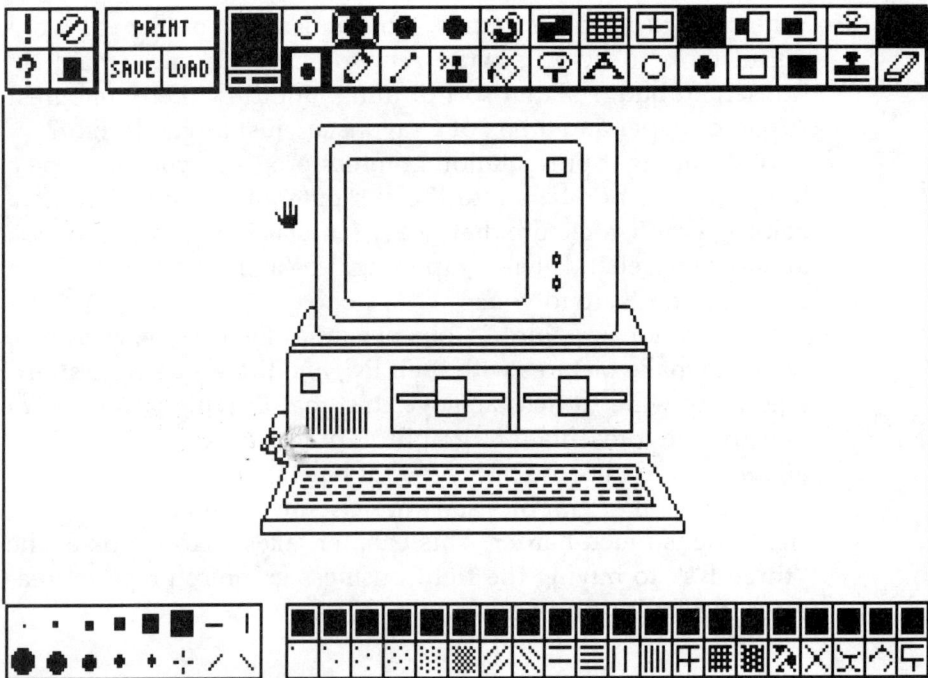

Figure 5-1.
Painting program example.

more than a simple electronic easel. You're given a blank pad (the screen), a palette of shapes, patterns or color, a brush, and some other artist tools. As illustrated in Figure 5-1, you pick a brush, "dip" it into a color or pattern, and start spreading paint over the screen.

Freehand painting programs, which generate pictures out of dots, are enhanced by the addition of user-selectable options to automate the drawing process. With these, the computer takes an active part in making the pictures.

The main applications of a painting program are:

- To create symbols for pictographs
- To create pictures for image underlays
- To edit graphics digitized by a video digitizer or page scanner
- To modify a chart on a dot-by-dot basis

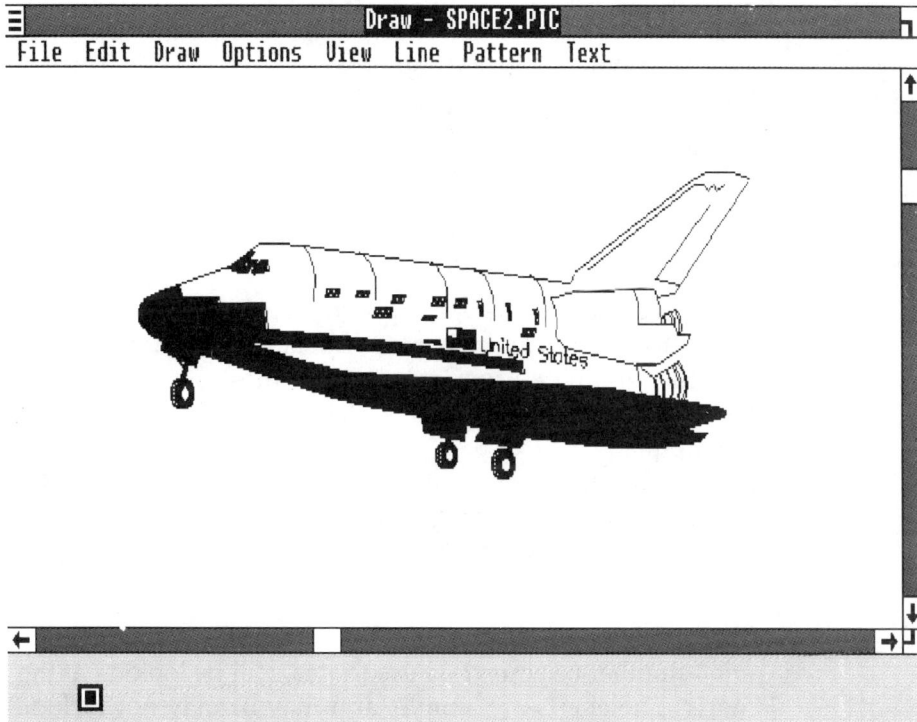

Figure 5-2.
Drawing program example.

Drawing

Drawing programs are more structured than painting programs, although you can often draw the same types of images with both. Drawing packages create graphics out of a series of simple shapes, including lines, squares, and circles. The way you place the shapes on the drawing pad determines the appearance of the finished graphic.

Advanced drawing programs are designed for computer-aided design and are not suitable for most work with presentation graphics. The less complex drawing programs, such as the one in Figure 5-2, allow control of the exact size and placement of the objects on the screen, providing a set of rulers marked off in whatever graduations you desire. Many of the better programs let you zoom in close, to make fine adjustments, then zoom back out to finish the picture.

The main applications of a drawing program are:

- To create symbols for pictographs
- To create pictures for image underlays
- To modify a chart on an object-by-object basis

Presentation Graphics

Business presentation graphics programs are those that turn numbers into pie, bar, and other kinds of statistical charts. By far, presentation graphics programs are the most popular of the bunch, because almost everyone works with numbers they'd like to see simplified.

The flexibility that a presentation graphics program provides varies from package to package. In general terms, this flexibility largely determines whether the program is for analytical or presentation graphics.

- Analytical graphics are for use when you, and perhaps a small number of your close associates, will be looking at the charts. The charts are simple, and may or may not include titles, legends, or other textual annotation. Integrated programs such as Lotus 1-2-3 produce analytical graphics.

- Presentation graphics are for use when you plan to show your charts to a variety of people, possibly for the purpose of selling or persuading. Presentation graphics are full of flourishes, like text, color filling, annotations, and so forth. Most all stand-alone charting programs produce presentation graphics.

If you don't have control over the labels, titles, chart position, color, and other elements of the graph, the program is for analytical graphics work. The more options a program provides, the more flexible it is, and hence, the more personalized the charts can be.

Presentation graphics software also varies in the number and type of charts it can produce. Almost all of them can create simple bar, line, and pie charts. Better programs can create exploded pie charts, histograms (frequency distributions), scatter (XY) graphs, stock market plots, and more.

A few advanced presentation graphics programs are designed to create complex statistical charts, and plot such things as regression lines, modes, means, and moving trends. Of course, just about any charting program can create these types of line and dot graphs, but you have to do all the calculations yourself.

Mapping Software

A special kind of graphics software makes maps. The maps show statistics such as the population spread across the country, areas where crime is high, and the mean temperature over parts of the nation. Statistical map-making software is helpful for government agencies, insurance companies, advertising firms, research organizations, schools, financial institutions, and others that deal with data that spans a geographic area.

Most map-making software contains a database, organized by state, county, city, ZIP code, and general census data (for the United States and other parts of the world). All this information for the entire country or world spans many disks, and each disk is often available separately. There's no need for a disk that contains the database for Kentucky, for example, if your business deals only with California, Oregon, and Washington. Most map programs let you add to the database and the database is regularly updated.

Also included with the map-making software are boundary files, used to draw geographic features such as county, state, country, and ZIP code outlines.

With the data base information and the boundary files, you can construct a map that shows just about anything. For example, consult the database for the minimum drinking age in each state. Identify the colors for each minimum age and display the map. On the screen appears a map of the United States, color-coded to the minimum drinking ages for each state. Depending on the capabilities of the software, you can pull out states, zoom in close, focus on just some states, and more.

Finished maps can be printed with a printer or plotter. A color output device lets you use the color capabilities of the map-making software to the fullest.

Establishing Your Needs

Before you can shop for a business graphics program, you must first establish your needs. There's no sense buying a program with features you don't want. Likewise, it's a waste of money to buy a program that's too weak to serve your needs. You can establish your needs based on the following criteria:

- *Audience.* If you'll be the only one viewing your graphs, there's probably no need to get a program that can create fancy presentation-quality charts.
- *Chart types.* Not every graphics program produces the same charts. Get one that can generate the chart types you need or use the most.
- *Time constraints.* Preparing fancy presentational graphs takes time. Generally, the more elaborate the program features, the longer it takes to generate a chart. However, many programs let you save chart settings for use later on.
- *Level of expertise.* If others will be using your program, consider their level of computer expertise. The more basic the graphics program is, the easier it is to use for those in your office with little or no computer skills.

Features

What should you look for in a good business graphics program? Following are a number of basic considerations:

Color or Black and White

Not all graphics programs can handle color, either on the screen or on paper. If you want color, make sure the program supports it. Of course, to display color, your computer will need a color monitor and video display board. To print color, you'll need a color printer of one kind or another.

Remember that the computer screen and printed result can be different. The picture you view may be limited to monochrome only (because of a limitation in the program or your computer system), but the printed output can still be in living color.

Hidden Features and Capabilities

Some basic and very important features are hidden, or seem so obvious that they're often overlooked. Some things you'll want to consider include ability to create text files, whether or not you can fit more than one chart on a page or screen, and the maximum number of data series you can plot at one time.

Don't Forget Text

Text charts are very popular. In fact, they're used more often than any other type of graphic. Most graphics software do text as a matter of course. If you can type in a title, label, or annotation with the program, you can make a text chart with it.

A more effective program will let you choose among various fonts, text sizes, and styles, as in Figure 5-3. You may need a

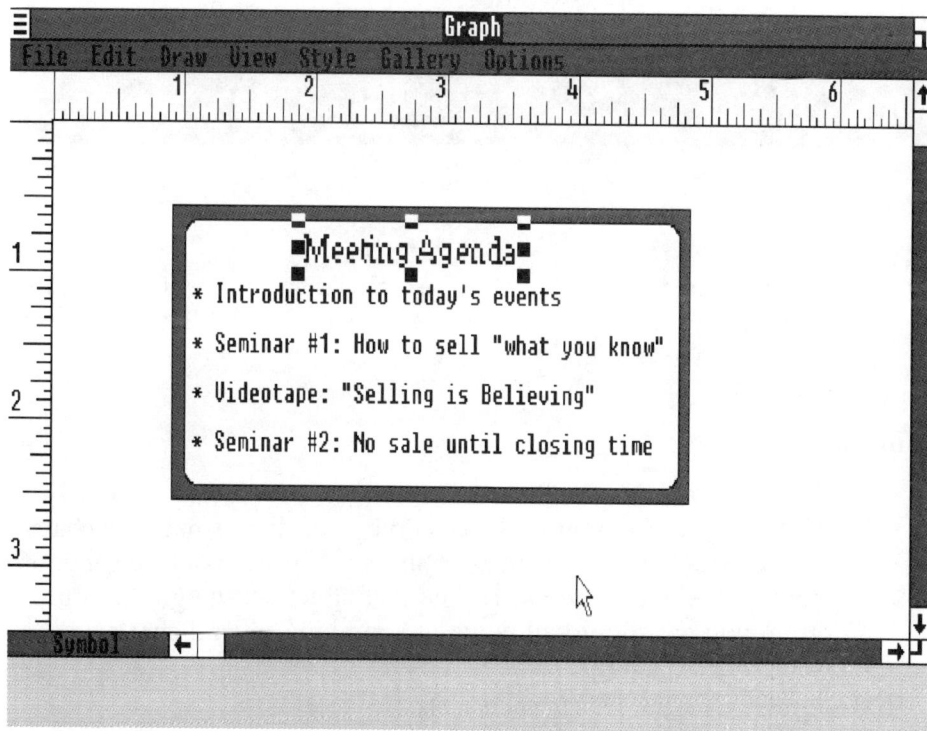

Figure 5-3.
Text chart.

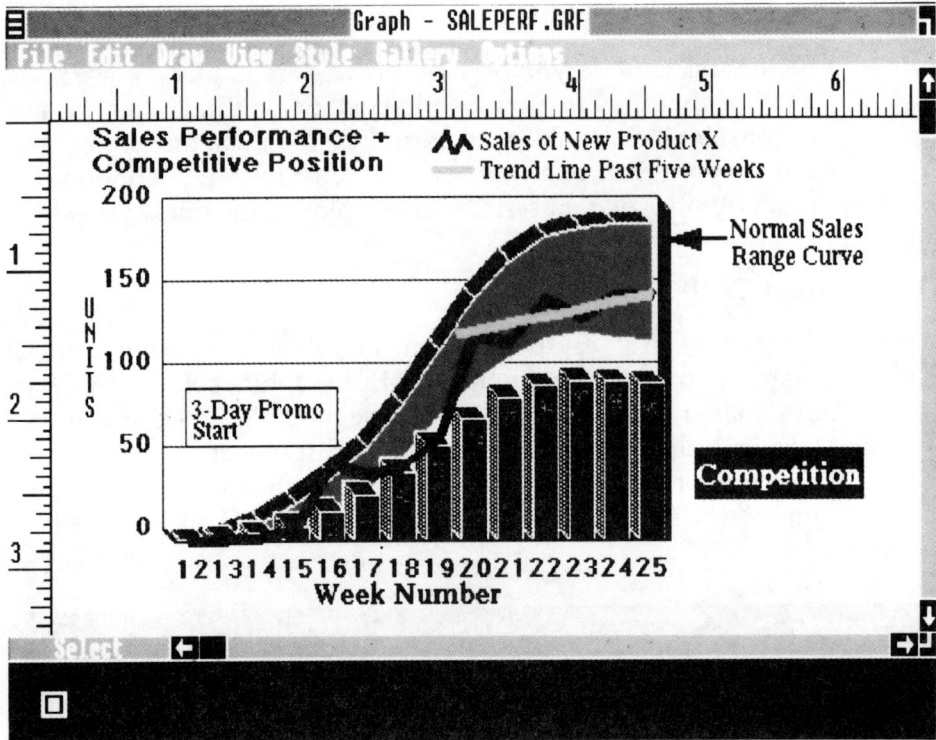

Figure 5-4.
Combo charts.

stand-alone program for this. Text charts should be limited to no more than six lines of six words each, so you can fill up the frame with large lettering.

Combining Charts

You can't always fit all the information you want to convey in a single chart. You might, for example, plot three small line charts side by side, as in Figure 5-4, to show the growth of three of your company's departments. To be most effective, the graphics program you get should allow you to combine several charts on the screen or on a page.

Number of Data Series

Presentation graphics programs are limited not only in the variety of charts they produce, but in the number of data series per chart they can accept (one data series is a complete set of numbers, not the numbers themselves). Look for a program that can accept no fewer than six data series for bar and column charts, and a dozen or so for line charts.

Data Interchange

If you regularly plot lots of data created by a spreadsheet, inventory, or a database program, you should consider automatically transferring the data from these applications to your graphics program. You'll save time in the long run and you'll be plagued with fewer errors.

In order for the graphics software to accept the numbers from the alien program, the data must be in a format it can understand. The simplest program lets you "cut and paste" tabular numerical data. You cut the data out of the source program and paste it into the graphics program. Most spreadsheet, accounting, and database programs generate tabular data. Most programs that operate under the Windows environment allow easy cut-and-paste transfer of data.

Many of the more advanced graphics programs can read the data file generated by your other software. Following are a number of file formats used:

- DIF, which stands for data interchange format, is used by many electronic spreadsheet and data management programs. It was popularized by VisiCalc, the first electronic spreadsheet program. If your program normally saves files in a proprietary format, it may also be able to store the data in a DIF file, for use with the presentation graphics software.

- WKS and WK1 are worksheet documents prepared by Lotus 1-2-3, Symphony, and a number of other electronic spreadsheet programs.

- SYLK is used by most Microsoft electronic spreadsheet and data management programs. It is similar to DIF in that it is a special file format not normally used by the applications program. It can be used when you want to transfer data from one program to another.

- TIFF is a graphics interchange format used by many page scanner and page layout programs. It is also supported by a number of presentation graphics programs.

- PostScript is a printing language used with many laser printers. A PostScript file format can be created in one program (such as a drawing package) and attached to the presentation graphics program.

Numerical Analysis

You may save all the number crunching you do for your electronic spreadsheet program, but it's nice to have a business graphics program that can analyze the data you've fed it, and provide a visual representation of that analysis.

At the very least, the program should be able to compute trends, as shown in Figure 5-5. All the program is doing is averaging the numbers. It's a simple task for the computer, a time-consuming one for you. If you deal in stocks, you may want to

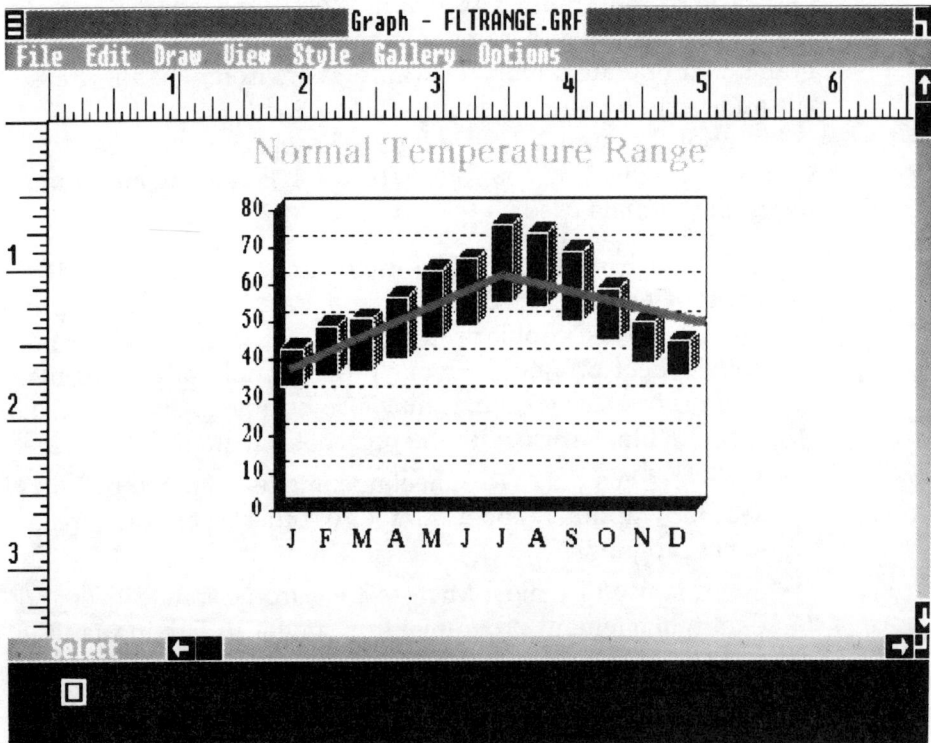

Figure 5-5.
Trend line.

consider a moving average, one that allows you to track only the latest 20 or 30 numbers.

For more elaborate work, you'd need a program that can do linear regressions, fitted exponential curves, standard deviations, correlation coefficients, cumulative sums, and the others in the long and sometimes tedious list of statistical analysis.

Freehand Drawing

Most of the charts you create with your graphics program will be ready to show, with no alteration required. With others, you may want to add a flourish here and there, such as change the columns in a column chart to coins, place a picture behind an area chart, or add a frame around the entire graph. To do this, you'll need a program that allows freehand drawing.

A growing number of presentation graphics programs offer the ability to add graphic elements to the basic chart. If your presentation graphics program lacks this feature, you can use a stand-alone painting or drawing program.

Clip Art and Symbol Libraries

Many graphics programs—presentation, painting, and drawing—come with or have available a selection of clip art, ready-made images you can include in your own charts. A sampler is shown in Figure 5-6. You can edit the clip art (erase parts, change colors, and so forth) to fit your requirements. A number of independent companies offer additional clip art libraries, with hundreds of images per disk. Just make sure the clip art files are compatible with your painting program.

Design Flexibility

You don't want to be restricted to a certain chart design or layout. Steer away from programs that let you assign a chart type, enter numbers, and little else. To be an effective chart maker, you'll want full control over the placement, size, and type style of the title, X- and Y-axis labels, annotation, and other text. You'll also want to be able to freely choose the patterns, symbols, and colors used in your charts.

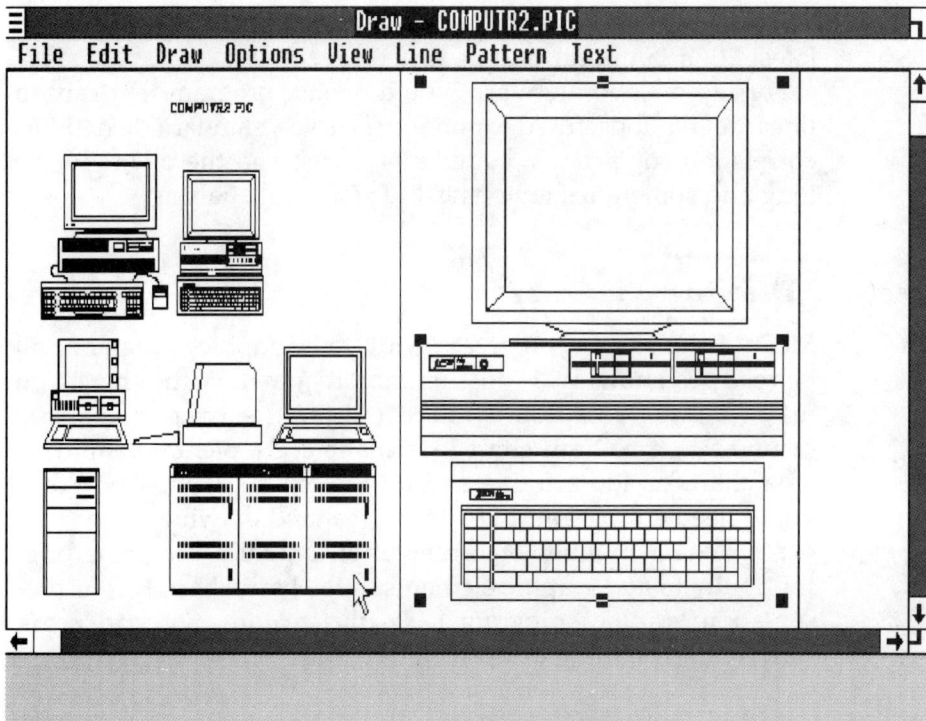

Figure 5-6.
Clip art enhanced graph.

Presentation Features

Creating business graphics is only half the game. Showing them to your associates is the other. If you plan on presenting your charts personally to an audience, consider using your computer as a slide carousel. For this your graphics program must have a "slide show" feature. If it does not, you'll need a separate software package to do the job.

The simplest type of slide show program merely steps through the charts you've created. A script you write before the presentation tells the program which charts to use, and in what order. The presentation can be either free-running, with a predetermined delay between each slide change, or interactive, requiring you to press keys to advance each frame.

The more elaborate business graphics and slide show programs offer Hollywood-style special effects. Instead of cutting from one chart to another, you can slowly fade from one to the other.

Presentation features, and how to use them, are covered in detail in Chapter 10.

Driving the Program

The more features a graphics program has, the more complex it is to use. Like any computer program, there are several techniques used for interacting with graphics software. *Command-driven programs*, where you type in a string of keywords to control the program, were popular a few years ago. But they're becoming rare today. Command-based programs are difficult to learn, and it's almost impossible to remember all the commands, especially if you don't regularly use the software.

Menu-driven programs are now the most popular because they present all or nearly all the possible command choices right on the screen. Many of the menu-driven programs use pop-up or pull-down menus, as shown in Figure 5-7, that appear after you

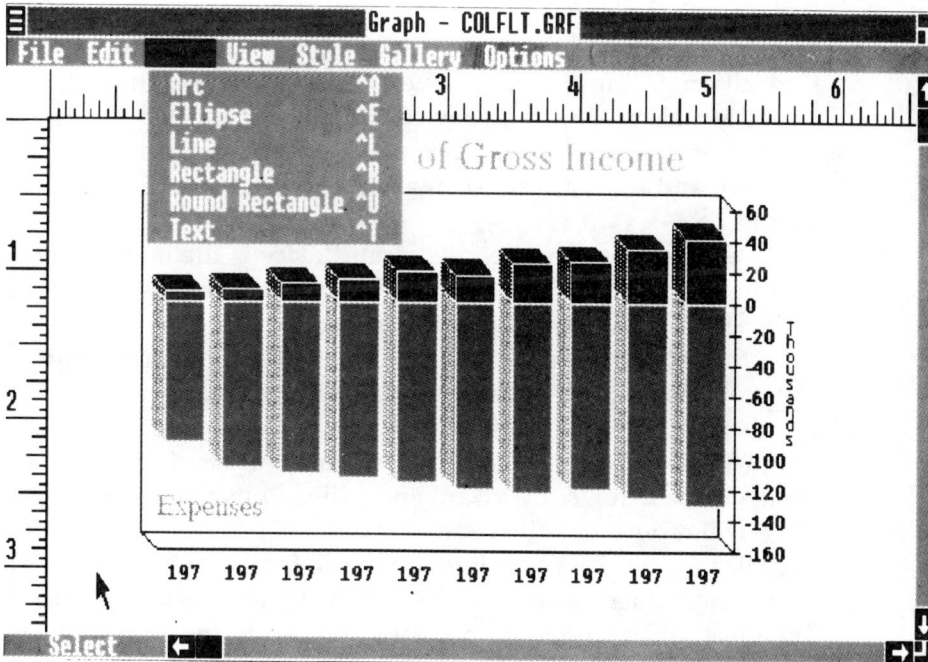

Figure 5-7.
Sample menu.

strike a certain key. You can then choose from among the list by pressing a key on the keyboard.

Alternate Input Support

Many of the latest presentation graphics programs let you use an *alternate input device* to control them, such as touch tablets, mice, and light pens to draw with a computer. If you're going to be doing a lot of graphics work, especially freehand embellishment, you should consider getting a program that supports a mouse or other alternate input devices. Of course, your computer must be able to use one of these devices.

Mouse Basics

An increasing number of graphics programs require the use of an alternate input device. Even those programs that don't need an alternate input device are greatly assisted by one. Commands are more easily made, graphics are more readily drawn, and the software seems like a natural extension of the hand.

The most popular alternate input device is the mouse, first pioneered by Xerox in the 1970s. The mouse, as shown in Figure S5-1, is standard equipment on many computers, including the Apple Macintosh and IIGS, the Commodore Amiga, and others, but it is extra on the IBM PC and compatibles.

Using a mouse requires a period of adjustment. Those accustomed to using a keyboard for data entry and commands may find the mouse awkward and stifling, but continued practice will reduce the objections.

Mice for the PC come in many basic forms. Apart from the inner workings (discussed elsewhere in this chapter), mice connect to the computer in a variety of ways, including:

- *Controller board*. You install a board in one of the expansion slots in your computer. The mouse then connects to the board.

- *Serial port.* The mouse connects to one of the serial ports installed in your computer.

- *Mouse socket connector* (IBM PS/2 computers only). The mouse, equipped with a special round connector, attaches to the mouse port jack on the back of the computer.

The IBM PC and compatibles are not specifically designed to work with alternate input devices like the mouse. So even if you have a mouse connected to the computer, it will not operate without a driver program. The driver program is installed into the computer's memory either when the computer first starts or when you run a program.

To have the driver automatically load when you start the computer, place the name of the driver program in the AUTO-EXEC.BAT file. For example, if the driver is named MOUSE.COM, place "MOUSE" on a line by itself in the AUTOEXEC.BAT file on your DOS disk or hard disk. Your PC DOS manual explains how to do this. Alternatively, you can enter the name of the mouse driver each time you want it loaded into the computer.

Some mouse drivers are system device files. These have names such as MOUSE.SYS and are placed in the CON-FIG.SYS file of your DOS disk or hard disk. You cannot manually load a .SYS file by typing its name from the keyboard.

Mice for the PC and clones have from one to three control buttons. Most presentation graphics software use only one or two buttons; the third (typically the middle one) is left unused. Many commands or functions require that you press two of the buttons at once (this is called *chording*). Be sure to press both buttons simultaneously, or the results may not be as expected.

Other software uses just one button. You select certain commands and functions by clicking a button (usually the left one) several times in rapid succession. This is called *double* or *triple clicking,* depending on the number of times you press the button. Double and triple clicking requires practice, too, or the software may not behave as you want. Carefully read the instruction manual that came with the program to learn the mouse techniques that you must use.

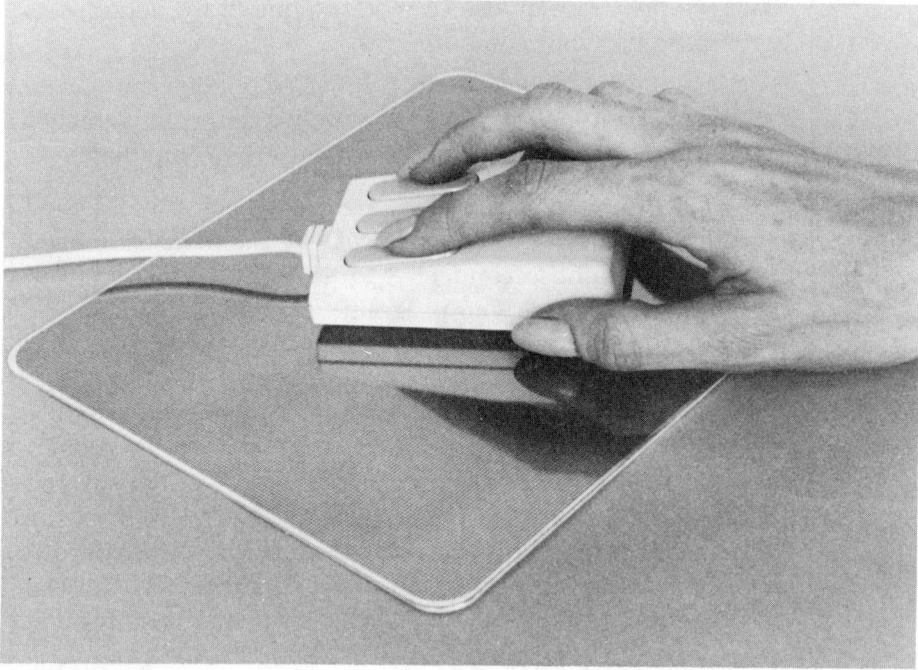

Figure S5-1.
Typical mouse.

Alternate Input Devices and How They Work

Here is how mice, light pens, and touch tablets work.

Mouse

There are two major types of mice: mechanical and optical.

- *Mechanical mouse.* The typical mechanical mouse is actually a *mechanical/optical hybrid*. When the mouse is moved across a flat surface, a ball in the underside rotates, turning two rollers. Attached to the roller is a disk with slits (called a *light chopper*). The light from a light emitting diode (LED) shines through the slits; a photodetector on the other side senses the on/off light beam pulses as the disk rotates, and provides this data to computer.

- *Optical mouse.* The optical mouse skids over a plastic pad. LEDs and photodetectors provide the sensing to pick up a series of fine hash marks in the pad.

Graphics Tablet

Four types of graphics tablets are in wide use: analog, digital, electrostatic, and potentiometer.

- *Analog.* Most low-cost analog touch tablets work by *resistance* (some by capacitance). A resistive wire micromesh forms a touch sensitive coating on the inside layer of two facing panels. Pressing anywhere on the face of the pad presses the layers together, creating a resistance. The computer reads the resistance and determines the correct point of contact.

- *Digital.* The digital pad has hundreds (and sometimes thousands) of *digital switches*—contact points that touch when the surface of the pad is depressed. The output of the switches are relayed to the computer for position processing.

- *Electrostatic.* A circuit sends sequential high-voltage pulses through a grid. When the stylus comes into contact with the pad, a coil in the tip of the stylus picks up a pulse through *induction*. The received pulse is sent through the stylus and to the computer via a connecting wire. The timing of pulse determines the point of contact on the pad.

- *Potentiometer.* Graphics tablets that use mechanical arms employ highly accurate *potentiometers* mounted in the joints of an arm. When the arm is moved, the resistance value of the potentiometer changes. This change is read by the computer as direction and distance of travel.

Light Pen

An *electron beam* in the video screen sweeps across the face of the tube hundreds of times each second. The sweep is from the left to the right and top to bottom (as viewed on the outside of the tube). A *photodetector* mounted in the tip of the light pen detects when the beam passes by and sends a pulse to the computer. The computer compares the pulse with the timing of the video beam and determines where the pen is located on screen.

Help!

Despite the claims of software publishers, no business graphics program is so simple that "a child could use it." If it's that simple, it probably lacks the features you want and need for your professional presentations. Learning how to use the program, and finding answers to your questions, are the domain of the instruction manual, on-line help screens (if any), and phone or mail customer support.

Manual

The printed instructions on how to use the program should be clear and concise, especially if many people in your office will be using it. A poorly written or unorganized manual means that it takes much longer to learn the program. Time isn't always on your side, and it's a poor business graphics program that demands too much of your time.

There is no absolute right and wrong way to write and present an instruction manual. Browse through the manuals of the graphics programs you're interested in, and note how ideas, concepts, and instructions are conveyed. Also note if the manual has:

- A table of contents
- Adequate illustrations
- A glossary
- An index
- A quick reference card or section

On-Line Help

On-line help—a sort of "manual on disk"—is useful whenever the real instruction manual isn't near and your question is a simple one. To call up the on-line help, you press a key, and instructions are flashed on the screen. On-line help comes in two general flavors: interactive and context-sensitive.

With interactive on-line help, you call up the help screen and choose a topic from a master menu. With context-sensitive on-line help, the program initially provides instructions for the task it thinks you're trying to accomplish. If it isn't the help you wanted, you can still call up the main menu and choose the topic manually. Context-sensitive on-line help saves time, but it isn't a necessity.

The text that goes along with the on-line help facility can easily fill up an entire disk. If the software you like has a help feature, see if the help files are on the same disk as the program. Otherwise, you may have to swap disks in and out of the computer's disk drives whenever you call for help.

Customer Support

Some questions can't be answered by a manual or the on-line help screens. You need outside assistance, and your dealer or the publisher of the program should be there to answer your questions. Since it's difficult for a dealer to know every software package he or she sells, you'll not likely get much technical help from your local computer store. The better source is the program publisher, who often maintains a staff for the express purpose of answering questions about the product.

Most software publishers maintain a phone-in customer support line. The line may be toll free, but most often, you'll have to foot the bill for the phone call.

A number of software publishers charge a fee for customer support. There's often no charge for the first 30 to 90 days of using the program; after that time, you pay a flat fee for each phone call you make. The rate varies, so make sure you get all the facts about customer support before you purchase the program.

System Requirements

Like people, no two business graphics programs are alike. And neither are the hardware requirements for making the program work. To get the most out of the program, make sure you have enough random access memory (RAM), the proper number and type of disk drives, the correct version of DOS, and compatible video controller boards, monitors, and printers.

RAM

Most presentation graphics programs require a minimum of 128K of RAM. If your computer doesn't have that much memory, you'll need to add it in order to use the program. If you use a RAM disk or print spooler software, you'll need enough memory to run the graphics program as well as some for storing RAM disk and print spooler data.

Disk Drives

Nearly all business graphics programs require two double-sided disk drives. Very few will work on a single-drive computer, and those that do usually require you to swap disks in and out of the drive during use. If you have a hard disk, you'll want to make sure the program can be copied to it. Some business graphics programs are copy protected and have no provision for transferring the program data to your hard disk.

Hard Disk

The complexity of some presentation graphics programs requires the use of a hard disk drive. The program comes with so many files that the software spans five or more floppy disks, and swapping the disks in and out of a drive is either inconvenient or not practical. If you don't already own a hard disk drive, you'll need to add one to your computer before you can adequately use the program. You can install the hard disk drive yourself or have your dealer do it.

DOS Version

The average business graphics program is designed to be used with PC-DOS version 2.X or 3.X. Check the manual that accompanies the program for more details. If the software requires DOS 2.0 (or later), earlier versions of DOS—such as 1.1—may not work properly with it. You'll need to invest in a later version to run the program.

Video Display Board

All business graphics programs require the use of a video display board capable of graphics. This includes:

- Hercules monochrome graphics adapter
- Color graphics adapter
- Enhanced graphics adapter
- Video graphics array adapter

You'll also need a suitable monochrome or color monitor. See Chapter 6 for more information about monitors and video display boards.

Printer and Plotter

Printers and plotters work by receiving writing or drawing codes from the computer. If it can't understand the code, it can't make

```
MC.COD           MC.DAT           MC.SYS           FONTLIST
CHART.COM        CHART.PIF        F00225.RFT       F00230.RFT
F00235.RFT       F04830.RFT       F04837.RFT       F04843.RFT
F06625.RFT       F06630.RFT       F06635.RFT       F13025.RFT
F13030.RFT       F13035.RFT       F001.SFT         F017.SFT
F033.SFT         F081.SFT         F129.SFT         F145.SFT
F209.SFT         MC.INI           6SHOOTER.GPD     AMPLOT.GPD
ANA6500.GPD      ANADEX.GPD       APLASER.GPD      APPLOT.GPD
CALMOD84.GPD     CDI.GPD          CI3500.GPD       CLRJET.GPD
COLORPRO.GPD     COLORSCR.GPD     DATP80X0.GPD     DATP80X1.GPD
DMP29.GPD        DMP40.GPD        EPSON.GPD        EPSONHI.GPD
FUJITSU.GPD      HERMES.GPD       HIEPSON.GPD      HIHERMES.GPD
HIHPLSR.GPD      HIHPLSR2.GPD     HIIBMCLR.GPD     HIIBMGR.GPD
HIIBMPRO.GPD     HIJX80.GPD       HILQ1500.GPD     HILQ2500.GPD
HINECP5.GPD      HITI850.GPD      HITI855.GPD      HP7470A.GPD
HP7475A.GPD      HP7510A.GPD      HP7550A.GPD      HPLSR.GPD
HTOSHCLR.GPD     IBMCLR.GPD       IBMGR.GPD        IBMPRO.GPD
IBMQUIET.GPD     IBMXY749.GPD     ITO8510A.GPD     ITO8510S.GPD
JX80.GPD         LASERGR.GPD      LQ1500.GPD       LQ2500.GPD
LTOSHCLR.GPD     MAGICORP.GPD     MATRIX.GPD       MP2000.GPD

TRANSFER LOAD filename: HP7510A.GPD              read only: Yes(No)
                 load:(All)Data Format
Enter filename or use direction keys to select from list
L1    List                         100% Free NL Microsoft Chart:
```

Figure 5-8.
Printer/plotter choices.

charts. Your presentation graphics program must be compatible with your printer or plotter and supply the proper operating code.

Most programs offer a menu of printers and plotters they are compatible with, such as that in Figure 5-8. You choose your model and the program takes care of supplying the proper operating codes. When choosing a graphics program, make sure your printer or plotter is on the list.

Printer/Plotter Driver

All printers and plotters require a software driver to reproduce graphics. The driver is the interface between the graphics software and the output device. The driver allows the charting program to be used with a nearly unlimited selection of printers and plotters.

Your presentation graphics must come with a driver for your brand and model of plotter or printer. If a driver is not included, consult your dealer or the publisher of the software. In many cases, a driver for another printer or plotter can be used. For example, many plotters use the Hewlett-Packard Graphics Language (HPGL) and are compatible with at least one of the HP plotters, such as the HP7575. If your plotter falls into this category, you may use the HP7475 driver.

Most laser printers have built-in emulation. Under software control, they emulate any number of popular printer types, including the Diablo 630 (daisywheel), Epson MX or FX (dot matrix), and Hewlett-Packard LaserJet. If you are using a laser printer, you must first set the proper emulation, say, to Epson FX series printer. The driver for the presentation graphics program will then be able to properly communicate with the printer.

C H A P T E R   6

Graphics Adapters and Monitors

E X E C U T I V E   S U M M A R Y

There are six popular graphics display adapter standards in use on the IBM PC and clones: monochrome display adapter, Hercules monochrome graphics adapter, color graphics adapter, enhanced graphics adapter, video graphics array, professional graphics adapter. Each type of adapter requires a special type of monitor.

The resolution for color graphics on the IBM PC begins at 320 by 200 pixels (for the color graphics adapter) and extends to 640 by 400 pixels (for the video graphics array). Up to 256 colors can be simultaneously shown on a video graphics array board (out of a possible palette of 262,144 hues).

Color RGB monitors are the best choice for all-around graphics/text work because they provide color and the clearest picture. Video bandwidth and dot pitch play an important role in the sharpness of the image displayed on a monitor.

Imagine going through life cross-eyed and short-sighted—without the benefit of corrective lenses. Yet millions of computer users spend countless hours behind an ill-fitting computer monitor, staring at blurred letters and smeared colors. No wonder most users complain of eye fatigue, nausea, and headaches after spending the better part of the morning crouched behind a computer.

If you're serious about graphics work on your IBM PC or compatible, you need the right monitor. That monitor, in turn, must be connected to the proper type of display adapter board. You'll find all you need to know about how to choose the best display adapter board and monitor in this chapter. The IBM PC and clones offer many alternatives, and you must carefully weigh each choice based on your needs. If you already have a monitor and display adapter, read this chapter to make sure they are compatible with your presentation graphics software.

Video Display Adapters

With the exception of the IBM PS/2 computers, the IBM PC requires a separate *video display adapter* to connect to a monitor. The computer itself has no means to interface to a display. One such display adapter board is shown in Figure 6-1.

There are five main types of display adapters and all but one are suitable for graphics work:

- Monochrome display adapter
- Hercules monochrome graphics adapter
- Color graphics adapter
- Enhanced graphics adapter
- Video graphics array

Note that there are more display adapter types than the six listed above. However, these represent the adapters that are supported by most presentation graphics programs. If you choose another adapter type, be sure it works with your monitor and software. A listing of features and capabilities of each type of board is provided in Table 6-1. With all display boards, the proper monitor must be used or no picture will result. In some cases, using a monitor with the wrong kind of display board will ruin the board and monitor!

Figure 6-1.
Sample display adapter.

Monochrome Display Adapter

The *monochrome display adapter (MDA)* was first introduced when the IBM PC came out in 1981. It has no provisions for graphic display except for a series of special text characters (these characters are sometimes used in certain software programs to draw boxes, lines, etc.). The MDA is not suitable for use with presentation graphics software. If your computer has this adapter, it must be exchanged for one of the types listed below.

Hercules Monochrome Graphics Adapter

The *Hercules monochrome graphics adapter (HMGA)* is an MDA with the added provision of graphics capability. The graphics are in monochrome only but at high resolution of 720 by 384 picture elements (pixels). About 50 percent of the presentation graphics

Table 6-1.
Display Board Cross Reference.

Table 6-1. Display Adapter Modes and Attributes

Monochrome Display Adapter (MDA) Display Modes

Mode	Type	Colors	Resolution	Text Cell	Text Layout	Comments
7	Text	Mono	720 x 350	9 x 14	80 x 25	

Color Graphics Adapter (CGA) Display Modes

Mode	Type	Colors	Resolution	Text Cell	Text Layout	Comments
0 & 1	Text	16	320 x 200	8 x 8	40 x 25	
2 & 3	Text	16	640 x 200	8 x 8	80 x 25	
4 & 5	Graphics	4	320 x 200	8 x 8	40 x 25	
6	Graphics	2	640 x 200	8 x 8	80 x 25	

Enhanced Graphics Adapter (EGA) Display Modes

Mode	Type	Colors	Resolution	Text Cell	Text Layout	Comments
0 & 1	Text	16	320 x 200	8 x 8	40 x 25	
2 & 3	Text	16	640 x 200	8 x 8	80 x 25	
4 & 5	Graphics	4	320 x 200	8 x 8	40 x 25	
6	Graphics	2	640 x 200	8 x 8	80 x 25	
7	Text	Mono	720 x 400	9 x 16	80 x 25	
B	Font loading internal mode					
C	Font loading internal mode					
D	Graphics	16	320 x 200	8 x 8	40 x 25	
E	Graphics	16	640 x 200	8 x 8	80 x 25	
F	Graphics	Mono	640 x 350	8 x 16	80 x 25	
10	Graphics	16	640 x 350	8 x 14	80 x 25	
13	Graphics	16	320 x 200	8 x 8	40 x 25	Extended mode
14	Graphics	16	640 x 200	8 x 8	80 x 25	Extended mode
16	Graphics	16	640 x 350	8 x 14	80 x 25	with minimum 128K

Video Graphics Array (VGA) Display Modes

Mode	Type	Colors	Resolution	Text Cell	Text Layout	Comments
0 & 1	Text	16	360 x 400	9 x 16	40 x 25	40 x 25
2 & 3	Text	16	720 x 400	9 x 16	80 x 25	80 x 25
4 & 5	Graphics	4	320 x 200	8 x 8	80 x 25	Double-scanned to 320 x 400
6	Graphics	2	640 x 200	8 x 8	80 x 25	Double-scanned to 640 x 400
7	Text	Mono	720 x 400	9 x 16	80 x 25	80 x 25
B	Font loading internal mode					
C	Font loading internal mode					
D	Graphics	16	320 x 200	8 x 8	40 x 25	Double-scanned to 320 x 400
E	Graphics	16	640 x 200	8 x 8	80 x 25	Double-scanned to 640 x 400
F	Graphics	Mono	640 x 350	8 x 16	80 x 25	
10	Graphics	16	640 x 350	8 x 14	80 x 25	
11	Graphics	2	640 x 480	8 x 14	80 x 25	
12	Graphics	16	640 x 480	8 x 16	80 x 25	
13	Graphics	256	320 x 200	8 x 8	80 x 25	Double-scanned to 320 x 400

Table 6-1 (Continued)

Special Modes

Mode	Type	Colors	Resolution	Text Cell	Text Layout	Comments
8	PCjr graphics	16	160 x 200	--	--	
9	PCjr graphics	16	320 x 200	8 x 8	40 x 25	
A	PCjr graphics	4	640 x 200	8 x 8	80 x 25	
15	Graphics	Mono	720 x 348	8 x 14	80 x 25	Hercules EGA mode

43 lines EGA 50 lines VGA 8 x 8 cell

programs support the HMGA board. Hercules pioneered the standard, but compatible boards are now available from other manufacturers.

Color Graphics Adapter

The *color graphics adapter (CGA)* came out with the MDA when the IBM PC was first introduced and was designed to satisfy the educational and home markets. The CGA has two modes: text and graphics. In graphics mode, the board displays monochrome alphanumeric characters and graphics with a resolution of 640 by 200 pixels. In full-color mode, the board has a resolution of 320 by 200 pixels and can display a maximum of four colors. Those four colors are out of a total palette of 16 hues. The CGA is supported by nearly all presentation graphics programs.

Enhanced Graphics Adapter

The *enhanced graphics adapter (EGA)* offers higher resolution than the CGA, and more colors. EGA boards come with different amounts of memory, from 64K RAM to 256K RAM. With a full 256K RAM, an EGA board can display up to 16 colors simultaneously out of a total palette of 64 colors. Resolution is 640 by 350 pixels. The EGA is supported by most presentation graphics programs.

Some manufacturers make "super" EGA adapters that have extended resolution up to about 800 by 600 pixels. Many graphics programs support the super-high resolution mode, but a software driver is necessary to ensure compatibility.

EGA boards are *downward compatible* with the CGA. If the software cannot support EGA resolution, the display adapter shifts to CGA mode. Most all EGA boards have one or two RCA phono jacks, similar to the CGA adapters. However, these jacks do not provide composite video output, as found in the color graphics adapter. In most cases, the jacks are connected internally to an expansion bus on the EGA card.

Installing RAM Chips

The enhanced graphics adapter can support a maximum of 256K of random access memory (RAM). With 256K RAM, 16 colors can be displayed at the same time on the screen (out of a palette of 64 possible colors). Not all enhanced graphics adapters come with the full complement of 256K, but the extra memory can be easily installed in most boards. To upgrade the board, you install additional memory chips in empty integrated circuit sockets. There is no soldering involved and the process is relatively easy.

However, there are some caveats and general rules you should follow when installing RAM chips. Careless handling of the chips destroys them, and finding a faulty chip can be difficult. For best results, install the chips slowly and carefully the first time, and avoid problems. Here are the details.

Types of Memory Chips

EGA boards may accept either 64K-bit or 256K-bit memory chips (some use specialty RAM chips, but these boards are rare). Notice the word "bit." RAM is measured in the number of bits stored, not bytes. To calculate the bit capacity of a RAM chip into bytes, divide by 8. Refer to the documentation that came with your graphics adapter on the type of memory chips that are required.

Both the 64K-bit and 256-bit chips are further rated by their *access time*—the time it takes to deliver a piece of information to the computer when requested. Access times are expressed in *nanoseconds* (ns). Most graphics boards need RAM chips with an access time of 120 to 150 nanoseconds, or faster.

Avoid using RAM chips with access times of 200 nanoseconds or more.

Shop Wisely

Where you get the RAM chips will largely determine how much money you'll save. Local computer dealers sell RAM chips but the cost can be high. Your best bet is a local electronics store or mail order electronic specialty companies. These mail order firms advertise in magazines such as *Radio-Electronics* and *Modern Electronics* and accept credit card and COD orders. Some addresses are given in Appendix C, Sources.

Shopping the electronics supply houses can be a bit confusing for the uninitiated. If you're having trouble finding what you want, call the company and you should be able to get courteous help.

If you're shopping the ads, you'll find that most of the bigger ads list the various components under separate headings. You'll locate what you want under "Dynamic RAMs." If you find no such heading, look for the notation 4164 (for 64K-bit chips) or 41256 (for 256K-bit chips). These numbers may also have a suffix, such as -20 or -15. These suffixes indicate the access time of the chip. For example, the number 4164-15 indicates a 64K-bit chip with a 150-nanosecond access time.

Installing the Chips

Before opening the protective plastic bag holding the RAM chips, be sure to discharge any static electricity from your body by touching the metal chassis of a grounded appliance. Static can destroy the innards of a RAM chip.

To install the chip, first locate the *clocking notch* cut into one end of the IC. You'll need to line this notch up with another notch in the empty socket. If you reverse the chip in the socket, and turn the power to your computer on, you'll damage the chip and it will have to be replaced.

Grasp the chip by its plastic edges—not by its metal leads—and gently insert it into the socket. Apply even downward pressure. If the chip starts to go in crooked, gently lift it back out and try it again. If you've having trouble seating the chip into the socket, gently rock it back and forth to ease it all the way in. Sometimes, the leads of the IC will be bent slightly outward and won't fit into the socket. If this is the case, gently squeeze the leads together a bit with your fingers. If, for some reason, you must take the chip out of the socket, grasp the chip by the ends and pull up. You may need to pry a stubborn chip out of the socket with a nail file.

Of course, there are special tools for inserting and removing RAM chips. Radio Shack sells an IC inserter remover; other stores carry a similar tool. The tools make the job of plugging in your own RAM chips more convenient. The tool can easily pay for itself by avoiding costly damage.

Before you close up your computer, double-check your work. If you're not filling up all the sockets, are you sure you used the right ones for the amount of memory you're adding? Are the chips all the way in their sockets? Is their orientation correct—notch matches notch? If all seems okay, you can put your computer back together, and turn it on.

Video Graphics Array

The *video graphics array (VGA)* is built into the IBM PS/2 computers and is also available as an add-on board for the IBM PC and compatibles. The VGA has many modes and resolutions, up to 640 by 480 pixels and 16 colors. When displaying medium-resolution graphics (320 by 200 pixels), the VGA can output up to 256 colors out of a total palette of 262,144 hues.

The VGA adapter requires its own special type of monitor that can operate at a horizontal frequency of 31.49 kHz, with either analog or digital signals. Some monitors are expressly designed for use with VGA boards, although the trend is toward using a multiple frequency monitor (see below) that can adjust the proper horizontal and vertical frequency rates.

As with the EGA board, the VGA is downward compatible with both the CGA and EGA standards. To maintain the proper aspect ratio when displaying lower resolution graphics, the VGA board *double scans* each horizontal line. Instead of displaying the standard 640 by 200 pixels of the CGA, for example, the VGA displays 640 by 400 pixels.

> ## *Horizontal and Vertical Frequency*
>
> All monitors operate at specific frequencies. These frequencies are important—the higher the frequency, the greater the bandwidth; so the more resolution the monitor has.
>
> CGA monitors have a *horizontal frequency* (also called the scan rate or line rate) of about 15.75 kHz (kilohertz, or 15.75 thousand times per second). Horizontal frequency rates of 18 to 30 kHz are used for EGA and VGA boards. The video frequency of the monitor must exactly match the video frequency signal put out by the computer, or serious incompatibility problems can result.
>
> Monitors are also rated by their *refresh rate*, or vertical frequency. The typical monitor has a refresh rate of 60 Hz, although some higher resolution types have refresh rates of 70 Hz.

Other Display Board Types

The *professional graphics adapter (PGA)* provides all the functions of VGA boards, in addition to some added modes. The PGA standard was developed by IBM and released at the same time as the EGA board, but its cost has prevented it from becoming a popular standard.

Some low-end IBM PS/2 computers use a *multicolor graphics adapter (MCGA)*. This is a limited subset of the VGA adapter, offering much the same as the standard CGA board but also 320 by 200 pixels with 256 simultaneous colors. The extra colors require an analog monitor.

A few third-party companies, including Tseng Labs and Plantronics, have developed graphics boards that have caught on to some degree with software developers. Both of these boards require special monitors (or a multiple frequency monitor, as discussed later in this chapter) and a software driver.

How They Work

The operation of a graphics display adapter is relatively simple. First, the board intercepts a stream of code produced by the computer. This code, in turn, is translated into a visual signal by the electronics on the controller.

In essence, data from the computer is in the form of coordinates (such as 75, 100), which means that there is to be a pinpoint of light on the TV screen 75 spaces from the left and 100 spaces from the top. It is the job of the controller to translate data coordinates into a visual signal—bits and bytes into pinpoints of light.

In the case of a color image, the computer sends out the same data coordinates, but in sets of three. To produce a given color, the three primary TV colors—red, green, and blue—are mixed together. The final job of the graphics controller is to deliver a clean, sharp picture to a compatible monitor.

It is important to keep in mind that with presentation graphics, the resolution of the image you see on the monitor is usually far less than the resolution you'll see printed on paper. This is especially true if the graph is printed with a laser printer or high-quality color pen plotter (both discussed in detail in Chapter 7). The graph you see on the monitor can have jagged lines and pale color, but when printed out, the lines will be smooth and the colors rich and bold.

Combination Boards

A number of graphics adapter boards include some or all of the five display types mentioned above. A common board is the *4-in-1 EGA adapter*. This board includes:

- Monochrome graphics adapter
- Hercules monochrome graphics adapter
- Color graphics adapter
- Enhanced graphics adapter

You may select the mode of operation either by setting a set of switches and/or jumpers on the 4-in-1 board or via software, depending on the adapter. You may use up to two different types of single-frequency monitors, such as a monochrome and EGA monitor, or you may use a multiple-frequency monitor (see the section below).

How to Choose a Graphics Adapter Board

Just like buying a new car, picking the best graphics adapter board means looking for the important elements that make it a worthwhile product. It also means asking a lot of questions and doing some detective work. Does the board run smoothly? Does it seem well made? Does it appear as if the dealer will support it? Does it do everything you need it to do? A *no* to any of these queries should steer you to another choice. Here's what to look for in a solid, reliable graphics adapter board, and why it pays to choose carefully.

Features and More Features

You already know that there are several standards of graphics adapter boards—Hercules monochrome graphics, CGA, EGA, and VGA. The board you buy must be compatible with the software you are using and with your computer monitor.

In addition to the graphics standard, there are additional features found in many display boards. EGA boards come with installed memory of between 64 and 256K. With 256K, you can view up to 16 colors simultaneously. Most EGA boards let you install additional memory, but not all do. If the board has less than 256K, and you think you may want to have the full color feature someday, be sure that additional memory chips can be added.

Most all CGA and EGA boards have a built-in interface for a light pen. If you plan on using a light pen, be sure the board has the proper connector on it. The connector can't be easily added to a board that lacks light pen compatibility.

The Quality Goes in . . .

Not all graphics adapter boards are quality-made products. If you look carefully, you can spot many manufacturing defects. To inspect the board, hold it by the edges only, and look first on its *back* side, the part that has no components on it. What you should see is a collection of bright, silver solder joints, with perhaps a bit of the metal leads of the components peeking through.

You *shouldn't* see lots of tiny wires coursing through the back side. These "jumpers" are signs of a hurried board design, or a design that proved faulty when the boards were manufactured. Likewise, there shouldn't be too much of the component leads sticking through the solder. The longer the lengths of the leads, the more chance that some of the leads will bend and touch one another, possibly causing severe damage to the board and your computer.

The components on the graphics board are soldered onto the foil. The *foil* is a thin sheet of copper that serves as the "wires" for the circuit board. Some of these joints may be incomplete. With an incomplete joint, there's either no solder at all, or the solder doesn't touch the component lead or foil.

If the board doesn't seem to be working properly, you can sometimes spot an incomplete soldering job by jiggling the components one by one and watching for the ones that are loose. Another common problem is excessive solder applied to the board. This can lead to solder "bridges," which effectively short out the board, rendering it useless. You can detect bridges that have been caught by the manufacturer by looking for spots on the back of the board that look scraped. A couple of scrapes won't mean anything, but if the board you're interested in has lots of scrapes, it reveals poor workmanship.

Next, visually inspect the components on the board. Unless they're designed otherwise, all the components should be flush with the board. Many expansion boards are double-sided, that is, they have been soldered on both the component and lead sides. Inspect the solder joints on the component side as you did before.

Test Driving

If the graphics board looks satisfactory (as most will), it's time to test drive it. Ideally, this should be done at the dealer's. This makes it easier to choose another board if you run into a problem, or decide that you don't like the product after all.

With the dealer's help, if possible, try out the board and

make sure each of its functions work. Use it with a monitor that supports the functions of the board, including extra colors or resolution.

A Question of Support

You may need some help getting your new graphics board properly installed in your computer. Take a look at the manual that accompanies the board to see if installation seems like something you can handle. Most boards are easy to install and you probably won't have any trouble with yours. But a few may come with bad documentation, or require unusual installation. If so, it's best to seek the help of a pro.

If you purchased the board from a dealer, ask the dealer to install it in your computer. You'll have to bring your computer into the store for this, of course, since few dealers offer on-site service. The dealer may charge you for installing the board, but it shouldn't be more than $25 to $40.

If you can't get a dealer to help, or don't want to pay the installation fee, seek out the advice of a knowledgeable friend, or attend a local users' group meeting and ask for help. The members of most users' groups are more than happy to lend a helping hand, and they're often more knowledgeable about computers than dealers.

Good after-sales support is important, particularly if you have a problem with the graphics adapter later on. You'll want a dealer who will provide answers to your questions, offer assistance when something doesn't work right, and help you repair the board if something breaks.

If a reliable dealer isn't around, you'll have to contact the manufacturer for help. Some expansion board makers don't have a customer support telephone line; so if you don't have a dealer to refer to, you'll be out of luck. The moral: If you aren't going to buy the board through a dealer, at least make sure you can contact the manufacturer in case of trouble.

For your peace of mind, try out the support number *before* you purchase the board. If the number is out of order, or you can't get a straight answer to even a simple question, you'll know to stay clear of that graphics adapter.

Installing a Graphics Adapter Board

Imagine an automobile where you can switch the transmission from manual to automatic, add another two or three cylinders to the engine, or change the body of the car from a hard top to a convertible. You can't do that with any car yet invented, but the same idea has already come to computers—in the form of expansion boards.

The graphics adapter is one such expansion board that lets you change the characteristics of your computer. You can "redesign" your computer without needing a service technician, soldering iron, or complex set of schematics. Keep these tips in mind when installing a graphics adapter card.

Work Area

Before you install a graphics adapter in your computer, make sure you have plenty of elbow room. Working in a cramped space invites trouble. Work only at a well-lit table, covered with carpeting or soft fabric. A sheet of antistatic foam, if you have it, is even better. Before working inside the computer, *be sure that the power to the computer is off and that the AC cord is unplugged.* This is vitally important for both you and your computer.

Starting Work

The cover of the PC and some PC compatibles is fastened by screws. Remove them using the proper type screwdriver. An increasing number of PC clones have flip-up tops, so no screwdriver is required.

The integrated circuits (ICs) and other components on the board can be damaged by static electricity. You carry with you a static charge wherever you go (even if the weather isn't dry), so before you take your computer apart or handle the board, first discharge the static from your body. The best way is to touch the metal chassis of any grounded appliance.

Switch Settings

Most graphics adapters need to be configured before you can install them inside your computer. Almost all boards use one of two methods for changing their operating characteristics: miniature DIP switches or jumpers.

- DIP switch blocks look like integrated circuits with tiny switches on top.
- Jumpers are removable plastic and metal tabs that sit astride two connector pins.

No matter what your board uses, read the instructions carefully on how to set the DIP switches or jumpers to conform to your computer and setup. Many of the EGA boards available let you define the *initial start-up mode*—whether the board behaves as a monochrome adapter, CGA, or EGA when you first turn it on. Other switches or jumpers let you select the type of monitor you are using. Be sure to set this switch correctly if you are using a TTL monochrome monitor. This type of monitor can be *severely damaged* if the board is set to CGA or EGA operation.

Depending on the type of board you install, you may need to reset some of the DIP switches in your computer (there are no switches in the IBM AT or clones or IBM PS/2 computers). On the IBM XT and clones, there is one set of eight DIP switches. Switch numbers 5 and 6 tell the computer which type of display adapter and monitor is installed. For most graphics adapters, set the switches as shown in Figure S6-1. A number of multimode EGA boards require that you set both switches to the OFF position.

Installing the Board

Once you've set up your board and compter to accept the graphics adapter, you can install it in an empty expansion slot. With the IBM PC or clone, you can put just about any board in any slot. Your only restriction will be the length of interconnecting cables and the placement of other boards.

If you're installing a full-length card into an IBM PC or clone, remove the bracket cover beside the slot you've chosen to use. If the board came with a plastic card guide, attach it to

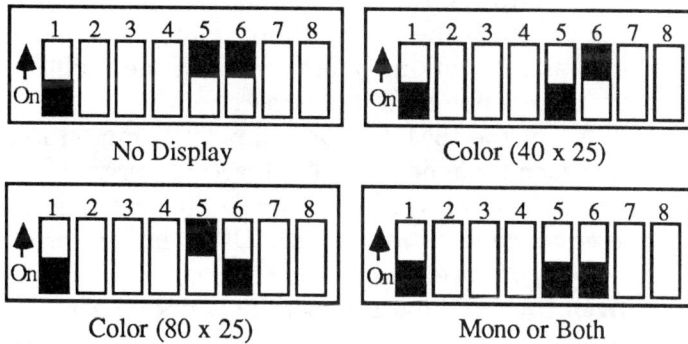

Figure S6-1.
DIP switch settings.

the inside chassis opposite the expansion slot that you are using.

Handle the board by the edges, making sure you don't touch the components or the narrow strips of metal on the edge connector. When inserting the board, be careful to line up the edge connectors of the card with the expansion slot. If the expansion slot has never held a board before, the contacts inside it may be unusually stiff. An extra measure of pressure may be required to seat the board inside the connector. Though you may need to press down to get the board into place, never force it. If you're having trouble inserting the board, look to see if there are any obstructions, and then try again.

Once the board is in place, press down firmly but gently to make sure the board is seated all the way into the connector. Then attach the mounting bracket to the chassis.

Testing

Before you close up the computer, inspect your handiwork and look for potential problems. Is the board all the way into the expansion slot? It should be. Are all the cables firmly attached? Make sure they are. Are there any brackets or other metal objects touching the card or computer circuit board? If so, correct the problem now.

If everything looks all right, replace the cover onto the computer, plug the AC cord back into the wall outlet, plug the monitor into the display adapter socket, and turn the computer on. With the PC and most clones you'll be notified if things aren't working properly when the built-in diagnostic tests sense a potential problem.

Users of the IBM AT (or compatible) must run a software utility each time the computer is reconfigured. The AT SETUP program lets you communicate to the computer the changes you've made to its insides. SETUP is entirely prompt driven, so it's easy to use.

Even if everything seems to be working satisfactorily, you should run your diagnostic software. The diagnostics will be able to check the memory, serial and parallel ports, graphics adapter, and so forth.

The final test is making sure that all your software works properly. Watch for any inconsistencies, like errors you've never encountered before or sluggish operation. If you find an operational problem, see if the manual included with the board has a troubleshooting section. Look up the problem there. If you can't pinpoint the problem check your installation one last time, and then refer to your dealer or the manufacturer.

Program Compatibility

Even though the VGA and EGA are downward compatible with lower resolution graphics standards, certain programs may not work with them. For example, an EGA board running in CGA mode may not work with a graphics program that sends the display information directly to the adapter, bypassing the computer's Basic Input/Output System (BIOS).

This direct link is favored by many programmers because it speeds up operation of the program, but it also causes serious compatibility problems. The moral: If the program is written specifically for a CGA or EGA board, it may not work with a higher resolution adapter. Check first to make sure or contact the publisher of the software.

Computer Compatibility

IBM PCs that left the factory prior to October 27, 1982 will not work with an EGA or VGA board. The BIOS contained on the motherboard of the computer will not recognize the EGA or VGA boards and must be replaced. You can order a replacement BIOS from any authorized IBM dealer, but you will have to remove the existing BIOS chip from the computer (your dealer can do it for you if you are unsure which chip it is). Your PC will then be useless until the new BIOS arrives.

Alternatively, you can purchase a PC-compatible BIOS from most any dealer that distributes computer and electronic parts (check the Yellow Pages). These BIOS chips are used in PC compatibles, and many are quite good. Imagine—using a clone BIOS in a real IBM PC! If you are not sure of the age of your PC, you can readily check it using a program such as Mace Utilities or Norton Utilities.

Types of Monitors

There are three major types of graphics monitors to choose from, enabling you to better match the right monitor with the right job. The five major types of computer monitors are:

- Digital monochrome
- Color composite
- Color digital RGB
- Color analog RGB
- Multiple frequency color

A monitor cross-reference chart appears in Table 6-2.

Table 6-2.
Monitor Cross Referencing.

Table 6-2. Monitor and Attributes

Monitor Type	Input Signal(1)	Min. Resolution(2)	Horz. Sync Rate	Vert. Sync Rate	Min. Bandwidth(3)
Digital Monochrome	TTL	720 by 350	18.432 kHz	50 Hz	16 MHz
Color Composite	Analog	250 x 200	15.75 kHz	60 Hz	8 MHz
Color Digital RGB/CGA	TTL	640 x 200	15.75 kHz	60 Hz	14 MHz
Color Digital RGB/EGA	TTL	640 x 350	15.75 & 21.85 kHz	60 Hz	16 MHz
Color Analog RGB	Analog	640 x 350	15.75 kHz	60 Hz	16 MHz
VGA	TTL or Analog	720 x 480	31.49 kHz	70 Hz	30 MHz
Multiple Frequency Color(4)	TTL or Analog	720 x 480	15.5 - 35 kHz	50-70 Hz	30 MHz

Notes:
1. TTL = Transistor-to-Transistor Logic (digital signals)
2. Minimum resolution required to display text/graphics from display board
3. Minimum bandwith required to display text/graphics from display board
4. Typical monitor; models may vary

Digital Monochrome

In essence, a *digital monochrome* monitor is much like a black and white TV, but with several important differences. First, monochrome monitors can't tune into broadcast television channels. They can only receive signals from the computer they are hooked up to.

Second, not all monochrome monitors display white images on a black background. To reduce contrast, many monochrome monitors display green images on a black background. Other models are available with amber characters on a black background. These usually cost 10 to 20 percent more than green screen monitors, but in all other respects, are the same.

Third, monochrome monitors for the IBM PC and compatibles are designed to accept digital signals. These signals are transmitted from the display adapter and interpreted by the monitor as text or graphics.

Monochrome monitors can be used for business charting purposes provided you use a display adapter with Hercules graphics capability. A standard monochrome graphics adapter will not display graphics.

Composite Color

The *composite color* monitor is so-called because the signal they are designed to receive from the computer combines all the information necessary to display stable, color pictures. In operation, the three TV colors (red, green, and blue) are combined with synchronization pulses, the latter of which are required to prevent a rolling or jittery picture.

Composite monitors are about twice as expensive as the average monochrome models. In most cases, the more expensive units have a crisper, sharper look, and employ some type of auto-color correction circuitry. Most, but not all, have built-in audio amplifiers and speakers.

Color composite monitors can be used with most color graphics adapters. A RCA phono terminal on the back of the adapter is used to connect the computer to the monitor.

Color Digital RGB

Color composite monitors can't deliver fine detail in the images they show and are only moderately useful in business presentation graphics. Minute details, such as small text in a pie graph, don't show up well. The *color digital RGB* monitor provides clear, sharp pictures. The technical difference between RGB and composite monitors is a rather simple one, but the visual differences between the two are marked. Instead of separating the colors from a combined video signal, as composite models do, RGB monitors are designed to accept individual red, green, and blue color signals from the computer.

Depending on the type of display adapter used, digital RGB monitors are limited to displaying no more than 8 to 64 colors.

There are two subtypes of digital RGB monitors. One type operates with a horizontal frequency of 15.75 kHz and is designed to connect to a color graphics adapter. The monitor displays up to 16 colors. The other type operates with a horizontal frequency of 15.75 kHz in addition to 21.85 kHz. This type is made to work with an enhanced graphics adapter and displays up to 64 colors. You may use a 15.75 kHz frequency monitor with an EGA board, but you will be limited to CGA resolution and color.

Color Analog RGB

Many digital RGB monitors are restricted to displaying a maximum of 8 to 64 colors. When used with a color graphics adapter, for example (16 colors), each of the three colors is either on or off, or at half intensity.

Color analog RGB monitors can display many more colors—millions, in fact—because the signals being fed to it by your computer can be continuously variable, instead of just on and off, as shown in Figure 6-2. The video graphics array and professional graphics adapters are designed to work with either digital or analog RGB monitors. With the VGA adapter operating in analog mode, you can view up to 256 colors simultaneously on an analog RGB monitor. The total palette is 262,411 colors.

Most analog RGB monitors are dual-function: You can switch between analog and digital modes by flicking a switch.

Multiple Frequency Color

To suit a variety of needs, there are several *multiple frequency color* monitors available that automatically adjust to the horizontal and vertical scan frequencies generated by the graphics dis-

Digital RGB Monitor

1 0 0 1 1 0 1 0 0 1 1

Signal through
cable is digital --
composed of 1's
and 0's only

Connecting
Cable

Analog RGB Monitor

Signal through
cable is analog--
continuously
variable

Connecting
Cable

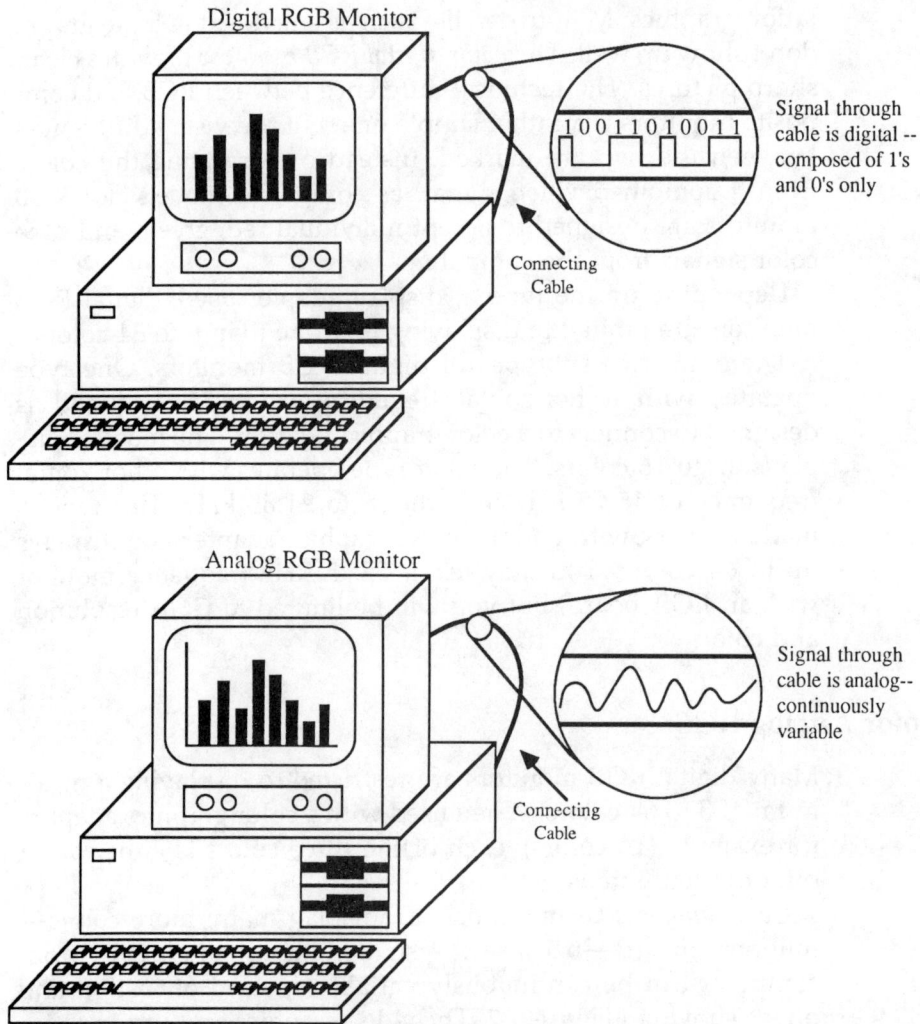

Figure 6-2.
Analog/digital signals to monitor.

play adapter. The operating limits vary from monitor to monitor, but typically span 15.5 to 35 kHz for the horizontal frequency rate and 50 to 70 Hz for the vertical scan frequency rate. This allows you to use one monitor for all the types of display adapter boards discussed in this chapter.

With most multiple frequency monitors, the frequency selection is automatic: You just plug the monitor into the display adapter and turn the computer on. The monitor automatically adjusts for the output frequencies of the display adapter board. With other models, you must manually select between operating frequencies.

Text Cells

When not displaying graphics, all the graphics boards revert to a *text mode*. The text characters are stored on the board and appear on the screen in a *text cell*, as shown in Figure 6-3. The size of this cell, and the arrangement of characters in the cell,

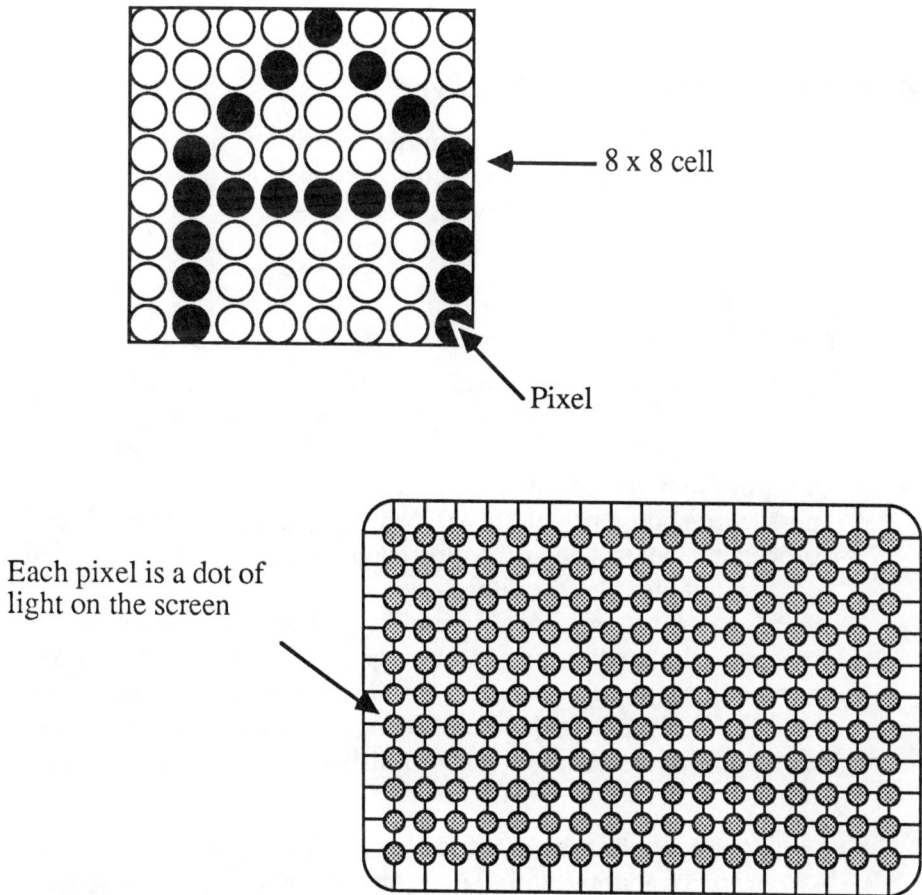

8 x 8 cell

Pixel

Each pixel is a dot of light on the screen

Figure 6-3.
Text cell.

determines how clear the characters are. Unless you plan to use your computer solely for graphics work, you should at least consider the clarity of the text display. If you use the display adapter and monitor in a text application, such as word processing, your eyes will tire if the characters are not fully formed.

Consult Table 6-1, above, for the size of the text cell in each display board. Also consider the type of monitor you are using. A monochrome monitor, or a monitor that has a *single-beam monochrome switch*, is best when viewing text. When using a color monitor in color mode, the text may lack a definite outline. The three TV colors (red, green, and blue) may not be perfectly aligned to make a white letter, and so the character appears blurred.

Choosing the Right Monitor Type

How do you know which monitor is best for your needs? Are there quality differences between various monitors of the same type? How do you know when you're getting a good monitor? Let's take each question in turn.

Which Monitor Is Best?

Your choice of monitor will depend on the kind of display adapter you have in your computer. If you have yet to select a display adapter, base your choice of monitor on your computer. Suppose that you use your computer mainly for producing business correspondence with a word processing program. Word processing doesn't require color or graphics, so a monochrome display adapter and monitor is suitable.

However, you're probably reading this book because you're interested in creating presentation graphics. While a color monitor is not absolutely necessary for business graphics work, it can be helpful, especially if you're using a color printer or plotter, and you want to see how the finished chart will look when printed.

- For monochrome graphics, use a Hercules monochrome graphics adapter and digital (or *TTL*) monochrome monitor.
- For color graphics, use a color graphics adapter, enhanced graphics adapter, or video graphics array board and a suit-

able monitor. For the greatest flexibility, invest in a multiple frequency monitor.

Quality Differences Among Monitors

With monitors, you get what you pay for. The average low-cost monochrome monitor, for example, delivers a far more inferior picture than a higher cost model. Spend a few extra dollars for a higher-end product, and you're almost assured of getting a crisper picture.

Picture Resolution

You'll be most concerned with the monitor's ability to display clear, sharp pictures. One important key to picture clarity is the monitor's *resolution*. A monitor with a high resolution can produce a cleaner, sharper picture than a monitor with a low resolution.

With computers, the term "resolution" usually refers to the number of individual pixels that are created to create an image. The resolution of the color graphics adapter is 640 horizontal by 200 vertical pixels, as shown in Figure 6-4. To adequately display

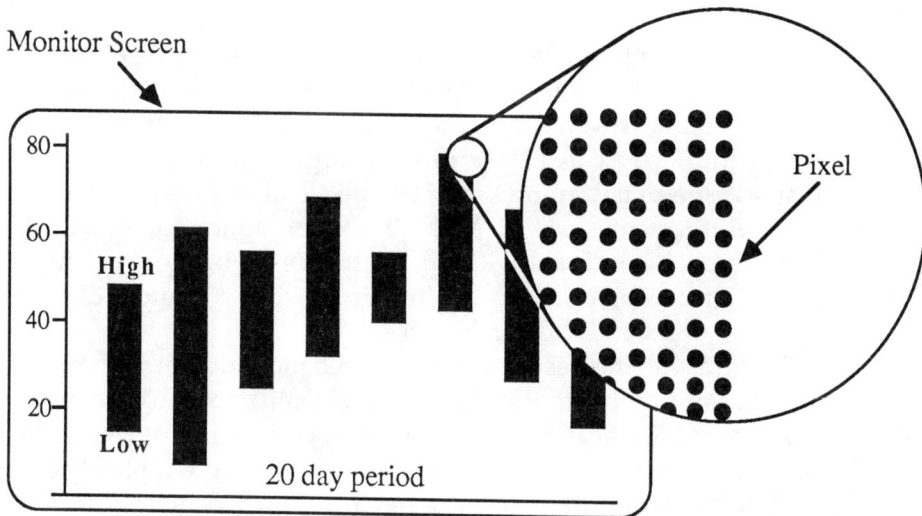

Figure 6-4.
Resolution matrix.

all the pixels in color and monochrome mode, you need a monitor with a resolution of *at least* 640 by 200 pixels. Any less and the pixels will smear into one another.

Many monochrome and color monitors don't display pixels as discrete dots of light, but rectangular bars. Resolution with these monitors is often quoted as lines rather than pixels. Still, the same rule of thumb applies: the higher the number of lines, the higher the resolution.

Bandwidth

The more pixels splashed on the face of the monitor, the higher the resolution, or sharpness, of the picture. But the *bandwidth* of a monitor is what controls the number of pixels that can be adequately displayed on the screen at once. Therefore, bandwidth is the real element that determines resolution.

What's bandwidth? Think of a video picture as a collection of sounds from a symphony orchestra. You're probably aware that most humans can't hear very low or very high sounds. This is the bandwidth of hearing. Our ears pick up sounds within the range of human hearing; all others are left for the dogs. Video bandwidth is much the same. But instead of high- or low-pitched sounds, video bandwidth deals with picture detail. High-frequency video information is actually the very fine detail in the picture.

The average home television set has a theoretical video bandwidth of 4.2 MHz (megahertz, or millions of cycles per second). In practice, however, the figure is more like 2 or 3 MHz. At this bandwidth, you can barely discern large, half-inch letters. To display fine-detail graphics—more pixels at once—you need a bandwidth of at least 12 MHz (a color monitor for the CGA board must have a bandwidth of at least 14 MHz). For very high resolution graphics work, a monitor with a bandwidth of between 18 and 30 MHz is required.

To find out the resolution and the bandwidth of a monitor (resolution and bandwidth go hand in hand), refer to the manufacturer's specifications sheet (sometimes a catalog sheet; other times contained in the instruction manual packed with the monitor). If you don't find what you need, ask your dealer. When all else fails, contact the manufacturer directly.

Keep it foremost in your mind that you'll want to balance the bandwidth, and hence the resolution, of a monitor with your computer system. If your computer puts out only medium resolution graphics, it's hardly necessary to have a very high resolution monitor.

Convergence

Technically speaking, resolution refers to video bandwidth and the number of pixels (or lines) that show up distinctly on the screen. But there are other elements that contribute to a "sharp" or "fuzzy" picture. One is *convergence* and deals mostly with color monitors. Monochrome monitors employ a single electron gun to produce characters on the screen; color monitors have three such guns, or least one gun that produces three streams of electrons.

For proper, focused display, the beams in a color display must converge on the same point on the screen (in actuality, it is not the *exact* same point, but a closed cluster of three points, as illustrated in Figure 6-5). A poorly designed or built monitor may exhibit poor convergence; so the individual colors that make up the image can look separated. In some cases, all the monitor needs is a tweak of a control or two. In others, the problem is part of the monitor design and is not correctible.

Edge-to-Edge Sharpness

Another picture clarity consideration is what's commonly referred to as *edge-to-edge sharpness*. Most manufacturers rate

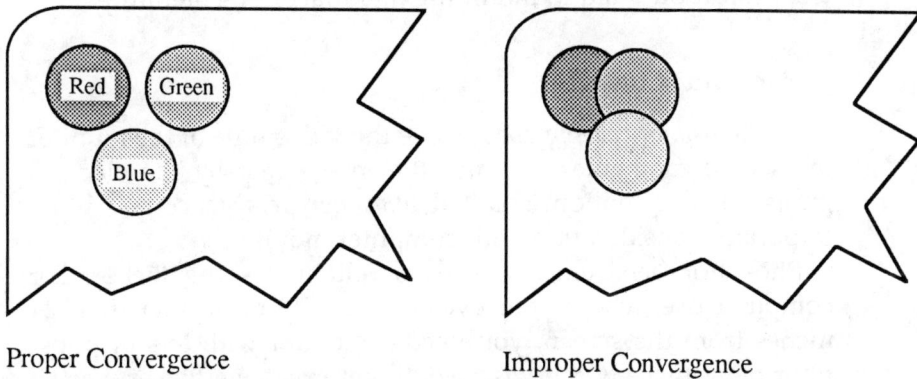

Proper Convergence   Improper Convergence

Figure 6-5.
Proper/improper convergence.

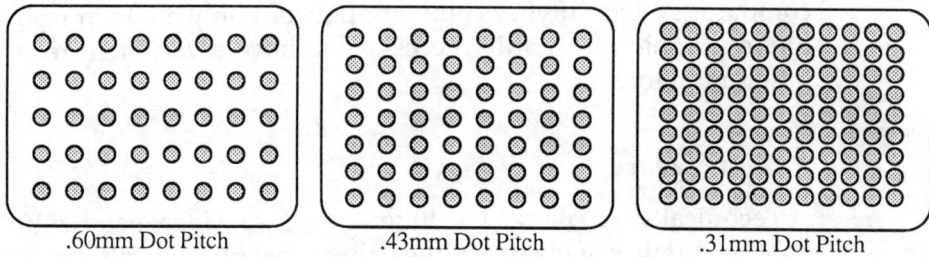

.60mm Dot Pitch   .43mm Dot Pitch   .31mm Dot Pitch

Figure 6-6.
Dot pitch examples.

their wares by the picture the monitor delivers at the center of the screen, which looks best. Computers splash text and pictures across the entire face of the monitor, so you must be sure the edges of the display also look sharp.

Dot Pitch

Overall sharpness can also be determined by the *dot pitch* of the monitor. Plainly speaking, the dot pitch, which is expressed in millimeters, is the vertical distance between the centers of two pixels, as in Figure 6-6. In a color monitor, the dot pitch is measured as the distance between two pixels of the same color.

With a wide dot pitch, the pixels will be spaced further apart; a grainy, low resolution appearance is the bottom line. The average dot pitch for a TV set is about 0.90 millimeter. Moderate quality computer monitors have a dot pitch of about 0.43 mm; higher quality monitors, 0.31 mm or less. Like resolution, this is a specification often found in the manufacturer's literature.

Phosphor Coating

The *phosphor coating* used inside the video tube of the monitor is used to momentarily retain the image cast by the electron gun(s). This retention is called *phosphor persistence* and is an important consideration with computer monitors.

Phosphor persistence lessens or eliminates the flicker. For computer use, where your eyes are usually no further than 24 inches from the screen, you need a monitor with lots of phosphor persistence. Otherwise, you'll get excessive flicker, particularly when viewing very high resolution graphics.

At the same time, beware of too much of a good thing. Too

much phosphor persistence can cause some unsettling side effects. This is particularly true of amber- and green-screen monochrome monitors. If the text and graphics appear to fade in and out instead of flashing on and off, the screen has excess phosphor persistence. If you use your computer for text-based applications only, you're probably okay. Not so with graphics— especially animated graphics. You'll want a monitor with far less phosphor persistence so the images don't "dissolve" into one another.

One Size Fits All?

The majority of computer monitors are available in three basic sizes: 9, 12, and 13 inch. A number of monitors have tube sizes of 15 to 20 inches; they can be used for presentation graphics applications but are primarily intended for use with computer-aided design and desktop publishing programs.

In all cases, the size of the monitor screen is measured diagonally, from one corner to the opposite, as shown in Figure 6-7.

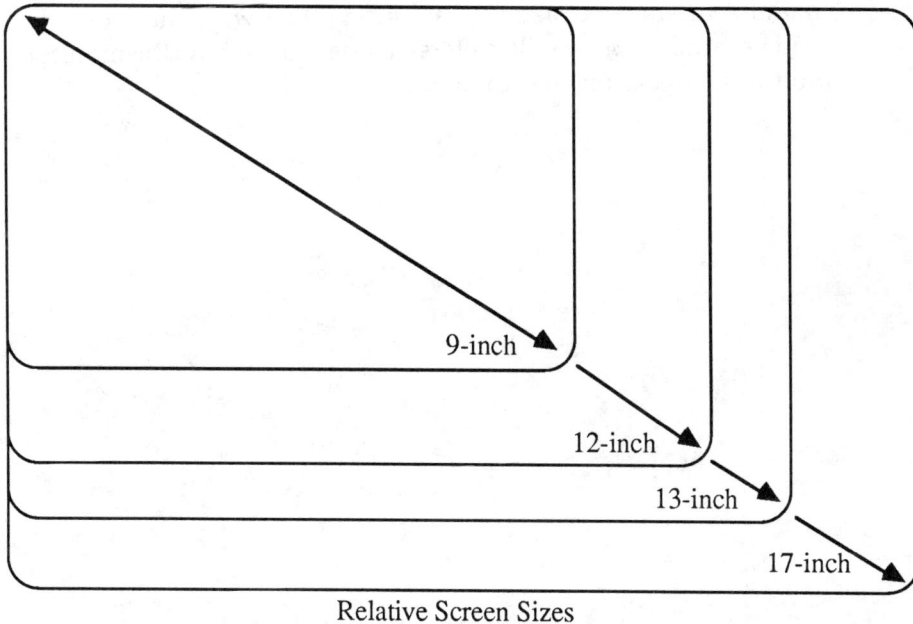

9-inch

12-inch

13-inch

17-inch

Relative Screen Sizes

Figure 6-7.
Three sizes, stacked to show dimensions.

Table 6-3.
Monitor Conversion Chart.

If the screen size of the monitor you're interested in is measured horizontally and vertically in millimeters, use this chart to convert it to the older fashioned diagonal-in-inches measurement.

Screen size (H by V mm)	Diagonal (inches)
148 X 111	9
216 X 162	12
240 X 180	13
300 X 226	17
348 X 261	19

This goes back to the old TV sales days and naturally takes into account the rectangular shape of the picture tube. Some monitor manufacturers have taken to measuring their wares horizontally and vertically, *and* in millimeters no less. To see how the monitor you want stacks up, see Table 6-3.

On Paper with Printers and Plotters

E X E C U T I V E   S U M M A R Y

Both printers or plotters can be used for creating business graphics. There are four main types of printers suitable for business graphics: impact dot matrix, ink jet, laser, and thermal transfer. Except for the impact dot matrix variety, these printers can print directly onto overhead transparency material.

Of the three major types of plotters—drum, flatbed, and hybrid—the hybrid variety is by far the most popular. Multiple-pen plotters automatically change pens on command from software.

Printer speed is most often expressed as the number of characters that can be printed in one second or the number of pages that can be printed in one minute; plotter speed is expressed as the length of a line the plotter can draw in one second. Laser printers are the fastest of the breeds, with a print speed of six to eight pages per minute.

Printers and plotters hook up to the computer via its parallel or serial interface port, and sometimes via a special controller card (laser printers). The printer or plotter must be compatible with the software running on the computer for it to generate graphics.

Only a few short years ago, computer industry pundits claimed that the office of the 1980s would be paperless. The completely electronic office, they said, would conduct business through computers. Important business mail, reports, memos, and presentations would be in the form of thousands of tiny bits of data sent through complex webs of computer links.

So far, the electronic office hasn't happened, nor anything that closely resembles it. In fact, today's businesses are producing more printed material than ever. It is estimated that each day, U.S. businesses create 600 million pages of computer-generated output. That's not counting 235 million photocopies and 76 million letters produced daily. Many of these pages are printed to be saved for future reference. File cabinets around the country hold an estimated 21 trillion sheets of paper.

Until the vision of the electronic office becomes a reality, we'll have to make do with making printed copies of the data we crunch, munch, and bunch on personal computers. By themselves, however, average computers lack means to create permanent paper copies. That's the job for a printer or plotter.

Though today's computer printer or plotter is easy to use, choosing the right one for the job can be a tough task. Do you need color, or will black and white output be fine? How big will your charts be and will the printer or plotter accept the proper size of paper? Will you need to make overhead transparencies? What types of output devices are compatible with your computer and software?

Tough questions.

So here are the answers. Because printers and plotters are so different, they are covered separately in this chapter. The first portion of the chapter is devoted to printers, the second to plotters. Finally, you'll learn how to hook up a printer or plotter to your computer, how to make sure it is compatible with your system, and how to choose the right paper and supplies for it.

Printers

Just about any printer will work with a word processor or electronic spreadsheet program; not so with a graphics program. Not only must the printer be compatible with your computer, but it must perfectly support your graphics software. The printer must also be well suited to the type of graphics that you'll be doing.

Your Printer Parade

In the world of graphics, there are four different types of printers to choose from. The printers capable of graphics output are:

- Impact dot matrix
- Ink jet
- Laser
- Thermal transfer

A fifth major type, letter quality or daisywheel printers, are not suitable for graphics work, so they are not included in this discussion. Each type of printer has its advantages and disadvantages. Note that while laser printers provide the best overall resolution, there are no affordable models that can produce color output.

All the printers generate text and graphics out of dots. The size and closeness of the dots determine resolution.

Impact Dot Matrix

Impact dot matrix printers are by far the most popular of the four types. They're relatively inexpensive, they last a long time before they break down, and they're fast. A typical dot matrix printer is shown in Figure 7-1.

With most impact dot matrix printers, characters and graphics are made by the movement of microsized needles—stacked one on top of the other in a printhead—across the page. As the printhead sweeps by, as illustrated in Figure 7-2, the printer actuates some of the pins, which strike against an inked ribbon (hence the term "impact dot matrix"), leaving individual dots on the paper.

Because of the way they create letters and numbers, dot matrix printers aren't always the best choice for making text printouts. But they're perfect for graphics, because the dots on the paper represent dots on the computer screen, as depicted in Figure 7-3.

Most dot matrix printers print more dots on the page than the computer can display on the screen; so the resolution of a graphic is often better on paper than it is on the computer. The typical resolution of an impact dot matrix printer is 100 to 150 dots per inch. You see less than half that on the computer screen.

Figure 7-1.
Typical dot matrix printer.

Dot matrix printers vary in the size of dot-producing needles (also called wires). The thicker the needles, the more coarse the final printout will be. Generally speaking, the cheaper printers have larger needles, and aren't always well suited for fine graphics work, even if they're credited with such an ability.

Some of the latest dot matrix printers have printheads with 12 to 24 needles. With these models, the needles are necessarily smaller, so the finished graphic looks better, as you can see in the close-ups in Figure 7-4.

To print graphics, the printer must have a *bit-mapped* capability. Nearly all dot matrix printers have a bit-mapped capability, but the feature works differently from printer to printer. This is why a graphics program may work perfectly with one printer brand or model, and not with another. If you have a presentation graphics program, be sure it works with your printer.

Most dot matrix printers print black on white paper. A small number are capable of color printing. These typically use a three-

Paper

Ribbon

Platen

Wires (needles)   Printhead

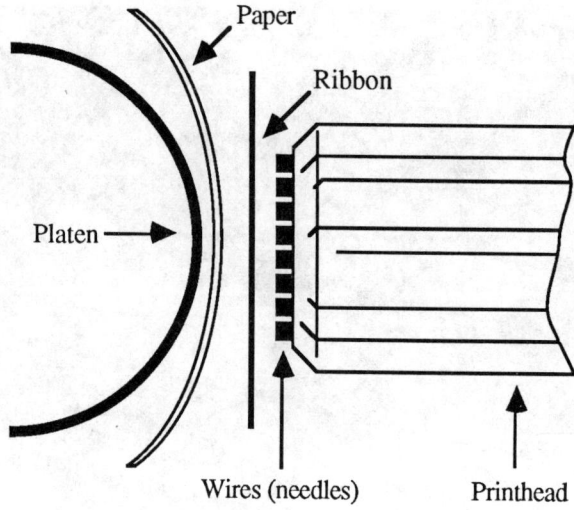

Dots are created one column
at a time as the
printhead sweeps by

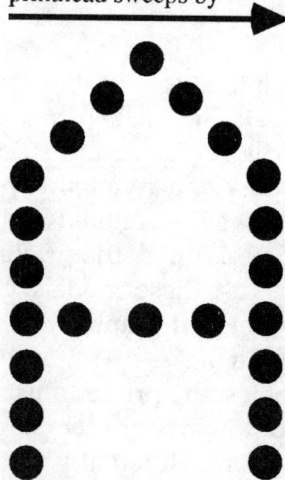

Figure 7-2.
Dot matrix printhead drawing.

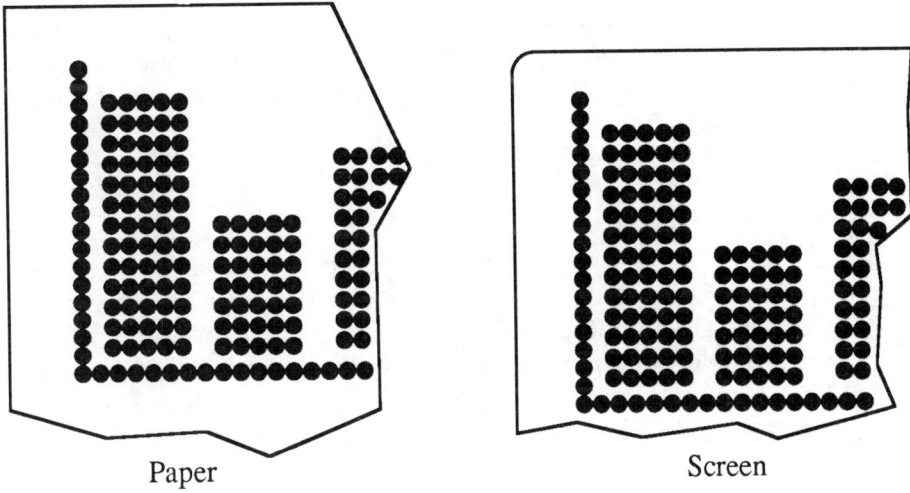

Paper   Screen

Figure 7-3.
Graphic of dots on screen/paper.

24-wire printhead   9-wire printhead

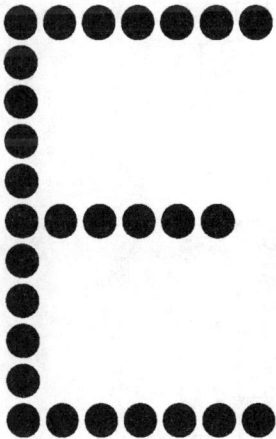 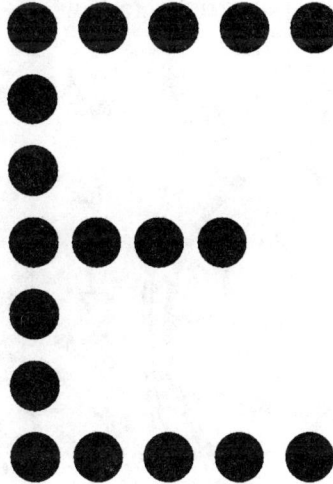

Figure 7-4.
Graphic close-up with thick/thin print needles.

or four-color fabric ribbon. More colors are created by going over the graphic two or more times, each with a different color. The color mixing isn't perfect, and as the ribbon gets older the ink gets lighter.

Ink Jet

Ink jet printers use a process whereby a fine spray of ink is applied directly on the page from one or more high-pressure nozzles, as illustrated in Figure 7-5. In a way, the ink jet units are a type of dot matrix printer, except that the resolution (number of dots) is much higher, because a shot of ink can make a smaller—and hence more defined—mark than a mechanical needle.

Many of the better ink jet printers produce characters of very fine quality, with resolutions of 150 to 250 dots per inch. This includes both text and graphics. They also can print in color. Like impact dot matrix printers, most all ink jet models use three or four colors and mix them to produce other hues.

There is yet another benefit to ink jet printers: They can print directly on plain paper or on clear acetate film. The inks used for printing are transparent, so they're perfect for making overhead transparencies. However, with all their advantages, most ink jet

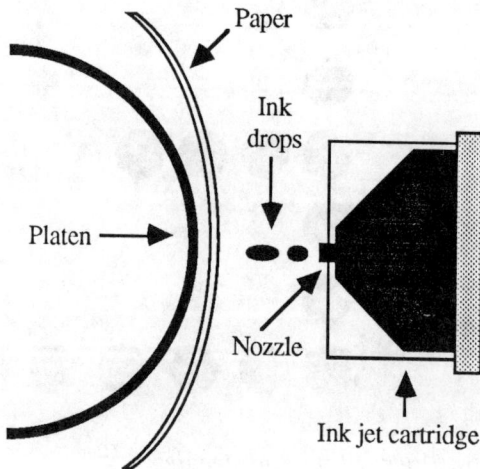

Figure 7-5.
Ink jet head drawing.

printers suffer from a serious disadvantage: They can be notoriously slow to print out graphics. More on printer speed later.

Laser

Laser printers are perhaps the most sophisticated form of non-impact printers. Laser printers, like the model in Figure 7-6, actually draw each dot of a graphic onto a photosensitive drum, which is then used as a master to make a paper copy (laser printers are based on standard plain-paper copier technology, and in fact, often use the same mechanical innards found in office and home copiers). Laser printers can print on paper or overhead transparency film.

The dots that make up the text and graphics of the finished laser printout are extremely small. Resolution on most laser units is 300 dots per inch, about twice that of a typical dot matrix printer. Some of the more expensive laser printers, the ones that cost over $10,000, have resolutions of over 600 dots per inch.

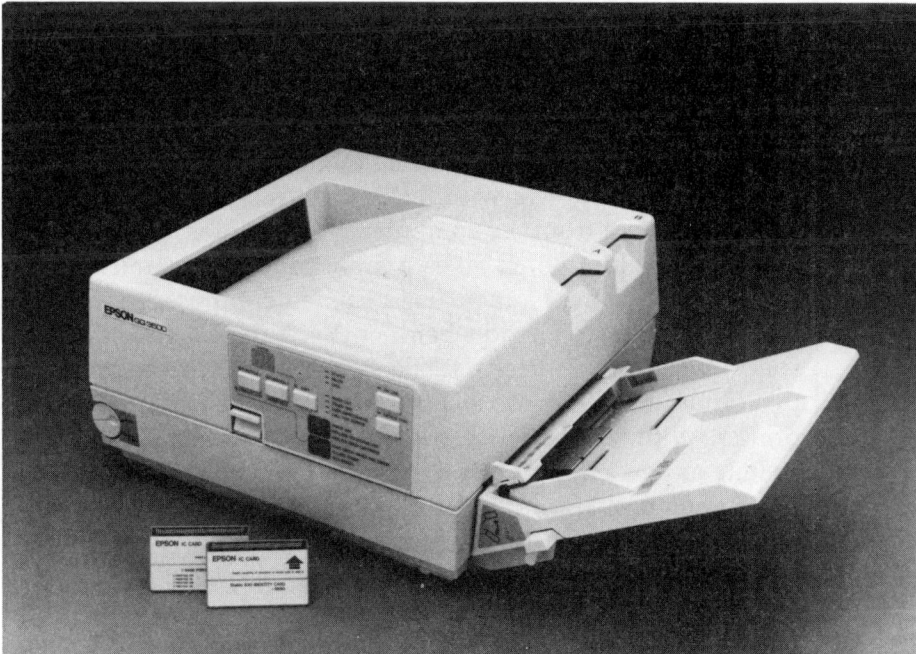

Figure 7-6.
Typical laser printer.

Many laser printers have a page description language built-in. This language allows the printer greater flexibility when used with many types of applications, such as presentation graphics, desktop publishing, and computer-aided design.

Proper Form with Page Description Languages

Most computer software send data to a printer in the form of ASCII characters. To print an "H," the program sends the code for an H. Similar codes are sent for the other characters in the alphabet, as well as control sequences, for adjusting line spacing, font size and style, page breaks, and so forth.

Presentation graphics and page layout programs that combine text and graphics work a little differently. Two methods are commonly in use: raster image and page description. Raster images are like the pictures on TV—they're made up by a series of dots aligned in a sequence of rows. This includes text, illustrations, and graphic embellishments such as lines and boxes. All the dots are printed in high resolution by the laser printer.

The biggest problem with raster images is the time it takes to send the data from the computer to the printer. Each dot on the page is a bit, which takes a finite time to transmit to the printer. An 8½ by 11 inch page can be composed of up to 8,415,000 dots (at 300 dots per inch resolution). Even at high-speed parallel port speeds, it takes over 16 seconds to transfer this amount of information from the computer to the laser printer. With slower serial port speeds, the transfer can take as long as several minutes.

Another problem is that the computer must translate the page you've created to the raster image, which is time consuming in itself.

A better approach is the page description language. Instead of sending the image dot by dot, the computer sends the page as ASCII text and graphics "primitives"—basic codes that describe the size and shape of graphic objects. A page description language interpreter in the laser printer intercepts this information, converts it into dots (very quickly), and processes it into an image for printing.

The most common page description language is PostScript, written by Adobe Systems of Palo Alto, California. PostScript is used in the Apple Laserwriter, the QMS PostScript series of laser printers, the Allied Linotype 101P and 300P typesetting machines, and literally dozens of other laser printers and output devices.

The computer "talks" to PostScript with English-like commands, such as those shown in Figure S7-1, and yet the final output produces graphics as shown in Figure S7-2. All programs that have or support a PostScript printer driver will work with any PostScript-compatible output device. PostScript graphic objects, font arcs, even bit maps, can be drawn in any scale, rotated this way and that, and positioned on the page—in a matter of seconds.

Not all presentation graphics programs for the IBM PC support PostScript, but many do. If you have a PostScript-compatible laser printer, or plan on getting one, be sure your graphics software also supports PostScript.

If you have a yen for programming, you can write your own PostScript code. Several books are available that explain PostScript programming. With your own code, you can modify the images from your business graphics programs and create a wide variety of special effects, such as filled and rotated text, special logos, and more.

Because of their high resolution, laser printers need a considerable amount of random access memory (RAM) to store and manipulate the graphics they print. A basic laser printer comes with 512K of RAM, which provides enough memory for a full-page resolution of about 150 dots per inch. For a full-page resolution of 300 dots per inch, the printer needs a minimum of 1 megabyte. Many laser printers come with 1.5 to 2 megabytes of memory. Some of this memory is used to store fonts that are *downloaded* from the computer prior to printing.

```
gsave  %Line
137 109.5 0 false false 0 fixcoordinates
newpath
0 -71.5 moveto 0 71.5 lineto
1 setlinewidth 0 setgray stroke
grestore

gsave  %Line
247.887 182 0 false false 0 fixcoordinates
newpath
-112.112 0 moveto 112.112 0 lineto
1 setlinewidth 0 setgray stroke
grestore

gsave  %Line
242.5 434 0 false false 0 fixcoordinates
newpath
-117.5 0 moveto 117.5 0 lineto
1 setlinewidth 0 setgray stroke
grestore

gsave  %Rectangle
172 121.5 0 false false 0 fixcoordinates
36 121 dorect
gsave 0 setgray eofill grestore
1 setlinewidth 0 setgray stroke
grestore

gsave  %Polygon
226 113.5 0 false false 0 fixcoordinates
/counter 0 def
/pointList 10 array def
-17.986 -68.5 addpt
18.013 -68.5 addpt
18.013 68.5 addpt
-17.986 68.5 addpt
-17.986 -68.5 addpt
newpath
pointList dopoly
closepath
gsave 0 setgray eofill grestore
1 setlinewidth 0 setgray stroke
grestore
```

```
gsave  %Polygon
280 142.999 0 false false 0 fixcoordinates
/counter 0 def
/pointList 10 array def
-18.068 -39 addpt
17.931 -39 addpt
17.931 38.999 addpt
-18.068 38.999 addpt
-18.068 -39 addpt
newpath
pointList dopoly
closepath
gsave 0 setgray eofill grestore
1 setlinewidth 0 setgray stroke
grestore

gsave  %Polygon
334 129 0 false false 0 fixcoordinates
/counter 0 def
/pointList 10 array def
-18.367 -53 addpt
17.632 -53 addpt
17.632 53 addpt
-18.367 53 addpt
-18.367 -53 addpt
newpath
pointList dopoly
closepath
gsave 0 setgray eofill grestore
1 setlinewidth 0 setgray stroke
grestore
```

Figure S7-1.
PostScript sample code.

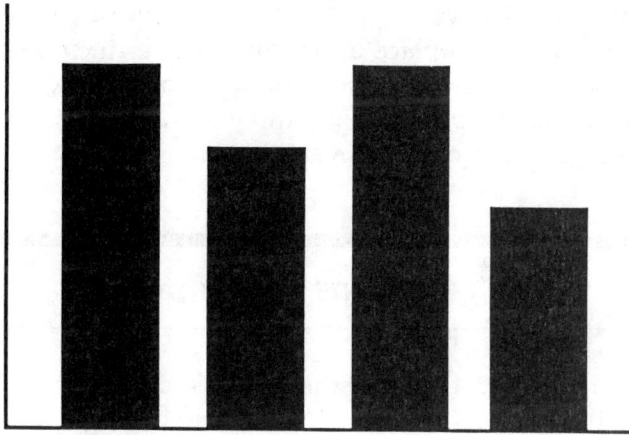

Figure S7-2.
PostScript Graphic result.

Thermal Transfer

The thermal transfer printer is a big cousin to the older fashioned thermal printer. In a thermal printer, images are created by passing a metal or ceramic printhead over a temperature-sensitive paper. Points in the printhead get hot and "burn" a dot on the page. Thermal transfer printers also use a heat-producing printhead, but temperature-sensitive paper is not required. The image is imparted to the paper with a waxy inked ribbon. The printhead heats the ribbon, and the ink melts onto the paper, as shown in Figure 7-7.

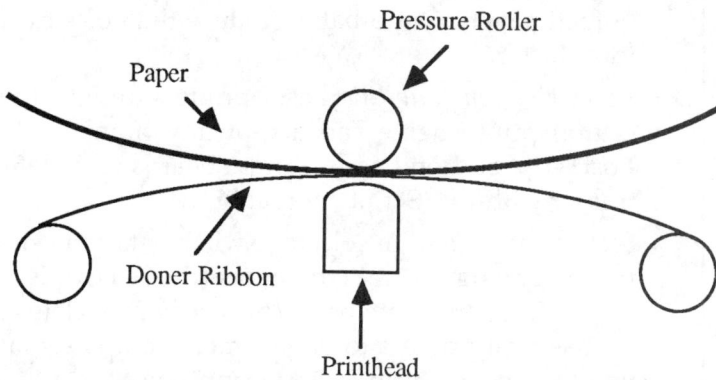

Figure 7-7.
Thermal transfer printhead drawing.

Print resolution varies, but even the least expensive thermal transfer models can place up to 200 dots per inch on the page. The ribbon of a thermal transfer ribbon can be black or color. For color printing, the printer mixes three or four basic colors to produce a palette of from 7 to over 30 hues.

Add-Ons for Printers

If you're not satisfied with the features of your printer, investigate the add-ons available for it before buying a new model. Often, accessories are available from the original manufacturer or third-party manufacturers that greatly add function and versatility to an old printer. Consider these add-ons:

- *Sheet feeder.* A sheet feeder automatically inserts cut sheets into the printer. You don't have to be there to load each new sheet into the printer. A bin collects the printed pages in collated order. Many sheet feeders have several bins that accept different paper stock.

- *High-capacity paper cartridge.* Many laser printers have only one paper cartridge that holds 100 sheets of paper or less. Larger capacity cartridges are available that hold from 250 to 500 sheets.

- *Sound baffles.* If your dot matrix printer makes too much noise, enclose it in a sound baffle. These fit on top of the table or computer stand and allow easy access to load and unload paper. Sound baffles reduce the noise by a significant factor.

- *PostScript compatibility.* Laser printers designed with the Canon print engine can accept any number of several PostScript add-on boards. These boards provide the laser printer with PostScript compatibility.

- *Selector switches.* A selector switch lets you share one printer among several computers (the selector is different from a local area network). The selector also lets you connect several printers to one or more computers, allowing you to select the printer you want to use.

Printer Speed

For presentation graphics, you'll want the fastest printer you can get, because even the average graph can take up to 5 minutes to print. Most manufacturers rate the speed of a printer by the number of characters it can print in 1 second. Character print speed has little meaning when pounding out graphics, but it can serve as a guide to help you determine if a given printer will be fast enough.

Generally speaking, a printer with a character print speed of under 25 characters per second will be too slow for most presentation graphics work. The slower the printer, the longer it will take to print out even a simple graph. If printing becomes a time-consuming hassle, you'll avoid it. Of course, if your demands aren't stringent, or if you don't plan on making too many charts and graphs, a slow printer may not be a nuisance.

On the average, laser printers are the fastest of the group discussed above, because the image is drawn by a beam of light. Accept laser print speeds with skepticism, though, since the print speed is usually just a measurement of the rate of paper transfer through the printer. The speed often doesn't take into account the time the computer needs to send the printer the graphics information. A laser printer with a stated top speed of eight pages per minute can usually output two to three finished pages per minute.

Print speed with impact dot matrix printers varies widely— from a low 50 cps for the inexpensive models to over 300 cps for the expensive ones. Print speeds of 120 to 180 cps are about average with impact dot matrix printers.

Ink jet and thermal printers are the slowest of the bunch. Many units top out at 30 characters per second, even less when preparing a color printout because the printhead has to go over the same area two or more times.

Other Speed Considerations

Speed is also determined by:

- The rate the printer advances each line (called *slew rate*)
- Whether or not the printhead can lay down graphics when going in both directions

A slew rate of 4 to 6 inches per second is about average for medium-cost printers, though you could get by with a slower rate without a noticeable decrease in overall speed. A printhead that can print from left to right and right to left (called *bidirectional*), will complete a picture about 20 to 30 percent faster than a *unidirectional* (left to right only) printer.

A warning: Many printers are bidirectional, but the graphics software driving it may not be "intelligent" enough to feed it bidirectional graphics information. This effectively reduces the printer to unidirectional mode.

Selection Criteria

There are several factors you'll want to consider when purchasing a printer, no matter what type it is. First, you'll want to think about the maximum width of paper you'll be using. Most printers are equipped with a 10-inch carriage and can accept paper no larger than 9½ inches wide. For wider printouts, get a model with a 15- or 17-inch carriage.

The second factor is the type of paper feed mechanism the printer uses. The feed mechanism is simply the way the printer

Figure 7-8.
Printer with pin feed clamps.

pulls the paper along so it can print on it. Like standard type-writers, many printers have friction feed: The paper is squeezed through rubber rollers.

Pin feed or tractor feed mechanisms, like the one shown in Figure 7-8, are used with perforated paper. The pin mechanism grasps the paper by the holes and yanks it through the printer. Pin feed is good when doing lots of printing (there's no need to worry about misalignment) and is also helpful for nongraphics work such as printing on check stock, mailing labels, and so forth.

Being able to use continuous form stock is a definite bonus when speed is important. When working with a single-sheet friction feed printer, you must be present to load and unload paper, and it takes a considerable amount of time to insert the new page, line it up, and resume printing. To be effective, the pinfeed mechanism should be adjustable, to allow for various widths of stock.

It should be remembered that, by their nature, thermal, thermal transfer, ink jet, and laser printers are capable of producing only one copy at a time. Impact printers, on the other hand, can generally produce as many as six copies at once.

Printers and How They Work

The four major types of printers work in vastly different ways. Here is a brief overview of the technologies behind each.

Impact Dot Matrix

Dot matrix printers form text and graphics by impacting a series of needle-sized wires against the ribbon and paper. The number and size of the needles determine print resolution. Many dot matrix printers have nine printing needles (or wires), but an increasing number have 18 and 24. When printing high-resolution text and graphics with nine needles, the printhead may pass over the same lines two or more times. At each pass, the needles fill in the spaces between previously made dots.

The size of the needles in the printhead limit the resolution of the printer. A "large" printing needle is about 0.014 inch. A "small" printing needle is about 0.007 inch. The needles can't be any smaller or they will pass through the ribbon and directly hit the paper. Not all printing needles are round. Some dot matrix printer designs use oval-shaped needles. The shape helps fill in gaps.

Thermal Transfer

Thermal transfer printers use a multilayered heat-sensitive ribbon. When one or more all-electronic elements encased in the printhead heats up, it melts the waxed-based ink and transfers it directly to the paper. The transferred ink cools quickly. Pressure exerted by the printhead fuses the ink permanently onto the paper. Thermal transfer printers have from 9 to over 26 heat-producing elements in the printhead. The more elements, the finer the printing.

Color images are created by overlaying the three subtractive colors—yellow, cyan (blue/green), and magenta (red/blue)—onto the paper. Most thermal transfer printers can also be used with silver direct-thermal paper.

A new wrinkle in thermal transfer technology, called resistive transfer, comes from IBM. Instead of passing heat through a ribbon, the IBM Quietwriter passes minute pulses of electricity. A special layer in the all-black Quietwriter ribbon reacts to the electrical charges and turns the voltage spikes into heat, depositing ink at just the right places. Text and graphics are printed as extremely small dots. The thimble-sized printhead inside the Quietwriter has 40 heat-producing elements in it, enabling it to have a resolution exceeding 350 dots per inch.

Ink Jet

There are two kinds of ink jet printers: continuous flow and drop-on-demand.

- With continuous flow, the faster of the two, a steady stream of ink shoots through a control electrode, which breaks up the flow into a series of tiny, evenly spaced, droplets. The droplets then pass through a deflection electrode. When the electrode is turned off, the drops hit the paper. When turned on, the drops are deflected into a gutter, where the ink is then filtered, degassed, pressurized, and reintroduced into the ink supply. About 2 percent of the ink emitted by the nozzle ever hits the paper.

- With drop-on-demand, the ink is forced into a holding bladder by pressure from a miniature ink reservoir. To place a dot on the paper, voltage is applied to a piezo-electric element or tube. Peristaltic pulses from the forward expansion of the vibrator increases the pressure inside the bladder, which forces a spurt of ink to flow out the nozzle. The piezoelectric element contracts when the voltage is removed, and the pressure is reversed, to keep ink from oozing out when not wanted.

Other drop-on-demand actuation processes involve impulses of hot air, created inside the printhead, that form bubbles to expand the ink out the nozzle; pressurized air that carries the ink droplets out of the printhead and onto the paper; and electrical currents that pressurize and vaporize the ink to force it out of the nozzle.

The least expensive ink jet printers have only one ink channel, so a full line of text has to be made with several passes of the printhead. This makes text printing painfully slow—on the order of 15 to 25 cps. Multichannel ink jet printers, with 4 to 32 nozzles, print faster.

Color ink jet printers, which are becoming very popular, have three or four channels, one for each of the three subtractive primary colors: yellow, cyan, and magenta (and sometimes a separate channel for black). With ink mixing, ink jet printers can produce up to seven distinct colors, plus more with dithering. Black and colored inks are stored in a removable cartridge.

Laser

Laser printers use a helium-neon gas or solid state laser to paint a series of dots on a rotating photoconductive drum, as illustrated in Figure S7-3. A spinning polygonal mirror or holographic scanner reflects the modulated (on/off) laser beam across the drum. To create a page, the drum first passes a cleaner, which scrapes off old toner. The drum is subsequently charged with high-voltage current and then exposed to the laser light.

Next, the drum passes a developing station, which contains the toner powder. Powder adheres to any spot where the laser beam has hit. Finally, the drum makes contacts with the paper via a transfer corona, which transfers the powder from the drum onto the paper. Pressure and heat rollers fuse the toner to the paper.

Laser printers have high resolution—a minimum of 300 dots per inch. This resolution makes the print look nearly typewritten or typeset, but under close inspection, you can still spot the dot-by-dot makeup of the print.

There are three main factors in increasing resolution:

- The laser light has to be focused more precisely. This requires better lasers and more precise imaging optics.

- Due to the physics of the drum, there is always a tell-tale "halo" that appears around the spot where the laser beam has struck. The halo reduces the overall resolution.

- The dry toner used in the printing process has a finite granularity. To increase resolution, the toner particles must be made smaller.

Other printers based on electrostatic design include light-emitting diode (LED), liquid crystal shutter (LCD), and ion deposition. In the LED system (see Figure S7-4), as used in many laser printers manufactured by NEC, a narrow strip of light-emitting diodes spans the width of the photoreceptor drum. The LEDs turn on and off to create an image.

In the LCD system, circuits control a clear liquid crystal display, which is similar to the kind used in digital watches, but light can pass through it. Light goes through the clear portions of the shutter, but it's stopped by the opaque portions. The image exposed onto the drum is then developed and transferred to paper as with a standard laser printer. The ion deposition system uses an ion generator to apply pinpoints of charged particles directly on the surface of the photoreceptor drum.

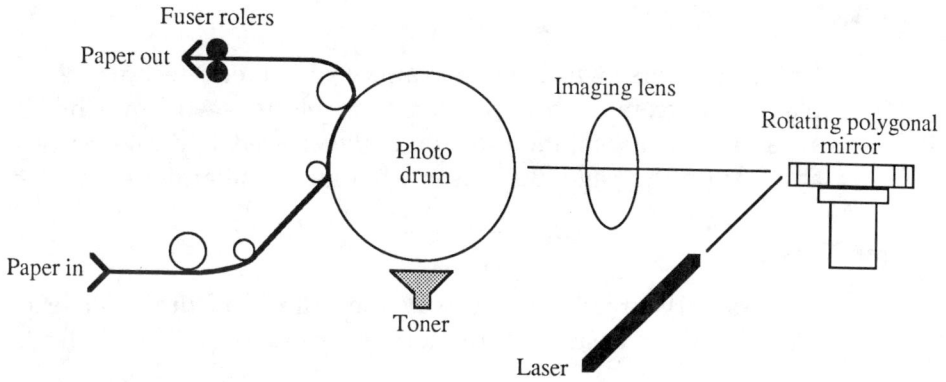

Figure S7-3.
Laser insides.

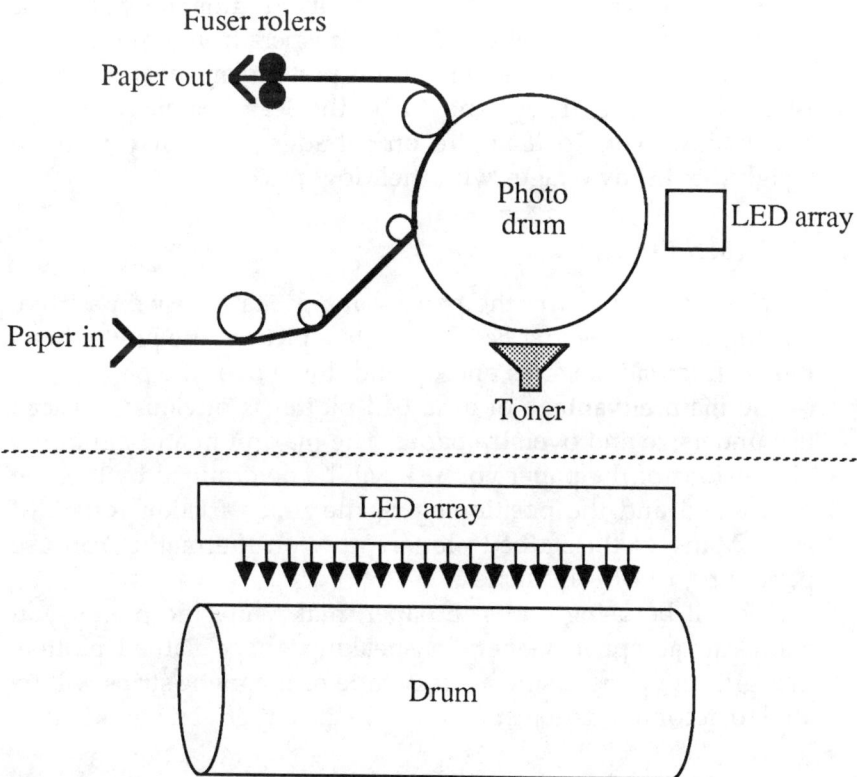

Figure S7-4.
LED print system.

Plotters

Unlike printers, which use a variety of esoteric techniques to place characters on a sheet of paper, plotters work much the same. All use a pen, mounted on a *plotter head*, to draw pictures and text on the page. But this is where the similarities end.

Plotter Types

Plotters vary greatly in the way they draw pictures and text. There are three basic types of plotters: drum, flatbed, and hybrid.

Drum Plotters

With a *drum plotter* you attach the paper to a cylindrical drum. The drum rotates back and forth when plotting. To complete the picture, the pen carriage shuttles horizontally, from one side of the drum to the other. Drum plotters get the job done, but they can't be used with long or short paper. In addition, the paper has a tendency to slip out of the drum's graspers from time to time.

Because of their limitations, drum plotters are nearly nonexistent these days. They tend to be the least expensive of the bunch, however, so if you're on a budget, you may want to weigh the disadvantages with their low price.

Flatbed Plotters

With a *flatbed plotter* the paper remains stationary on a fixed, flat surface—the *plotter bed*. To create a picture, the plotter head moves from side to side, and up and down over the paper.

The main advantage of a flatbed plotter is obvious: You can use undersize and oversize paper. The maximum and minimum dimensions of the paper you use will be determined by the size of the bed and the positioning of the unit's friction rollers (if any). Many of the flatbed plotters now on the market can use paper up to 11 by 17 inches.

If you'll be using odd-size paper, make sure the plotter you want can accept it. Generally speaking, those flatbed plotters that grip the paper using a sticky tape or magnetic strips will be able to accommodate just about any size paper you want to use.

Hybrid Plotters

The *hybrid plotter*, shown in Figure 7-9, is modeled after the flatbed plotter but with a twist: the paper moves in and out of

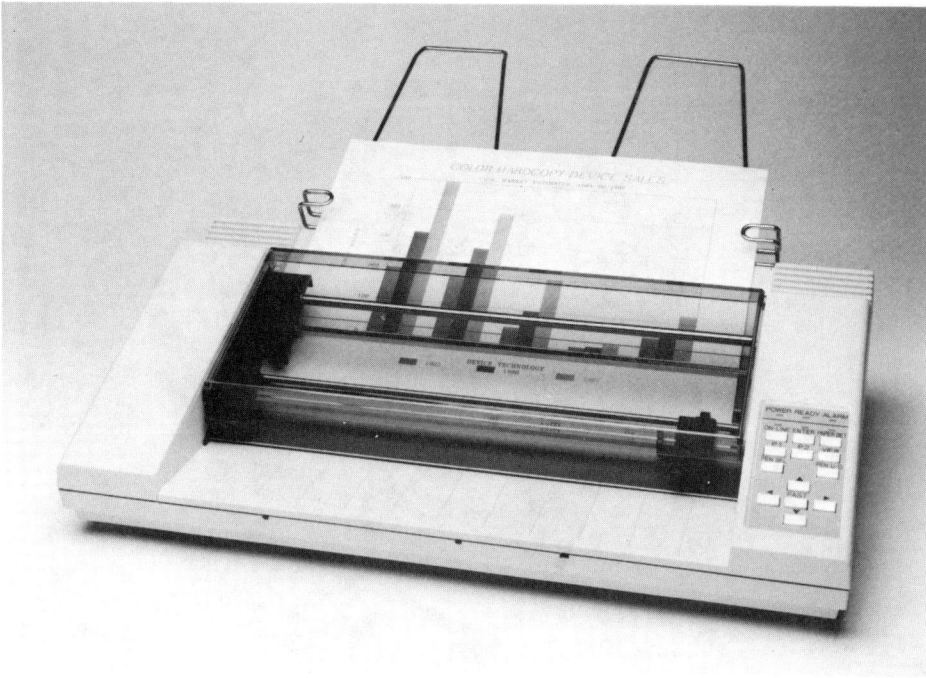

Figure 7-9.
Hybrid plotter.

the machine while the plotter head sweeps over the page horizontally. Most hybrid plotters can take paper sizes of up to B to C, but because all the units use rollers to pull the paper through the machine, most cannot accept paper smaller than 8 by 10 inches.

How Many Pens?

The most basic, and least expensive, plotters can handle only one pen at a time. You load the pen into the pen holder, then tell the plotter to go to work. Few plotters have single, nonchangeable pens, but these are rare and are typically for specialty computers, like ultracompact portables.

The hottest trend these days is the multipen plotter. These units store from two to eight pens in a *carousel*. To change colors, the plotter puts one pen away and grabs another. The carousel can be attached to the plotter head (the most efficient design) or can be positioned off the bed (see Figure 7-10). You can, of course, make a plot with more colors than the number of pens

Figure 7-10.
Pen carousel.

your plotter can accept. Most graphics software let you stop the plot to change pens.

Most plotters use a special pen design, so it's unlikely that you'll be able to use the pens from one plotter with another (exceptions do exist, though you may need to purchase an adapter). This means you're at the mercy of the plotter manufacturer to supply the variety of pens you need. At the very least, you'll want to be sure that there are plenty of colors to choose from, and that the pens are available with both water- and oil-based ink. For more about inks, see the section on Printer/Plotter Accessories.

Plotter Speed

Like computer printers, plotters work at different speeds. Some are notoriously slow, plotting a single graph in over 10 minutes. Others are speed demons, plotting the same graph in under 3 minutes. There are a number of variables to consider when grading plotting speed.

First and foremost is the *speed of the plotter head,* which is usually expressed in inches per second. Low-end units have plotter head speeds of between 4 and 8 inches per second (ips), the better ones from about 8 to 20 ips. Manufacturers often state the speed of the head when it's traveling in either the x or y axis. Occasionally, the speed will be given when the head is traveling diagonally. Obviously, the speed specification will be a little better in this case, since the plotter head is moving in two directions at once.

Another important criteria for judging speed is the *acceleration of the plotter head.* If it takes a long time for the head to come to full writing speed, the graph will take a while longer to create. Plotter head acceleration is given in g's. Most plotters have accelerations of from 0.5 to 1 g, the better ones from 1 to 6 g's.

Graphing Quality

Accuracy is a vital issue with plotters. The more accurate the plotter can draw a picture, the better it will look, because lines will match up and colors won't bleed into each other. Plotter accuracy is rated by resolution, sometimes termed *addressability* or *step size.*

Resolutions of 0.001 inch (excellent) to 0.004 inch (good) aren't uncommon. You can't really tell the difference between a plotter that has a resolution of 0.001 or 0.004 inch without a magnifying glass, but you *can* tell the difference between plotters that have a 0.004- and 0.025-inch resolution. Your best guide is your own eyes. Study the output of the plotters you like, and see if the accuracy is good enough. Figure 7-11 shows how a diag-

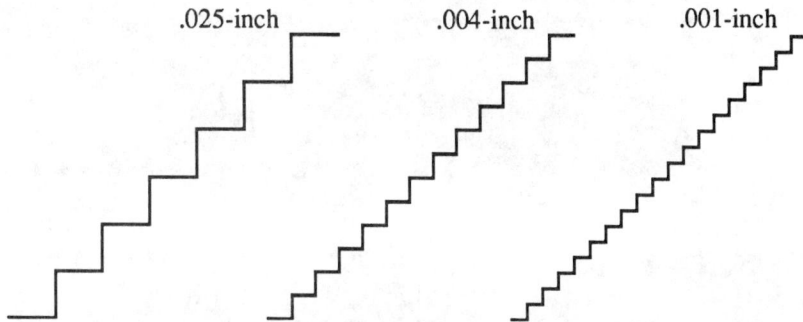

Simulated plotter resolution at approximately 100X magnification

Figure 7-11.
Plotter output with different resolutions.

onal line (the toughest test for a plotter) might look if magnified about 100 times.

Tied to resolution is *repeatability*, or the plotter's ability to hit the same place on paper twice with its pen. Repeatability is usually measured in millimeters and is taken with and without a pen change. Average repeatability without a pen change is about 0.2 mm. With a pen change the repeatability is often from 0.2 to 0.4 mm.

Hi-Tech Hookups

You've chosen a printer or plotter and are ready to go to work. But there's still the question of how to hook it up to your computer. You'll want to make sure your printer or plotter can connect to your computer, and that you have the right cabling for the job.

Parallel Interface

Most printers and plotters come with either one of two types of interfaces, adapters to allow them to hook up to your computer.

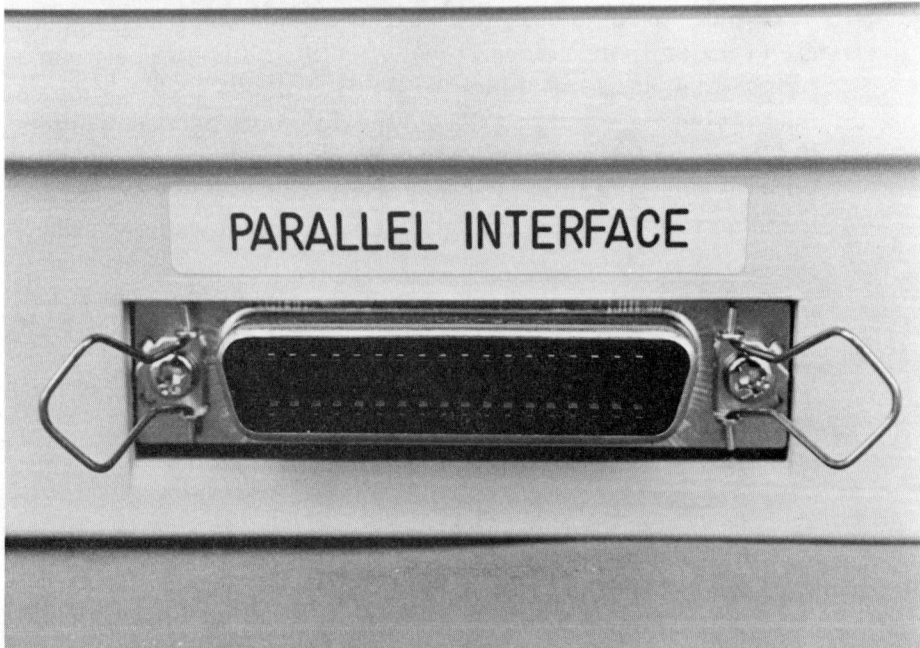

Figure 7-12.
Centronics connector.

By far, the most common is the parallel interface. It's also the easiest to use. Just hook a cable between the computer's parallel interface and printer/plotter, and you're done.

Still, there *is* the question of using the right cable. Most parallel-based printers and plotters use what's known as a Centronics-type connector, illustrated in Figure 7-12. Your dealer should have a cable that will stretch between the parallel port on your computer to the printer or plotter. If not, you may have to special order the cable.

Serial Interface

Some printers and most plotters come with serial interfaces, which are far tougher to match to a computer. Most serial interfaces use the same type of connector known as a DB-25, as shown in Figure 7-13, but there's no guarantee that your printer and computer will comply. Once again, it's a question of finding the right cable.

There's also the question of setting up the proper communi-

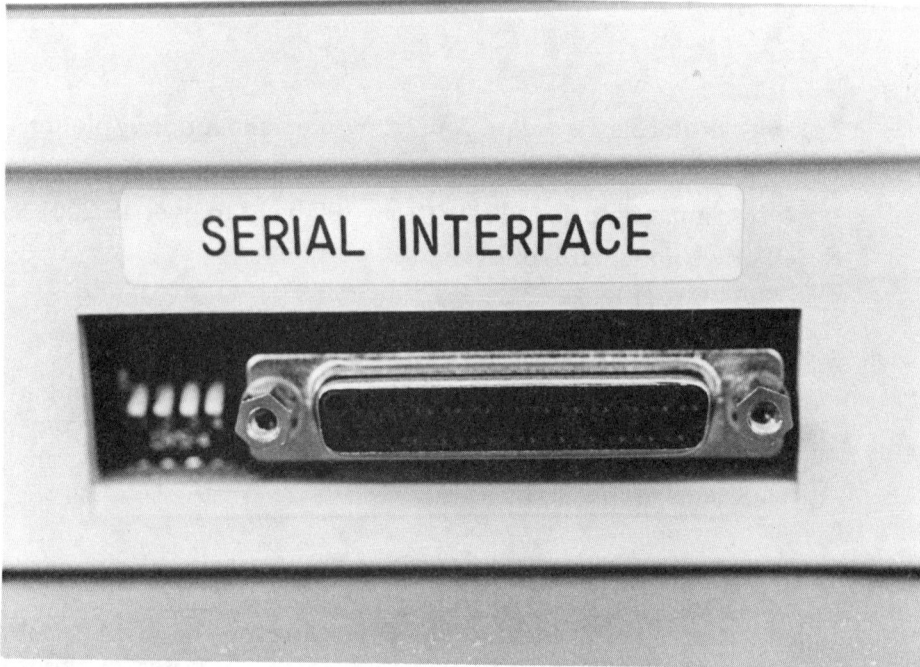

Figure 7-13.
DB-25 connector.

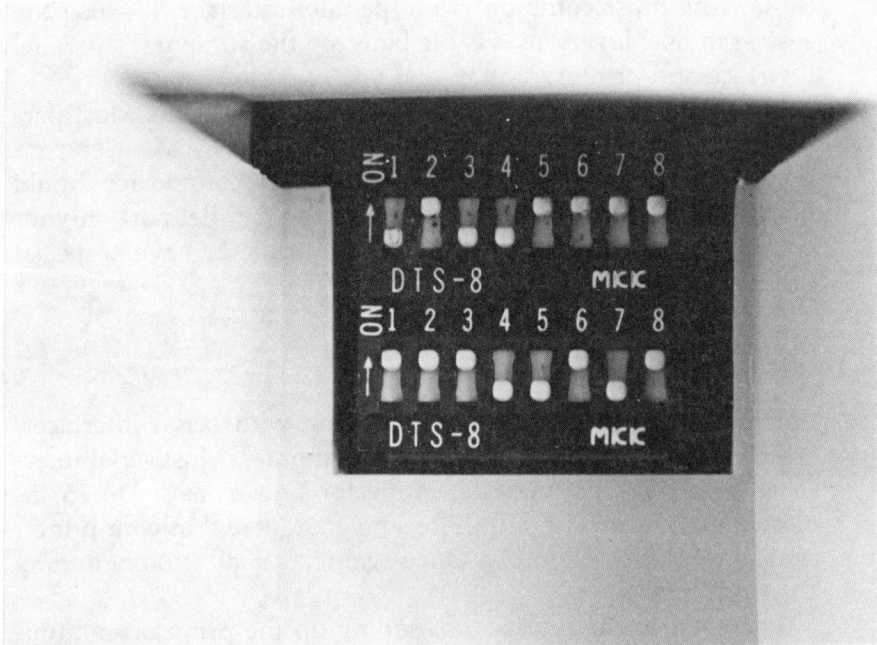

Figure 7-14.
DIP *switch close-up.*

cations protocols between your computer and printer/plotter. Parameters to set include:

- Transmission or baud rate (from 300 baud to over 19,200)
- Parity (none, odd, or even)
- Stop bits (1 or 2)
- The number of bits in each data "word" (7 or 8)

These parameters are set on the printer or plotter by flicking a set of miniature DIP switches (see Figure 7-14). With the computer, the parameters are set with the help of a utility program or with your graphics software.

Controller Card

Many laser printers for the IBM PC and clones have a special controller card that must be installed in the computer. Without the card, the printer won't function. The controller contains the interface for connecting to the printer as well as memory and other circuitry for proper operation. Depending on the design of the controller card, the laser printer may be limited to use by no more than a single computer (many laser printer users like to share the one printer among many computers).

Maintaining Your Printer or Plotter

Your computer is nearly all electronic, and it doesn't need rigorous periodic cleaning and maintenance to keep it in tip-top shape. But that doesn't apply to everything in your computer system. Your printer—whether it be dot matrix, daisywheel, ink jet, or laser—is mostly mechanical, and you must treat it with care and diligence. A clean printer is a happy printer; besides, your printer lasts longer and works better when it's clean.

There are several cleaning and maintenance steps you can do to keep your printer and plotter in good working order. These steps are simple, don't require special tools or know-how, and cleaning supplies are commonly available.

General Cleaning

When not in use, it's a good idea to place a dust cover over your printer or plotter. This makes sense because most printers/plotters are used a relatively short period of time each day. If you don't want to keep removing and replacing the cover every time the printer or plotter is used, at least keep it on overnight. As always, avoid smoking around your computer gear. The smoke and nicotine can settle on mechanical and electrical parts, making cleaning that much more difficult. If you must smoke, install a filtered air cleaner near your workstation or use a "smokeless" ashtray.

Even with a cover, dust can never be avoided; some dust always sneaks by the best protective measures. A soft painter's brush, about ½ to ¾ inch wide, can be used to wipe away the loose dust that accumulates on the exterior of the printer/

plotter. Be sure to get all the nooks and crannies around the switches, ventilation holes, and levers.

Hard to reach areas can be cleaned with a can of compressed air (available at most photographic and computer stores). When using compressed air, blow the dust *away* from the printer; avoid pushing dirt further inside the machine. In place of the compressed air you can use a vacuum cleaner to scoop up the dust. A household vacuum with a soft brush attachment works well, or you can use one of the miniature battery-operated vacuums.

If dirt or grime piles up on the exterior of the printer or plotter, use a household spray cleaner, like 409 or Fantastik, to wipe up the gunk. Don't spray the cleaner directly on the printer; spray the cleaner on a sponge, then apply the sponge to the surface of the unit.

Follow the same general steps when cleaning inside the printer (plotters generally have no access to an internal mechanism). Remove the various covers and hatches as needed to access the printing and platen area. Most printers have two or three covers that can be readily removed when you require access to the inside. Under most circumstances, you do not need to disassemble the printer to clean it. In fact, this may void the warranty and may cause more problems than it is worth.

Avoid the use of cleaning solutions inside the printer. They act to remove necessary lubrication. Additionally, if the solution leaves a residue, it could cause problems in operation.

Cleaning the Printer Platen

The platen is the large rubber roller that feeds the paper through the printer. The platen receives a lot of abuse during printing, but you can easily rejuvenate it and restore it to almost-new condition.

The platen is rubber and needs a special cleaner. You can buy a can of rubber cleaner/rejuvenator at most typewriter repair shops. The bottle will last several years if you keep the cap on tight. To use it, soak the cleaner onto a corner of a piece of cotton or other white cloth, then wipe the platen from side to side. Roll the platen around to get all of it. The cleaner will dry within seconds.

With some printers, you can remove the platen from the printer. This makes cleaning the platen easier. While the platen is out, clean the small rubber guide rollers that pinch against the platen.

Do not clean the platen with alcohol or alcohol-based products. Alcohol acts to dry up the rubber, making it brittle.

Cleaning Plotter Rollers

Many hybrid plotters have rollers that grasp the paper and pull it through the plotter mechanism. These rollers can develop a glaze that can cause the paper to misfeed. Use the rubber rejuvenator on the rubber roller. You can apply the cleaner with a cotton swab or small clean rag.

Some plotters are equipped with abrasive grid rollers. They do not generally require cleaning, and in fact can be harmed by it.

Cleaning the Printhead

Depending on the volume of printing you do, you'll want to clean the printer's printhead every 6 months to a year. Cleaning will remove caked-on paper dust, ink, and other foreign material. The process of cleaning varies depending on the type of printer you have.

Dot Matrix

Dot matrix printers are the most prone to the effects of accumulated paper dust and dried ink. In a dot matrix printhead, small needles selectively strike against the ribbon, making an inked impression on the paper. After time, ink and paper dust can clog up the workings of the printhead, reducing print quality.

To clean the printhead, first remove the ribbon and blow excess particles away with a can of compressed air. Most dot matrix printers have a head-to-platen adjustment lever. This lever moves the printhead closer to or farther away from the platen, depending on the thickness of the paper you are using. Move the printhead as far back as you can. Additionally, if you can remove the platen, do so. It will make accessing the printhead easier.

Soak a cotton or sponge swab in alcohol and *gently* scrub the printhead clean (make sure the printhead is cool before you touch it). If you can't reach the front of the printhead, use an alcohol spray cleaner, the kind designed for cleaning audio and video tape heads. Repeat the process until the printhead is completely clean.

Ink Jet

The cleaning procedure for ink jet printers depends on the machine. You should consult the user's manual that came with the printer for more information. Basically, you will want to clear the print element and nozzles of any dried ink. If the printer has not been used for a while, the ink lines may be clogged, and you'll have to flush them out. Follow the manufacturer's instructions on how to do this.

Laser

Laser printers are really plain paper copiers with a laser light imaging source. You clean laser printers as you would the plain office paper copier.

If your laser printer uses replaceable cartridges, follow the manufacturer's recommended service interval. On most laser printers, the cartridge lasts 2,000 to 3,000 pages. An indicator on the cartridge shows you if it needs replacing. Or, replace the cartridge if you notice consistently poor print quality.

If the printer uses toner bottles, replace them as indicated. Wipe or vacuum spilled toner. This keeps the machine clean and easier to use, and helps promote better looking printouts.

Regularly inspect the insides of the printer. Use a small vacuum to get rid of paper dust and other foreign objects. Be careful with the internal parts of the printer, especially the small transfer and corona wires (these are mostly hidden on cartridge-based printers). Follow the maintenance procedures provided by the manufacturer on cleaning the internal parts, including rollers, fuser, and drum.

Software Compatibility

Hooking up a printer or plotter to a computer is the easy part. For graphics printing, you've got to make sure that your printer or plotter will work with your software. A number of graphics programs are compatible with a variety of popular output devices. Usually, you must "install" a printer/plotter driver—a special utility program included with the software package—before your can use the graphing application. The driver serves to interpret the information provided by the software for use with your specific printer or plotter.

If you haven't yet purchased a printer or plotter, a good way to go about it is to choose your software first. Note which makes and models the program(s) support, then get one of those units. You might want to try the program with the printer or plotter models you like, to make sure that the quality of the printout is up to par and that the unit operates fast enough for your needs.

Standard Plotter Compatibility

Because of their popularity, plotters from Hewlett-Packard and Houston Instrument have become de facto standards in the computer industry (the Hewlett-packard HP7475 is by far the most popular). To help ensure software compatibility, plotters made by a variety of other manufacturers often use the command language built into the Hewlett-Packard (known as *HPGL*) and Houston Instrument machines. The compatibility is not always 100 percent, however, so you'll want to test the plotter thoroughly with your software before you sign the check.

Printer/Plotter Accessories

Using a printer or plotter is much like owning an automobile—you have to keep feeding it paper, ribbons, and other supplies to keep it running; and like an automobile, your choice of "fuel" will greatly determine the overall operating costs.

Ribbons

The majority of printers use a ribbon of one type or another. Fabric ribbons last the longest and are the cheapest, but they yield the poorest results, especially when printing graphics. A few impact dot matrix printers use Mylar ribbons. Like their name implies, Mylar ribbons don't use fabric but Mylar plastic, coated with a special ink or dry carbon. Two types of Mylar ribbons are in use today: long-lasting multistrike (the printing mechanism goes over the same part of the ribbon several times) and the more expensive but higher quality single-strike. Both kinds are about 30 percent more expensive than their cloth cousins.

If you go through a lot of fabric ribbons, there are several "tricks" you can try to extend their useful life. One is to lightly spray the ribbon material with WD-40, an oiless lubricant available from most hardware stores. The solvent acts to regenerate the ink dried in the ribbon, allowing you to extend the life of the ribbon by 30 to 50 percent.

A better way to save money on ribbons is to re-ink them yourself. Re-inkers are priced at about $50; the ink bottles cost around $2 each and last through several ribbons. Buy a "blank" ribbon and a set of colored inks, and you can make your own custom color ribbons.

Whether you are re-inking or using WD-40, remember that you'll eventually wear out the cloth of the ribbon. Another way to save money is to purchase repacked ribbons—new cloth in used cartridges. A number of companies specialize in repacking ribbons; look in the Yellow Pages under Data Processing for a list of ribbon repackers near you. The quality is every bit as good as a new ribbon. Most ribbon repackers offer a money back guarantee just in case you're nervous about using a "preowned" ribbon.

Ink and Toner Cartridges

Ink jet and laser printers don't use ribbons, but that doesn't mean you don't have to buy supplies for them. Ink jet printers use ink cartridges that you literally plug into their sides. When the ink is depleted, you replace the cartridge.

Cartridges for ink jet printers can be hard to find, and are usually available only through your computer dealer or from the printer manufacturer. It will take a while for most office supply and mail order firms to carry a wide selection of ink jet cartridges at any appreciable discount. Fortunately, most cartridges hold enough ink for several reams of paper, and the overall cost for the cartridges isn't much more than Mylar ribbons.

Figure 7-15.
NEC print engine drum.

Laser printers are based on plain paper copiers, but they don't use the same type of toners and drums as your office copier uses. You must use a toner cartridge especially designed for your laser printer. The toner/drum cartridge for the laser printers based on the Canon print engine lasts for 2,000 to 3,000 pages. Some mail order firms specialize in refilling the cartridges with new toner. Check Appendix C for available sources.

Laser printers based on Ricoh and NEC print engines don't use a single cartridge that houses the photosensitive drum and toner. The toner is added separately into a *hopper* and the drum, shown in Figure 7-15, is replaced only when needed.

Plotter Pens

Most plotters use specially designed pens that fit no other model. As a result they're hard to find and can be expensive. Find a source and buy an extra set of pens for a rainy day. Plotter pens usually come in a variety of thicknesses (thin, medium, thick), and with different ink chemistries.

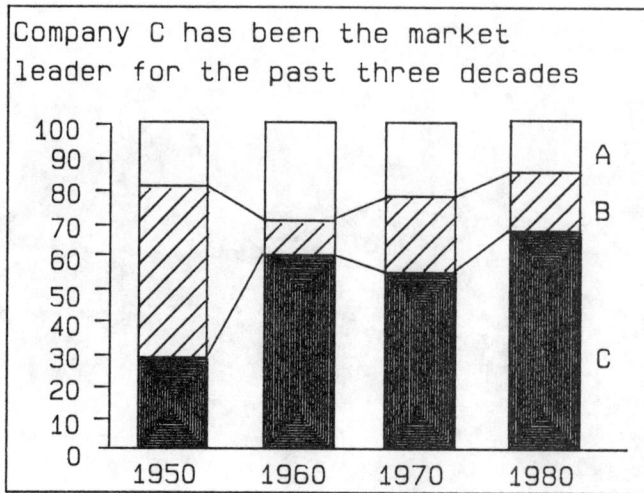

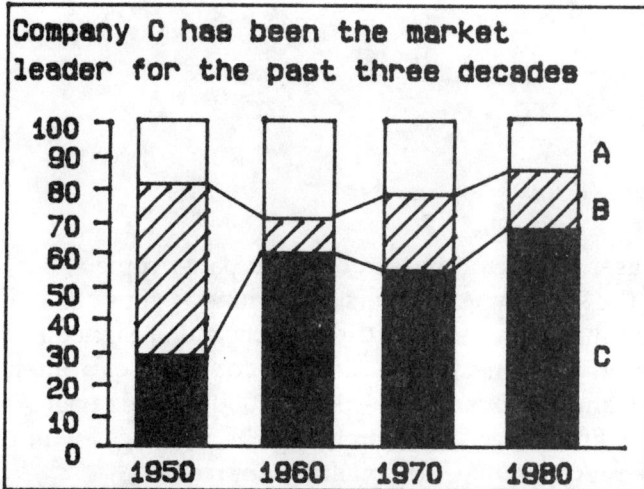

Figure 7-16.
Graph drawn with hard/soft tips.

When plotting on plain paper, use the standard water-based ink pens. Load in a set of oil-based pens when using overhead transparency film. The hardness of the tip of the pen (nib) will largely determine how long the pen will last. The harder the tip, the longer the pen will last, but the lines drawn with it will be thinner. Figure 7-16 shows a small graph produced with a hard and soft tip pen. The clarity of the picture is enhanced with the soft tip pen.

Some plotter pens are refillable. You pop the top off the pen and squeeze more ink into it out of an applicator bottle. The refillable pens are more difficult to use but represent a savings if you make many graphs over the course of a year.

Paper Stock

With the exception of a few specialty models, most printers and plotters can use a wide variety of paper stock—from plain paper to gummy-back labels to clear acetate film for overhead transparencies. Your choice of stock will largely depend on the job you're doing and the capabilities of your printer or plotter.

For rough draft work with your printer, buy continuous form pin feed paper, the cheaper the better. Your printer will need a tractor mechanism to use pin feed paper, of course. For final drafts, get a box of 20-pound, plain white continuous form paper with razor perforations. When you tear the holes off the paper and separate each sheet (called debursting and decollating in computer parlance), the edges are smooth and clean.

Of course, if you need the best quality paper available, or need a special watermarked or coated stock, you'll need to use cut sheets. Find a good supply from your local stationers, or look in the Yellow Pages for a factory-direct paper outlet. Whenever possible, buy paper locally; shipping charges from discount mail order firms can eat up savings quickly. Textured, rag-content paper is suitable for dot matrix printers only. The fibers of the paper diminish print quality when used with thermal transfer, ink jet, and laser printers.

Judging Paper Quality

The paper you use in your printer plays an important part in the quality of copies you obtain. Good quality paper needn't be expensive, and it goes a long way in improving the looks of your copies. Following are some things you should know about paper and printers.

Paper Weight

Besides size, paper is graded by weight. Most printers, copiers, and typewriter/word processors use paper weighing 18 to 20 pounds (abbreviated #). Thinner, lightweight papers have a weight of 16 or 17 pounds, and bulky papers have a weight of 25 to 30 pounds. This limited range is the approximate minimum and maximum paper weight that most printers can handle. Unless the printer is specifically made for it, you can't feed extra light or heavy paper through it, or the paper will jam.

Paper Content

Common printer paper is made of wood pulp, called bond, with no cotton or "rag" content. Bond paper is suitable for most applications, but if you need a better look and feel, load the copier with a rag-content paper, like the kind used in letterheads. Avoid fancy linen or all cotton papers; print quality may be impaired.

Color Paper

Color paper can be used to separate sections of reports, or to indicate the level of revision of a document. Most all color papers, except construction art paper, can be used with a printer.

Note that the color is not colorfast in some papers. If the paper is exposed to moisture or heat, the colors may fade, shift, or bleed. Be sure the colors are permanent or you may not obtain the results you are looking for. Worse, the colors may rub off inside the printer. The residue must be cleaned or subsequent printouts may be tinged with color.

White paper comes in grades of whiteness. Bright white paper is often made by mixing ultraviolet optical brighteners with superbleached pulp. Most people prefer a more subdued white paper, because it is easier on the eyes. If you need a specific brightness, check with the local stationary or paper supply store.

Paper Quality

Experts can judge the quality of paper by touch, sight, even smell. Unless you have specific training, it's difficult to tell a "good" paper from a "bad" paper. But you can evaluate a given paper by using it for a while with your printer. Buy a ream of several brands and try each. Note how well the printer accepts the paper, and whether the print quality gets better or worse. This is particularly important with laser printers.

When choosing paper, try to compare a new sheet with the sample sheet. Apart from a little bit of soil left behind from handling, the sample should look like the fresh sheet. Be on the lookout for yellowing. Also examine how well the sample has stood up to being fondled. Most bond papers will show creases and dog ears rather easily, but a good rag content paper will hide them.

Paper Finish

Bond paper has a smooth, even texture. Holding it up to the light, you can see the splotches of pulp from manufacture. The smooth finish is what makes bond paper ideally suited for printing. The ink or toner sets evenly on the surface of the paper, with no distortion.

Paper with some rag content will have a definite texture, perhaps even a linen weave. This texture, while making the paper "feel" better in your hands, may actually produce inferior results on almost any printer except a good impact dot matrix model. If you want to use a rag paper, get one that has little surface texture. Avoid highly polished papers (like slick magazine pages), as the ink or the toner may not set well on the surface. You can test this by making a sample print and rubbing the page with your finger. Little or no ink or toner should rub off.

Remember that cotton rag papers have a higher moisture content than plain bond paper (the cotton absorbs moisture much more readily). When this moisture is driven out by the fuser heater in a laser printer, it causes the paper to curl. If the curl is excessive, it may remain there forever and will detract from the finished product.

Most laser printers can use just about any type of paper stock, including overhead transparencies, but you can't use extra slippery or extra thick paper. You run the risk of jamming the printer. Also, avoid using heat-sensitive "sticky-back" paper (the kind often used for drafting), since the fusing mechanism in the laser printer can melt the backing, creating a sticky, oozing mess.

Most laser printers use an optical switch that senses when paper is feeding through the mechanism. This switch is blocked when paper passes by. Clear acetate film or overhead transparency material will not adequately block the switch, so the laser printer may jam. If your printer uses an optical paper switch (as opposed to a mechanical switch), be sure to order overhead transparency film that has a white stripe painting on one end. Should your laser printer not accept any clear overhead transparency film, make a paper print and copy it on a plain paper copier. Fill the copier with the transparency film.

Most all thermal transfer and ink jet printers require a special polyester-based paper. Bond paper with a heavy rag (cotton) content yields unacceptable results. Why? The cotton fibers of the paper are extra long and absorb the ink along their entire length. On paper, the printed result can look splotchy and uneven. Most major paper suppliers offer polyester-based paper and overhead transparency film.

Making Slides and Viewgraphs

E X E C U T I V E   S U M M A R Y

Overhead transparencies are good for presentations to small audiences (under 30 people) in a small room. Slides can be shown to any size audience, as long as the room is big enough and the slide projector can shine an image large and bright enough for everyone to see. Overheads can be made from a plotter or printer. Impact dot matrix printers can't be used for making overheads, but ink jet, thermal transfer, and laser printers can.

Plain paper and infrared copiers can also be used to make overheads from paper originals. You can make color overheads with a plain paper copier by switching toner cartridges or using special color transfer film.

Slides can be produced by photographing a printout, snapping a picture of the computer's screen, or using a video film recorder. When shooting the computer's screen, use a monitor hood or tripod to keep the camera steady.

Many of the charts you create with your personal computer will be for your own use. You may, for example, decide to chart a row of numbers just so you can analyze the relationship between them. But business graphics are also for sharing, for presenting your ideas to others. If you're giving an oral presentation, you'll need slides or overhead transparencies for displaying your graphs to your audience (you can also use your computer as a kind of electronic slide carousel; see Chapter 10 for details).

The process of converting a computer-generated chart to a slide or overhead transparency isn't terribly difficult, but there are certain tricks to the trade. You also need the proper supplies, or you'll be foiled from the start.

Overhead Transparencies

An overhead transparency, or *viewgraph*, is a large 8 by 10 inch acetate sheet used with an overhead projector, like the one in Figure 8-1. A light from the projector shines through the sheet

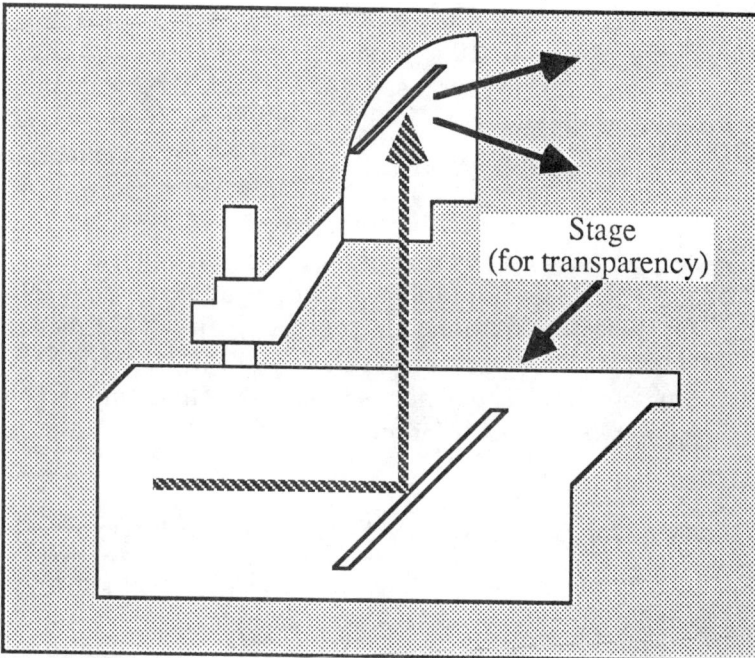

Figure 8-1.
Overhead projector, with overhead.

and is directed into a lens and onto the screen. Because they give off so much light, overhead projectors are ideal for use in semilit rooms.

In addition, overhead projectors permit a lot of useful interaction. The sheet is large and easy to handle. Overhead projectors are designed with an open "stage" (the part you rest the transparency on), so it's easy to write directly onto the overhead or point to an item on the chart with a pencil or pointer.

Between slides and overhead transparencies, overheads are the easier of the two to create. You can make a transparency directly with a plotter or with most printers. Transparencies can also be made from material printed on paper with a plain paper or infrared copier.

Overheads with a Plotter

It's easy to make an overhead with a plotter. If the plotter has multiple pens, you can make colored overheads. Plotters for personal computers are available in two basic sizes: for plotting on paper up to 8 by 10 inches or 11 by 17 inches. The smaller plotters are perfect for the job, since you won't be making overheads larger than 8 by 10 inches. Whatever plotter you choose, it must be able to accept transparency sheets. A plotter that looses its grip on the overhead won't be any use to you.

The pens in a multipen plotter are removable, and you can insert any color pen into the plotter's pen carousel. That means you're not stuck with plotting with basic colors. You can draw with any ink, as long as there's a pen for that color.

Most business graphics programs let you assign colors prior to plotting; others don't. In any case, there's no reason that you must stick to the palette specified by the program. You can easily switch the red pen for a blue one. The computer and plotter won't know the difference.

Color Output from a Single Pen Plotter

If your plotter can't automatically change pens, you can still make full-color charts. The technique involves manually swapping pens, so the plotter you use must be able to accept additional colored pens.

1. While in the charting program, assign colors to parts of the graph, as usual. Instruct the program to pause between color changes (most graphics programs allow for this).
2. Insert the first color pen to use and start plotting.
3. When the program pauses the plotter, *carefully* change the pen, being sure not to upset the position of the plot head or the viewgraph.
4. Resume plotting until the next pen change. Change the pen again as you did before. Continue this procedure until all the colors are plotted.

The Right Supplies

Standard plotter pens for drawing on paper aren't suitable for drawing directly onto acetate film. Soft point, oil-based pens work best with overhead transparencies. Most manufacturers offer a variety of pens with different tip thicknesses, hardnesses, and ink chemistries for their plotters. Choose the right one for the job.

If you're not getting acceptable results when using an oil-based pen, you may need to slow down the drawing speed of the plotter. Some graphics programs let you assign a maximum plotting speed to better match the optimum writing speed when using transparency film. If you can't control the plotting speed via software, you may have to fiddle with the setup switches on the plotter.

You can use just about any type of clear acetate material, as long as it is uncoated. Avoid using overhead transparency material designed for use with plain paper copiers. Many of these have a silicone coating that will cause the ink to smear. Instead, use write-on transparencies, or acetate designed for use in plotters.

When the overhead is done, always mount it in a frame, as shown in Figure 8-2. The frame makes it easier to handle the overheads and blocks out excess light. Frames also let you attach overlays and reveals.

Overheads with a Printer

Impact dot matrix printers can't print on acetate film. Not so with ink jet, thermal transfer, and laser printers. These models can

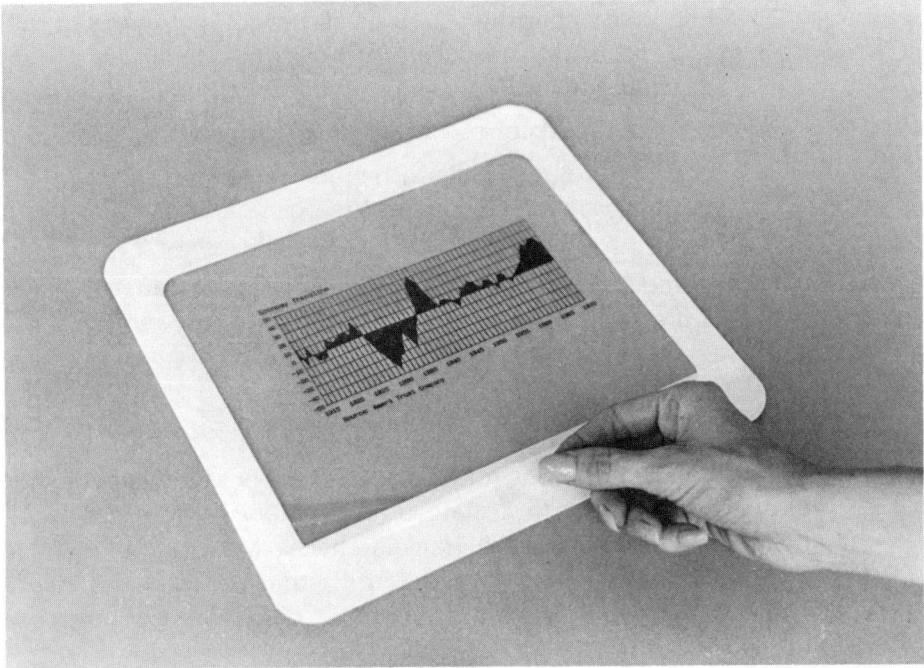

Figure 8-2.
Mounting overhead in frame.

print directly on acetate with no smearing, special ribbons, or other chemicals. All three yield superior results.

A number of ink jet and thermal transfer printers can print in color. If you want color output, make sure you're using a color ribbon or cartridge, and that the graphing software is compatible with the printer.

As with plotters, your choice of transparency material makes a big difference. Use only uncoated acetate. If you haven't yet purchased a printer, check the models you're interested in to make sure they accept acetate sheets. The printer should grasp the sheet firmly, with no slippage.

Overheads with a Plain Paper Copier

There may be times when you can't or don't want to create over-heads directly with a printer or plotter. Plain paper copiers can be used to make clear and sharp overheads. Print or plot the original (in one color only), load the proper transparency material into the copier, and make a copy. It's as simple as that.

Types of Transparency Sheets

Different copiers require different types of transparency material. There are three or four general types; check with an office supply store for a type compatible with your copier.

Transparencies for plain paper copiers come clear or colored—red, green, and blue. The colored ones help break up the monotony of an "all-white" presentation, but should be used with discretion. Don't switch from color to color too often.

Most plain paper copiers use an optical switch that senses when paper is feeding through the mechanism. This switch is blocked when paper passes by. Clear acetate film or overhead transparency material will not adequately block the switch, so the copier may jam. If your copier uses an optical paper switch (as opposed to a mechanical switch), be sure to order overhead transparency film that has a white stripe painted on one end.

Copying Tips

When making transparencies with a plain paper copier, copy the art onto plain paper first, to make sure the graphic is centered on the page and that the copying mechanism is operating properly. When you're satisfied with the copy, load the transparency sheets.

Large, black areas on your graphic can pose problems for all but the best copiers. Instead of black bars, you may get washed-out gray ones. If you're using a less-than-sterling copier, avoid large black areas in your chart whenever possible. Use hatching, patterns, or outlines instead.

The original should be as dark as you can make it. If it's light, make another printout using a fresh ribbon. If you must write on the original, use a dark, felt-tipped pen. Avoid using pencil or colored pens. And, whenever possible, use a regular copy setting on the copier. The darker the setting, the more chance there is of picking up paste-up marks and splotches from the original.

Embellishing with Color

You can add impact to black and white transparencies by adding a bit of color. The easiest way is to use markers or colored acetate overlays.

For markers:

1. Make the chart as usual, but fill the chart elements (bars, columns, areas, pie slices) with white.
2. Print or plot the chart as usual, and make an overhead of the paper copy.
3. Fill in the chart elements with a felt-tip pen recommended for use with acetate (these pens are available from most office supply stores).
4. Let the ink dry fully, and then cover the colored side with a blank sheet of acetate. Tape the two together and mount them on a frame.

For acetate overlays:

Colored pens aren't suitable for filling large areas since you can see the marks left by the pen tip. For big areas, use colored acetate overlays. The film is available in packs with a rainbow of assorted colors.

1. Make the chart as usual, but fill the chart elements (bars, columns, areas, pie slices) with white.
2. Print or plot the chart, as usual, and make a copy of it onto a transparency.
3. Choose a color to use and lay the sheet on top of the overhead (be sure to stick the proper side against the overhead; one side of the color sheet is coated with a light adhesive, the other side is not). Press out any air bubbles with your fingers.
4. With a hobby knife, cut along the edges of the graphic elements, as shown in Figure 8-3. Don't press down too hard or you'll cut through the overhead.
5. Remove the excess color sheet. You can use different colors for other graphic elements if you like.
6. Spread out any remaining air bubbles with your fingers, then sandwich a plain sheet of acetate over your graph. Tape them together and mount them on a frame.

Full-Color Charts

Color copiers (and laser printers) are available but they are expensive. You can create color transparencies from a copier in a number of ways:

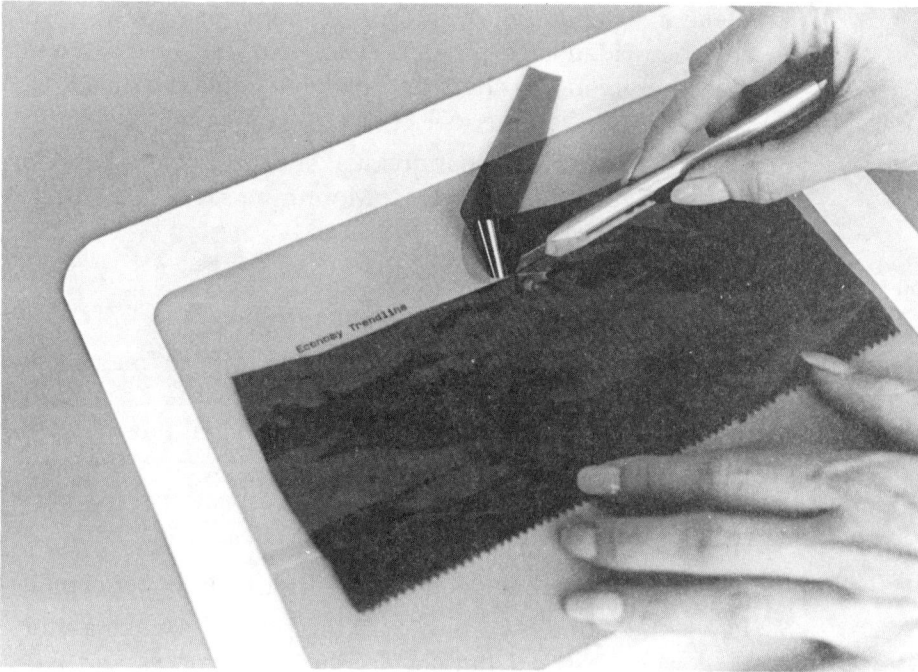

Figure 8.3.
Using overlay.

Color Toner Cartridges

Use this method if your copier or laser printer accepts cartridges with different color toner.

1. Create the graph and copy it into a drawing or painting program that lets you manipulate the image. Make several copies of the graphic, one for each of the colors that will be in your overhead. Name each copy with one of the colors.

2. Open up one of the copies, let's say the one named "green," and erase all the elements that *won't* be colored green. For example, erase everything but the bars in a bar chart. Make a print of it.

3. Repeat the procedure for the other colors (one for the title and one for the grid and axes lines, for instance). You should end up with several paper copies. Each copy represents one of the colors of the final overhead. Elements on one copy should not be present in the others.

4. Make a separate overhead of each copy, using a different color cartridge each time. That is, take the "green" copy, load the green cartridge, and make a single overhead. Do the same for the other colors.

5. Carefully match up the individual sheets of colored acetate and sandwich them together. Mount the set on a transparency frame.

Kroy Kolor

Kroy Kolor is a unique material that adds color to images created with a plain paper copier or laser printer. The Kroy Kolor system consists of a set of colored sheets (several dozen colors are available) and a transfer machine. The dye from the color sheets adhere to the parts of the page or overhead that has been imaged with toner. To add color to an overhead transparency:

1. Image a transparency with a printer or plain paper copier.

2. Lay a sheet of Kroy Kolor over the print. To make a multicolored chart, cut the sheets into small pieces and tape them over specific elements of the chart.

3. Feed the chart through the transfer machine. When finished, remove the transfer sheets.

You can also create multicolor charts using several layers of overhead transparency film. Follow the directions given above for color toner cartridges. Use a different color transfer sheet for each printout. You can effectively sandwich four or five transparencies together.

Overheads with an Infrared Copier

Infrared copiers use heat instead of light to reproduce images. Overhead transparencies are available for infrared copiers, too, and in a greater variety than with plain paper copiers. There's the standard black image on clear or colored stock (red, green, blue), as well as clear image on black stock, clear image on red stock, and colored image (red, green, blue, and purple) on clear stock. 3M is the major manufacturer of infrared copier supplies. Check with a local 3M dealer for more information on what's available.

Color Overheads

3M makes a unique colored film called Type 288. This film creates a colored image on a clear background (most viewgraph films for plain paper and infrared copiers create black images on a colored background). Type 288 film comes in a rainbow package of four different colors—red, blue, green, and purple.

You can make a full color transparency from a black and white original by following the steps outlined above for making color overheads with a plain paper copier. But instead of switching toner cartridges, switch to a different color transparency sheet. The images Type 288 film creates are semitransparent; so some color mixing is possible, but the results aren't always predictable.

Slides

Overhead transparencies are fine for presentations to small groups, but they fall short when addressing more than 30 or 40 people in a large room. And, by their nature, overheads are not designed for elaborate "multimedia" shows, since you must manually swap the transparencies on the projector.

Slide presentations let you show your work to a large group—up to several hundred people if the room is big enough. If you have several projectors, you can gang them up with a dissolver or controller (covered in more detail in Chapter 10) for making a flashy multimedia presentation.

You can make slides of your charts in a variety of ways, from photographing a printout to sending your charts to a graphic arts house for digital typesetting.

Photographing a Printout

To photograph a printout onto 35mm film, you'll need a copy stand and camera with a lens that can focus down to about 7 inches. A tripod is optional, as long as the exposure is shorter than $\frac{1}{60}$th of a second. Here's what to do:

1. Make the printout, then place it on the stage of a copy stand or tape it to a copy board. Adjust the lights so that they're on either side of the printout, and at a 45 degree angle to it, as shown in Figure 8-4.

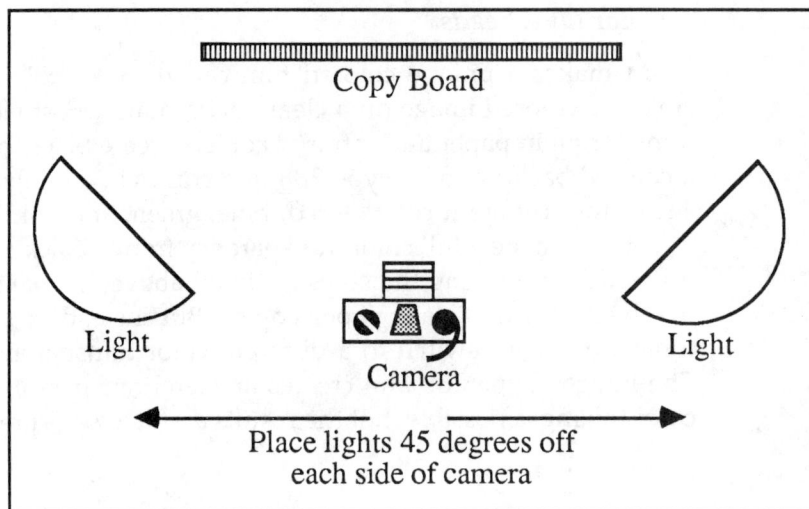

Figure 8-4.
Copy stand layout.

2. Frame and focus the camera. If your camera has a macro capability, use it. If you can't get the image in focus, you may need to attach a close-up lens to the camera's lens.

3. Use your camera's built-in meter to take an exposure reading. The exposure will be a little low, since the camera will compensate for the bright white background of the graphic. Add another one-third to one-half f/stop, to be sure that the film picks up the darker portions of the image. A better way is to use an 18 percent gray card (available at photo stores) and take the exposure off it.

4. Squeeze off the shot. Bracket your exposures by shooting two additional frames, one a half stop over the recommended exposure, another a half stop under.

If you are using color film, and the lights in your copy stand are the incandescent photoflood variety, you'll need to attach an 80B color compensation filter to your camera lens. Without the filter, the pictures will have an excessive orange glow. The filter will cut down the light reaching the film by about one-third an f/stop, so remember to take this into consideration if you're setting the exposure manually.

Black and white film requires no filtration, nor do you need it if the copy stand is equipped with electronic flash.

Photographing the Computer Monitor

An easier method than shooting a printout is to aim the camera directly at your computer's monitor and shoot away. Just about any 35-mm camera will do; it's the lens that makes the difference.

You'll obtain the best results if you have a zoom lens with a close focus (not a macro) capability. This will allow you to aim, frame, and shoot with the greatest flexibility and without having to be too far away from the screen. Zoom lenses with 35-mm to 70-mm focal lengths yield the best results without undo distortion (squeezing or stretching the center of the picture). You can also use a standard 50-mm lens equipped with a 1+ or 2+ diopter close-up lens.

1. Mount the camera on a sturdy tripod and set the shutter speed at no faster than one-eighth of a second (a noticeable bar will appear across the screen with faster shutter speeds).

2. Dim or turn off the room lights and adjust the brightness control on the screen so that it's comfortable to your eyes.

3. Use the camera's built-in exposure meter to set the f/stop, or use the recommended indoor light setting for the film you're using (see the instruction sheet packed with the film). If your camera has an automatic flash, turn it off or cover it up completely. The flash will wash out the screen.

4. Take a picture of the screen. For safety, shoot a couple of extra frames one-half f/stop over and under the recommended setting. If you take pictures of the screen regularly, you'll get to know which setting is right for your camera, lens, and monitor, and you won't have to waste film bracketing the exposures each time.

Most computer monitors give off excess blue light (your eyes compensate for it so you don't notice it). If your color pictures are too blue for your liking, use a yellow 81A, B, or C filter.

Monitor Hoods

The point-and-shoot method described above works fine most of the time, but if you find yourself photographing the computer screen frequently, get a monitor hood. Monitor hoods, like the one in Figure 8-5, consist of a plastic box that fits around the

Figure 8-5.
Sample monitor hood.

computer's video screen. At the other end of the hood you place the camera.

The hood, which includes its own built-in close-up lens, provides enough physical support that you don't need a tripod. And since it blocks out ambient light, you don't need to turn off the room lights. Shooting with the hood is the same as shooting without one. On your first roll, bracket the exposures.

Film Recorder

Perhaps the best way to shoot your computer's screen is with a video film recorder, a device that includes its own very high resolution monitor. Whatever you see on your computer screen is captured on film in vivid detail.

Several models of film recorders are available. Some hook up to your computer via the composite video output jack on the display adapter board. Others hook up to the RGB output of the video card. The RGB connection generally provides a crisper image, but you're limited to the colors that the graphics controller card can generate (usually 4 or 16).

Cameras and Camera Backs

Most film recorders come with their own 35-mm camera. You simply load the film and start shooting. With others, you must attach a separate camera. You'll need a lens adapter so you can attach your camera to the recorder. The adapter is available from the manufacturer of the recorder.

A few video film recorders have a lens and shutter built into them, but lack a camera back—the part that holds the film and advances it. You can change the camera back to switch to another type of film. You could, for example, shoot a roll of 35-mm film with a 35-mm camera back, then switch to a Polaroid film back for shooting instant pictures.

Film and Exposure

For slides, use either Kodachrome 40, Ektachome 100, or Ektachrome 160 (or another manufacturer's comparable slide film). Ektachrome film has a slight blue cast to it (especially noticeable when shooting computer screens) but you can have it processed anywhere. Kodachrome film needs to be processed by Kodak or some other large photographic lab.

If you are in a big hurry, use Polaroid instant slides. You need the Polaroid autoprocessor system to develop the slides. Image quality is excellent and you get finished slides in less than 5 minutes. Color or black and white (standard or high-contrast) slide films are available for the autoprocessor system at most photographic stores.

If your camera doesn't have a built-in meter, use a hand-held meter and take a reading of the illumination of the screen. Remember that these exposure settings are average. Experiment with a spare roll and adjust the settings to your particular camera, lens, and computer monitor.

Computer-Slide Service Bureaus

If your time schedule allows, you may send the charts created by your presentation graphics program to a computer-slide service bureau. The service bureau makes a 35-mm slide or overhead transparency print using their high-resolution video film cameras. Turnaround is usually 48 hours or less and express service and delivery are available. A number of computer-slide service bureaus are listed in Appendix C.

Some service bureaus are set up to accept charts created with a number of popular graphics programs. Check first for compatibility before sending in your data. However, most service bureaus do not accept charts created with a program other than their own proprietary software. As with all presentation graphics software, the features of the service bureau programs vary. Part of the task of choosing a good computer-slide service bureau is making sure their software is satisfactory for your needs.

If you don't have the time or inclination to create the charts yourself, you may specify the chart type and data and have the service bureau make the graph from scratch. The cost is usually higher for this service because it requires an artist to generate the chart.

Whether you supply the complete chart or just the data, you can connect to the service bureau by mail or modem. Prepare the chart or data on a standard 5¼- or 3½-inch IBM PC format diskette and label it clearly. Data transfer via a modem is more involved but if you are in a hurry, you save time and express delivery charges. Most computer-slide service bureaus have specific telecommunications software for use with their system; contact them for more information.

Modem Basics

Modems are used to connect two distant computers together for the purpose of sharing data, programs, or both. For presentation graphics, you'll use a modem to send or receive chart data between offices of your company or to transmit chart information to a computer-slide service bureau. The modem connection is most often made through standard telephone lines.

Most modems attach to the computer via an RS-232C serial port. They are powered either by the electricity flowing through the telephone line, by a separate AC power cord, or by an internal battery. The IBM PC and compatibles can accept *card modems*. These are printed circuit boards that contain all the necessary modem electronics. They attach to the computer in one of the expansion slots and do not need a separate power supply or serial port (the modem *does* occupy one of the two COM port addresses of the computer, so you can have only one other serial port installed in the PC).

Modems connect to the telephone in two ways: directly and acoustically. *Direct-connect modems* run in-line between the telephone wall jack and the telephone instrument. Many direct-connect modems available today can be programmed to place and answer calls. These are often referred to as "smart" modems. Most smart modems are "Hayes" compatible (named after a popular maker of modems) and use the *Hayes AT* command set. This compatibility, which is not always complete despite claims by the manufacturer, assures the modem of working with a variety of software.

Acoustic-connect modems, which can't be used to dial or answer the phone, have a pair of rubber cups that accept the handset of a standard desktop telephone. Acoustic-coupled modems are usually used when you can't tap directly into the phone line.

Modems transmit and receive data at a variety of standard speeds, all expressed in *baud*, or bits per second (BPS). The slowest is 300 baud, which equals 30 text characters per second. Most modems in use today operate at 1200 baud, or 120 text characters per second. The latest modems for personal computers work at 2400 baud (240 characters per second). To work properly, both modems on either end of the phone line must be operating at the same speed.

Modems send and receive data in two discrete sets of tones. The first modem in the link uses one set of tones; the second modem uses the other set. These sets are referred to as "answer" and "originate." Almost all modems are capable of both answer and originate operation, but not all are. Older models operate in originate mode only.

Connecting a modem to your computer and phone isn't enough to establish a communication link. The computer must be told that it's going to be conversing with another PC. A communications program establishes the proper link. Communications programs run from the very simple to the very complex. At one end of the spectrum are simple programs that instruct the computer to send and receive data. At the other end of the spectrum are sophisticated programs that let you save the data received by the mode, or to command a smart modem to dial the phone or answer a call.

A software program that supports the *XMODEM* communications protocol is recommended when transferring numerical data or graphics through the phone lines. The XMODEM protocol, endorsed by nearly all communications programs, monitors the phone line and detects transmission errors. Data is sent again if an error occurs.

Digital Typesetting

For pristine graphics printouts, try a phototypesetting service. You send a disk filled with your chart documents to the typesetter, and they send back the pictures professionally typeset on PMT film. Turnaround time is under 1 week. Digitally typeset screen images are ideal when producing an ad or brochure.

The typesetter expects the picture documents you send in to be in a specific format, usually captured with a proprietary "screen saver" program. Consult with your typesetter for details.

Most digital typesetting is in black and white, but color separations (separate pieces of film for each of the four process colors) are also available. The price is higher than monochrome images. Because the graphic has already been color separated, however, it's one less step a printer must do when preparing your ad or brochure, so you can save money in the long run.

Graphics in Written Reports and Oral Presentations

E X E C U T I V E   S U M M A R Y

There are five important steps in preparing material for written or oral presentations: Analyze the message, simplify the message, set length limit, add sparkle to the writing, and review the document.

The layout of the finished document can be in one, two, or three columns. The one-column layout is best suited when the document is typewritten. Use headings and subheadings at logical places in the document to break up long passages of text. A dot matrix printer (impact or nonimpact) can be used to print the final draft. But the quality of the print must be high, preferably indistinguishable from typewriter print.

The keys to planning a successful oral presentation are budget, lead time, audience size, audience sophistication, audience contact, sequence flexibility, and pacing. A chart should remain projected on the screen for as long as it takes for you to talk about it—but no longer. Turn off the overhead projector when changing transparencies.

You've spent hours, perhaps days, compiling data, crunching it with your computer, and churning out striking business graphics. Don't blow all your hard work by dumping the charts carelessly in a meaningless report, or by flashing them mechanically on a screen before the bored eyes of your colleagues.

The art of successful business graphics is a two-step process: creating and presenting. You've done the creating part; now comes the equally important job of presenting those graphs to others. The best, most ingenious charts in the world pale to mediocrity when presented haphazardly.

If you read nothing else in this book, read this chapter. It provides short tricks, tips, and pointers on how to present your charts and graphs effectively. The chapter is divided into two parts. The first part, Charts into Print, details everything you need to know about including charts in memos, reports, and other written documents. Charts on the Silver Screen, the second part, discusses the proper technique of setting up business meetings and giving oral presentations. We've saved a separate chapter, Chapter 10, for advanced presentation techniques using your computer.

PART ONE: CHARTS INTO PRINT

Follow these suggestions when preparing charts for a report, newsletter, and other printed material.

- *Analyze.* Analyze your message to make sure it is clearly definable. Make an outline.

- *Simplify.* Simplify the message and the document outline so that only the pertinent facts remain. Avoid preaching or teaching.

- *Set length limit.* Establish a length for the document and stick to it as much as possible.

- *Add sparkle to the writing.* Write in the present tense and in the active voice. Whenever possible, enhance the document by using metaphors, anecdotes, and examples.

- *Review the document.* When you are done, review the document and pass it along to a colleague to get a second opinion.

Fundamentals of Layout

With the text written and finalized, it's now time to consider the format of the finished product. This step has become an integral part of business communications because of the proliferation of desktop publishing software. These programs let you design the layout for your manuscripts. Of course, you may reproduce the document in standard single- or double-space typewritten manuscript style using your word processor. But you may desire a more polished look not available in your word processor. You'll need a page layout program to create the special layouts you want.

Single or Facing Pages?

Before you can design a page layout, you must consider the form of the finished document. Pages printed on one side and bound together with a single staple are probably best left to the single-column, double-spaced manuscript layout. If the pages are bound along one edge like a book, however, you can choose a one-, two-, or three-column format.

Multiple-column layouts are best suited when the document will be printed on both sides of the pages. Open the document anywhere and the layout consists of two *facing pages*. For best results, there should be some kind of unity and symmetry between the two facing pages.

One Column

It's perfectly acceptable to prepare a document in a single-column format, especially when the page is typewritten or printed with a daisywheel or dot matrix printer. Typewriter and printer fonts really don't lend themselves to multicolumn treatment, because the characters are so large.

Don't be afraid of extra white space around the text, as illustrated in Figure 9-1. In fact, the blank areas of the page are about as important as the text areas. Feel free to reduce the width of the single column to create extra white space. You can use the wide "marginal" area for headings. You're also free to extend your graphics beyond the margins of the columns.

Single-column text can be written flush right, flush left, or justified (both right and left margins flush). If you use a word pro-

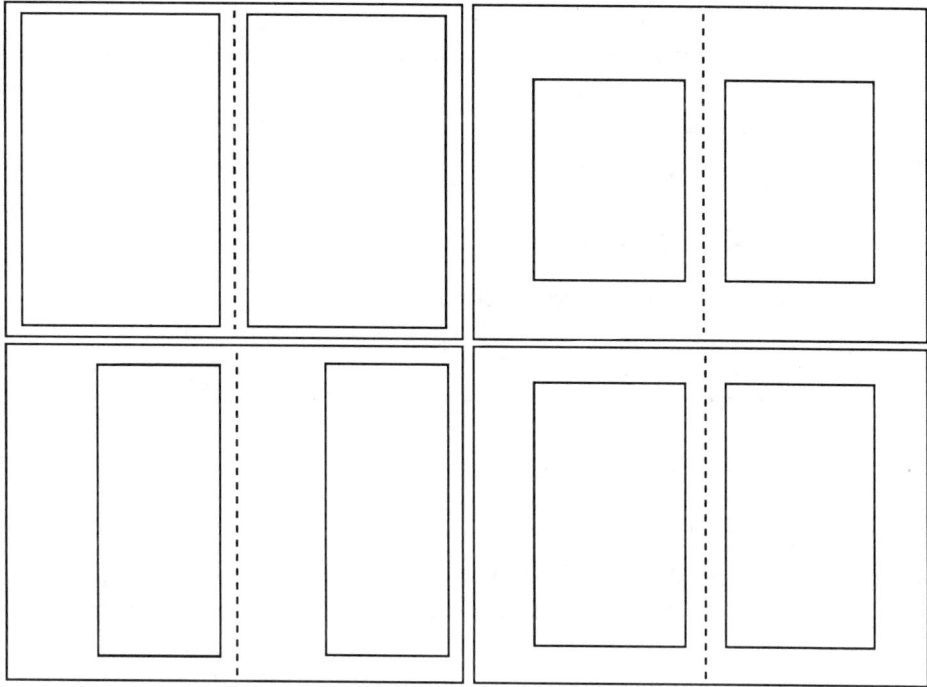

Figure 9-1.
Several single-column layouts.

cessor or page layout program with autojustification, try to avoid the extra large spaces that the program puts in to stretch the line between both margins. Hyphenate words whenever possible to close up the gaps.

If your page layout program has kerning and tracking capabilities, use them. Kerning is shown in Figure 9-2 and is adjust-

VA LT Ta Kerned

VA LT Ta Not kerned

Figure 9-2.
Kerning example.

ing the space between two adjacent characters to improve the appearance of the document. Tracking is used with justified margins and is adjusting the space between all characters in the line to bring them closer together or further apart. Tracking helps prevent large gaps between words.

Two and Three Columns

If the document is professionally typeset or prepared with a laser printer, the size of the text will likely be smaller than if the document is prepared on a daisywheel or dot matrix printer. If there are more than 55 characters per line, it's a good idea to chop up the text by dividing it into two or three columns.

Two- and three-column layouts, like the ones in Figure 9-3, seldom leave room for extra white space, and graphics are more difficult to position. In both a two- and three-column layout, graphics can stretch between the columns if necessary. Some word processing programs accept graphics that are wider than

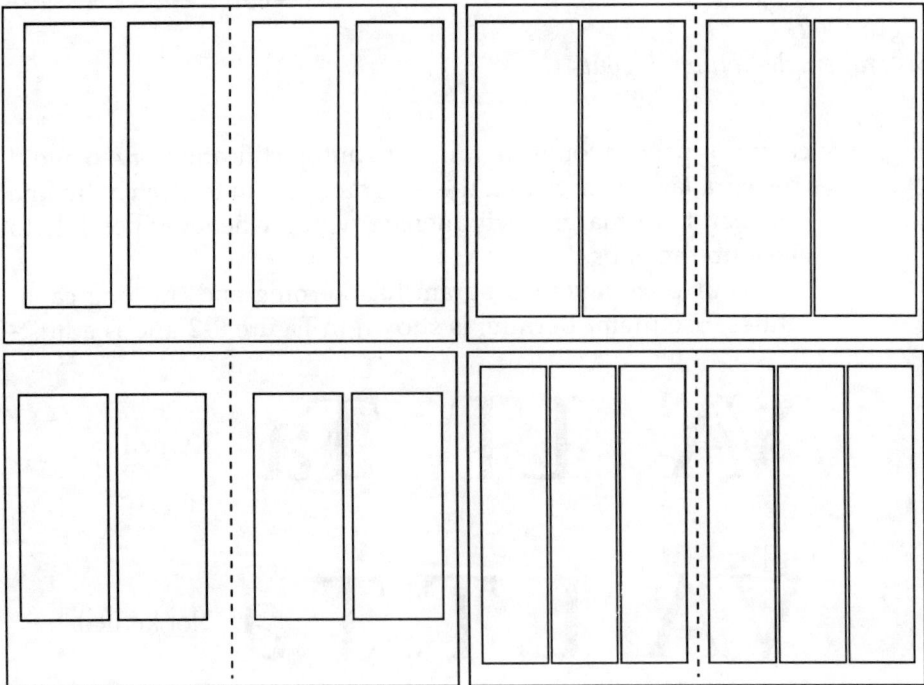

Figure 9-3.
Two- and three-column layouts.

the columns, but not all can. Use a desktop publishing program for elaborate page layouts.

Headlines and Headings

Each major section of your document should be highlighted with a title or headline. Use uppercase, underlining, or boldface (or all three) to set the headline apart.

Separate large chunks of text at logical points with headings and subheadings. This makes the document easier to look at and helps the reader find information faster. Pick a format for the headings and stick with it. For example, major headings can be in all uppercase, minor headings in upper- and lowercase, and so forth. Adding headings is very important if you're using a two- or three-column page layout because it helps break up the narrow columns.

Inserting the Charts

Depending on your time and resources, you can insert the charts into the written report with the help of a word processor, a page makeup program, or—as a last resort—with old-fashioned scissors and glue.

Word Processor

Many of the latest versions of word processors for the IBM PC and compatibles can combine text and graphics on the same page. The easiest way to use a graphics-capable word processor is to finalize the text, then use the program's "clipboard" feature to cut and paste the pictures into the document. The cutting-and-pasting procedure varies from program to program. But to be most flexible, you should be able to select the portion of the chart you want, and paste just the cropped section into the word processing document. The process is made easier if you use a mouse or other alternate input device to define a cutting or cropping box.

Page Layout Program

A word processor lets you write text and insert pictures within the document, but most programs limit you to specific page

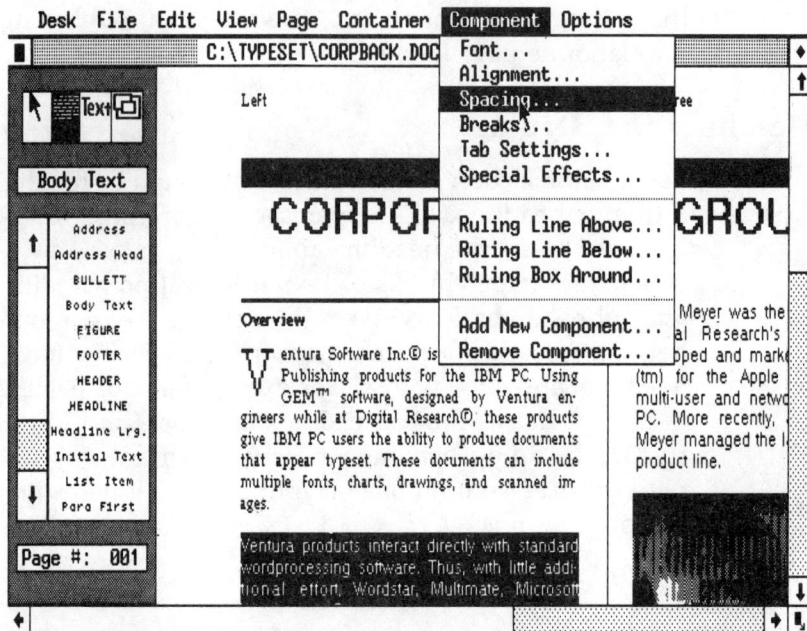

Figure 9-4.
Page layout screen.

designs. A page makeup program lets you format words and pictures in just about any way you choose. You define the look of each page of the document as if you were arranging toy building blocks on the living room floor. You can mix different column widths, overlap pictures, combine various fonts and font sizes, and more. Page layout programs are ideally suited when using one of the multiple-column layouts described in the previous section. Figure 9-4 shows a document in preparation.

Page layout programs are the cornerstone to desktop publishing and have become increasingly popular. They are, however, more difficult to learn and use than a word processor and often require the use of a mouse cursor positioning device (or some other alternative input device, like a light pen or graphics tablet).

Scissors and Glue

Lacking a word processor that can integrate words and picture, or a page layout program, your alternative is a pair of scissors and a bottle of glue. You won't get any awards for your hi-tech approach, but manually cutting and pasting the charts into your report is certainly the cheapest way to go. The major disadvantages: You can't easily change the layout of the finished page (without repasting) and you run the risk of pasting the graphics crooked on the page.

When preparing the manuscript, measure the artwork and leave a blank space accordingly. You may need to print several drafts before the spacing is correct for all the charts. You can use rubber cement, paper glue, or hot wax (applied with a hand waxer) to place the artwork on the page.

The Printout

Most daisywheel computer printers let you choose the size and style of the type. Just about any 10 or 12 pitch typestyle will work. Courier 10 pitch or Letter Gothic 12 pitch are two good choices. The main consideration is that you are consistent. Avoid mixing typestyles in one document. Possible exceptions include captions for charts, footnotes, and page numbers. Be sure the ribbon is fresh and use good quality paper.

Dot matrix printers *can* be used for the final document, but only if the printer can produce sharp, well-defined characters. Most bargain dot matrix printers are primarily designed for draft work only. Some better dot matrix printers have a "letter quality" or "near-letter quality" mode. There is some improvement in these modes, but not always enough for a professional-looking report.

The main advantage of using a dot matrix printer is that you can mix text and graphics on the same page. Daisywheel printers cannot print graphics at all, forcing you to manually place the charts using scissors and glue.

Laser printers represent the best of both worlds. They can mix text (of all sizes) and pictures on the same page, and the final result looks professionally typeset. A number of page makeup programs (see above) are designed for use with laser printers.

If the resolution of the device is high enough, you can also use a thermal transfer or ink jet printer. These printers are also ideal if you are printing the charts in color. Make separate printouts for each copy of the report or document.

Reproduction

If you are preparing multiple copies of your documents, you can either print each copy separately or reproduce them on a plain paper copier or on an offset printer. As a general rule of thumb, make original printouts when preparing only a few copies (less than five or six) of a reasonably short document, and you're not manually pasting the graphics on the page. Original printing is also necessary if the graphics are in color. Otherwise, reproduce the document.

Plain Paper Copies

Copies made with the office copier should be fine for most applications, but be sure the copier has a fresh and ample supply of toner. Try a few test sheets to see if the copier is up to par. Look especially at large black areas. These tend to fade into gray when reproduced on a less-than-sterling plain paper copier. If you have no other choice—you're stuck with the copier you have—you may want to consider redoing the charts and replacing any solid black areas with a lighter tone of gray.

Few plain paper copiers reproduce in color, but if you have a color copier, or have access to one, it can be used to reproduce charts printed in color. A number of copy services offer color copies; the price is generally $1 to $3 per page. If color copying does not yield acceptable results, print the charts separately and bind them in the center or at the end of the document.

Offset Printing

If you're distributing more than a few hundred copies of the document, you'll want to consider offset printing. Offset printing yields higher quality prints and if you are making enough copies, the printing costs are reduced. Your local print shop can also fold and bind the printed documents for you.

Finalizing Camera-Ready Artwork

The original pages of your document, complete with charts, serve as camera-ready artwork for the plain paper copier or off-

Figure 9-5.
Various halftone screens.

set printer. When duplicated on an offset printer, a negative—or plate—is made of each page. The plates are then put in the printer and copies run off. Text and line art, which include your charts, can be photographed directly onto the plate without any intermediate steps.

The same isn't true for photographs. Black and white photographs must first be *screened,* a process that breaks up the many gray areas of the picture into dots of varying size. This is necessary because printing presses print only black; the black dots substitute for the many gray levels in a picture.

Halftone screens are used to convert the grays to dots. The dot spacing in halftone screens vary from course to fine, as shown in Figure 9-5. A course dot screen is used in newspaper printing. The finer screens are for higher quality printing on coated paper. Your printer will do the actual screening, but you must specify the type of screen you want to use. For regular offset printing on plain paper, you should specify a No. 75 screen, which provides good results with a minimum of smearing. Higher quality paper can support a finer screen.

Facsimile by PC

Deadlines are a part of business, and sometimes there is no time to prepare a presentation and mail it to a client or a business associate. When even the overnight express services aren't fast enough, you can still get your point across with a facsimile—transferring the image of each page over the telephone lines.

If you already own an IBM PC or AT, or a clone equipped with PC-standard expansion slots, you can add facsimile capability to your office. The addition of one of the new breeds of fax expansion boards can turn an IBM PC or compatible into a facsimile machine.

Several such expansion boards are available that slip into an empty expansion slot in the PC and use the computer's memory and screen to store and display pages. Received documents appear on the screen, and they can be stored onto magnetic disk or transferred to paper with a suitable dot matrix printer.

Pages can also be sent to other facsimile devices (stand-alone or computer) from your PC. The pages can either be screen images captured into the computer's memory or text documents transferred to fax-equivalent images.

If you have an optical scanner, you can use it to process the image of the pages into the computer. This way, you don't have to use documents prepared by the computer. You can transfer anything that you can fit into the scanner, including signed contracts, text/graphic reports, newspaper and magazine articles, you name it.

The best part about a PC-based facsimile is that the devices work in the "background," while you're writing with a word processor or calculating with an electronic spreadsheet. As long as the fax board is connected to the phone lines, you can send and receive documents with almost no intervention on your part. Keep reading for more on PC-based facsimile expansion boards.

Why Fax?

Facsimile offers a cost-effective alternative to overnight and messenger services. Even if you have lots of pages to send to someone, the cost savings may still be in your favor if you use the fax machine, even if the call is long distance. As an example, it costs approximately $2.50 for a 5-minute phone call from Los Angeles to New York. In that 5-minute period, 5 to 10 pages can be transmitted via fax. If you are sending a long letter or 5- or 10-page report, the total cost is $2.50.

PC-based fax boards let you save even more money with unattended dialing. The machine is loaded with the documents to send and a list of phone numbers to call. The fax machine then calls each number, sending the proper documents to the fax machine (stand-alone or PC-based) on the other end. With unattended calling, you can take advantage of the lower rates in the evening or even on weekends.

More About Fax

Facsimile, the science of transmitting an image of a document and reconstituting that image at another place, is nothing new. In fact, facsimile was invented over 100 years ago, by Alexander Bain, but an adequate transmission scheme (like the telephone) was not around so the idea languished.

Many years later, electrostatic fax machines started to appear, and in the 1960s, standards for their design and communication protocol were established by the Consultative Committee for Telephone and Telegraph (CCITT).

The first fax machines, labeled *Group I*, were the slowest of them all, taking from 4 to 6 minutes to transmit a single letter-size page. *Group II* machines improved on the speed somewhat, decreasing the transmission time to 2 to 3 minutes.

Both Group I and Group II faxes use analog technology to send images from one location to the other. The latest and most popular scheme, digital transmission, is embraced by all *Group III* facsimile devices. The transmission for a Group III fax is under 1 minute. Most letter-size pages are transmitted in 30 to 40 seconds. All PC facsimile boards operate in all three modes—Groups I, II, and III.

A Look at Fax Boards

At its most basic level, the PC fax board is a high-speed modem, operating at a top speed of 9,600 baud (the transmission speed can be slower if the phone connection is poor). Extra circuitry on the board, as well as software running on the computer, convert the text and images viewed on the PC into fax format, or vice versa. That's why you can't use a regular modem to send and receive facsimile documents.

Many of the documents you send through the fax board will be in text-only ASCII format. All the boards currently out have an automatic ASCII-to-fax conversion feature, so any text document you see on screen can be transmitted down the phone lines.

Since facsimile is graphic-based, the recipient sees the characters of the document in picture format. If the receiver also has a PC fax board, the received image is a graphic, not a text document. You need optical character reader (OCR) software to convert the graphic image of the characters into true editable text. OCR software is available as an extra-cost option on most fax boards.

If the text does not need to be manipulated, it can be printed on most dot matrix or laser printers. Most boards come with software drivers that support a wide range of printers.

The benefit of fax is fully realized when transmitting and receiving documents that have both text and pictures. Text and graphics are treated the same by the fax system, so you never have to worry about incompatibilities between the receiving and transmitting stations. It also doesn't matter if the transmitting station is a PC-based fax and the receiver is a stand-alone fax. Both communicate with the same protocols and procedures.

Using a Scanner

Stand-alone facsimile devices scan an original that you insert into a slot in the machine. An optical system in the fax breaks down the page into hundreds of horizontal lines and transmits the lines serially though the phone link. PC-based fax boards have no optical system so they cannot scan originals. If you need to send printed documents through the fax system, you need a desktop scanner.

Scanners are typically used in desktop publishing systems as a way to convert original artwork into computer data, so that pictures can be merged with text onto a desktop published page. All scanners have a maximum image resolution exceeding the requirement needed to send fax documents. The highest resolution of Group III fax transmissions is approximately 200 by 200 dots per inch. Desktop scanners have an upper resolution of 300 by 300 dots per inch (some are even higher).

If you already have a scanner, it costs you nothing to use it with the fax board. However, if a desktop scanner is not among the repertoire of your computer system, and you need to transmit copies of original documents, you must add its cost to the price of the fax board. The advantage of purchasing a separate fax board and scanner over a stand-alone fax machine is that you can use the scanner for other applications.

Fax boards install in your computer like any other expansion card. The boards currently available are full-size so you need a full slot to accommodate one. Since the board is really a modem, it functions as a serial COM port. If you already have a serial port in your computer, you must assign the fax board as COM2. In normal operation, you cannot plug in the board if you have two COM ports already installed. You must disable one COM port or the computer will not function properly. This can be a problem if you have a serial port installed for a plotter or printer and another installed for a modem (or use an internal modem). A few models of fax boards, including the Datacopy MicroFax, also function as a Hayes-compatible telephone modem.

All fax boards connect to the phone lines via a standard RJ-11 modular jack. If your phone system lacks this stype of jack, you must have one installed. Office phone systems may have a different type of connector, especially if rotary phone lines or multiple phone extensions are available from one phone cable. Most phone service companies can install the required RJ-11 jack for a minimal charge.

PART TWO: ON THE SILVER SCREEN

The same suggestions apply for presenting your graphics in person as they do when including charts in written documents. Refer to the beginning of Part One, above, for suggestions on how to plan and prepare for oral presentations. In addition to the points made previously, consider the following when going before an audience with your presentation graphics.

Audience Participation

Most presentations are interactive and require the participation of those attending. Be sure everyone who should be at the meeting can come.

Type of Presentation

There are many types of presentations, but only one is right for any given meeting. What is your message and its purpose? Define the message and purpose and gear the presentation around it. For example, a sales meeting will entail a different kind of presentation than a training session.

The Required Tools

By giving some thought to the nature of your presentation, you can more easily decide on the finished form of the graphics, the type of media to use, and the equipment and facilities you'll need for giving the presentation.

Budget

Your budget will largely determine the type of media and use for the graphics, and the equipment you use to show them. Overhead transparencies are cheap to produce but they may not be what you want for your presentation. If you have the budget, consider 35-mm slides.

You can also use your computer to display the charts. This requires a "slide-show" program and, if the audience is large, a projection TV or LCD overhead projection panel (see below). See Chapter 10 for more information using your computer as a slide carousel.

Slide shows using 35-mm slides can be costly to produce, not only in film and processing costs but also in equipment purchase or rental. An elaborate multimedia show requires, at the very least, several slide projectors and a dissolve unit.

Lead Time

Overhead transparencies can be made in a flash; slides take longer because the film must be developed after it's been exposed (exception: Polaroid instant slide film).

Audience Size

Slide shows are ideal for large audiences, as long as the projector is powerful enough to throw a bright image on the screen. A presentation to a large audience (more than 30 people) requires a big meeting room or auditorium, which precludes the use of overhead transparencies. If the audience is a small one—under 10 people, you may consider producing the graphics on flip charts and do away with projections altogether. A number of business graphics programs can print on extra large paper, when used with the proper type of plotter.

Sophistication of Audience

The more sophisticated the audience, the slicker the presentation must be. The same is true for an audience that you're trying to woo, like a potential client. Flip charts and overheads may be unsuitable; use either a slide projector or a computer.

Audience Contact

Presentations designed to elicit a certain response require intimate audience contact. Slide presentations don't offer this, because it's necessary to darken the room. Slides also make it hard to interact with the graphic being shown on the screen. Free-running presentations—those recorded on videotape or programmed in a multimedia slide show—also don't provide much audience interplay.

Overhead transparencies, on the other hand, provide a great deal of audience contact. Overheads can be projected in semilit rooms. The overhead is openly available for you to point to and mark on.

Sequence Flexibility

Even the best planned presentation sometimes need to be reorganized. Both slides and overheads let you easily change the sequence of the visuals. If you're using more than two slide projectors, make sure that you update all the slides so the continuity isn't disturbed.

Presentations recorded on a video cassette recorder or filmed on a slide strip can't be edited. The order of visuals presented by a computer can be changed, but it requires rewriting the playback script.

Setting Up the Meeting Room

Prior to giving your presentation, you should be sure the meeting room is ready, and that all the equipment is functioning properly and ready to go. If you have a choice, arrange the seating according to the diagrams in Figure 9-6. It allows everyone to see both you and your graphics.

Sound Check

If using a PA system check it out. Remember that bodies absorb sound, so when the room is full of people, the volume level you thought was perfect may be too low. Adjust the volume control so that it's just a little loud. Remember to keep the speakers away from the microphones. A microphone placed too close to a speaker causes annoying howling feedback.

Equipment Check

If you're using either a slide or overhead projector, make sure it's plugged in, aimed at the screen, and properly focused, and keep an extra bulb handy. Murphy's law says that projector bulbs go out only when the presentation is about to begin.

Media Check

If you're using a slide projector, quickly run through the carousel to make sure all the slides are mounted properly. There's nothing more embarrassing than a slide projected upside down. If you're using overheads, flip through them to make sure they're

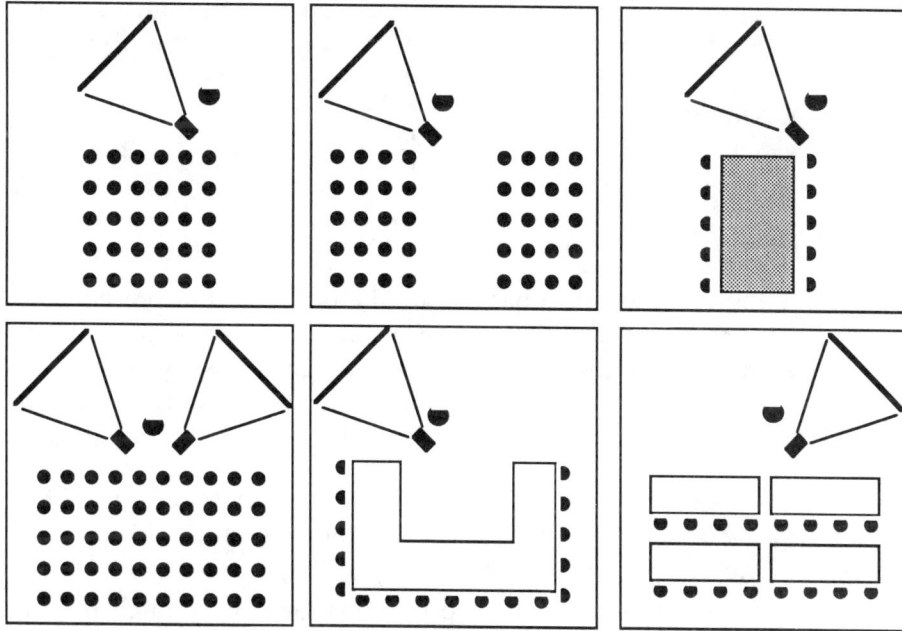

The Right Ways

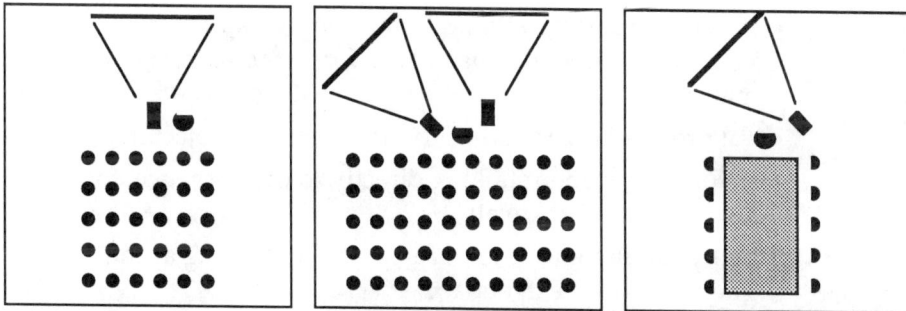

The Wrong Ways

Figure 9-6.
Preferred seating arrangement.

still in the correct order. If the overheads are mounted in a frame (which they should be), jot down the frame number of each transparency in one corner.

Light Check

Lastly, dim the room lights and project one of your charts and go to the back of the room. Can you see the graph clearly enough? If not, darken the room some more. If the lights are controlled by dimmers, note the knob setting (use a pencil) so you can quickly dim the lights to the proper level during the presentation.

Show Time

The moment of truth has come. The time for your presentation has arrived, and your audience single-files into the meeting room. There's no time for second thoughts now. Approach the podium, greet your audience, and begin the show. Here are some tips to make sure that you appear cool and professional:

- Avoid scheduling a meeting close to 12 noon or much after 4:30 in the afternoon. The midmorning and midafternoon hours tend to be the best.
- Limit the presentation to less than an hour. A half hour is even better.
- Start on time.
- If you're standing at a podium, don't grasp the edges. Keep your hands free and use them for expression, as you normally do.
- Talk to the audience, not to the screen or projector.
- If you're shy about talking directly to the audience, focus on a spot on the back wall.
- Tell your audience the purpose of the meeting at the outset. Then stick to the agenda.
- Keep your hands out of your pockets and don't rattle coins or keys.
- Refer to your notes, but avoid gluing your eyes to them.
- Involve the audience as much as possible. Ask questions that elicit a group response.
- If you find you're running late, or that your audience is getting restless (is it approaching 12 noon?), speed up the pace, or take a 10-minute break.
- If the meeting was called to initiate action, assign tasks and set deadlines.
- Finish on time.

Using Slide and Overhead Projectors

So much for the general guidelines on giving professional presentations. The focus of this book is on preparing and presenting business graphics and there are plenty of specifics you should know about. First and foremost is the proper use of slide and overhead projectors.

Slide Projector

If you're using a slide projector, use a remote control to advance the slides. Also:

- Despite what you may have heard or read, there is no "maximum" time that a slide should be projected on the screen. It's not 30 seconds, 20 seconds, or 10 seconds; it's the time you need to get your idea across, and no longer.
- Use a light pointer (a flashlight that projects an arrow) to point to key spots on the chart.

Overhead Projector

Overhead projectors were designed so that you can interact with the graphic being displayed on the screen. Use this feature whenever you can. Here are some other guidelines.

- When using an overhead projector, turn it off momentarily when you change overheads. This helps emphasize points and avoids the screen glare when there is nothing on the projector stage.
- Use a pen, pencil, or pointer to point to specific areas on the chart.
- Use a nonpermanent marking pen to write directly on the transparency. If the ink or toner on the overhead smears, cover it with a blank transparency, and write on the blank.
- If you're addressing specific points highlighted in a word chart, cover the transparency with a piece of cardboard and reveal only one line of the chart at a time.
- For added flair, use 3M Color Highlight film. Lay a sheet of this dark blue film over your chart. With the special marking pen provided with the film, write or highlight portions of the chart. The highlighted areas quickly turn a striking bright yellow.

- As with a slide projector, there is no maximum time a graphic should remain on the screen. When you're done talking about it, go on to the next chart or turn the projector off.

Study Material

Ideally, you want your audience to leave the presentation with your idea firmly cemented in their minds. One way to ensure this is to provide a synopsis or outline of your talk to the audience. The handout material needn't be elaborate; in fact, it can be a duplicate of your working outline and a few of the more important charts you presented to the audience. Provide extra space in the outline for notes.

Record Your Performance

This presentation isn't likely to be your last; at least, let's hope so! There's always room for improvement. You can best analyze your performance if you make a videotape of your presentation. If you don't own a VCR and camera (or a camcorder), rent one; the cost is less than $30 a day. Be sure there's enough light in the room to make adequate pictures.

CHAPTER 10

Advanced Presentations

EXECUTIVE SUMMARY

There are three general approaches to an enhanced visual presentation: recorded visuals, multimedia slide projection, and computer-generated slide shows. You can tape charts and graphs using a video camera, or by hooking the computer directly up to the VCR. The signal from the computer may not be compatible with the VCR. Use a color processor or RS-170 adapter to modify the signal generated by the computer for use with the VCR.

The basic multimedia setup consists of two slide projectors and a dissolve unit. The projectors must be compatible with the dissolve unit. Dissolve units can be controlled manually or programmed via computer control or sync tape.

A slide show program is all that's required to use your computer as an electronic slide carousel. You should use multiple monitors or projection TVs when presenting your show to a large audience. You can also use an LCD screen panel with an overhead projector. The panel connects to the computer and displays a facsimile of the video screen.

The first movies were nothing more than short, single-take scenes, photographed by an immobile camera. There was no editing, no unusul special effects, no fancy camera work. But because the medium was so new, audiences flocked to see the latest arrivals. The corner nickelodeon was never empty.

As the motion picture industry matured, new techniques were refined. Movies became a combination of art and science. The "look" of film was improved dramatically, and audiences were no longer interested in watching a movie just to see actors jump up and down on the screen. They had gotten a taste of the "classy" movie, and they wouldn't settle for anything less.

Now, more than ever, our eyes are bombarded daily with high-tech multimedia imagery. Even the average breakfast cereal commercial is a breakthrough in computer-manipulated film-making. Our eyes have become so accustomed to flashy computer graphics, moving images, and brightly colored animation, that we expect to see it everywhere.

With time and the right tools, you can add some high-tech sorcery to your presentations. It's not hard and the results can look spectacular. In this chapter, you'll learn about some of the techniques for adding a polished Hollywood-style look to your business graphics presentations. This chapter centers on three approaches: recorded visuals, multimedia slide projection, and computer-generated slide shows. So, without further delay—lights, camera, action!

Recorded Visuals

A video cassette recorder (VCR) and a camera are all that's required to preserve your presentation on videotape. Depending on your computer equipment, you may not need the camera.

How would a recorded presentation come in handy? Let's say you're exhibiting at a convention. You'd be hard pressed to stand up all day and deliver the same speech hour after hour. Both overhead and slide projections require at least a semilit room, which means you'd have to conduct the presentation in a darkened booth. Record your presentation, and you can play it back all day, nonstop. You can set up several television monitors around the booth, to catch the eye of the show attendees walking by.

Another example is mass-producing a presentation. Each copy

of your tape costs as little as $6, so you can afford to distribute your presentation as widely as you like.

Camera and VCR

Perhaps the easiest way to capture your charts and graphs on tape is to aim a camera at the printouts and record each one in the proper order. Use your printer or plotter to make paper copies, as usual. The best way to photograph each chart is tack it on a copy stand, as illustrated in Figure 10-1. The camera should be on a tripod to keep it steady. If you read Chapter 8, Hot Shots: Making Slides and Overheads, this setup should be familiar to you. It's the same arrangement used to take still pictures of printouts. For more details on using the copy stand, see Chapter 8.

You'll want to time the duration that each chart remains on the screen. Use a stopwatch and your VCR's Pause button while recording. Most high-end VCRs, including camcorders, provide clean, jitter-free edits when you start and stop the deck using the Pause button. If your machine doesn't, you'll want to consider renting a professional-level VCR so you can make cleaner edits.

You can add sound to your presentation if your VCR (or the one you're renting) has an audio dub capability. Briefly, audio dubbing lets you record or replace the soundtrack without disturbing the picture. If the VCR records in stereo, or has a sound-

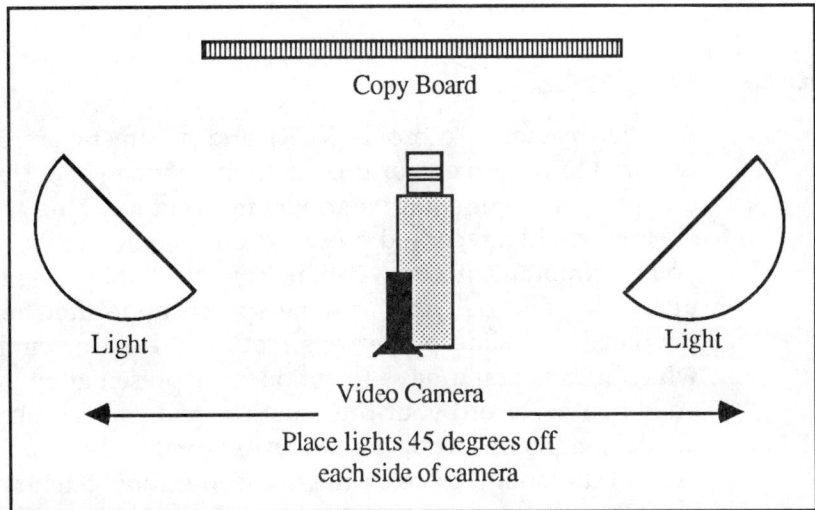

Copy Board

Light

Light

Video Camera

Place lights 45 degrees off
each side of camera

Figure 10-1.
Copy stand setup.

on-sound feature, you can record your voice on one channel and a music background on the other channel.

Step by Step: Camera to VCR

Here's how you might record a short presentation:

1. Set up the camera, VCR, copy stand, and artwork as illustrated in Figure 10-1.
2. Insert a blank tape into the VCR and record 30 seconds of black (no picture). This is easy to do; just keep the lens cap on the camera.
3. Place the VCR in Pause mode, remove the lens cap, and focus on the first chart. Release the Pause button and record the chart.
4. Put the VCR in Pause when you have enough of the chart recorded, and change graphics. Release the Pause button once again and record the second chart.
5. Continue the process until all the charts are on tape.
6. Replace the lens cap and record 30 seconds of black at the end of the tape.
7. To add sound, rewind the tape, plug in a microphone (the higher the quality the better), and set the recorder in Audio Dub mode. Record the narration.

More than Charts

There's nothing that says your presentation is limited to just charts. Throw in a picture of your office or factory between a column graph that shows worker productivity. Pictures you tape can be color prints or slides. When taping slides, use a *telecine adapter*, as shown in Figure 10-2. The adapter lets you tape an image projected by a slide projector. You can also use the adapter to tape Super-8 movies. Because the movie projector and video system are not in synchronization, the recorded image flickers slightly.

Computer to VCR

If your computer is equipped with a color graphics adapter (not an enhanced graphics adapter) outfitted with a composite video output jack, you may be able to hook your computer directly into

Telecine adapter

Video camera

Slide projector

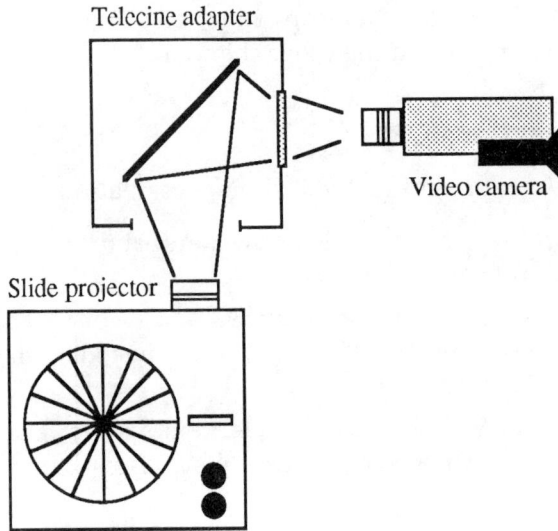

Figure 10-2.
Telecine setup.

the VCR. Use a phono-to-phono cable, available at your computer dealer's or nearby stereo store. Be sure to plug the cable into the VIDEO IN jack on the VCR, as shown in Figure 10-3.

To record your charts, all you have to do is display them on the screen as usual. What you see on the screen is automatically sent to the VCR. For best results, create all your charts and save them on disk. While making the graphics, save a blank screen. You'll use this to add the blank leader to the head and tail of the tape.

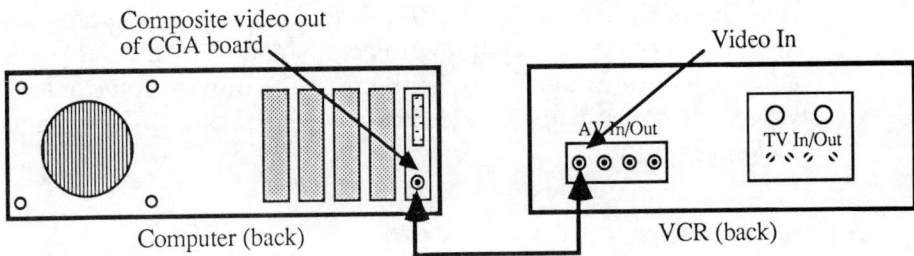

Composite video out
of CGA board

Video In

AV In/Out

TV In/Out

Computer (back)

VCR (back)

Figure 10-3.
Computer to recorder.

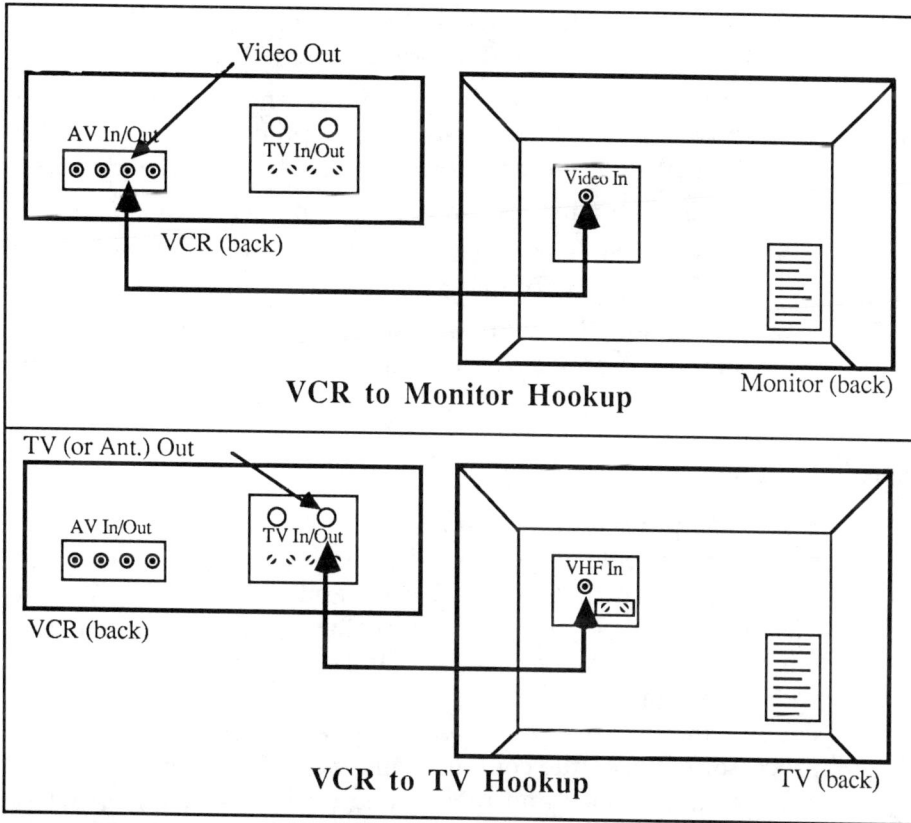

Figure 10-4.
VCR to monitor/TV.

Test to see that you're getting a picture by hooking up a monitor or TV to the output of the VCR. When using a monitor, connect it to the VIDEO OUT jack of the VCR; when using a TV, attach it to the VCR via the VHF OUT connector (see Figure 10-4). If you have a picture, make a test recording of the first chart. Wind back the tape and view the results.

Step by Step: Computer to VCR

Follow these steps to record your presentation:

1. Insert a blank tape into the VCR. Bring up a blank picture on your computer screen (an empty screen). Record 30 seconds of black (no picture).

2. Pause the VCR and recall the first chart from disk. Release the Pause button and record the chart.

3. Pause the VCR when you have enough of the chart recorded, and retrieve the next graphic from disk. Release the Pause button once again and record the second chart.

4. Continue the process until all the charts are on tape.

5. Bring up the blank picture again and record 30 seconds of black at the end of the tape.

6. To add sound, rewind the tape, plug in a microphone, and set the recorder in Audio Dub mode. Record the narration.

Possible Problems

Direct computer-to-VCR recording works most of the time, but not always. Problems can occur because your computer may not put out a signal that the VCR can handle. The most common malady is too strong a signal coming into your VCR. The picture might roll and jitter, and there may be a buzzing sound in the speaker of the TV.

You can combat this to some degree by hooking up a color processor between the computer and VCR. The processor, available at Radio Shack and most video dealers (cost under $200) allows you to manipulate the colors and brightness level of the picture.

Another approach is to add an RS-170 adapter between the computer and VCR. These are designed to electrically modify the substandard signals generated by some color/graphics video boards for use with a VCR. Contact your dealer for more information about RS-170 adapters.

Tips on Editing

To edit video tape, you must set up a dubbing system with two VCRs, and precisely time when each deck turns on and off. You play back the shots on one VCR, in the order that you want them, and re-record them on another VCR. You can use this method, for example, to insert live action scenes into your presentations. Connect the two VCRs as shown in Figure 10-5. Use separate audio and video cables for the best picture and sound.

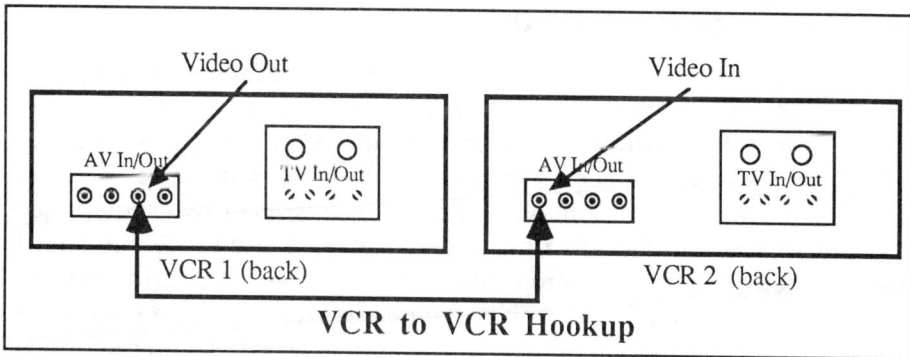

Figure 10-5.
Dubbing setup.

Taping Considerations

With either shooting method—camera-to-VCR or computer-to-VCR—you can make additional copies of the tape by using two VCRs and recording from one to the other. Use the same hookup procedure outlined in VCR-to-VCR dubbing, above.

Avoid making copies of previously copied tapes. The image quality decreases greatly with each successive copy. You can also send your tape out to be duplicated. The cost varies, depending on the length of the presentation, but it's usually under $30 per tape.

Here are some more tips:

- Record only at the fast speed, that is, SP on VHS decks, B-I or B-II on Beta decks. You get lower quality when recording at the slower speeds.

- Use a high-grade tape for the original. Subsequent copies will turn out better.

- Be sure the VCR is in good working condition before taping. Clean the heads with a commercial head cleaning tape prior to recording.

- If you're using a video camera, make sure there is enough light to make a good picture. If the picture looks grainy or washed out, use brighter lights or move the lights closer to the artwork.

Multimedia Slide Projection

A multimedia presentation involves two or more slide projectors and electronically switching between them to create an animation effect. All the projectors are pointed at the same screen. Not all projectors need be focused on the exact same spot.

The most basic multimedia setup consists of two slide projectors and a dissolve unit. The dissolver is used to easily switch between the two projectors. This requires, of course, that the projector have a dissolver connector and that it be compatible with the dissolve unit you're using. Kodak Ektagraphic projectors are the most common projectors used in multimedia presentations; high-end models from other manufacturers are also available. For greatest flexibility, the projectors should be outfitted with zoom lenses.

In operation, projector A has all the odd-numbered slides, and projector B all the even-numbered slides. The dissolve unit advances the slides one at a time, alternating between the two projectors. The final result is a playback of slides in perfectly interlaced order—1, 2, 3, 4, and so on.

Dissolve units offer three basic transitions between slides, dissolve, cut, and fade.

- In a dissolve, slide A slowly dims out of view while slide B slowly appears. You can vary the speed of the dissolve from very slow to very fast.
- In a cut, slide A abruptly replaces slide B.
- In a fade, slide A slowly dims out. After a short period of time, slide B slowly appears. Like dissolves, you can vary the speed of the fade.

Fancy Dissolve Units

More elaborate dissolvers can control up to 6 or 12 slide projectors and can be programmed electronically or with the aid of a control tape (which can also carry the narration, so the slide cues are synchronized with the words). The more projectors, the harder the presentation is to produce, and of course, the more expensive it is. You'd be wise to stick with two projectors until you become more proficient at multimedia presentations.

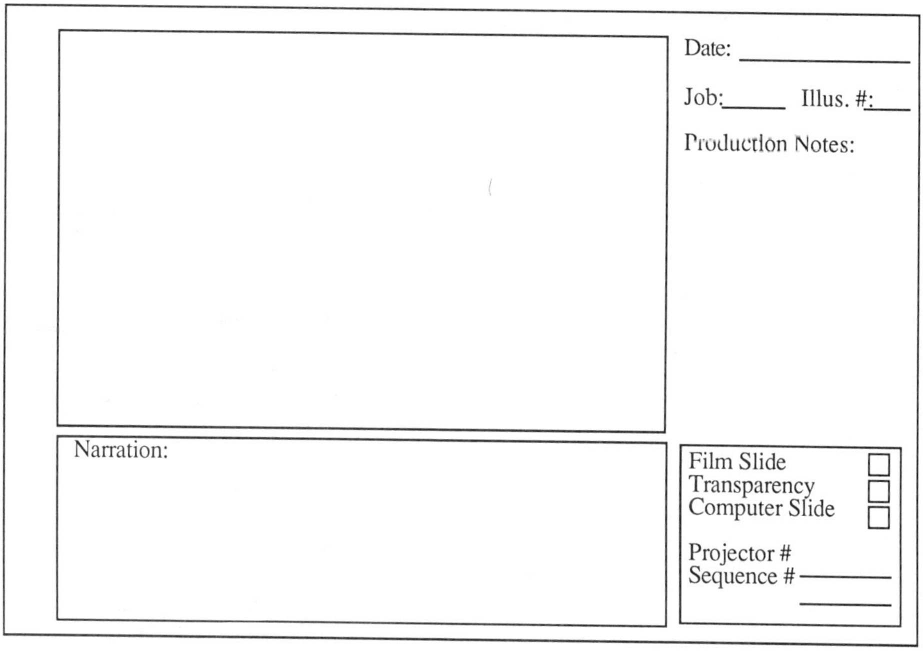

Date: _____

Job: _____ Illus. #: ___

Production Notes:

Narration:

Film Slide ☐
Transparency ☐
Computer Slide ☐

Projector #
Sequence # _____
          _____

Figure 10-6.
Full-page script style 1.

Scripting

Like any other presentation, a multimedia show requires planning. The script for a multimedia presentation must be complete, with the small details mapped out. Write an outline of the presentation, and prepare the visuals according to the outline (these can include graphs, word charts, photographs). With the visuals in hand, begin the scripting process. You can use one of the forms on the following pages if you'd like. Figures 10-6 and 10-7 show two formats you can use to script your presentations.

Curtain Time

Multimedia presentations require precision, so it's important that you give yourself plenty of time to set up and get yourself ready. At least an hour before your presentation, set up the projectors and aim them at the screen. If the show is programmed, do a dry run to make sure the cues are still correct. If the dissolver will be

Narration: _____
_____
_____
_____
_____
_____
_____
_____

Narration: _____
_____
_____
_____
_____
_____
_____
_____

Narration: _____
_____
_____
_____
_____
_____
_____
_____

Narration: _____
_____
_____
_____
_____
_____
_____
_____

Figure 10-7.
Full-page script style 2.

manually controlled (which someone else should do so you can concentrate on the presentation), be sure everyone concerned understands the cues. Distribute copies of the cue sheet/script so all concerned know what they are doing.

Computer-Generated Presentation

Computers are for more than just creating business graphics. With the right software, they can be used to present your charts as well. Used creatively, your computer can be an inexpensive and very workable alternative to an elaborate multimedia setup.

A number of business graphics programs also include a "slide-show" feature. Stand-alone programs specifically designed for personal computer slide-show presentations are available as well, and usually with fancier features. In either case, you create the charts and graphs in the usual manner and save them on a disk. Once all the visuals are complete, you write a "script" to string them together. A playback command or separate program reads the script, pulls the charts from the disk in the correct order, and displays them one at a time on the screen. Your computer becomes a sort of high-tech slide carousel.

The display format of the slide show determines the minimum requirements for the playback computer. If the slide show is generated using 320 by 200 pixel CGA-quality charts, it can be played back on any system that has a color graphics capability. But if the slide show is generated using 640 by 350 pixel EGA-quality charts, it can be played back only on a computer equipped with an EGA display and adapter.

Slide-show programs push the PC to its processing limit. The special effects and animation (see below) require computational power and you may notice that the slide show progresses faster on some computers than it does on others. Generally, you achieve the best results when using an IBM PC AT or a PC AT/XT using a coprocessor speedup board.

Because the images are stored on a disk, large slide shows need a hard disk drive. Create a subdirectory for the show files (as discussed in Chapter 11) to keep them separate from your other data. If you are sharing the slide show with others, try to fit as many files on a single diskette as you can. Group the files logically so that disk swapping is not required. For example, if the show spans over two disks, put the first half on one disk and the other half on the second disk.

Automatic Scripting

Slide-show programs must be told which charts on the disk to show, and in what order. You specify each visual in a script, which you can add to or edit at any time. The script includes other information as well, such as the duration the graphic is to remain on the screen and the type of transition between visuals. The scripting function is handy because it forces you to plan your presentations. Once the show is scripted, you can play it back and test it for smoothness and continuity. If you find a mistake or problem, you can easily correct it.

Special Effects

The basic slide-show programs, or the business graphics generating software that provide a slide-show capability, have limited transitions. You're usually limited to direct cuts between slides. The more elaborate slide-show programs let you choose from a variety of transitions, including:

- Wipes, where one chart replaces another
- Dissolves, where one chart slowly dims while another concurrently appears
- Fades, where the chart slowly goes from full brightness to complete darkness

The computer can change slides very quickly. Many programs allow you to keep an image on the screen for a tenth of second or less. You can use this feature to create animation. Suppose the visual on the screen is a pie chart with a slice missing. You can animate the pie slice so that it joins the rest of the chart, as in Figure 10-8. This requires you to make several separate frames. In each one, the slice moves closer and closer to the rest of the pie.

Other Uses

You needn't keep the finished slide show to yourself. Computer-generated presentations are perfect for distribution to others. You can fit the script and visuals on one or two disks and mail

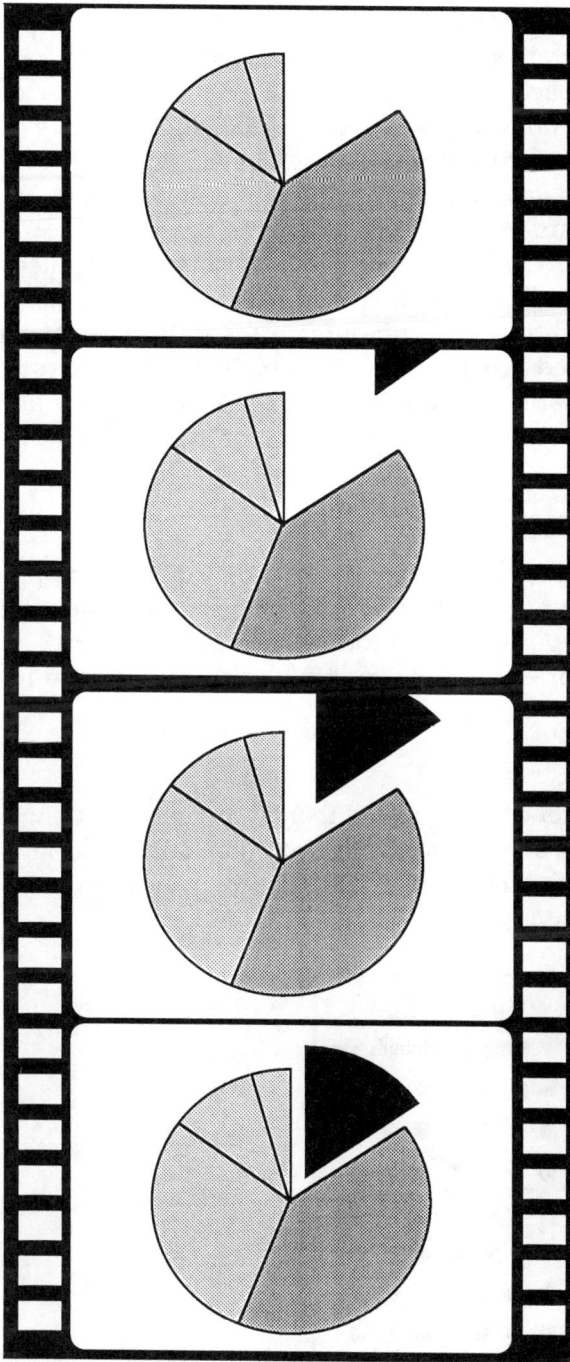

Frame 1

Frame 2

Frame 3

Frame 4

Figure 10-8.
Animated pie chart.

it anywhere. Most slide-show programs have a separate play-back program that reads the script and runs the presentation. The playback program is usually non-copy protected and the program publisher gives you the green light to make distribution copies of it for inclusion in your show.

By now, you've probably thought that if you can capture individual charts with a VCR, you can use a video recorder to tape a slide show. The advantage of recording a computer-generated slide show is that you don't have to start and stop the VCR between slides. The computer plays back the show exactly as you scripted it. This approach is handy when you can't lug your computer around with you. See the section above on making a taped presentation for notes on recording with a VCR.

A Question of Screen Size

You can use a regular computer monitor when giving your presentation to one or two people. Larger groups will require more monitors, positioned so that there's at least one 12- or 13-inch monitor for every three people, as shown in Figure 10-9.

Projection Sets

If the audience is big (more than 20 people), you'll want to consider using a projection TV. If you'll be talking during the show, position the screen off to one side, the way you do when giving

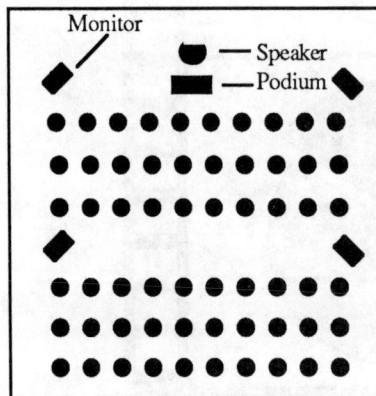

Figure 10-9.
Multimonitor setup.

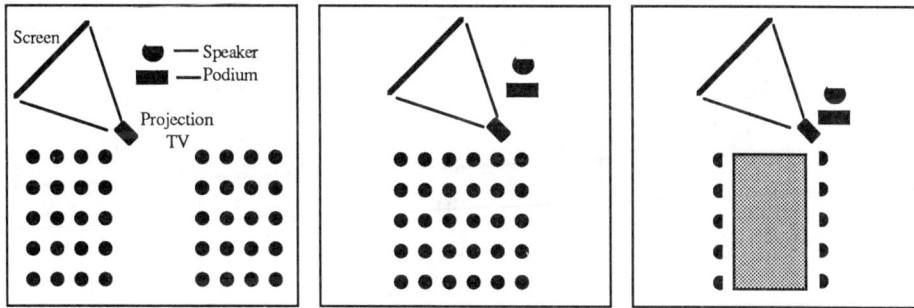

Possible Big Screen TV Arrangements

Figure 10-10.
Projector screen setup.

a presentation with an overhead projector (see Figure 10-10). You and the projection TV screen won't be competing for the attention of the audience.

Projection units are bulky; so it's difficult to take your computer-generated show on the road (of course, you also have to take your computer or VCR along, so the load can quickly get burdensome). In addition, projection TVs don't have the same resolution as computer monitors. Avoid small text or graphics whenever possible. If you must project fine text, use a high-resolution computer-grade projection monitor. Most computer-grade projection monitors are monochrome (green on black or white on black) only.

Lap-Top Computers and Graphics Presentations

An ideal adjunct to an on-the-road graphics presentation is a portable computer, particularly the compact briefcase or *lap-top* variety. Lap-top computers have been around for a long time, but the first machines were not suitable for business applications because of limited memory, screen display, and disk drive storage.

Now, lap-top computers routinely come with memory exceeding 256K, with a choice of sophisticated mass storage options, including hard disk drives and MS-DOS compatibility, meaning that they can run on all of the programs designed for the IBM PC.

Among the latest improvements in lap-tops are:

- *Larger and brighter display screen.* The typical lap-top screen displays a full 80 columns by 25 lines and CGA resolution of 320 by 200 pixels (some display up to 640 by 200 pixels).

- *More memory.* Almost all applications programs, including presentation graphics and slide-show programs, require at least 256K of RAM. The current crop of lap-tops, most being designed to run off-the-shelf IBM PC software, come with or have provisions to accept memory in excess of 256 K. Most can take up to 640K, and a few can accept Expanded Memory Specification (EMS) memory.

- *High-capacity drives.* For several years MS DOS-compatible lap-top computers have used 3½-inch floppy disks, which store up to 720K of date. IBM's embrace of this smaller format has ensured that off-the-shelf software is available. A number of sophisticated lap-tops even come with built-in 20 or 30 megabyte hard disk drives.

- *Longer battery life.* Batteries haven't improved much in the last few years, but the lap-top computers are built with circuits that don't consume as much power. When used on a lap-top equipped with a 3½-inch drive, a set of batteries lasts 4 to 6 hours on one charge. Of course, the computer can always be plugged into a wall when a power outlet is nearby.

LCD Panels

Several companies, including Kodak, manufacture or market a unique liquid crystal display (LCD) panel for use with overhead projectors. The LCD panel connects to the color graphics adapter (or comes with its own board) and acts as a kind of video screen. Instead of emitting light, however, parts on the panel transform from clear to a solid gray, as determined on the screen image.

When placed on the stage of an overhead projector, the solid gray portions block light; the clear portions pass it. Resolution is limited to CGA or EGA, depending on the model. Most of the panels available measure about 10 by 14 inches, with a screen area of about 9 by 6 inches. That's less than the average viewgraph (up to 8½ by 11 inches), but the screen area is sufficient for most presentations. You can use the panel with a standard desktop PC or a portable PC.

The main advantage of the LCD panel over the projection TV is one of cost. The panel is much less expensive than a projection television system. Other advantages:

- You don't need a special high-reflectance screen; any wall or screen will do.
- The panel can be used with any overhead projector setup.
- The panel is compact, allowing you to take it with you, especially if you are equipped with a portable PC.

LCD panels don't produce color—the picture appears as a dark blue on white. But you can colorize the display by using colored acetate film. Place the film under or over the panel and the entire picture takes on the hue of the acetate. By placing a piece of clear acetate over the screen, you can draw with colored markers during your presentation.

Setting Up a Graphics Workstation

E X E C U T I V E   S U M M A R Y

The basic business graphics workstation consists of the computer with at least 256K of RAM (preferably more), a graphics display adapter, monitor, and output device—a printer, plotter, or film recorder. Extra memory in the computer, when not used for the presentation graphics program, can enhance operation. The memory can be applied as a RAM disk or RAM cache, or can hold RAM-resident desk accessory software. All three speed up the computer and make working with it more productive.

Work disks are custom application disks you devise that have just the programs and files you need. You may have several work disks, each containing a copy of your presentation graphics program and special files.

A hard disk drive lets you store programs and data files for fast and easy retrieval. Each major application should be placed in its own subdirectory. The copy protection placed on some programs prohibits their installation on a hard disk drive.

A coprocessor board speeds up the operation of your computer. The board is particularly important with presentation graphics, because number-crunching and drawing time for charts may be extremely slow on certain computers.

Four representative presentation graphics programs— Freelance Plus, Chart-Master, Microsoft Chart, and Windows Graph—show how typical software is integrated with the PC and exemplifies the features and capabilities found on the latest graphics packages.

If you are a heavy user of presentation graphics (or plan on being one), you'll find that your work will go faster and more efficiently if you take the time to turn your IBM PC or compatible into a kind of graphics workstation. The ideal graphics workstation utilizes each resource of the computer to its fullest, taking advantage of the wide variety of hardware and software available to make your job easier.

In this chapter, you'll learn how to fine-tune your computer to make it run smoothly and efficiently with your presentation graphics program and other software. You'll learn how to effectively use a hard disk drive, how to squeeze extra power from the computer's RAM, the benefits of a coprocessor board, and more.

The Graphics Workstation

At a minimum, your graphics workstation will consist of:

- IBM PC or compatible (this includes a PC, XT, AT, or PS/2)
- Graphics display adapter
- Monochrome or color monitor

You'll also need an output device of one kind or another if you plan on making permanent copies of your charts. The most popular output device is the printer (dot matrix, ink jet, thermal transfer, or laser). Other output devices include pen plotters and film recorders.

Although not an absolute requirement on all presentation graphics programs, a mouse or other alternate input device allows you to easily choose commands and manipulate elements within the chart.

Memory

The computer needs a minimum of 256K of random access memory (RAM), preferably more. With the low cost of RAM chips, there is really no reason not to outfit the computer with the full complement of 640K, the maximum that DOS can handle.

If you own an IBM PC or XT, you must fill the memory on the motherboard (either 64K or 256K), then use an expansion board for additional RAM. You cannot add the expansion board until all the memory sockets on the motherboard are full. Most IBM PC compatibles, as well as the PC AT, can accept the full complement of up to 640K RAM on the motherboard. You do not need a separate memory expansion card.

When expanding the memory of the PC or XT, remember to change the DIP switch settings or the computer will not realize that additional memory has been added. When expanding the memory of the AT, you must run the SETUP program to reinitialize the computer and inform the computer that it has more memory at its disposal.

RAM Disk

RAM disk software partitions a portion of the computer's RAM as an electronic disk drive. Data is temporarily stored in memory rather than on a disk. The benefit of a *RAM disk* is its speed. You can store and retrieve data on a RAM disk several hundred times faster than with mechanical disk drives. That saves you time and makes you more productive with your computer.

Of course, you use the memory as a RAM disk only if your applications programs do not require it. Most presentation graphics software need from 256 to 320K of RAM to operate, leaving extra memory for a RAM disk. Figure 11-1 shows how

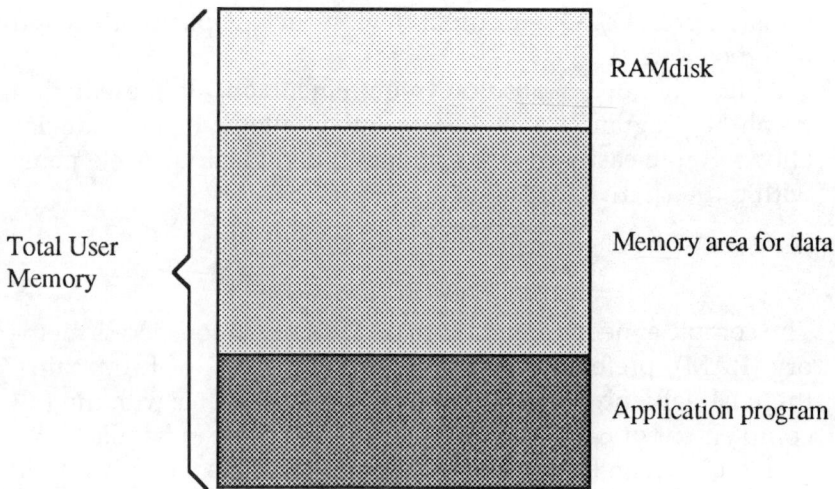

Figure 11-1.
RAM disk in stack.

the memory might be partitioned off in your computer when a RAM disk is installed.

If you want to save the data in the RAM disk, you must copy it to a floppy disk before you turn the computer off. Once the power is turned off, information in the RAM disk is forever lost.

You need a utility to partition the extra RAM in your computer as a RAM disk. Both commercial and public domain RAM disk utility programs are available. Public domain programs may be obtained through a mail order service (see the latest editions of the computer magazines for names and addresses) or from a local PC computer user's group.

Most all RAM disk software allow you to specify the size of the "disk." You can set the size in even 1K-byte increments or large chunks, usually 8K, 16K, 32K, or 64K increments. Even though the standard PC drive stores 360K of data, the RAM disk needn't be this large. You want a disk large enough to store the files you are currently working with. A 128K to 192K RAM disk is sufficient for most applications.

RAM Cache

RAM cache is a small portion of memory (usually 32K or less) reserved to hold bits and pieces of programming code. The idea of the cache is that repetitive tasks are stored in RAM, where they can be retrieved by the computer much faster than data can be retrieved from a disk. RAM caching is particularly helpful if you own a hard disk drive. With the cache installed in memory, you'll notice that the drive works even faster than before. Note that some hard disk drive systems have their own cache memory and don't need (or can't use) extra.

Like RAM disk software, RAM cache programs are available commercially or through the public domain. The better programs let you assign just about any portion of memory to caching. Normally, you don't need a cache larger than 32K, but if you are not using a RAM disk, you can safely expand the cache size to 64K or even 128K without risk of stealing too much RAM space from your applications programs.

RAM Resident Programs

Popular desktop accessory programs, such as Borland's Side-Kick, reside in memory even when you are using another application. *RAM resident* desk accessory programs are handy time savers because they allow you to stay in the current application. You don't have to quit, start another program, work with it, then transfer back to the original application.

Desktop accessory software is sometimes referred to as *terminate-and-stay* (or TSR) programs. You may use RAM resident programs as long as you have the memory for it, but you will likely not have room if you also use a RAM disk or RAM cache (which, all things considered, are probably more important).

If you use a RAM resident program, be sure that you test it fully with all your programs. It is not unusual for the RAM program to interfere with the normal operation of the computer, causing a failure or worse, a loss of data on a disk. If the RAM resident program lets you load only certain accessories into memory, such as a notepad, on-screen clock, or address book, pick only those that you need. If you don't use the other accessories, leave them out of the memory.

Loading RAM Software

RAM disks, RAM cache, and RAM resident programs should be loaded automatically whenever you start the computer or begin a session with your applications software.

To load the programs at startup, include the name of the utility in the AUTOEXEC.BAT file on your DOS disk or hard disk. If you don't already have an AUTOEXEC.BAT file, you can easily create one with the following:

- Type COPY CON: AUTOEXEC.BAT
- Press RETURN.
- Enter the name of the program (such as "RAMDISK" or "RAMCACHE"), just as if you were typing the name to manually run the program.
- Press Return when you are through.
- Press the F6 key twice, then RETURN.

The AUTOEXEC.BAT file is now complete. You can examine its contents by entering TYPE AUTOEXEC.BAT and pressing the Return key. If you already have an AUTOEXEC.BAT file, you'll erase it if you follow the instructions above. If the file is short, reenter the information into the new file. If it is long, use a text editor or word processor to add just the lines for the RAM disk or RAM cache.

Some RAM disk and RAM cache software function as system drivers and have a file extension of .SYS (programs end with .COM or .EXE extensions). System drivers cannot be invoked by entering the program name but must be placed in the CONFIG.SYS file, which is also located on your DOS disk or hard disk. If you don't already have a CONFIG.SYS file, create one using the procedure outlined above (this time, type COPY CON: CONFIG.SYS). If the CONFIG.SYS file already exists, examine its contents first, then duplicate it when creating the new file. Alternatively, use a word processor or similar program to edit the existing CONFIG.SYS file.

To load the RAM disk, RAM cache, or RAM resident programs when you start your application, create a batch file. The programs must be executable and have either a .COM or .EXE file extension (*not* a .SYS file extension). You can include just about any number of programs in the batch file. The computer will execute each program in the batch file in turn. Your applications program should be last in line. All batch files end with a .BAT file extension.

To create a batch file:

- Type COPY CON: and the name of the batch file, such as GRAPH.BAT. You can use just about any name for the batch file, as long as it ends with .BAT.
- Enter the name of each program you want to run. Type them as if you were manually running the programs.
- Press the RETURN key after each program name.
- Put the name of the graphics program at the end. The computer will run this program last. Press Return.
- Press the F6 key twice, then RETURN.

You can examine the contents of the batch file with the TYPE command, as illustrated above. If the batch file is long, use a word processor or text editor. To run the batch file, type its name, as if it were a program (to the computer it *is* a program). The computer will execute each program in turn. If there is a problem, edit the batch file to correct it, and then try again.

Any good book on PC DOS explains the topics of the AUTOEXEC.BAT, CONFIG. SYS, and batch files. Refer to one of these books for more information.

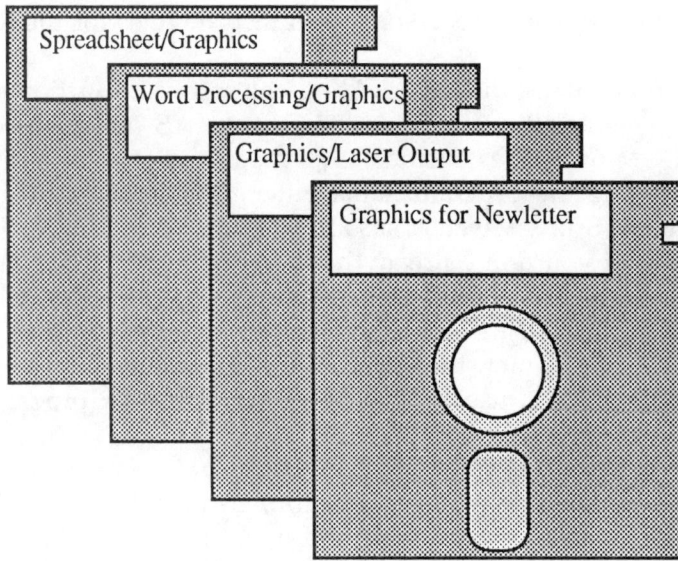

Figure 11-2.
Custom disks concept.

Making Work Disks

A *custom work disk* is a disk engineered for a core task, such as creating presentation graphs and integrating them into a word processing document. Figure 11-2 shows the basic idea of custom disks. With a custom disk, you avoid the disk swapping necessary when alternating from one application to another, and because all the tools you need for the task are within easy reach, your efficiency with the computer will skyrocket.

Some Guidelines

Though there aren't many rules for developing custom work disks, there are a few tips you'll want to consider. As much as possible, try to keep your applications on a single disk, even if you have more than one disk drive. Often, you'll be using the second drive for capturing data files, or for switching off to other custom-task disks when you're through with one job and starting another.

Of course, you can't always stick to the "one-disk" approach. Some of the bigger applications come on two or more disks, although the main program is contained on only one disk. The other disks include support files that are not always necessary for using the program. If necessary, create a work disk that consists of two disks.

Most tasks will require that you combine two or more applications on a disk. You're biggest enemy will be limited disk space—fitting all the applications you want on a 360K or 720K disk (users of the IBM AT or clones have up to 1.2 megabytes of disk storage space). Still, there are several ways around this limitation.

First, you can free up some space by removing extraneous files. These include "README" files, help files that you no longer need, and driver files for devices that you don't use. You can also substitute some desk accessory programs for full-fledged applications. Instead of using a full word processor to prepare text for your charts, for example, use a notepad desk accessory.

Some PC programs are copy protected, so you can't easily make extra work copies. Backup utilities overcome most copy protection schemes so you can make additional work disks. Because of the way most copy protection plans work, however, you may not be able to fit two or more protected applications on a single disk.

When constructing your own disks, be on the lookout for "program interaction." The PC is a little like a person. Instead of drugs, it's uncomfortable when you combine certain applications or accessories on one disk. If the computer ceases to operate, or data is lost, experiment with different program combinations until you find the right mix.

Using a Hard Disk Drive

It used to be that a *hard disk drive* was a nice thing to have, but you didn't absolutely need one. If required, you could sneak by with just two floppy disk drives, and swap disks in and out of the drives as you worked with a program.

The complexity of the average presentation graphics program—or just about any of the new software for the PC—makes using a hard disk practical and time saving. It is estimated that approximately 30 percent of all PC and compatibles owners now have a hard disk drive, and—because the prices of hard disk drives are falling—this percentage is rapidly increasing. With a hard disk, you don't need to worry about making custom work disks because all your programs and files are within easy reach.

The capacity for hard disk drives for the PC range from a low of 10 megabytes to over 100 megabytes. Common drive capacities are 20, 30, and 40. The 20-megabyte capacity is popular with the IBM PC XT or compatibles, the 30- and 40-megabyte drives are popular with the IBM AT and PS/2 computers. Regardless of your make or model of computer, a 20- or 30-megabyte drive should be sufficient for most applications.

Hard disk drives require installation on both a mechanical and software level. The instructions that come with the drive explain how to properly install it and set it up for data. Once the drive is installed, format it with system files and copy the files from the DOS disk on to it. This enables the hard disk to act as the startup device. You no longer need a DOS disk to start the computer.

Because hard disk drives can store so many files, it is imperative that you store your applications and data in individual *subdirectories.* How you set up each subdirectory is up to you, but most users establish a different subdirectory for each major application. For example, all the files for your word processor are stored in one subdirectory, all the files for the presentation graphics program are stored in another, and so forth. You'll find a number of good books on hard disk management. Refer to one of these for more details on establishing and using subdirectories.

Note that some presentation graphics programs are copy protected, and may not allow you to transfer them to a hard disk. Some copy-protection schemes are based on the *key-disk* system. The program *can* be copied to the hard disk, but the copy is not an exact duplicate of the original on the distribution diskette. When you run the copy on the hard disk, the software knows it is not an original, and you are asked to temporarily insert the distribution diskette into the floppy disk drive. The program then checks to be sure that the original is a good copy, and you are allowed to proceed.

Other copy-protection systems do not permit the program to be transferred to another disk, either floppy or hard. The resulting copy, if it can be made, will not run. However, copying utilities are available that let you get around this limitation. You use the utility to install a copy of your applications program on the hard disk drive. Additionally, some graphics programs software comes with their own hard disk installation program. You can use the program to install and remove copies of the protected software from work disks and hard disk drives.

Organizing the Workstation in Your Office

The design of the IBM PC and compatibles allows for a relatively compact arrangement of the system components. The hard disk drive and expansion boards fit into the computer enclosure, and the monitor can rest on top. If the monitor is extremely heavy (as most multiple frequency and large screen monitors are), place a monitor stand over the computer. This prevents the monitor from bending or breaking the case of the computer.

Additional components of the system include a printer or plotter, or another output device, such as a film recorder. Because of short cable lengths, these peripherals should be placed as close to the computer as possible.

As a general rule of thumb, the cable for a parallel interface peripheral should not be over 6 to 8 feet long. Likewise, the cable for a serial interface peripheral should not be over 8 to 10 feet long. If you need a longer cable length, purchase an extension and try it for a day or two. If you notice that the peripheral is acting strangely, then the cable is too long and it must be shortened.

A typical arrangement for a presentation graphics workstation is shown in Figure 11-3. Space is provided for a mouse; you can change the placement of the mouse to the left side of the keyboard if you are left-handed. Plan for additional desk space if you use a graphics tablet.

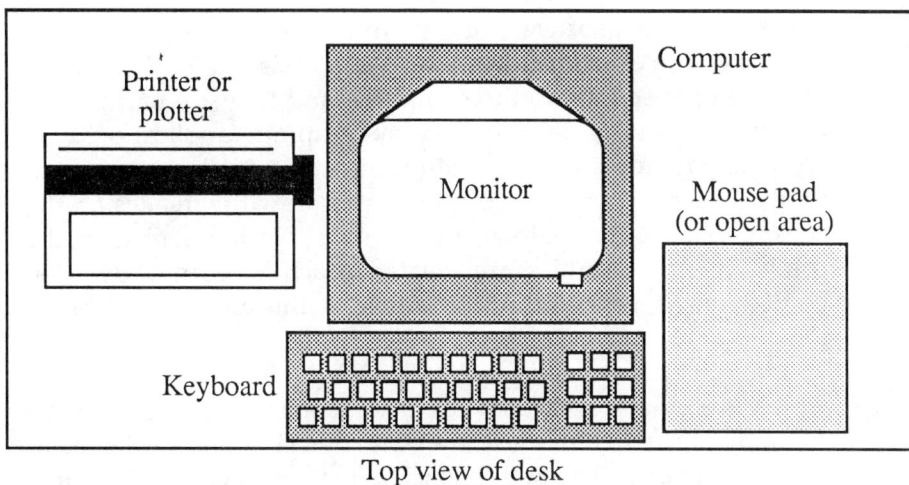

Top view of desk

Figure 11-3.
Workstation arrangement.

Coprocessor Boards

There are two elements of a computer's *microprocessor* (the main processing chip) that determine its computing power:

- Its *architecture*, or the number of bits it can digest at one time
- Its *clock speed*, the rate at which the microprocessor works

The higher the number of bits, the faster the number crunching. That's one reason why the IBM AT, which has a true 16-bit microprocessor (the Intel 80286), is faster than the IBM XT (and most clones), which has what is effectively an 8-bit microprocessor (the Intel 8088). The PC and nonturbocharged clones have a clock speed of 4.7 MHz, or 4.7 million cycles per second. The newest models of the AT are about twice that. The higher the clock speed, the faster each computational instruction is carried out.

If your computer is too slow for your needs, or it can't run a piece of software that you want to use, you might be able to improve matters by adding a *coprocessor*. Coprocessors come in several forms. Some are single integrated circuits, such as the 8087 or 80287 math chip (the 8087 is for the XT; the 80287 is for the AT). Others are small circuit boards that are added over the motherboard, and still others are full expansion boards that fit into one of the slots in the computer.

Basically, coprocessors alter the personality of your computer by using a different microprocessor that either speeds up operations or allows the computer to run a different set of software (such as Apple II software or CP/M programs).

Most coprocessors available today are designed for the express purpose of speeding up the computer, and they are particularly useful when used in presentation graphics applications. By nature, graphics are computation-intensive, and a slow computer takes a long time to compute and draw the images on the screen. With a coprocessor, or *speedup* board, installed in the computer, the graphics are created much more quickly. You don't have to wait around so much as the computer does its thing.

A favorite coprocessor for the IBM XT or XT clones is the 8087, which is a single integrated circuit that snaps into place on the computer's motherboard. It goes into a socket intended specifically for the chip. The 8087, which sometimes goes by the name of *floating point match coprocessor*, is engineered to crunch numbers several times faster and more efficiently than the stock 8088.

It's important to remember, however, that many off-the-shelf programs, like the older release of Lotus 1-2-3 (release 1A) don't make use of the 8087. Many presentation graphics programs use the 8087, but some don't. Be sure to check the program's manual before investing in the 8087 chip.

Most coprocessors are expansion boards you insert into the computer. The board plugs into an empty slot, and a cable or connector attaches to the 8088 socket. The 8088 chip on the computer's motherboard is removed and stored for safekeeping, or *piggybacked* onto the speedup board.

The processor on a speedup board may be any of several types: The NEC V-20 or V-30, the Intel 8086 (the true 16-bit version of the 8088), or the Intel 80286. The 80286 is the same chip used in the IBM AT. The V-30 and 8086 chips provide a 10 to 50 percent increase; the 80286 can speed up the computer by several hundred percent.

Note that not all clones can support extreme speed increases. A coprocessor board with an 80286 chip operating at 10 or 12 MHz, for example, may outrun other circuits in the computer. The circuits most likely to lag behind are the RAM chips. If you use a high-speed coprocessor board, make sure the RAM chips are the fastest possible—150 nanoseconds is the absolute slowest chip you can use; 65 to 100 nanoseconds is even better.

Speedup boards equipped with the 32-bit Intel 80386 are available for the IBM AT and clones. This chip has a clock speed of 12 to 16 MHz (some operate as high as 20 MHz) and dramatically increases the performance of the computer.

Graphics Program Overview

Following are overviews of four popular graphics programs. You'll find what they do, the kinds of charts they produce, and how they interface to the computer. These overviews serve to show you how each program uses the resources of the PC and illustrate the kinds of features and capabilities that are found in the latest presentation graphics packages.

Lotus Freelance Plus

Freelance was originally designed to be used with Lotus 1-2-3, as a way to embellish the analytical graphs created by that pro-

WE PUSH RENT A CAR

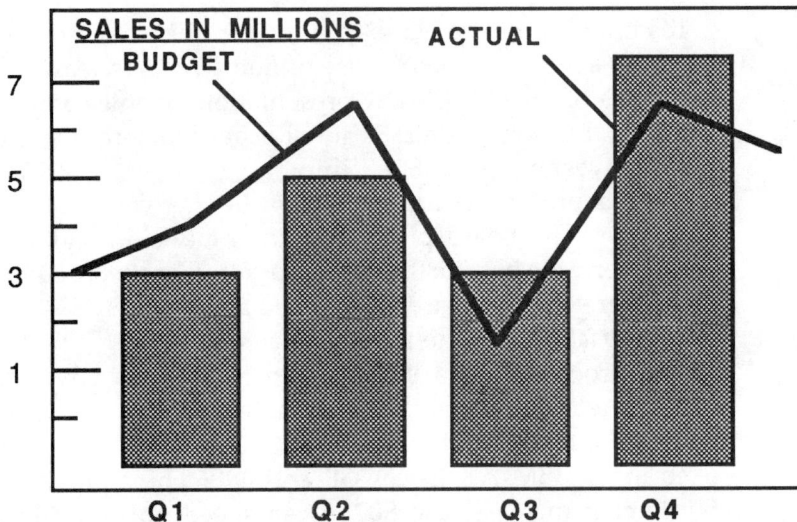

Figure 11-4.
Freelance example.

gram. But Freelance Plus also has all the tools necessary to create charts from scratch (the early version of Freelance did not provide adequate original chart-making tools).

The graphing facilities include column, bar, line, pie, and dot charts. You may enhance any chart with the drawing tools provided. You can, for example, add boxes around charts as borders, connect the segments of a stacked bar chart with lines, and add text to any graph. An example of a Freelance Plus chart is shown in Figure 11-4.

The program includes a library of more than 500 common symbols; you can place a symbol anywhere on the graph. As an added feature, Freelance Plus comes with maps of each of the 50 states. Additional map sets of the United States, divided by county, major city, or three-digit ZIP code, are also available. You can resize or edit any symbol to better suit your needs.

You can enter data directly into Freelance Plus by typing it into a templatelike worksheet. But the real strength of the program comes from its ability to directly read Lotus 1-2-3 and Symphony worksheets. The program readily accepts the 1-2-3 .PIC graph files, or you can transfer the entire contents of the worksheet. This allows you to perform powerful computations on the numbers using 1-2-3 or Symphony, rather than transfer the results for charting with Freelance Plus. The program also reads Ashton-Tate dBase files.

Freelance Plus can also be used to dress up the charts created by another Lotus presentation graphics program, Graphwriter. Graphwriter produces area, bar, bubble, Gantt, hi-low, pie, dot, and text files, and supports additional fonts, but it doesn't have complete control over chart element position and size.

All the chart elements can be manipulated using the various commands in Freelance Plus. The commands are located in a menu at the top of the screen, as in 1-2-3. You select a command by typing or by pointing with the cursor keys. With the various commands you can resize or reposition individual labels, titles, text, and legends. You can also separate and manipulate individual bars, columns, and pie slices. Additional type styles are included to change the font and size of text.

You can maneuver the chart elements using keyboard commands, but it is easier with an alternate input device, such as a mouse or graphics tablet. Using the freehand graphics tools is made easier with a mouse or graphics tablet as well. Freelance Plus supports a variety of alternate input devices; software drivers are included for most popular types.

Finished charts created by Freelance Plus can be printed using a dot matrix, ink jet, or laser printer. Among the popular brands, the program supports the Epson and Okidata dot matrix printers and the Hewlett-Packard LaserJet. Plotter support is also provided; drivers are included for the Hewlett-Packard HP7470 and HP7475. You can use a non-HP plotter as long as it emulates HPGL. Numerous film recorders are supported by Freelance Plus, including the Polaroid Palette and General Parametrics VideoShow.

Freelance Plus requires at least 384K of RAM to operate and a minimum of two disk drives. The symbol library and support files are on separate disks, and for the greatest ease of use, a hard disk drive is recommended. The program can be used with a CGA, EGA, or Hercules monochrome graphics adapter, and suitable monitor.

Ashton-Tate Chart-Master

Chart-Master was one of the first presentation graphics programs for the IBM PC, and for years it served as a benchmark

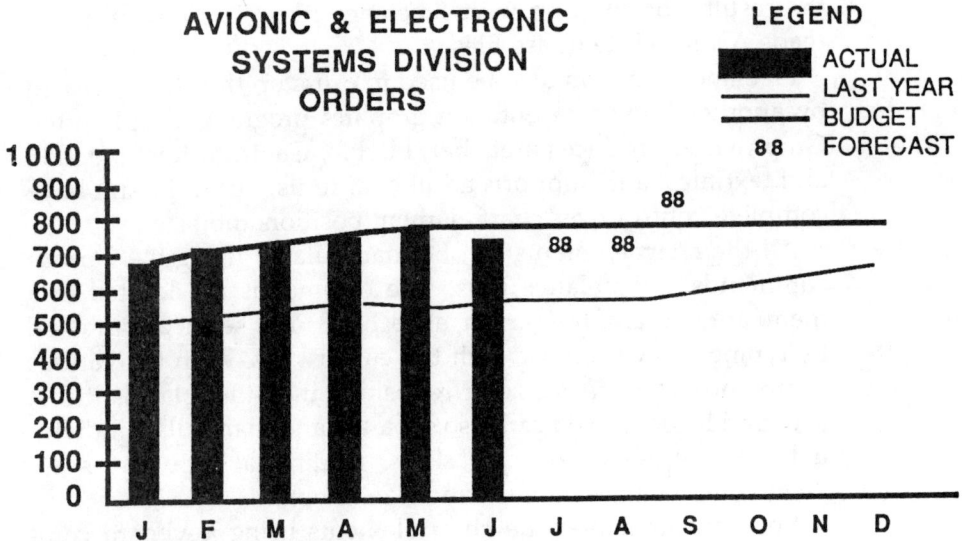

Figure 11-5.
Chart-Master example.

for the category. To keep up with the times, new versions of Chart-Master have come out and the program is now sold by Ashton-Tate, makers of dBase III.

Chart-Master can create all the usual chart types, including column, bar, line, dot, area, and pie graphs. An example of a Chart-Master graph is shown in Figure 11-5. You can mix two or more charts together to create a composite graph or you can plot several charts side by side on the same page. An options menu allows you to custom design almost every aspect of the graph, such as hatching, grids, axis scaling, and location of each chart element. The options menu provides nine pages of selections and choices.

Chart-Master embraces the menu-driven approach. To create a chart, you select the Create a Chart command in the menu. You are then led through a series of input screens, from chart title through data input. You define the chart type and enter the values for each element of the graph. As you enter text information you are provided an additional set of options for displaying the text in any of eight fonts, 16 sizes, and with or without justification, color, and underlining. You can also select any piece of text for boldfacing or underlining.

If the chart data is already in another form in a different application, you can use Chart-Master's Datagrabber facility to retrieve it. The program can directly read files stored in DIF, SYLK, and ASCII formats. After importing the data, you highlight the data you want to graph.

The program supports the Hercules monochrome graphics adapter, color graphics adapter, and enhanced graphics adapter. Chart-Master automatically checks the identification of the graphics adapter and adjusts its resolution accordingly. When an EGA board is installed, you can sample the printout in high resolution or with one or two color palettes in medium resolution. Chart-Master does not include any freehand drawing tools, so a mouse or other input device is not a requirement. The program needs at least 320K of RAM for complete operation.

Chart-Master supports some 80 output devices, including dot matrix printers (including models from IBM, Epson, C.Itoh, and Okidata), Hewlett-Packard HP7475 and compatible plotters, ink jet printers, laser printers (such as the Hewlett-Packard LaserJet), and film recorders (Polaroid Palette, Hewlett-Packard 7510A image recorder, and General Parametrics VideoShow).

Ashton-Tate sells a number of other presentation graphics-related programs in the "Master" series. These include Diagram-Master, for generating flowcharts, organization charts, Gantt charts, and similar diagrams; Map-Master, for making customized map charts; and Sign-Master, for producing text-only graphs.

Microsoft Chart

Microsoft Chart was an early pioneer in "correct" presentation graphics. Its designers were careful to follow the standard conventions and regulations that give presentation graphics their maximum credibility. The newest release of Chart includes advanced features such as 3-D graphics and data sharing.

Chart requires a minimum of 320K of RAM and one of the following graphics adapter boards: Hercules monochrome, EGA, or CGA. While the program comes on several disks, only one is used during actual making (after using the tutorial and setup programs), so a hard disk drive is not required. Two floppy drives should be used, however, one to hold the program disk and the other to hold the data disk. Chart supports any mouse compatible with the Microsoft Mouse (bus, serial, or In-Port connection), as well as a graphic tablet or light pen with mouse emulation.

A number of output devices are supported by Chart, including the Hewlett-Packard LaserJet (laser printer), PaintJet and ThinkJet (ink jet printers), C.Itoh 8510 dot matrix printer, Epson FM, MX, and LQ series, IBM Graphics printer and Quietwriter (thermal transfer) TI 850 and 855, HP 7570 and 7475 plotters, and Houston Instruments DMP-29 and DMP-40 plotters. Chart can interface to color film recorders, such as the Polaroid Palette and General Parametrics VideoShow.

You enter data for the charts in an Entry screen. The Entry screen lets you type text for the categories and numbers for the values. Alternatively, you can import data from Lotus 1-2-3, Ashton-Tate dBase, or Microsoft Multiplan files. Chart understands ASCII, SYLK, and DIF file formats.

At all times a set of commands appear at the bottom of the screen. You access the commands via the keyboard or mouse. Once the data is entered, you select a chart to create. Chart supports a gallery of eight basic graph types, including area, bar, column, hi-lo, pie, line, and dot. You can mix and match charts on the same page or combine them to make composite graphs. An example graph from Microsoft Chart is shown in Figure 11-6.

After the basic graph is complete, you may enhance it using the various commands in Microsoft Chart. You select individual chart elements with the mouse, thus identifying the objects you want to modify. For example, selecting the title allows you to change the position, font, size, and style of the title text. You can similarly change the pattern and color of chart bars, columns, pie slices, and lines, the position and characteristics of legend and axis scale test, line weights and patterns, symbols, text frames, and so forth. You can variably control the spacing between the bars and columns in bar/column charts, from zero space to a full overlap.

Micrografx Windows Graph

Windows Graph is compatible with Microsoft Windows. It's easy to use and welcomes chart revision and creative embellishment. Windows Graph combines the convenience of generating charts in Lotus 1-2-3 with the rich gallery of chart types and customization of Microsoft Chart.

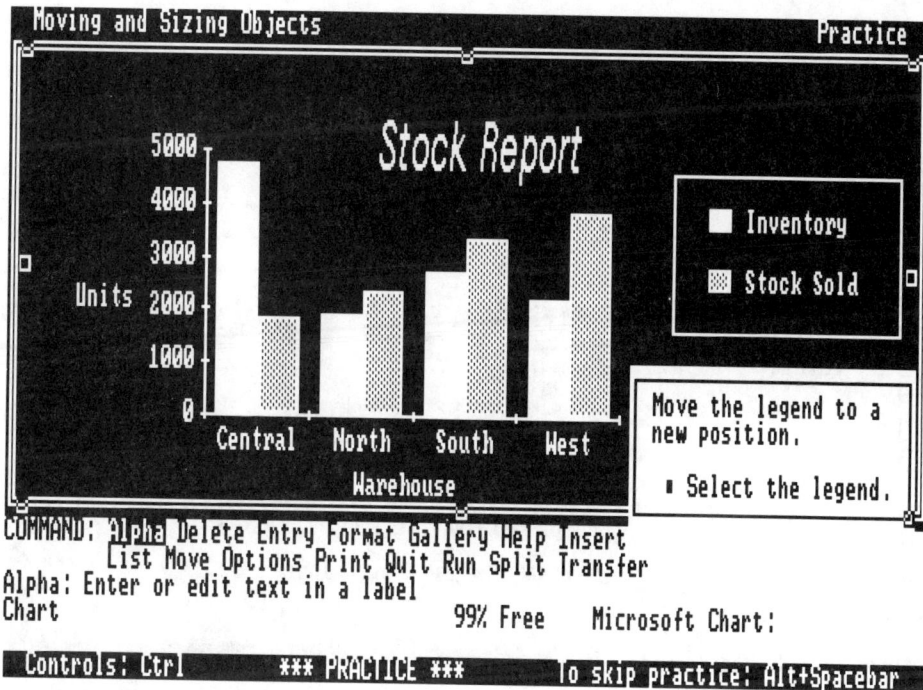

Figure 11-6.
Microsoft Chart example.

Windows Graph can generate all major types of charts, and it allows you complete freedom over how the chart appears on screen and on paper. A sample Windows Graph chart is shown in Figure 11-7. The program can be used with or without Windows and requires a minimum of 512K RAM; 640K is even better. A hard disk is recommended. You install the program onto the hard disk following a menu-driven setup procedure.

The setup program allows you to specify the type of graphics display, printer, and pointing system (if any) that you are using. Windows Graph works with color graphics, enhanced graphics, or Hercules monochrome graphics adapters.

Most popular printers are supported, including the Epson FX and MX line, the Okidata 92/93/192/193 (IBM or Standard), IBM Graphics, IBM Prowriter, C. Itoh 8510, Toshiba P1351, NEC P2/P3, Hewlett-Packard Laserjet (and Laserjet Plus), and Apple Laserwriter. A PostScript driver is included to take full advantage of the Laserwriter's font and graphics capabilities. The driver can also be used with other PostScript-compatible

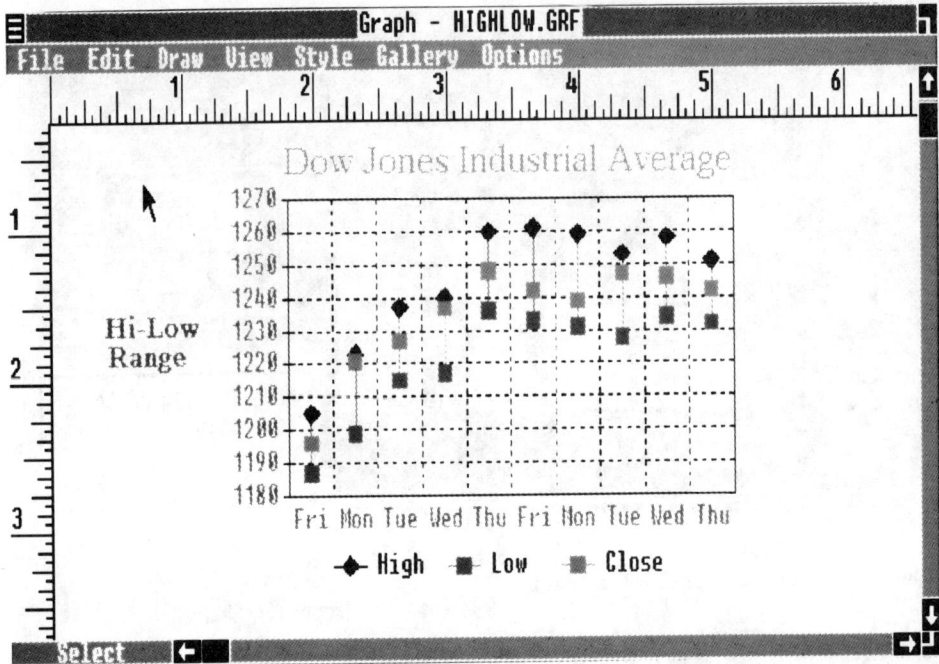

Figure 11-7.
Windows Graph example.

devices. Windows Graph comes with drivers to run the Hewlett-Packard HP7470, HP7475, and HP7550 plotters. Other multipen plotters can be used as long as they emulate the HP line. The program can be used with various mouse systems and light pens.

Window Graph incorporates the familiar Windows user interface, so the program screen is familiar. At the top of the screen is the menu bar; the chart window is blank and ready for a new graph. In normal view, you see approximately 6 by 3½ inches of the entire 8½ by 11 inch sheet of paper.

Windows Graph uses a Lotus 1-2-3–like worksheet to contain the data for the chart. Open the worksheet window (menu or keyboard) and you are provided with a worksheet. You enter text and labels into the worksheet like you do with 1-2-3 or most any electronic spreadsheet program. Each column holds labels or a series of data for the graph. You can have just one series or several.

Once the data has been entered into the worksheet, you choose the type of chart to create. Windows Graph makes seven basic types of graphs: area, bar, column, line, pie, dot, and table. You choose the type from a gallery and select one of four common variations. You can also custom design your own variations and save them for use later.

The program allows full modification of the chart and you can edit the chart data at any time. Clicking on an element of the chart, such as a column in a column chart, allows you to make changes to that element. Another command lets you change the color of bars, columns, areas, symbols, and all other chart elements. You can similarly change the fill and line pattern, line width, and background. Chart attributes—grid, data organization, scale, and so forth—can also be modified. A Projection command lets you turn a regular 2-D chart into a 3-D chart.

Besides customizing the chart and adding a 3-D effect, Windows Graph provides a number of features you can use to add creative embellishments, including chart overlays and freehand drawing tools (use the mouse or light pen with these).

As a Windows-compatible program, Windows Graph follows most of the Windows user interface conventions. You can load Windows Graph with any other Windows-compatible application. Windows Graph supports DDE, or Dynamic Data Exchange. Various commands are supported through DDE, including Load, Redraw, Clear, Update, and Save. With DDE, you can update, redraw, transfer, and save graphs while in another application.

Chart Types and Their Uses

To show one thing, one time:

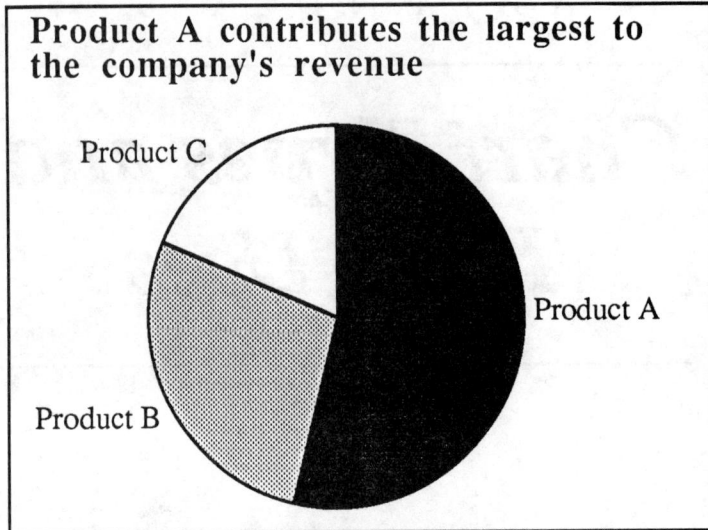

Figure A-1.
Pie Chart.

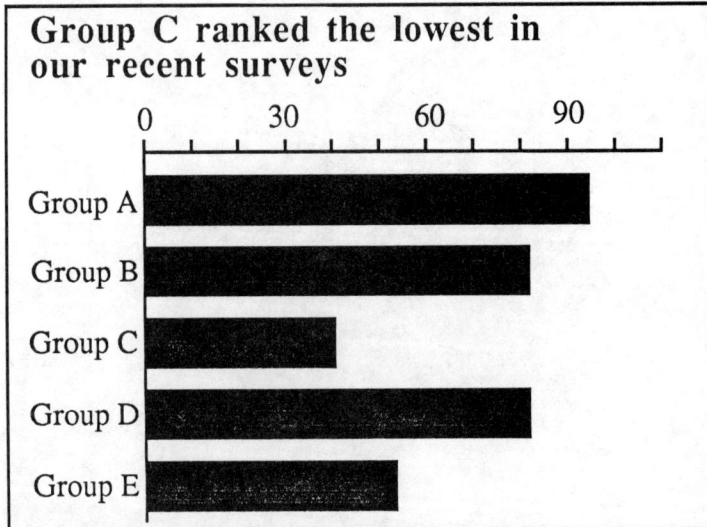

Figure A-2.
Single Bar Chart.

To show one thing, many times:

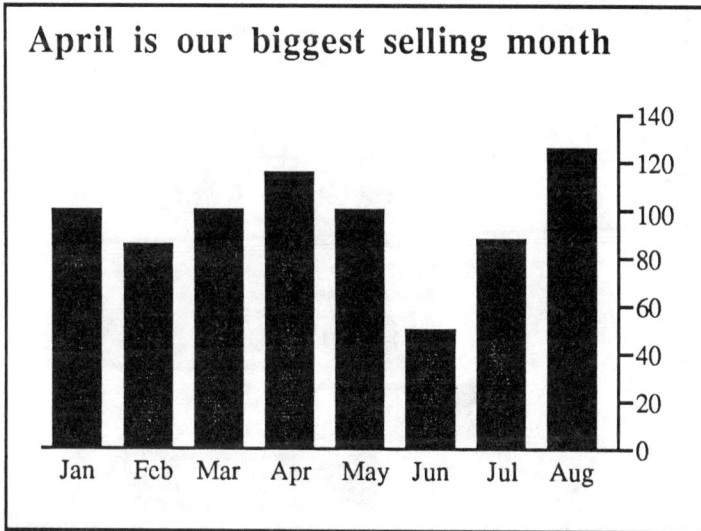

Figure A-3.
Column Chart.

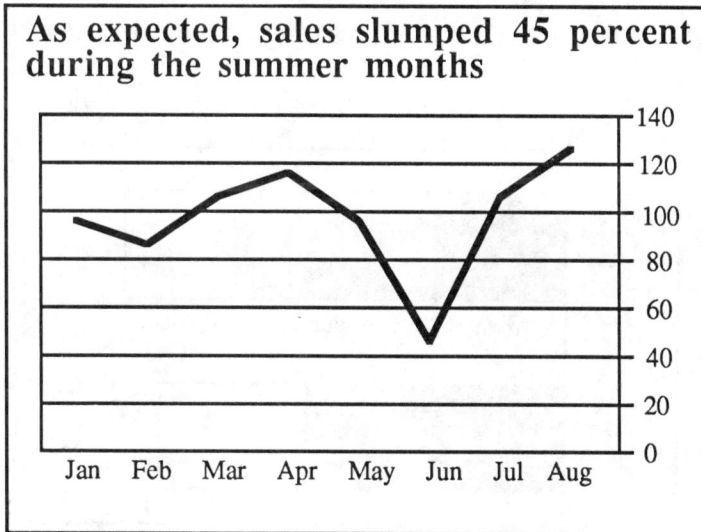

Figure A-4.
Line Chart.

To show many things, one time:

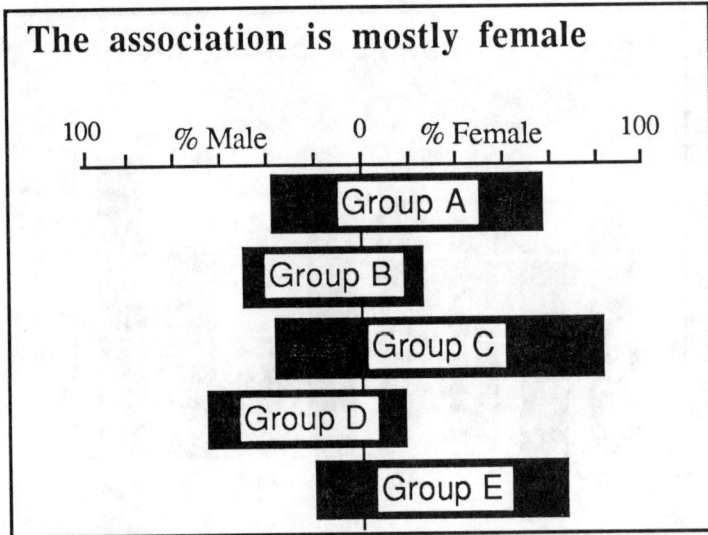

The association is mostly female

100   % Male   0   % Female   100

Group A

Group B

Group C

Group D

Group E

Figure A-5.
Stacked Bar Chart.

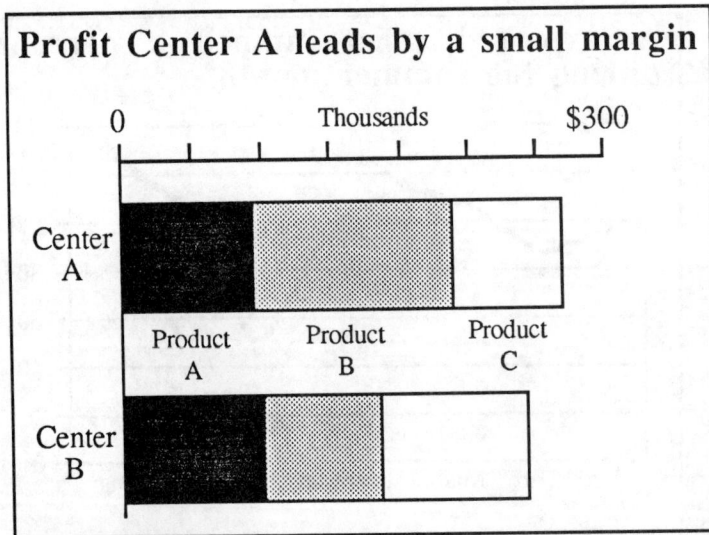

Profit Center A leads by a small margin

0   Thousands $300

Center A

Product A   Product B   Product C

Center B

Figure A-6.
Sliding Bar Chart.

To show many things, many times:

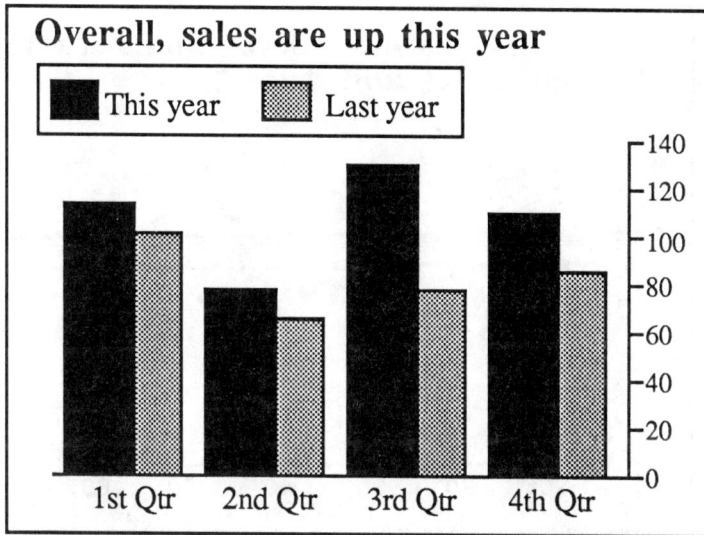

Figure A-7.
Multiple Column Chart.

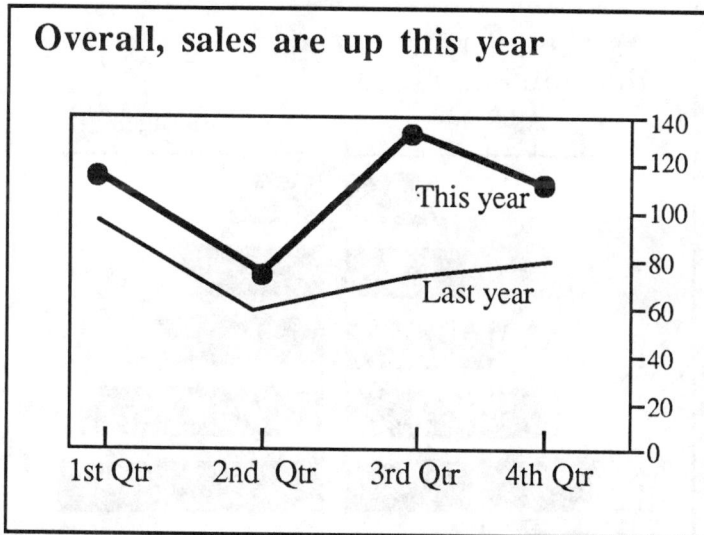

Figure A-8.
Line Chart.

To show frequency:

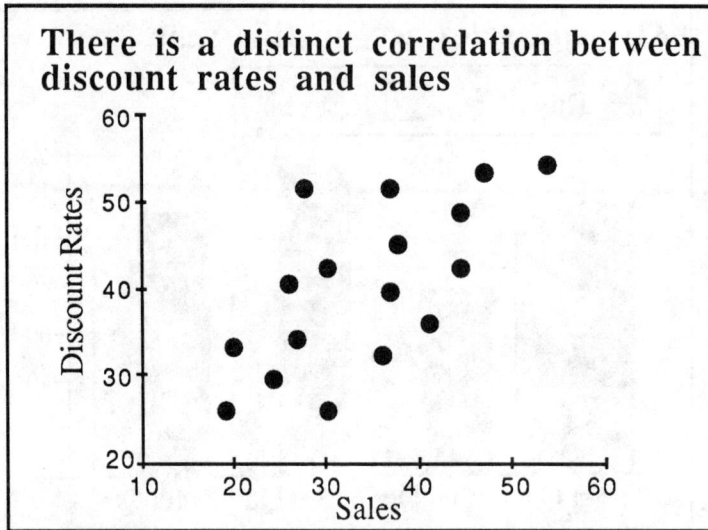

Figure A-9.
Dot Chart.

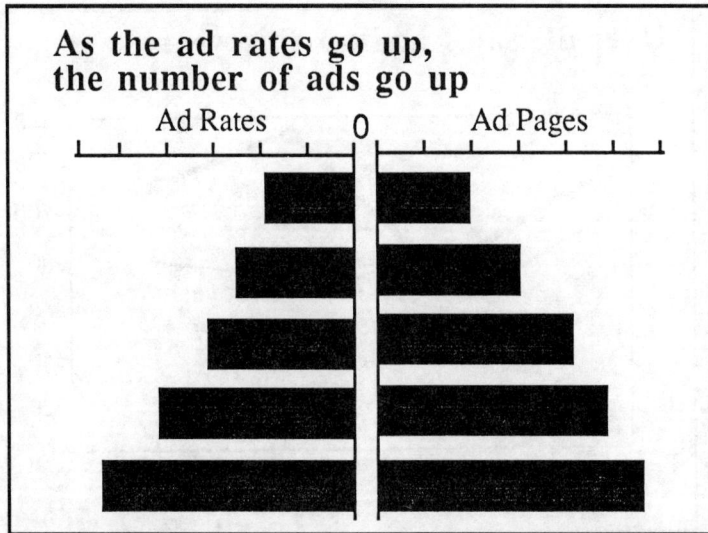

Figure A-10.
Paired Bar Chart.

APPENDIX B

Further Reading

Choosing the Right Chart, Integrated Software Systems Corp. (ISSCO), 1984.

Designing a Good Graph, Integrated Software Systems Corp. (ISSCO), 1984.

Designer's Guide to Creating Charts and Diagrams, Nigel Holes; Watson-Guptill, New York.

How to Lie with Statistics, Darrell Huff; W. W. Norton, New York, 1954.

Say It with Charts, Gene Zelazny; Dow Jones-Irwin, Homewood, IL., 1985.

The Visual Display of Quantitative Information, Edward Tuft; Graphics Press, (for consistency) 1983.

APPENDIX C

Sources

Abaton Technology Corp.
1526 Cloverfield Blvd.
Santa Monica, CA 90404
(818) 905-9399
Image scanner

ACT (Applied Color Technology)
21 Alpha Road
Chelmsford, MA 01824
(617) 256-1222
Color ink jet printer

Adobe Systems
1870 Embarcadero Road
Palo Alto, CA 94303
(415) 852-0271
PostScript page description language; typefaces for PostScript-compatible printers

Advanced Computer Products, Inc.
PO Box 17329
Irvine, CA 92713
(800) 854-8230
(714) 558-8813 (in CA)
Memory chips and computer components

Advanced Graphics Software
333 W. Maude Ave., #105
Sunnyvale, CA 94086
(408) 749-8620
SlideWrite graphics presentation software

Aldus Corp.
411 First Ave. South, Suite 200
Seattle, WA 98104
(206) 662-5500
PageMaker page makeup program

Allied Linotype Co.
425 Oser Ave.
Hauppauge, NY 11788
(516) 434-2000
Professional phototypesetting systems

Analytical Software
10939 McCree Road
Dallas, TX 75238
(214) 340-2564
Boardroom Graphics business graphics program

Apple Computer, Inc.
20525 Mariani Ave.
Cupertino, CA 95014-2094
(408) 996-1010
Laserwriter PostScript-compatible laser printer

Application Techniques, Inc.
10 Lomar Park Drive
Pepperell, MA 01463
(617) 433-5201
Turbocharger for PrtSc command; graphics extender

Applied Technologies
806 Forest
Olathe, KS 66061
(913) 782-1249
Color transfer sheets

Art Machine Inc.
611 Broadway, #613
New York, NY 10012
(212) 505-6400
Computer-slide service bureau

AST Research
2121 Alton Ave.
Irvine, CA 92714
(714) 863-1480
TurboScan page scanner; TuroLaser laser printer (PostScript and non-Post-Script versions); CGA- and EGA-compatible display boards

Ashton-Tate
Graphics Products Center
20101 Hamilton Avenue
Torrance, CA 90502-1319
(213) 329-8000
Graphics preparation software including Map-Master, Sign-Master, Diagram-Master, and Chart-Master

ATI Technologies
3761 Victoria Park Ave.
Scarborough, Ontario, Canada
(416) 756-0711
Graphics display boards

AT&T
Electronic Photography and Imaging Center
7351 Shadeland Street, Suite 100
Indianapolis, IN 46256
(800) 858-TRUE
High-resolution video digitizer

Autographix, Inc.
100 Fifth Ave.
Waltham, MA 02154
(617) 890-8558
Slide Expert business graphics; computer-slide service bureau

Aztek Inc.
17 Thomas
Irvine, CA 92718
(714) 770-8406
PCchart presentation graphics program; computer-slide service bureau

Bell & Howell Co./Quintar Division
411 Amapola Ave.
Torrance, CA 90501-1493
(800) 320-5231
(213) 320-5700 (in CA)
Graphic Express freehand painting program

Boca Research, Inc.
6401 Congress Ave.
Boca Raton, FL 33431
(305) 997-6227
Graphics display adapters

Boeing Computer Services
PO Box 24346 M/S 7W-05

Seattle, WA 98124-0346
Boeing Graph 3-D presentation graphics package

Brightbill-Roberts & Co.
120 E. Washington Street, Suite 421
Syracuse, NY 13202
(315) 474-3400
Graphics Partner painting program; Show Partner and Show Partner F/X electronic slide presentation software

Brilliant Image
141 W. 28th Street
New York, NY 10001
(212) 736-9661
Computer-slide service bureau

Business and Professional Software
143 Binney Street
Cambridge, MA 02014
(800) DIAL-PBS
(617) 491-3377 (in MA)
Graphics packages including PBS Business Graphics (presentation graphics) and 35mm Express (slide presentation)

Business Systems International
20942 Osborne Street
Canoga Park, CA 91304
(818) 998-7227
LaserSoft/PC page makeup program

C. Itoh Digital Products Inc.
19300 S. Hamilton Ave., Suite 110
PO Box 9085
Torrance, CA 90508
(213) 327-2110
Dot matrix and laser printer systems

CalComp
2411 W. LaPalma Ave.
Anaheim, CA 92801
(800) CALCOMP
(714) 821-2000
Plotters

Canon U.S.A. Inc.
One Canon Plaza
Lake Success, NY 11042
(516) 488-6700
Printer systems: ink jet, laser; image scanner

Chorus Data Systems
PO Box 370
6 Continental Blvd.
Merrimack, NY 03054
(603) 424-2900
PC Eye video digitizer system

Community Research & Information Systems
75 E. Main Street
PO Box 1280
Riplet, NY 14775
(716) 736-4100
Polymaps map-making software

Compugraphic Corp.
200 Ballardvale Street
Wilmington, MA 01887
(800) 452-4526
Professional phototypesetting equipment

Computer Peripherals, Inc.
2635 Lavery Court, Suite 5
Newbury Park, CA 91320
(800) 854-7600
(805) 499-5751 (in CA)
Graphics display boards

Computer Support Corp.
2215 Midway Road
Carrollton, TX 75006
(214) 661-8960
Diagraph presentation graphics (with over 2,200 symbols), Diagraph Windows
(Microsoft Windows-compatible), and Picture Perfect

CompuVision International
PO Box 1287
Old Chelsea Station
New York, NY 10013-1287
(212) 213-0134
Giraph business graphics program

Concept Omega Corp./Thoroughbred Software Division
PO Box 1035
Somerville, NJ 08876
(201) 722-9565
ConceptR, ConceptG, and Thoroughbred Graph charting programs

Control Systems
2676 Patton Road

PO Box 64750
St. Paul, MN 558164
(800) 826-4281
ArtBrush freehand painting program

Cricket Software
30 Valley Stream Parkway
Great Valley Corporate Center
Malver, PA 19355
(215) 251-9890
Graphics and desktop publishing software

Data Color Graphics
9645 Webb Chapel Road
Dallas, TX 75220
(214) 350-9442
Computer-slide service bureau

Datacopy Corp.
1215 Terra Bella Ave.
Mountain View, CA 94043
(415) 965-7900
Image scanner

Dataease
12 Cambridge Drive
Trumbull, CT 06611
(203) 374-2825
Graphtalk presentation graphics

Data Transforms
616 Washington St.
Denver, CO 80203
(303) 832-1501
Fontrix font assortment package

Decision Graphics Inc.
PO Box 2776
Littleton, CO 80161
(303) 796-0341
DGI ArtShop plotter support and graphics program

Dest Corp.
1201 Cadillac Court
Milpitas, CA 95035
(408) 946-7100
Image scanners

Dick Smith Electronics
PO Box 8021

Redwood City, CA 94063
(800) 332-5373
Memory chips and computer components

Digital Research Inc.
60 Garden Court
PO Box DRI
Monterey, CA 93942
(800) 443-4200
(408) 649-3896 (in CA)
GEM-compatible graphics programs: GEM Draw Plus (drawing), GEM Paint
(painting), GEM Graph (presentation graphics), GEM WordChart (word chart)

DoKay Computer Products, Inc.
2100 De La Crux Blvd.
Santa Clara, CA 95050
(408) 988-0697
Memory chips and computer components

Eastman Kodak Co.
Dept. 620
Rochester, NY 14650
(800) 445-6325
LCD overhead projector computer screen

E-Machines, Inc.
7945 SW Mohawk Street
Tualatin, OR 97062
(503) 692-6656
Display systems

Emulex Corp.
3545 Harbor Blvd.
Costa Mesa, CA 92626
(714) 662-5600
CGA- and EGA-compatible graphics display adapters

Enertronics Research
1910 Pine Street
St. Louis, MO 63103
(800) 325-0174
(314) 421-2771 (in MO)
EnerCharts and EnerGraphics business graphics programs

Enter Computer Inc.
6887 Nancy Ridge Road
San Diego, CA 92121
(619) 450-0601
Plotters

Epson America, Inc.
2780 Lomita Blvd.
Torrance, CA 90505
(213) 539-9140
Printer systems: dot matrix, ink jet, laser, plotter

Everex Systems, Inc.
48431 Milmont Drive
Fremont, CA 94538
(415) 498-1111
Graphics display boards

Express Computer Supplies
2215-R Market St., #292
San Francisco, CA 94114
(415) 864-3026
Transfer ribbons

Facit Inc.
9 Executive Park Dr.
PO Box 334
Merrimack, NH 03054
(603) 424-8000
Plotters and printers

Fox & Geller
604 Market Street
Elmwood Park, NJ 07407
(201) 794-8883
dGraph III graphics program, data-compatible with Ashton-Tate dBase III and
Lotus 1-2-3

FTG Data Systems
10801 Dale Street, Suite J-2
PO Box 615
Stanton, CA 90680
(714) 995-3900
Light pens

Fujitsu Component of America Inc.
3320 Scott Blvd.
Santa Clara, CA 95054-3197
(408) 727-1000
Plotters, image scanners

General Parametrics Corp.
1250 Ninth Street
Berkeley, CA 94710
(415) 524-3950
VideoShow film recorder and software

Genigraphics
4806 W. Taft Road
Liverpool, NY 13088-0591
(315) 451-6600
Computer-slide service bureau

Genoa Systems Corp.
73 E. Trimble Road
San Jose, CA 95131
(408) 432-9090
CGA, EGA, and VGA compatible graphics display boards

Graphic Software Systems Inc.
9590 Southwest Gemini Street
Beaverton, OR 97005
(503) 641-2200
GSS-Chart presentation graphics program; GSS-Plotalk plotter utility

GTCO Corp.
7125 Riverwood Drive
Columbia, MD 21046
(301) 381-6688
Graphics tablets

Health Telematics Systems Inc.
1900 Dublin-Granville Road
Columbus, OH 43229
(614) 267-8100
LCD panel overhead projector screen

Hercules Computer Technology
2550 Ninth Street
Berkeley, CA 94710
(415) 540-0212
Hercules monochrome and color graphics adapter boards

Hewlett-Packard Corp.
3000 Hanover Street
Palo Alto, CA 94304
(415) 857-1501
ScanJet image scanner; LaserJet laser printer (PostScript and non-PostScript versions)

Hewlett-Packard Corp.
16399 W. Bernardo Drive
San Diego, CA 92127-1899
Plotters (619) 487-4100

Hewlett-Packard Corp.
Personal Software Division

3410 Central Expressway
Santa Clara, CA 95051
(800) 367-4772
(408) 749-9500
Graphics Gallery presentation business graphics software

Houston Instrument
8500 Cameron Road
Austin, TX 78753
(512) 835-0900
Plotters

IBM Corp.
Old Orchard Road
Armonk, NY 10504
(800) 447-4700 (dealer info)
Graphics software: PC Graphing Assistant (presentation graphics), PC Drawing assistant (freehand drawing), PC Storyboard (slide presentation)

IBM Corp.
Plotter Products
Box 3332
Danbury, CT 06813-1974
(800) IBM-PLOT
(203) 796-9600
Plotters

IBM Corp.
Information Systems Group
900 King Street
Rye Brook, NY 10573
Quietwriter thermal transfer printer
(914) 934-4000

IMSI
1299 Fourth Street
San Rafael, CA 94901
(415) 454-7101
Mouse systems

Intex Solutions
568 Washington Street
Wellesley, MA 02181
(617) 239-1168
3D graphics enhancer for Lotus 1-2-3

James River Corp.
Groveton Division
Groveton, NH 03582

(800) 521-5035
(413) 589-7592
Printer paper (formulated for laser, dot matrix, ink jet, thermal transfer, overhead, etc.)

JDR Microdevices
1224 S. Bascom Ave.
San Jose, CA 95128
(800) 538-5000
(800) 662-6279 (in CA)
Memory chips and computer components

Key Tronics
PO Box 14687
Spokane, WA 99214
(509) 928-8000
Keyboards and integrated keyboard systems (trackballs, graphics tablets)

Koala Technologies
269 Mt. Herman Road
Scotts Valley, CA 95066
(800) 223-3022
(408) 438-0946 (in CA)
Graphics tablet

Kroy Sign Systems
7560 East Redfield Road
Scottsdale, AZ 85260
(800) 521-4997
(602) 951-1593 (in AZ)
Kroy Kolor transfer sheets

The Laser Group
1300 Waverly Place
Joliet, IL 60435
(815) 727-2600
Mail-order Canon-cartridge refill

Lasergraphics Inc.
1761 Cowan Ave.
Irvine, CA 92714
(714) 660-9497
Film recorder

Lexisoft, Inc.
PO Box 1950
Davis, CA 95617
(916) 759-3630
SpellBinder desktop publishing program series

Lite-Pen Co.
12500 Beatrice Street
Los Angeles, CA 90066
(800) 634-1967
(800) 821-7807 (in CA)

Litepen Systems
Logitech
6505 Kaiser Drive
Fremont, CA 94555
(415) 795-8500
Light pens, mouse systems

Lotus Development Corp.
55 Cambridge Parkway
Cambridge, MA 02142
(617) 577-8500
GraphWriter presentation graphics and Freelance graphics enhancement software

MAGICorp
50 Executive Blvd.
Elmsford, NY 10523
(914) 592-1244
Computer-slide service bureau

Marketing Graphics Inc.
401 E. Main Street
Richmond, VA 23219
(800) 368-3773
(804) 788-8844
PC PicturePak image libraries for PC Storyboard and Show Partner presentation programs

Maynard Electronics
460 E. Semoran Blvd.
Casselberry, FL 32707
(305) 331-6402
Mouse systems

Media Cybernetics Inc.
8484 Georgia Ave.
Silver Springs, MD 20910
(800) 426-HALO (sales)
(800) 446-HALO (tech. support)
(301) 495-3305
Dr. HALO freehand painting program; Image-Pro image processing program; Nimbus presentation graphics program

Micrografx Inc.
1820 N. Greenville Ave.
Richardson, TX 75082
(214) 234-1769
Graphics programs: Windows Graph presentation graphics, Windows Draw drawing, In*a*Vision freehand painting

Microdisplay Systems
1310 Vermilion Street
Hastings, MN 55033
(800) 328-9524
Genius 15-inch full-page monochrome display

Micrographic Images Corp.
20954 Osborne Street
Canoga Park, CA 91304
(818) 407-0571
Display systems

Microsoft Corp.
16011 NE 36th Way
Redmond, WA 98073-9717
(206) 882-8088
Microsoft Chart presentation graphics program; mouse systems

Microrim
3925 159th Ave. NE
PO Box 97022
Redmond, WA 98073-9722
DB Graphics presentation graphics program, compatible with Ashton-Tate dBase III and R:base files
(206) 883-0888

Microtek Lab Inc.
16901 S. Western Ave.
Gardena, CA 90247
(213) 321-2121
Image scanners

Moniterm Corp.
5740 Green Circle Dr.
Minnetonka, MN 55343
(612) 935-4151
High-resolution graphics monitors

MSC Technologies Inc.
2600 San Tomas Expressway
Santa Clara, CA 95051
(408) 988-0211
Mouse systems

NEC Home Electronics, Inc.
Personal Computer Division
1401 Estes Ave.
Elk Grove Village, IL 60007
(800) 323-1728
Multisync multiple frequency color monitors

NEC Information Systems Inc.
1414 Massachusetts Ave.
Boxborough, MA 01719
(617) 264-8000
Laser printers (PostScript and non-PostScript versions)

New England Software Inc.
Greenwich Office Park 3
Greenwich, CT 06830
(203) 625-0062
Graph-in-the-Box RAM-resident graphics enhancement software

Number Nine Computer Corp.
725 Concord Ave.
Cambridge, MA 02138
(617) 492-0999
Graphics display adapters

Okidata
532 Fellowship Road
Mt. Laurel, NJ 08054
(609) 235-2600
Dot matrix and laser printers

Orchid Technology
45365 Northport Loop West
Fremont, CA 94538
(415) 490-8586
Graphics display boards

PCsoftware of San Diego
11627 Calamar Court
San Diego, CA 92124
(619) 571-0981
Executive Picture Show presentation software

PCPI (Personal Computer Products, Inc.)
11590 W. Bernardo Court
San Diego, CA 92127
(619) 485-8411
Laser printers, graphics display adapters

Panasonic Industrial Co.
Computer Products Division
2 Panasonic Way
Secaucus, NJ 07094
(212) 977-9400
Image scanner

Paperback Software International
2830 Ninth Street
Berkeley, CA 94710
(415) 644-2116
Draw-It freehand drawing program; VP Graphics business presentation graphics

Paradise Systems, Inc.
217 E. Grand Ave.
South San Francisco, CA 94080
(415) 488-6000
Graphics display adapters

Pencept Inc.
39 Green Street
Waltham, MA 02154
(617) 893-6390
Graphics tablets

Polaroid Corp.
Electronic Imaging Dept.
575 Technology Square
Cambridge, MA 02139
(800) 343-5000
Film recorder

Photographic Sciences Corp.
770 Basket Road
Webster, NY 14580
(716) 265-1600
Monitor screen camera

Presentation Technologies Inc.
743 N Pastoria Ave.
Sunnyvale, CA 94086
(408) 749-1959
Film recorder

Princeton Graphic Systems
601 Ewing Street, Bldg A
Princeton, NJ 08540

(609) 683-1660
Image scanners, monitors, and graphics display boards

Prosoft
7248 Bellair Ave., Box 560
North Hollywood, CA 91605
(818) 765-4444
Fontasy font generation and page makeup programs

QMS, Inc. (Quality Micro Systems)
One Magnum Pass
Mobile, AL 36618
(205) 633-4300
Laser printer systems (PostScript and non-PostScript)

Quadram
One Quad Way
Norcross, GA 30093
(404) 564-5566
CGA, EGA, and VGA-compatible graphics adapter boards

Questionnaire Service Co.
PO Box 778
East Lansing, MI 48823
(517) 641-4428
MAPIT map-making software

Quimax Systems Inc.
844 Del Rey Ave.
Sunnyvale, CA 94086
(408) 773-8282
Monochrome and color monitors

Qume Corp.
2350 Qume Drive
San Jose, CA 95131
(408) 942-4000
Printer systems: dot matrix, laser

Radius
404 East Plumeria Drive
San Jose, CA 95134
(408) 434-1010
Display systems

Rand McNally & Co.
PO Box 7600
Chicago, IL 60680

(800) 332-RAND
(312) 673-MAPS (in IL)
Randmap map-making software

Ricoh Corp.
5 Dedrick Place
West Caldwell, NJ 07006
(201) 882-2000
Laser printers

RIX SoftWorks, Inc.
18552 MacArthur Blvd., Suite 470
Irvine, CA 92715
(714) 476-8266
EGA Paint program

Roland/DG
Roland Corp.
7200 Dominion Circle
Los Angeles, CA 90040
(213) 685-5141
Plotters

Samna Corp.
2700 NE Expressway #C-700
Atlanta, GA 30345
(800) 831-9679
Decision Graphics presentation graphics program

Saratoga Electronics, Inc.
12380 Saratoga-Sunnyvale Rd.
Saratoga, CA 95070
(408) 446-4949
Memory chips and computer components

Sharp Color
400 North High Street
Box 175
Columbus, OH 43215
(614) 221-0502
Color ribbons

Sharp Electronics Corp.
Systems Division
10 Sharp Plaza
Paramus, NJ 07652
(201) 265-5600
Plotters

Siemens Communications Systems, Inc.
550 Broken Sound Blvd.
Boca Raton, FL 33431
(305) 994-8800
High resolution ink jet printers

Sigma Designs, Inc.
46501 Landing Parkway
Fremont, CA 94538
(415) 770-0100
Graphics display adapters, display systems

Softcraft, Inc.
222 State Street
Madison, WI 53703
(800) 351-0500
FancyFont laser printer fonts (HP LaserJet-compatible)

SoftKey Software Products Inc.
260 Richmond St. West, Suite 300
Toronto, Ontario, Canada M5V 1W5
(800) 263-5800
(516) 598-5033
Keychart6 presentation graphics software

Softstyle, Inc.
Hawaii Kai Office Bldg., #205
7192 Kalanianaole Hwy.
Honolulu, HI 96825
(808) 396-6368
Laser printer utilities

Softest, Inc.
555 Goff Road
Ridgewood, NJ 07450
(201) 447-3901
Softtype typesetting and layout software

Software Publishing Corp.
1901 Landings Drive
Mountain View, CA 94043
(415) 962-8910
pfs: professional, Harvard, and First Choice software series, each with graphics modules

STB Systems, Inc.
PO Box 850957
Richardson, TX 75085-0957

(214) 234-8750
Graphics display adapters

Stella Systems
444 N Michigan Ave.
Chicago, IL 60611
(312) 329-2400
Stella Graphics, Business Graphics, Business Graphics II programs

Summagraphics
777 Commerce Drive
Fairfield, CT 06430
(203) 384-1344
Graphics tablet, mouse systems

Taxan Corp.
18005 Courtney Court
City of Industry, CA 91748
(818) 810-1291
Plotters

Tech-nique
920 Alvion Ave.
Schaumburg, IL 60193
(312) 529-7888
Mail-order Canon-cartridge refill

Tecmar
6225 Cochran Road
Solon, OH 44139
(216) 349-0600
Graphics display boards

Three D Graphics
860 Via de la Paz
Pacific Palisades, CA 90272
(213) 459-7949
Perspective 3-D charting program

3M Meeting Graphics
3M Center; Audio Visual Division
Bldg. 225-3 NE
St. Paul, MN 55144-1000
(612) 733-1110
Computer-slide service bureau; overhead transparency supplies

Torrington Co.
59 Field Street

Torrington, CT 96790
(800) 654-5449
(800) 225-7219 (in CT)
(203) 482-9511
Mouse

Vectrix Corp.
2606 Branchwood Drive
Greensboro, NC 27408
(800) 334-8181
(919) 288-0520
Vectrix Paint freehand paint program

Video Seven Inc.
46335 Landing Parkway
Fremont, CA 94538
(800) 238-0101
(800) 962-5700 (in CA)
EGA and VGA-compatible graphics boards

Visual Communications Network (VCN) Inc.
238 Main Street
Cambridge, MA 2142
(617) 497-4000
Execuvision presentation graphics software

Warp Speed Computer Products
1101 E Redondo Blvd.
Inglewood, CA 90302
(800) 874-4315
(800) 826-1563 (in CA)

Western Graphtec Inc.
12 Chrysler Street
Irvine, CA 92718-2086
(800) 854-8385
(800) 624-8396 (in CA)
(714) 770-6010
Plotters

Wyse Technology
3517 N First Street
San Jose, CA 95134
(408) 433-1000
High-resolution monochrome and color monitors

Xerox Corp.
101 Continental Blvd.
El Segundo, CA 90245

(800) 822-8221
Ventura Publisher desktop publishing program

Zenographics Inc.
19572 MacArthur Blvd., Suite 250
Irvine, CA 92715
(714) 851-6352
Autumn and Mirage freehand and presentation graphics software

Z-Soft
1950 Spectrum Circle
Suite A-495
Marietta, GA 30067
(404) 980-1950
PC Paintbrush freehand painting program

Glossary

abscissa The horizontal or X axis of a chart, usually used for time intervals.

alphanumeric Both numbers and letters.

analysis Numerical calculations on numbers in a chart, for the purpose of revealing trends or relationships between those numbers.

analytical graphics Charts and graphs to provide the maker with more information, not for presentation.

animate To suggest movement with a series of slightly different images.

annotate To add notes to charts.

antialias To smooth jagged edges.

area graph A type of shaded line graph showing cumulative quantity.

arithmetic scale See *linear scale*.

ASCII American Standard Code for Information Interchange, a code ensuring compatibility between a computer and its programs.

aspect ratio The ratio of an image's height to its width.

axis One of the two perpendicular lines that create the scales of the graph, crossing at point 0 and theoretically going on forever.

bandwidth   A measurement of the detail and clarity a monitor and video controller board can produce.

bar chart   A bar chart used to compare different items at the same point in time.

baud rate   The speed at which data is transmitted, equal to bits per second.

bit-map   A picture made out of individual dots, as opposed to lines and other discrete shapes in vector- or object-based graphics.

body copy   The main portion of text in a document.

breakhead   Subheadings interspersed within the main text of a document.

buffer   A protective storage place in the computer's memory, often used to temporarily store graphic or textual information.

CAD   Computer-aided design or computer-assisted design, a tool for mechanical electronic design.

CGA   Color graphics adapter; a relatively low-resolution color graphics adapter board standard used in the IBM PC.

caption   Explanatory text that appears below a picture or illustration. Also called a cutline.

cartesian coordinates   A system for defining every point on a graph.

clip   To select a small portion of a design in order to change or manipulate it.

cluster   A group of chart elements, usually bars or columns, that represent similar items from different data series.

column chart   A chart that uses vertical bars.

complement   The contrasting color that creates a neutral when added to another color.

composite monitor   A monitor that receives its color and brightness information in one signal.

computer-aided design   See *CAD*.

coordinate   One of the pair of numbers used to specify a point on a graph.

CRT   Cathode ray tube, a TV-like screen used in computers to display text and graphics.

crop   To cut off the edges of an image.

cursor   A marker on the screen indicating where the next activity will take place.

cut   A picture or illustration.

data point   A numeric value on a graph.

data series   A complete set of numeric data.

descender   The part of a lowercase letter which drops below the line.

DIF   Data Interchange Format, a standard ensuring data accessibility between programs.

digitize   To turn a picture or diagram into a signal usable by a computer; a digitizer is a peripheral that reads or traces the diagram and translates it for the computer.

DIP switch   Dual Inline Package, a set of switches used to adjust peripheral equipment.

display   The image on the screen.

dither   Adding dots to a small area for the purpose of smoothing an image or creating additional characters.

DOS   Disk Operating System, the program used by the computer to enable it to work with all the other hardware.

dot matrix   A printer that creates characters out of dots.

dot chart   A chart showing the correlation between two numbers, also called an X-Y or scatter chart.

dots per inch   In printing, the number of image- or character-producing dots, horizontally or vertically, in a linear inch. Abbreviated dpi. Often used to refer to the resolution of a printer.

draw program   A software program that lets you draw pictures from discrete shapes. Draw programs are based on vector- or object-oriented graphics. See also *paint program.*

driver   A software program that enables a hardware device, such as a laser printer or mouse, to interface with a computer. Drivers are used when the computer may not recognize the peripheral connected to it.

drop cap   A large capital letter that starts off a paragraph at the beginning of an article or main section. An illuminated drop cap is a capital letter enhanced with graphics or design.

drop line   A line extending from a data point and connecting to the scale on the X or Y axis.

drum plotter   A plotter that moves a pen horizontally across a round cylinder.

EGA   Enhanced graphics adapter; a high-resolution color graphics standard used in the IBM PC.

elements   Graphics, text, lines, and other components of a finished chart.

filling   Adding a color or pattern to a specific area on a screen. Also, the calculation of numbers to fill in gaps or to extend before or beyond the series.

flatbed plotter   A plotter that moves a pen on an X and/or Y axis across a flat platen.

flush right/left   Composing lines so that they begin or end on the right or left side. The text is not stretched out so that it is equal on both sides (justified). Normal text is flush left (also called ragged right).

folio   Page number.

font   A typeface.

footer   Text that appears at the bottom of all (or nearly all) of the pages in a document.

frame   The complete picture, or the border around the graph. Also an individual video or film picture.

grayscale   Variations of gray tone or density, expressed as a percentage or ratio of black to white. Examples: Light gray is 20 to 30 percent (20 to 30 percent black), medium gray is 50 percent, dark gray is 80 or 90 percent.

graphic tablet   A flat drawing tablet.

grid   A regular pattern of perpendicular intersecting lines on a graph.

halftone   Any image that contains intermediate grays, as opposed to pure black on white (or vice versa).

hard copy   A printed or plotted result.

header   Text that appears on the top of all (or nearly all) the pages in a document.

hi-res   High resolution, the ability of a monitor or printer to show highly detailed graphics.

interface   The connection between two pieces of equipment.

I/O   Input/output, refers to interfaces.

justification The positioning of a block of text equally within margins.

kern To adjust the spacing between certain characters to push them apart or bring them together, in order to make them look better when printed on the page.

key An explanation of the symbols or codes used in the graph.

laser printer A printer that creates characters out of a razor-thin beam of light.

leading The blank space between typeset lines. Expressed in points.

legend Keys or notations explaining symbols used in a graph.

line chart A chart that uses lines to connect data points.

linear scale A scale that shows the amount of change, in equally spaced intervals.

logarithmic scale An axis scale for showing a rate of change, rather than an amount of change, with no zero point.

monochrome A monitor that shows difference in shading rather than in color.

moving average An average taken over a specific number of points on a line, smoothing out minor fluctuations.

object-oriented See *vector graphics.*

PC-DOS The operating system used by the IBM PC, controlling all the activity of the computer.

page description language A computer programming language that defines the size, format, and position of text and graphics on a printed page. PostScript is the most popular page description language used in personal computers.

page layout Electronic or manual compilation of formatted text and graphics on a page or series of pages.

paint program A software program that creates graphics out of dots. Paint programs are based on bit-mapped graphics. See also *draw program.*

palette A selection of available colors for use in graphs.

pan In computer graphics, to move an object or screen display back and forth or up and down in real time animation.

parallel port A type of interface that sends and receives information 8 bits at a time.

pel, pixel   Picture elements, tiny dots of light or ink that together form an image of a character or picture.

pica   A typesetting measurement; there are 6 picas to the inch. Often used to express space, distance, or length between elements in a chart or page.

pie chart   A circular chart showing the share of a total as the wedges of pie.

polygon   Any shape with three or more sides.

PostScript   A popular page description language used with many laser printers and some other high-resolution output devices (such as phototypesetting equipment).

presentation graphics   Quality charts, graphs, slide shows, etc., used to explain or present information to others.

RGB video   Red-green-blue monitor; each color signal is sent on a separate cable, resulting in higher resolution.

raster   The pattern of horizontal lines on a monitor which are selectively illuminated to form the dots that make up characters and images.

resolution   The sharpness of the image on the monitor or other computer device; the number of pixels that make up the screen display.

scale   To reduce or enlarge an image; the X or Y axis in a graph.

segmented bar/column   A bar or column chart with segments attached one on top of another. Used to show comparisons of the whole as well as the parts.

series   A data series.

serial port   A type of interface that transmits and receives information 1 bit at a time.

subheads   Minor headings showing the elements of the page.

tick mark   A mark used to call attention to a detail, to indicate value, or to serve as a minor division in a grid.

thermal transfer printer   A type of printer where heat or electricity transfers ink from a special ribbon to the paper.

2-D graphics   Two-dimensional graphics drawn on a single plane.

trend line   A prediction of trends beyond the known values.

VGA   Video graphics array, a very high-resolution color graphics standard used in the IBM PC.

variable   An item whose value can change.

vector graphics   An object-oriented graphics system based on the reproduction of discrete shapes. See also *bit-map.*

WYSIWYG   A popular acronym that stands for what-you-see-is-what-you-get. WYSIWYG defines the visual fidelity between the image on the computer display and the printed result.

weight   The thickness of a line.

X axis   The horizontal or abscissa axis of a graph, usually representing time.

Y axis   The vertical axis of a graph, usually representing value.

Z axis   The depth axis of a three-dimensional graph.

Index